Stephanie L. Larson
Tales of Epic Ancestry

HISTORIA

Zeitschrift für Alte Geschichte
Revue d'histoire ancienne
Journal of Ancient History
Rivista di storia antica

– – – – – – – – – – – – – – – – –

EINZELSCHRIFTEN

Herausgegeben von
Kai Brodersen/Mannheim
Mortimer Chambers/Los Angeles
Martin Jehne/Dresden
François Paschoud/Geneve
Aloys Winterling/Freiburg

HEFT 197

Stephanie L. Larson

Tales of Epic Ancestry

Boiotian Collective Identity
in the Late Archaic and
Early Classical Periods

 Franz Steiner Verlag Stuttgart 2007

Bibliografische Information der Deutschen Nationalbibliothek
Die Deutsche Nationalbibliothek verzeichnet diese
Publikation in der Deutschen Nationalbibliografie;
detaillierte bibliografische Daten sind im Internet über
<http://dnb.d-nb.de> abrufbar.

ISBN 978-3-515-09028-5

ISO 9706

CONTENTS

ACKNOWLEDGEMENTS

This book originated in 1997 at the Theban Ismenion, where I began questioning the basis for interpreting Boiotian federalism as a sixth-century phenomenon. This fundamental problem became the focus of initial research on my dissertation, the chapters of which reflected this original concern but also were expanded to address more complex issues of collective identity. I thank my director, Paula Perlman, as well as the members of my dissertation committee, each of whose individual expertise challenged me to reconsider material often previously studied: John Camp, Erwin Cook, Lisa Kallet, Jack Kroll, and Irad Malkin. Special thanks go to Irad Malkin for taking on this extra project despite hardly knowing me at all and to John Camp for his perennial generosity. Since those heady days of graduate school, this book has been encouraged and assisted by a number of other mentors and friends: Nancy Boukidis, Joe Day, Katie Faull, Renée Gosson, Greta Ham, Susanne Hofstra, John Hunter, Karl Kilinski, Kleopatra Kathariou, Kathleen Lynch, Emily Mackil, Ghislaine McDayter, Ben Millis, John Oakley, Guy Sanders, Albert Schachter, Gary Steiner, and James and Ioulia Tzonou-Herbst. In particular I single out June Allison, who commented on much of the manuscript; Molly Richardson, who saved me from innumerable editorial errors; and Mortimer Chambers, editor for *Historia* and an engaging correspondent.

The writing of this book and the addition of new material was made possible by a grant from the Loeb Foundation of Harvard University which allowed me to spend a year (2005–2006) at the Blegen Library of the American School of Classical Studies, an institution to which I owe a great debt. The American School provided the original funding for the graduate year in which I worked on the kernel of this project, and it is partly the School and its dedication to educating graduate students in the wholeness of antiquity that I wish to commemorate here. But first and foremost, I thank Ron Stroud, the Mellon Professor of Classical Studies in Athens 1996–1999, for encouraging me to pursue this research and for persisting in his mentorship since then. What he has taught me both about antiquity and the profession cannot be repaid. I also acknowledge Bucknell University for generous support for summer research as well as the Archaeological Institute of America, at whose annual meetings I have presented a number of ideas detailed in this book.

Finally, I thank my dear and beloved partner Kevin for sharing my life as well as my work, and to Maggie, my daughter, I dedicate this book in gratitude for teaching me about beauty.

All translations are my own unless otherwise noted. Transliteration generally follows Greek spelling, although in a few cases I have preferred a more familiar Latinate form.

INTRODUCTION

> "Boeotia, a canton hopelessly behind the times, a slow
> canton, as the nimble Attics would say, a glorious cli-
> mate for eels, but a bad air for brains. Large historical
> views are not always entertained by the cleverest minds
> ... and the annals of politics, of literature, of thought,
> have shown that out of the depths of crass conservatism
> and proverbial sluggishness come ... some of the finest
> intelligences, some of the greatest powers, of political,
> literary, and especially religious life."

> Basil Gildersleeve, from *Pindar: the Olym-
> pian and Pythian Odes*, viii. New York 1885.

> ἤνπερ φρονῇς εὖ, φεῦγε τὴν Βοιωτίαν.

> Pherekrates, fr. 171 (Kassel and Austin)

Early in the fifth century the Old comedian Cratinus invented a new term to
lampoon his neighbors to the north: Συοβοιωτοί.[1] Even the Theban Pindar, in
composing for an Athenian audience, refers to the piggish reputation of his
Boiotian compatriots.[2] Athenaeus records a host of additional jests at the Boiotians' expense from the fifth-century Athenian stage.[3] Despite widespread recording, however, this Athenian stereotype of the Boiotians offers little help in
assessing the reality of the Boiotian collective in the late sixth and early to mid-
fifth centuries BCE.

In the following chapters I thus explore the construction and articulation of
Boiotian collective identity in the second half of the sixth and the first half of the
fifth centuries BCE. Far from being the ignorant pigs of Athenian ridicule, at this
time the Boiotian *ethnos* claimed its identity through genealogy, traditions of
territory and epic, shared dialectical features, ties to panhellenic epic tradition,
shared symbolism, a common name, and common cult. These categories of self-
identification are no different from those used by other *ethne* at this same time.

APPROACH AND STRUCTURE

Given the spotty nature of evidence for archaic Boiotia in general, I have come to
rely on Smith's work on ancient *ethne* in particular, since his identifying criteria
for *ethne* are evident for the Boiotian *ethnos* at this time: a common myth of

---

[1] Cratinus, fr. 310 Kock 1880, 103.
[2] Pind. *Ol.* 6.90; fr. 83.
[3] Ath. 10.417.

descent, an association with a specific territory, a sense of solidarity, a shared history, a distinctive shared culture, and a collective name.[4] Hall and Malkin also stress the importance of heroic descent and traditions of territory in articulating collective identity.[5] I likewise accept the primacy of traditions of decent and territory as the main criteria for the Boiotian *ethnos*; the additional aspects of the collective that I discuss comprise secondary *indicia* of the group.

I thus begin with these two major criteria of collective identity. My first chapter concerns the genealogy of Boiotos, the eponym of the collective and a figure who was considered equal to various figures of significance in the Hellenic genealogy; he was also linked to specific Thessalian traditions. Notably, Boiotos also played a role in the tradition of Boiotian migration and territory, the second primary category of Boiotian collective identity which forms the core of the second chapter. By analyzing the tradition in the *Iliad,* Hesiod, the *Aspis*, and Thucydides, I conclude that the main elements of the Boiotian migration story had emerged by the Archaic period and maintained homogeneity through the Classical age. One of the tradition's primary strands involves maintaining a relationship between the Boiotians of the Late Archaic and Classical periods and the Βοιωτοί of the Trojan War tradition, as depicted specifically in the *Iliad's* Catalogue of Ships; its other main focus lies in further denoting Boiotian links to Thessaly. The two primary ethnic criteria of descent and traditions of territory thus complement and reinforce each other.

I continue by exploring various *indicia* of Boiotian ethnicity. In Chapter Three I consider the Boiotian shield, as seen primarily in the shared coinage of Boiotian *poleis* from the late sixth century onward. To this numismatic analysis I add the literary evidence for the link between Boiotians and shields, found in both the *Iliad* and the Theban *Aspis*, as well as evidence from archaic iconography, primarily sixth- and early fifth-century Attic vase painting. Together these sources suggest that through links to the Boiotian shield, the Boiotian *ethnos* publicly connected itself to epic tradition and specific heroes of the Trojan war, particularly Telamonian Ajax. At the same time the Boiotians may also have buttressed their status as manufacturers and possible exporters of raw metals and weaponry. In Chapter Four I reinforce Boiotian links to epic tradition by discussing the general relationship between the late archaic Boiotian dialect and epic and archaizing Greek. I conclude that by the Late Archaic period the Boiotians were actively maintaining a purposefully epic-style dialect which marked them as descendants of epic heroes and thus solidified the epicizing tendencies already noted in both their traditions of territory and use of symbol.

In Chapter Five I examine both internal and external use of the collective regional ethnics, Βοιωτοί and Βοιώτιος, since use of a common name is an important marker of ethnic identification in all periods of Greek history. This study, which includes both epigraphic and literary evidence, shows that the Boiotians did not begin using their collective name, either as a group or as a marker of individual association with that group, in a strictly political or military sense until

---

[4] See A. Smith 1986, 22–31.
[5] Malkin 1998, 134; Hall 1997, 20–26.

the middle of the fifth century BCE. Before this time the term can only be understood to denote the already well-documented cultic aspect of the Boiotian collective.

Given the structure of these chapters, I plainly accept Smith's model of a subjectively perceived core ethnicity. At the same time I welcome Barth's contextual approach to group identity now put forth most lucidly by Hall with regard to ancient Greece. Hall argues that groups construct themselves through the conceptual boundaries they create against others: "ethnic identity can only be constituted by opposition to other ethnic identities." As a social entity, "the ethnic identity of a group is only likely to become salient when confronted with at least one other group."[6] Hall and Barth reject the concept of core ethnicity, but to my mind the two approaches are complementary rather than mutually exclusive. Subjective elements of the core identity of a given group, which both shift and endure depending upon historical context, can be understood to result from both oppositional and aggregative forces.[7]

Smith's secondary concept of "ethnicism" approaches Hall's oppositional model of group identity. For Smith ethnicism comprises "a fundamentally defensive" move and arises when the "group's sense of ethnicity ... is challenged by shattering external events."[8] As Smith also remarks, collective identity can be generated "discontinuously, through significant myth-making encounters,"[9] such as sporadic territorial battles or traditions of such battles, as in the Boiotian tradition of the battle of Keressos, which I treat in my concluding remarks. These "myth-making encounters" in turn may generate or strengthen additional traditions of population movement, territory, and genealogical legitimation, as we also find in the case of the Boiotians.[10] Juxtaposing Smith's and Hall's models of such oppositional ethnicity provides a basis for my approach to the Boiotian collective in the Archaic and Early Classical periods.[11]

I follow this portrait of the Boiotian *ethnos* by questioning the *opinio communis* that attributes Boiotian solidarity at this time to an early political and military *koinon*. Through reanalysis of the literary accounts of Herodotus and Thucydides, and by juxtaposing additional epigraphic and archaeological evidence with the results of my study of Boiotian coinage and *ethnika*, I argue that it was not until the middle of the fifth century that the Boiotians transformed their collective by adding to it a permanent political and military federal system. By the mid-fifth century, then, three different types of community operated in Boiotia simulta-

---

[6] Hall 1997, 32–33, based on Barth 1969, 9–38; see also Malkin 1998, 60.

[7] See McInerney 1999, 9; Hall 1997, 19; Jones 1997, 131.

[8] A. Smith 1986, 55 (also 50).

[9] A. Smith 1986, 76, where he adduces the example of modern Russian identity.

[10] See A. Smith 1986, 51–52.

[11] Other scholars have taken a similar approach to the formation of group identity by blending the models of core ethnicity and oppositional ethnicity (e.g., Sekunda 2000, 331, 347 for the Polichnitai). In adopting a similar method I accept Malkin's revision of Hall's chronology for the rise of oppositional ethnicity within Greece. Malkin argues that oppositional identity had become part of the Hellenic world at the local level in the Archaic period and on the panhellenic level earlier than the early fifth century (Malkin 1998, 60–61).

neously: *ethnos*, *polis*, and *koinon*. Boiotia thus seems to have been a crossroads between north and south, between *polis*-dominated Attika and *ethnos*-oriented Thessaly. While concentrating on the construction of Boiotian collective identity in the Late Archaic and Early Classical periods, then, the present study also concerns the development of this tripartite social and political organization.

This work is the first monograph devoted to Boiotian ethnicity of the Late Archaic and Early Classical periods; in its offering I hope to stimulate further discussion on Boiotian ethnogenesis and community. At the outset, however, I note my debt to previous scholars who have done important work on various aspects of Boiotian history and culture: particularly John Fossey and Albert Schachter. Aside from their projects on Boiotian epigraphy, topography, and cult, other scholars have paid particular attention to the fourth-century Boiotian federation and to federalism in general, such as Roesch and Larsen, but no work on Boiotia has yet taken such an approach to the various categories of evidence in an attempt to define the late sixth- and early fifth-century Boiotian *ethnos*.[12]

Although isolating various criteria and *indicia* of ethnicity may overemphasize the discreteness of each category, with this framework I hope to stimulate further study into the interrelatedness of such markers of identity. However artificial these main categories may seem at first, I have felt their presentation imperative before further work on Boiotian ethnogenesis can proceed.

In approaching Boiotia as a regional collective, this monograph responds to and amplifies recent scholarship on ancient identities and community formation. The past decade has witnessed an increasing number of regional, as opposed to local or panhellenic, studies of ancient Greece, especially for early periods of Greek history.[13] As noted above, this present work builds on these approaches and also relies on recent studies of ancient Greek ethnicities, as well as other less specific works by scholars of ethnicity and identity whose vantage is not classical.[14] While all these previous works are significant in their various fields, none, not even Brock and Hodkinson's *Alternatives to Athens* (2001), treats Boiotia in the necessary detail.

SOURCES, METHODS, RESTRICTIONS, AND TERMINOLOGY

In examining the Boiotian *ethnos* at a discrete moment in time, I restrict myself to sources from the Late Archaic and Early Classical periods as much as possible. Although this body of evidence is often frustratingly slim and riddled with gaps, I have made use of every possible category of material: epigraphic, numismatic, iconographic, archaeological, and literary. It has been pleasantly surprising to note how often these seemingly disparate sources corroborate each other. Given these sources' inevitable breaks in continuity, however, I have at times naturally been forced into the realm of comparison and speculation, but my choice has

[12] Roesch 1965; Larsen 1968.
[13] E.g., Mackil 2003; Morgan 2003; Nielsen 2002; McInerney 1999; Nielsen and Roy 1999.
[14] A. Smith 1986; Barth 1969; Hall 1997; Jones 1997.

largely been between writing an account of Boiotia which includes conjecture or refraining from treating archaic and early classical Boiotia at all.

As much as possible I have analyzed the evidence in terms of Boiotian self-representation by using internal Boiotian sources. However, I have also adopted the now well-accepted view, as first put forth by Barth and Anderson, that aspects of collective identity result in part from the perceptions of outsiders.[15] It thus seems highly probable that the Boiotians internalized non-Boiotian perceptions. Non-Boiotian sources thus comprise part of the evidence adduced in the following chapters and will be shown to reveal much about the Boiotian *ethnos*. In this approach I owe much to Hall who stresses the simultaneous operation of both primordialist and instrumentalist views of collective identity.[16]

My reader may be surprised that one of the topics I do not treat separately but rather raise when relevant is Boiotian cult, although cult naturally played a significant role in maintaining the Boiotian collective and most likely in helping to create it internally. The exception is Chapter Five, in which epigraphic and literary use of the collective ethnics directly concerns Boiotian cult, particularly the cult of Athena Itonia. My hesitation in fully analyzing Boiotian cult stems from its thorough treatment elsewhere. Mackil has most recently addressed the internal coherence of Boiotia as a region through cult and the communication and interactions that Boiotian cult promoted. In light of such discussions, I have felt it generally unnecessary to rehearse similar arguments.[17] I also refrain from including yet another topographical or geographical study of Boiotia. I instead refer my reader to Fossey's and Pritchett's work on the area.[18]

As for terminology, I limit my use of the terms "ethnic" and "ethnicity," preferring instead more generic terms like *ethnos*, collective, and collective identity. I use the term *ethnos* in its ancient Greek sense of nonspecific collective instead of in its common use in Classics as a referent for a non-*polis* political community.[19] Since one of my primary goals lies in defining non-political aspects of the Boiotian collective, I have adopted such generic terminology in order to allow each term to acquire specific meaning in the particular context. When I do use the term ethnicity, I equate it only with those aspects of the Boiotian *ethnos* as defined in this book.[20] I do not intend to link the term to issues of race, which can only complicate a reconstruction of the archaic Boiotian imagined community.[21]

[15] Barth 1969; B. Anderson 1983; see also Malkin 1998, 55–58.

[16] Hall 1997, 19; for these categories and the history of approaches to ancient ethnicity, see Siapkas 2003, 13–14, 41–59, 175–206; Malkin 2001, 1–19; McInerney 2001, 51–73; McInerney 1999, 8–39; Malkin 1998, 55–61; Hall 1997, 1–33.

[17] For Boiotian cult, see Mackil 2003; Bonnechere 2003; Schachter 1967, 1978, 1981–1994, 1990, 1994; Daumas 1998; Scheffer 1992. For cult systems as formulative in communities, especially Phokis, see Morgan 2003, 107–163.

[18] Fossey 1988; Pritchett 1969, 1980, 1982, 1985.

[19] For this distinction, see Siapkas 2003, 12–13.

[20] For the genesis of the modern term ethnicity, see Malkin 1998, 55; Cohen 2000, 23 and n. 71; for its vagueness, see Karakasidou 1997, 19. Like Morgan and McInerney, I do not find the commonplace equation between the terms *ethnos* and ethnicity as troubling as does Siapkas (Siapkas 2003, 12–13 and notes 14 and 17).

I use the terms "federation" and "confederacy" in their strictest sense, as first defined by Larsen and reviewed and accepted by Nielson: a "proper federation" or a "confederacy" is a state "in which there is local citizenship in the smaller communities as well as a joint or federal citizenship in which the citizens are under the jurisdiction both of federal and local authorities."[22] I use the phrase "political and military federation" as an equivalent to "proper federation with citizenship requirements." These terms are to be distinguished from organizations like amphiktyonies and alliances as well as from "tribal" groups. My understanding of the term federation thus seems equivalent to what many historians call the Boiotian "first federation," or what Paul Roesch calls the "Confédération béotienne de l'époque classique."[23]

Jeremy McInerney's definitions of region and geographic region have partially informed my understanding of these terms. For McInerney the term region signifies a territory which had certain natural characteristics that in part helped to shape settlement and subzones within the area. This understanding does not mean that the natural environment caused events, but at the same time it is difficult to maintain that the geologic environment of Boiotia did not affect the number and placement of *poleis* or the dense habitation of certain areas. In my view these patterns in turn influenced dispersion of population, the independence of certain communities, interaction between various communities, even the size and power of some settlements, not to mention the emerging concept of the region itself.[24] Although I am not so much interested in determining how the Boiotian *ethnos* came to be, at the same time I also accept Paasi's concept of a social and collective region as a product "of the development of society" which undergoes "gradual transformation as spatial manifestation of social processes."[25] Both McInerney's spatial definition and Paasi's social categorization of region thus inform my use and understanding of the terms "collective identity" and "regional identity."

Setting aside issues of terminology, I return to the underlying problem addressed in the following chapters: the nature of the Boiotian *ethnos* in the Late Archaic and Early Classical periods. Although historians of Greek political development since Wilamowitz have by and large accepted the existence of a political and military Boiotian federation from the last quarter of the sixth century BCE, a few notable scholars have expressed serious doubts about such an approach. Cauer adds the following caveat to his description of a sixth-century Boiotian federation, for example: "über die urprüngliche Verfassung und die Competenzen des Bundes ist nichts von Belang bekannt."[26] Even Ducat, a champion of late archaic Boiotian military federalism, admits that there can be no

[21] On race and the term ethnicity, see Siapkas 2003, 201.

[22] Larsen 1968, xiv–xv, quoted by Nielsen 1996, 42; see also M. Hansen 1995, 31.

[23] Roesch 1982 and 1965; see also Salmon 1978.

[24] See McInerney 1999, 40–41.

[25] Paasi 1986, 121; see also 113–114 (Paasi's definition of region is more elaborate than this necessarily brief summary reflects).

[26] *RE* III, 1899, col. 643, s.v. *Boiotia* (F. Cauer).

definitive agreement about when the Boiotian federation arose, what it really was, and who was in charge.[27] Schachter has tellingly remarked, "the whole question of this Boiotian confederacy will have to be looked at anew."[28] Instead of reviewing the evidence normally adduced in discussions of early Boiotian federalism, however, in the following chapters I first turn to the various categories of self-definition of the Boiotian *ethnos*; these units of collective meaning will shed much light on the group's attitudes and activities during this period and will lead to a reassessment of sixth-century Boiotian federalism in the concluding chapter of this book.

[27] Ducat 1973, 59; see also Effenterre 1997, 135.
[28] Schachter 1981–94, vol. 2, 216, n. 1.

CHAPTER 1
THE GENEALOGY OF THE EPONYMOUS HERO Βοιωτός

καὶ μὴν ἐπὶ γε τοῖς προγόνοις οὐ μεῖον
Ἀθηναῖοι ἢ Βοιωτοὶ φρονοῦσιν.

Indeed the Athenians thought no less of
their ancestors than did the Boiotians.

Xen. *Hipparch*. 7.2–4.

It almost goes without saying that ancient Greeks were obsessed with genealogy. Traditions of common origins played a particularly vital role in articulating group definition in the Late Archaic period, especially for those communities which traced a collective identity back to an eponymous ancestor.[1] The Hesiodic *Ehoiai*, perhaps our earliest and most lengthy genealogical poem, even includes eponymous genealogies for such foreign and exotic peoples as the Skythians and the Lastrygonians.[2] Hall brings this ancient preoccupation with descent into clearer focus:

> ... genealogies were the instrument by which whole social collectivities could situate themselves in space and time, reaffirming their identity by appeals to eponymous ancestors such as Doros, Ion or Dryops, who were at the same time the retrojected constructions of such identity.[3]

Recent years have witnessed a flurry of writing about such culture-heroes; following M. West, Hall argues that the mid-sixth century saw an increase in interest in such genealogies on the whole. Sparta had already laid claim to territory via traditions of the Herakleidai, but Athenian allegations of descent from Ion gained prominence in this period,[4] as did interest in the stemma of Hellen's descendants.[5]

[1] A. Smith 1986, 22–25; see Nielson 1997, 145; Malkin 1998, 57, 61, 134; Nilsson 1951, 65–80.

[2] Hes. fr. 150, 15–16 and 26–27 MW. M. West includes this fragment among those tales from the *Ehoiai* which he considers late ("surely of the sixth century:" M. West 1985, 131). West's dates for these and other fragments of the *Ehoiai* confirm the late archaic importance of genealogies of eponymous figures and founders.

[3] Hall 1997, 41; for a reiteration, see Morgan 2003, 187. Hall distinguishes between genealogies of eponymous culture-heroes and land genealogies: the former indicating a social group (e.g., Danaios at Argos, Lakedaimon at Sparta); the latter concerning primarily topography and territory (e.g., Taygete at Sparta; Hall 1997, 53; Malkin had earlier made a similar observation: Malkin 1994, 6–7).

[4] Hall 1997, 44, see Solon, fr. 4 (M. West 1972), and Connor 1993, 198–200. Hall posits that by the 470s, Athens had adopted a myth of autochthony in opposition to the older myth of descent from Ion. This is one of the markers in Hall's shift "from an aggregative to an oppositional self-definition" (Hall 1997, 54).

Traditions about the eponymous figurehead of the Boiotians, Βοιωτός, thus naturally comprise an important aspect in defining the community; I thus turn to the genealogy of Βοιωτός in the Late Archaic and Early Classical periods.[6] As we will see, by this time Βοιωτός was considered a descendant of Poseidon and the Thessalian Aiolidai; through others in his family tree he was also connected to regional cult centers, west-central and central Boiotia, and perhaps even to the legend of Theban autochthony.

BOIOTOS' PARENTAGE

Interest in Boiotos' family tree can be traced back to the mid-sixth century through a fragment from the Hesiodic *Ehoiai*, a panhellenic work which M. West dates generally ca. 580–520 but which incorporates much earlier inherited material.[7] The fragment, preserved in Stephanos, briefly treats Boiotos' progeny:

> Ὀγχηστός ἄλσος· Ὅμηρος "Ὀγχηστός θ' ἱερὸν Ποσιδήϊον ἀγλαὸν ἄλσος" [B 506]. κεῖται δὲ ἐν τῆι Ἀλιαρτίων χώραι, ἱδρυθὲν ὑπὸ Ὀγχηστοῦ τοῦ Βοιωτοῦ, ὥς φησιν Ἡσίοδος.

> Grove at Onchestos: Homer: "Onchestos, the glorious grove and sanctuary of Poseidon." It lies in Haliartan territory and was established by Onchestos the son of Boiotos, as Hesiod says.[8]

Here, an Onchestos is Boiotos' son. As the fragment indicates, Onchestos is primarily known as the toponym for the main sanctuary of Poseidon in central Boiotia which appears in sources beginning with the Catalogue of Ships.[9] That it is the only sanctuary included in the Catalogue's primarily geographic description of Boiotia may indicate its cultic significance for the region as a whole. *The Homeric Hymn to Apollo*, one of the earliest of the *Hymns*, also includes the site in the catalogue of the stations on Apollo's journey through Boiotia:

> Ἔνθεν δὲ προτέρω ἔκιες, ἑκατηβόλ' Ἄπολλον, Ὀγχηστὸν δ' ἷξες, Ποσιδήϊον ἀγλαὸν ἄλσος.

> Then you went farther, far-shooting Apollo, and you came to the glorious grove of Poseidon at Onchestos (*Hymn. Hom. Ap.* 229–230).

---

[5] Hall 1997, 43–44, where he suggests Athenian influence. Hall provides two tables of the Hellenic genealogy, one from Hesiod and the other from Euripides.

[6] Ancient sources make clear that Βοιωτός was regarded as the eponym of the group, e.g., Diodoros who twice remarks that Βοιωτός gave his followers the name Βοιωτοί (Diod. Sic. 4. 67.2 and 4.67.6).

[7] For the date, see M. West 1985, 136 (where he also speculatively suggests a narrower date of ca. 540–520, based on the ending of the *Theogony*). For the earlier traditions, see M. West 1985, 100–103, 162–164, 181.

[8] Hes. fr. 219 MW (= Steph. Byz. p. 483.3 Meineke).

[9] *Il.* 2.506; Kirk 1985, 194.

Accordingly, Onchestios is an epithet of this particular manifestation of Boiotian Poseidon.[10] As we will see, later sources concerned with Boiotos' paternity explicitly and consistently name Poseidon as his father. The Hesiodic fragment indicates that these two figures had been clearly linked by the mid-sixth century, although the exact nature of their relationship remains undefined, perhaps because the genealogy needed no rehearsal before a panhellenic audience already familiar with its details.

The Boiotian Korinna is our first extant source to relate Poseidon and Boiotos directly as father and son. In presenting the fragment alongside the *Ehoiai*, I of course raise the vexed issue of her chronology. Dating Korinna has been a matter of some debate since 1970, when M. West challenged the biographical tradition, which describes Korinna as a fifth-century poetess and Pindar's contemporary;[11] West prefers to place her work in the Hellenistic third century on the basis of style, morphology, and subject matter.[12] Although Page too ultimately preferred this late date, in his 1953 edition of Korinna he could not have stated more coherently the fundamental issue surrounding her work: "Korinna must be treated as a law unto herself; we must never make inferences from the common tradition to Korinna, unless they can be verified by reliable testimony."[13] Yet inferences are precisely what underlie arguments for her late dating.

Stewart convincingly reopened the discussion in 1998 by substantiating Tatian's late reference to a fourth-century statue of Korinna through archaeological evidence previously left unconsidered by literary historians.[14] Stewart identifies a marble statuette of Korinna as a late fourth-century copy of a earlier original, "presumably Silanion's statue," mentioned by Pausanias but discounted

---

[10] Also see the later *Homeric Hymn to Hermes* (lines 186–212); Janko 1986, 43; Paus. 9.26.5; 9.37.1. Notably, a river Onchestos is recorded in Thessaly with its source at Krannon (*RE* XVIII, 1959, col. 417, s.v. *Onchestos*; E. Kirsten).

[11] See Campbell 1992, 18–23, testimonia 1–4.

[12] I cite the major proponents for each view. Advocating an early date: Gerber 1970, 394–395; Allen and Frel 1972, 26–30; Kirkwood 1974, 185–186 and nn. 278–280; Roller 1989, 123; Burzacchini 1992, 47–65 (see also Burzacchini 1991, 81–90 for more bibliography); Rayor 1993, 219 and n. 3; Teffeteller 1995, 1077, n. 22; Vottéro 1998, vol. 1, 202–203 (tentatively). Those advocating a third-century date include: Guillon 1958, 47–60; M. West 1970, 277–287 (who bases part of his argument on statements by Guillon); M. West 1990, 553–557; Campbell 1992, 1–3; Clayman 1993, 633–642; Segal 1998, 315–326 (although Segal does not argue unequivocally for the later date). Most recently, Schachter, who accepts Stewart, has argued for a fourth-century date during the Theban hegemony (382–373); although Schachter's reading is nicely based on Boiotian history and its possible relation to Korinna fr. 654, his brief intertextual reference to Sophocles as source for Korinna fr. 654.6 is unconvincing, as is his reference to M. West's tracing of the myth of Zeus' concealment by the Kouretes (Schachter 2005, 275–283). For the ancient evidence of Korinna's life, including her contemporaneity with Pindar, see Page (Ael. *VH* 13.25; Page 1953, 69–74). In his publication of the papyrus, Page himself does not come down on either side of the issue, although he argues strongly for a late date (Page 1953, 65–84).

[13] Page 1953, 29.

[14] For a vitriolic attack on Tatian as a source, see e.g., Page 1953, 73–74, n. 6.

in earlier literary considerations of the poetess.[15] J. Larson subsequently comple-
mented Stewart's argument by discussing Korinna's subject matter, her regionalism and her relationships to Hesiod, Pindar, Bacchylides, and genealogical poetry
in general, which, she remarks, situate Korinna quite "at home in the fifth century."[16] Larson also attributes Korinna's adherence to strictly local stories to her
status as a female poet writing for choruses of young women.[17] It follows from
the likely local occasion and the partially female audience of her poetry (the
female chorus) that Korinna's work would have differed both stylistically and in
subject matter from Pindar's *epinikia* and particularly from poetry written outside
Boiotia by non-Boiotian males for quite different occasions than local Tanagran
or even Boiotian festivals.[18] Given these reasonable objections to the rather more
subjective assignment of Korinna to the third century, I accept the early date for
the poetess and situate her in the early to mid-fifth century as Pindar's contemporary.

I return, then, to Korinna's fragment which links Boiotos to Poseidon as a
son, as quoted by Herodian (in discussing Boiotian use of τ in place of ς):

Κόριννα Βοιωτοῖ· τοῦ δὲ μάκαρ Κρονίδη, τοῦ Ποτειδάωνος Ϝάναξ Βοιωτέ.

As Korinna says in her *Boiotos*: *wanax* Boiotos, blessed descendant of Cro-
nos, son of Poseidon.[19]

This stemma is significant in itself, for it corroborates the link between Poseidon
and Boiotos made only implicitly in the *Ehoiai*. That we find it in Korinna is most
important, since the Tanagran poetess concentrated on epichoric traditions of
regional and local significance. That she composed a poem about the Boiotian
eponymous hero thus indicates his status in the region; her concentration here on
Boiotos' paternity signifies that his family tree was also considered important
enough to include in performance for a local audience of the early fifth century.

Further interest in Boiotos' parentage also appears early in the fifth if not
already in the late sixth century, the more commonly accepted date for Asios, a
Samian poet of hexameter genealogies.[20] Asios, who seems to have been quite
interested in Boiotian myth, gives the following brief account of Βοιωτός:

---

[15] Stewart 1998, 278–281 (quote from p. 280).

[16] J. Larson 2002, 56.

[17] J. Larson 2002, 58–59. For a strong opinion on Korinna's parochialism, see Page 1953,
45. Rayor fully discusses the misapprehension of Korinna's poetry based on gender (1993, 219–
231).

[18] For Korinna's audience, see Rayor 1993 and Henderson 1995.

[19] Korinna fr. 6 (Page); Herodian p.m.l. i II.8, II 917.15 L. Wilamowitz emended the line to
τοῦδε μάκαρ Κρονίδη τοῦ Ποτειδάωνος ἄναξ Βοίωτε (see Page 1953, 32).

[20] Huxley advocates the sixth-century date by convincingly connecting the characters and
geography of Asios' fragments to events and figures of the early sixth century (Huxley 1969,
95). He argues against the alternative late fifth-century date, since it is based only on the style
and tone of one of the less securely ascribed fragments (*FGrHist* 76 F 60 = Ath. 525 E–F); for
this argument, see Bowra 1957, 391–401, esp. 400; also Schachter (1981–1994, vol. 1, 59) and
Forrest 1956, 43, n. 3.

... καὶ Ἄσιος τὸν ποιητὴν φήσαντα ὅτι τὸν Βοιωτὸν "Δίου ἐνὶ μεγάροις τέκεν εὐειδὴς Μελανίππη."

... and the poet Asios says that beautiful Melanippe bore Boiotos in the halls of Δίου.[21]

Upon first reading, Zeus seems to appear as Boiotos' father, as Gantz proposes, translating the phrase Δίου ἐνὶ μεγάροις as "in the halls of Zeus."[22] While this meaning of the text is possible, Huxley suggests a better reading based on mythology often associated with the birth of Βοιωτός and appearing in Strabo. Although the later story of Βοιωτός and Melanippe in Euripides is set in Metapontum, Strabo provides a different version of the tale where Melanippe brings her child to Δῖος, the eponym of the Thessalian town Δῖον, where there was even a hero shrine of the Metapontian Μέταβος.[23] It is in this context that Strabo quotes Asios; the phrase can thus also be understood to mean "in the halls of Dios/ Dion."[24] This seems the preferable reading of the term here, given evidence for Boiotos' descent from Poseidon in our other late Archaic sources.

Asios identifies Boiotos' mother, Melanippe, but provides no information about her family tree. Later accounts indicate that in one established tradition, at least, Melanippe was a daughter of Aiolos, son of Hellen.[25] Our only other archaic source for Aiolos' family tree, the Hesiodic *Ehoiai*, does not include Melanippe as one of his daughters, nor can her name be restored to the catalogue through Apollodoros.[26] This omission indicates little about Βοιωτός, however, for all other ancient sources for Boiotos' genealogy connect him through his mother's line to Aiolos. Melanippe's absence in the *Ehoiai* thus likely reflects a variant tradition for her or Aiolos' family tree. It does not indicate that other Archaic versions of Boiotos' genealogy did not consider him a descendant of Aiolos.[27]

Hellanikos provides a later but complementary version of Boiotos' genealogy:

---

[21] Asios fr. 2 PEG (ap. Strabo 6.1.15). For Asios' genealogical interests, see Asios' genealogy of Astypalaia and Samos (Paus. 7.4.1), two important local figures from Asios' native island (Huxley 1969, 90–91). Here Meandrios fathers Samia, thus staking the island's claim to one of the most economically important Ionian river valleys. For Asios' Boiotian interests, note that five of Asios' twelve fragments concern Boiotian myth (frs. 1–5 Kinkel); some are quite localized (e.g., the genealogy of Ptoios, fr. 3) and propagandistic (Huxley 1969, 90–92).

[22] Gantz 1993, 734.

[23] Huxley 1969, 93.

[24] Strabo 6.1.15.

[25] See below on Euripides' *Sophe*; also Gantz 1993, 734.

[26] Hes. fr. 10a.96, 34 MW (1990). Gantz adds the two daughters of Aiolos mentioned by Apollodoros (Kalyke and Kanake) to Hesiod's fragmentary account of the other daughters, however (Peisidike, Alkyone, and Perimede; Gantz 1993, 168). To these five West adds the Aiolis of Hesiod fr. 10a.103 (M. West 1985, 61, n. 68).

[27] M. West's suggestion that Boiotos descended from Asopos is possible but unlikely given the consistency in other archaic versions of Boiotos' descent from Aiolos (M. West 1985, 102– 103, 181).

μετωνομάσθη δὲ Βοιωτία κατὰ μέν τινας ἀπὸ Βοιωτοῦ τοῦ Ποσειδῶνος καὶ Ἄρνης ...

According to some, Boiotia is named after Boiotos, son of Poseidon and Arne ... [28]

Two aspects of this account are important in this context. First, the fragment reiterates the tradition of Boiotos' relationship to Poseidon from the *Ehoiai* and Korinna. Boiotos' descent from Poseidon, in fact, remains a consistent factor in subsequent versions of his genealogy; its unwavering persistence in the tradition thus indicates its continued importance from the early sixth century onward.

Second, the accounts of Hellanikos and Asios at first seem contradictory, for in Hellanikos Arne is Boiotos' mother; Asios' Melanippe is not mentioned. As we will see, Arne is the name of the Thessalian and Boiotian communities involved in the tradition of Boiotian migration in which Boiotos played a role (Hes. fr. 218 MW). It is thus no surprise that Arne appears in Boiotos' genealogy by Hellanikos' time. Notably, West has suggested that the figure Arne may have been included in the earlier *Ehoiai* in the context of Boiotos.[29] Given the link between Boiotos and the migration-community of Arne in Hesiod, West's suggestion seems plausible, although unprovable. In terms of Boiotos' descent from Arne in Hellanikos, however, it is most significant that Arne, like Asios' Melanippe, was also considered a daughter of Aiolos in antiquity, at least in Diodoros.[30] It thus seems possible that Boiotos was thought to have descended from a daughter of Aiolos in our earliest two accounts of Boiotos' maternity: Asios and Hellanikos. The specific identity of this Aiolid, whether Melanippe or Arne, may have been a less important feature of the family tree. In sum, then, by Hellanikos' time Boiotos' father is still identified as Poseidon and his mother likely continued to be an Aiolid, as she had been in Asios. This set of parents was current by the Late Archaic period, either implied or directly noted (*Ehoiai*, Asios, Korinna).

In the last quarter of the fifth century, Euripides treats Boiotos' family in his tragedy *Melanippe Sophe*. Here Poseidon is again Boiotos' father, as in Korinna, and Melanippe is his mother, as in Asios.[31] To Poseidon Melanippe bears twins, Boiotos and Aiolos, whose birth, attempted murder, recognition, and rescue of their mother forms the core of the play and a second lost tragedy: the *Melanippe Desmotis*. What is most significant in this later context is Melanippe's genealogy: in the prologue to the *Melanippe Sophe*, she informs the audience that her father is Aiolos, son of Hellen.[32] Euripides thus corroborates the Aiolid identity of Boiotos' mother from the earlier sources which began being recorded in the late sixth century with Asios.

[28] Hellanikos *FGrHist* 4 F 51 (= Schol. *Il.* 2.494).

[29] M. West 1985, 102.

[30] Diod. Sic. 4.67.3–6.

[31] Eur. *Sophe*; for full discussion, see Webster 1967, 147–157, who dates the play to 422 BCE (Webster 1967, 117).

[32] Pseudo-Eratosthenes, citing Euripides, also makes Melanippe the daughter of Aiolos, although he changes the plot (Gantz 1993, 734).

BOIOTOS' CHILDREN

Although Boiotos' parentage is one of the most consistent and thus significant aspects of his family tree, it is also worth looking at the children that the late archaic and early classical sources attribute to him. These descendants are generally linked to important regional and local cult centers as well as to certain Boiotian areas and communities.

As noted above, Hesiod situates Onchestos, the founder and eponym of Poseidon's regional cult center, as Boiotos' son.[33] This link is noteworthy, for the early significance of the regional sanctuary is attested through both archaic literary and epigraphic references as well as in material remains (e.g., *Il.* 2.506). The relationship between Boiotos and Onchestos also gives Boiotos a certain resonance for the community of Haliartos, in whose territory the sanctuary of Onchestos lay, as the *Iliad* and other archaic poems attest. It may not be insignificant that the sanctuary of Poseidon Onchestios later became one of the central cult places for the Boiotian *koinon* and was chosen as the neighboring site for the federal *bouleterion*.[34] Hesiod's link between Boiotos and Onchestos, then, firmly ties Boiotos to a cult center active by the Late Archaic period and shared by fellow Boiotians from various poleis around the region.

Korinna too promotes Boiotos' progeny in a fragment quoted by a scholiast to Apollodoros; here the scholiast details the rationale behind the alternative name for Thebes, "Ogygia:"

Ὠγυγίας δὲ τὰς Θήβας ἀπὸ Ὠγύγου τοῦ <πρῶτον> βασιλεύσαντος αὐτῶν. Κόριννα δὲ τὸν Ὤγυγον Βοιωτοῦ υἱόν. ἀπὸ τούτου δὲ καὶ τῶν Θηβῶν πύλαι.

Thebes is called Ogygia after Ogygos who was their first king. Korinna says that Ogygos was the son of Boiotos. From him also are called the gates of Thebes.[35]

Aside from Korinna, no late archaic or early classical sources describe Ogygos. Thus, we must tentatively turn to later evidence, especially Pausanias, for speculation on Ogygos' potential earlier significances in Boiotian tradition. He is, as above, considered the first king of Thebes by Apollodoros' scholiast and an early Theban king by Aristodemos, who locates his grave near one of Thebes' seven gates from which it took its name.[36] Pausanias associates Ogygos with the primordial flood in Boiotia.[37] Ogygos thus seems to have been a figure associated with beginnings, perhaps especially of Thebes. The *Suda* attributes to Ogygos three daughters, the Praxidikai, whose collective sanctuary Pausanias sees at the edge of Haliartan territory.[38] As Schachter notes, two of Ogygos' daughters have

[33] Hes. fr. 219 MW (= Steph. Byz. p. 483. 3 Meineke).
[34] See Schachter 1981–1994, vol. 2, 206–221, for the details of the cult and site.
[35] Korinna fr. 8 (Page); Schol. Ap. Rhod. III 1177–1187a (Wendel).
[36] Aristodemos *FGrHist* 383 F 4.
[37] Paus. 9.5 (an Ogygos also appears in an Attic flood: Paus. 1.38.7).
[38] Paus. 9.33.4.

regionally significant cultic connections: Alalkomenia, associated with the sanctuary of Athena Alalkomenia near Haliartos, and Aulis, linked of course to the site of Artemis from which the Trojan expedition sailed.[39] The figure of Ogygos thus has ties to Thebes, Haliartos (west-central Boiotia), and Boiotia's eastern seaboard. We cannot be sure that these connections were known or promoted by Korinna in her earlier presentation of Ogygos as son of Boiotos, although it seems likely that at least the Theban royal connection would have been known from Korinna's time, since catalogues of royalty may have changed less over the centuries than other parts of Boiotian mythic tradition. But at least we can say that Boiotos' descendants were a topic of local interest for Korinna's audiences and that Boiotos was thought to have had at least two known sons by her time: Onchestos (Hesiod) and Ogygos (Korinna).

Later traditions include another regional figure in Boiotos' family; Diodoros, for example, makes Itonos the son of Boiotos.[40] Although we likewise cannot retroject this exact relationship back to the Late Archaic and Early Classical periods, it is suggestive that Itonos is mentioned in the quotation of another fragment of Korinna, a third attributed to her work on Boiotos:

Ἀρμενίδας δὲ ἐν τοῖς Θηβαϊκοῖς Ἀμφικτύονος υἱὸν Ἴτωνον ἐν Θεσσαλίαι γεννηθῆναι, ἀφ' οὗ Ἴτων πόλις καὶ Ἰτωνὶς Ἀθηνᾶ. μέμνηται καὶ Ἀλέξανδρος ἐν τῶι α' τῶν Κορίννης ὑπομνημάτων.

In his *Thebaika* Armenidas says that Itonos, the son of Amphiktyon, was born in Thessaly; from him come the city Iton and Itonian Athena. He is also called Alexandros in the first book of Korinna's memoranda.[41]

Although to the scholiast the Thessalian Itonos is not Boiotos' son, as he later appears in Diodoros, for Korinna Itonos at least seems to have been a figure worthy of inclusion; she had another name for him, but if the scholiast is right in equating the two figures, Itonos/Alexandros played some sort of role in Korinna's treatment of the eponymous Boiotos. Sources show that the Thessalian Itonos was an important figure in south-central Thessaly, of course;[42] he was also significant in Boiotian cult and was particularly visible through the well-documented and -studied Boiotian cult of Athena Itonia, an important patron goddess of the Boiotian collective from the Archaic period onward.[43] Korinna's Itonos/

---

[39] *Suda* s.v. Πραξιδίκη; Paus. 9.33.5; on the Praxidikai, see Schachter 1981–1994, vol. 3, 5–6.

[40] Diod. Sic. 4.67.7.

[41] Korinna fr. 7 (Page); Schol. Ap. Rhod. 1.551 (Wendel).

[42] See e.g., Simonides Keios *FGrHist* 8 F 1 (for the goddess Itonia). For the sanctuaries of Thessalian Itonia, some of the earliest attested in the region, see: Paus. 1.13.1; Polyaen. 2.54; Lazarides 1965, 311–313; Morgan 1997, 174. For full bibliography on the archaeology of Itonia in Thessaly, see Morgan 1997, 194, n. 31. Philia seems to have been particularly important. On this site as Arne, see Morgan 1997.

[43] See Schachter 1981–1994, vol. 1, 117–127, on Athena Itonia in general. For specifics, see Alk. fr. 324 Voigt (fr. 147 Page); Bacch. fr. 15 Snell; Pind. fr. 94b, 41–49; P. Ure 1927, 57; A. Ure 1929, 160–171; A. Ure 1935, 227–228; Sparkes 1967, 121; Maffre 1975, 432 (no. 1); Kilinski 1990, 45. For various proposals for the Itonion's location, see Foucart 1885, 428; Frazer

Alexandros thus ties Boiotos further to west-central Boiotia, to the *polis* Koroneia and, unsurprisingly, to the Boiotian cult of Itonia specifically. Through the
related cult figure of Itonia, Itonos' appearance also ties the Boiotians to south-
central Thessaly, as does their descent from an Aiolid, as I discuss below. Itonos
was of such stature in Boiotian myth, in fact, that in later tradition he seems to
have superseded Poseidon as Boiotos' father, as Pausanias records.[44]

In sum, then, by Korinna's time tradition ascribed at least two children to
Boiotos: Onchestos and Ogygos. The poetess also attests to Boiotos' familial
relationship to Itonos. Together these descendants link Boiotos to regional cult
centers as well as more local community territories, especially Haliartan and
Koroneian territory. By the early fifth century, then, Boiotos thus has emerged as
a figure of both general regional appeal as well as of specific epichoric importance.

SUMMARY AND DATE OF THE TRADITION

This evidence from the *Ehoiai*, Korinna, Asios, Hellanikos, Euripides, and the
later sources suggests that the precise identity of Boiotos' mother (Arne or Melanippe) is not a significant detail of his parentage. Rather, his maternal grandfather, Aiolos, is one of the most important family figures, for it is he who consistently appears as Boiotos' ancestor. The other crucial relation is Boiotos' father, Poseidon, attested explicitly in three of the four earliest sources for the
genealogy (Korinna, Hellanikos, Euripides). The Hesiodic *Ehoiai*, our fourth and
earliest source, hints at this link between Boiotos and Poseidon ca. 580 BCE.
When considered together, these earliest versions of Boiotos' family tree, which
appear in both Boiotian and non-Boiotian sources, suggest that Boiotos' maternal
descent from Aiolos had become a canonical part of his family tree by the late
sixth century (the time of Asios, our first source for this part of the stemma).
Boiotos' descent from Poseidon comes to light by the early fifth century (Korinna) but is hinted at already in the early sixth century by the Hesiodic *Ehoiai*.
Boiotos' children, likewise important for their ties to cult, also start appearing in
genealogies at this time.

The emergence of Boiotos' family tree during the Mid- to Late Archaic period should be considered together with the other nascent articulations of Boiotian group identity discussed in the following chapters (e.g., traditions of migration, shared symbolism, common dialect). The continued importance of Boiotos'
genealogy as established at this time and the subsequent usefulness of this
tradition of descent for the Boiotian collective is indicated by the fact that the
genealogy did not undergo significant change or transformation in later sources.

1898, 169–170; Pritchett 1969, 85–88; Buckler 1996, 62; Krentz 1989, 313–317; Spyropoulos
1972, 317–138; Spyropoulos 1973a, 385–392, 394; Spyropoulos 1973b, 5–6. For the relationship between Thessalian and Boiotian Itonia: Hekataios *FGrHist* 1 F 2; Strabo 9.2.29; Sakellariou 1990, 187. See also Chapter Five.

[44] Paus. 9.1.1; Pausanias gives no source other than "λέγουσι." Stephanos continues this
tradition, s.v. *Boiotia*.

PRIMARY CONSEQUENCES OF BOIOTOS' GENEALOGY

Aiolos

Boiotos' descent from Aiolos, a son of Hellen, has important ramifications. First, it makes Boiotos and his people Greek. This categorization is simple but not insignificant, for numbering the Boiotians among other groups of canonical Greeks gives the collective a traditional and respected pedigree. This situation resembles contemporaneous construction of Phokian genealogy; in the sixth century the Phokians appropriate the Aiakid Phokos as one of their eponyms, thereby placing themselves within the Hellenic family tree.[45] We see a similar appropriation of the Thessalian Aiolos in the genealogy of Boiotos.

Second, when Boiotos' status as grandson to Aiolos is superimposed upon the Hellenic genealogy, as attested in our earliest archaic source, the Hesiodic *Ehoiai*, Boiotos assumes a significant position:[46]

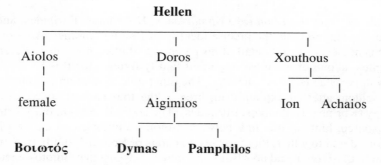

Here Boiotos becomes roughly contemporaneous with other significant descendants of Hellen, including Dymas and Pamphilos, eponymous heroes for two of the Dorian tribes, and Ion, eponym of the Ionians and a prominent figure in Athenian tradition. This generational arrangement implies that Boiotos was considered an important figurehead who represented the separate cultural group of the Boiotians. The panhellenic status of the *Ehoiai* indicates that Boiotos' designation of the Boiotians as a significant cultural collective was recognized both inside and outside the region by the sixth century.

When inserted into the later Euripidean stemma of Hellen, Boiotos belongs to the same generation as other eponyms of influential groups in the late fifth century: Ion, Doros, and Achaios.

---

[45] McInerney 1999, 144, where he lists further comparanda.
[46] For this table, see Hall 1997, 43 (Boiotos' position inserted here).

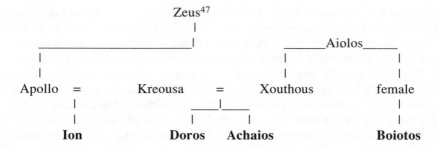

Together these sixth- and fifth-century stemmata of Boiotos clarify his importance as a mythological and cultural figurehead. It is reasonable to suggest, then,
that well before these periods the group named after Boiotos claimed equality
with other significant cultural groups: the Dorians, the Ionians, and the Achaeans.

Boiotos' descent from Aiolos plays a second crucial role for the Boiotian
collective by linking the group to Thessaly. During the Archaic period the descendants of Aiolos, especially his daughters and their children, were important
in traditions of north-central Greece, especially those concerning central Thessaly and the Iolkos region. M. West's chart of Aiolos' offspring from the *Ehoiai*
shows that three of Aiolos' five daughters and their families were associated with
various geographic regions in Thessaly.[48] It is natural that the ancestors of the
Boiotian eponym have Thessalian connections since the tradition of migration, in
which Boiotos was involved, also closely ties the Boiotians to south-central
Thessaly. Hellanikos' later version of Boiotos' genealogy further associates the
hero's family and the tradition of migration, for to Hellanikos Boiotos' mother is
Arne, the Aiolid who shares the name of the south-central Thessalian community
to which the Boiotians are connected in the migration story.[49] I will return to the
migration tradition later in this chapter and in Chapter Two; for now, it suffices to
note that Boiotos' genealogy links the Boiotian collective to southern Thessaly,
the very area considered their original home.

Aiolos holds further significance as an ancestor of Boiotos, for Aiolos' other
offspring concern archaic Boiotia specifically, as the names of his sons and
grandsons indicate. The *Ehoiai* lists Athamas, king of the Minyans and eponym
of the Boiotian Athamantine plain, as a son of Aiolos.[50] In the *Catalogue* Athamas seems to have sired Leukon, the eponym of the *Leukonis limne*, a name for
lake Kopais.[51] In the late sixth century Asios makes Athamas the father of Ptoios,

[47] See also Hall 1997, 43.

[48] M. West 1985, 60–63 (for the chart, see 61).

[49] Hellanikos *FGrHist* 4 F 51 (= Schol. *Il.* 2.494), quoted above in the context of Boiotos'
descent from Poseidon and Arne.

[50] Hes. frs. 68, 69, and 70.1–7; the earliest source for Athamas' connection to Minyan
Orchomenos is Hellanikos *FGrHist* 4 F 126 (= Schol. Ap. Rhod. III. 265: καὶ ῾Ελλάνικός φησι
τὸν ᾿Αθάμαντα ᾿Ορχομενὸν ῷκηκέναι); Pausanias mentions Athamas as the eponym of the
plain (Paus. 9.24.1). For a *stemma* of Aiolos' sons, see M. West 1985, 175–176.

the civic hero of the northeastern Boiotian *polis* Akraiphia.[52] Apollodoros too names Ptoios and Leukon as Athamas' sons and adds Schoineus, eponym of the Homeric town of Schoineis (*Il.* 2.497), a few miles to the north or northwest of Thebes.[53] In the *Bibliotheke* Erythros, the probable eponym for Homeric Erythrai (*Il.* 2.499), a community just south of Thebes, is also Athamas' son.[54] M. West has demonstrated that Apollodoros relies on Hesiod's *Ehoiai* for his arrangement and genealogies.[55] It thus seems reasonable to suggest that Schoineus and Erythros may have also been recorded as Athamas' sons in the *Ehoiai*. At any rate, the sons of Athamas are well represented in archaic sources and link Aiolos' male descendants, including Boiotos implicitly, to the geography of northeast and central Boiotia.

The end of the *Ehoiai*'s treatment of Athamas' family is fragmentary, but M. West argues that a final and unidentified son of Athamas was Minyas: mythical king, eponym of the Minyans, father of Orchomenos, and eponym of the most powerful archaic *polis* in northwestern Boiotia.[56] West's suggestion may be corroborated by another fragment from the *Catalogue* which concentrates on a list of Orchomenos' sons, one of whom is Aspledon, the name of another archaic Minyan community in northwestern Boiotia (*Il.* 2.511).[57] Presumably the *Ehoiai* treated the family of Orchomenos from its beginning and included the famous patriarch Minyas. It is likewise possible that Minyas was the grandfather of Amphion in the Hesiodic fragment 33a.6, in all likelihood the same Amphion who built Thebes with his brother Zethus.[58] Even if Minyas did not appear in the *Ehoiai*, however, the inclusion of the family tree of Orchomenos and of Orchomenos' sons highlights the early importance of this additional branch of the descendants of Aiolos. As noted above, the family of Athamas and his sons connect the progeny of Aiolos to central and northeastern Boiotia. Here the descendants of Aiolos' son Minyas also link Aiolos' family to northwestern Boiotia.

This brief look at Aiolos' family tree suggests that his immediate descendants played a significant role in Boiotian traditions in the Archaic period. Aiolos' sons ground the family in northwestern, central, and eastern Boiotia. His daughters establish Aiolian connections to Thessaly and thus call to mind the tradition of Boiotian migration from Thessaly in which Boiotos played a role, as we will see below. That the Boiotian eponymous figurehead is related to Aiolos as grandson in sixth- and fifth-century genealogies fits well into this scheme.[59] It may also be significant that claims of descent from a Thessalian figure are prominent in other

---

[51] Steph. Byz. s.v. *Kopai*; Hes. *Ehoiai* fr. 70.9 and 28.

[52] Asios fr. 3 Ki (= Paus. 9.23.6).

[53] Schachter 1981–1994, vol. 3, 15. My description is based on Strabo's location of the site: Strabo 9.2.22; Apollod. 1.9.2.

[54] Schachter 1981–1994, vol. 3, 15. In one source, however, Erythros is called Porphyrion.

[55] M. West 1985, 44–45.

[56] Hes. frs. 70.30 and 35; M. West 1985, 64 and 66.

[57] Hes. fr. 77 (= Steph. Byz. s.v. *Aspledon*).

[58] M. West 1985, 65–66 (see also the *stemma* on p. 175).

[59] In Diodoros' late account of Boiotos' wanderings, Boiotos inherits the throne of Aiolis from Aiolos himself; see Diod. Sic. 4.67.6.

areas of central Greece, for example, in Phokis, where one of the eponymous heroes Phokos hails from southern Thessaly.[60]

Poseidon

A second important figure in these earliest accounts of Boiotos' family is his father, Poseidon, who appears, as we have seen, as early as the *Ehoiai*. Boiotian Korinna's fragment, which makes the two father and son, is particularly illustrative of Boiotian attitudes toward their eponym. She addresses Boiotos as Κρονίδη, an epic term which in the *Iliad* is reserved primarily for Zeus but which is also perfectly natural for Poseidon. Through this designation Korinna thus sets Boiotos as a direct descendant of the Titans and brings him very close to the Olympians themselves in chronology and blood. Korinna also borrows the term Ϝάναξ from epic and with it gives Boiotos a title associated mostly with epic heroes, such as Agamemnon, Achilles, Nestor, and Priam, as well as divinities, including Poseidon, Zeus, Apollo, Hephaistos, and Hermes. These designations further indicate Boiotos' great significance as eponymous figurehead for the Boiotians and as semi-divine son of Poseidon.[61]

In the end, the majority of versions of Boiotos' parentage define the hero as the son of Poseidon and a daughter of Aiolos. The stemma's consistency testifies to the community's belief in the tradition and perhaps also to the age of the tradition itself.

CONCLUSIONS

In the Archaic period Boiotos was connected to cult figures of particular importance in central Boiotia, especially Poseidon and perhaps Athena Itonia. Evidence for these links begins with the *Ehoiai* and continues through the fifth century. Traditions of Boiotos' genealogy linking him to Poseidon and Itonia thus emphasize the collective importance of these regional cults.

Boiotos' family tree also concerns Thessaly, for he is consistently depicted as a son of an Aiolid, a family with significant ties to northeast and south-central Thessaly in the Archaic period. This Aiolid is sometimes identified as Arne. It is

---

[60] McInerney 1999, 145–146.

[61] Later accounts continued to emphasize Poseidon's paternity. Diodoros, for example, identifies Poseidon as Boiotos' father and, recalling Hellanikos and the Boiotian traditions of migration, claims Arne as Boiotos' mother (Diod. Sic. 4.67.3–6). Nikokrates (ca. 200 BCE) and Euphorion of Chalkis (third century) likewise repeat the Poseidon-Arne-Boiotos *stemma* (Nikokrates *FGrHist* 376 F 5; Euphorion fr. 113 Scheideweiler). Both Strabo and Hyginus' versions of Boiotos' family tree incorporate the *stemma* from Euripides' *Sophe*: Poseidon and Melanippe as parents of Boiotos and Aiolos (here Boiotos' brother; Strabo 6.1.15 [also our source for Asios fr. 2]; Hyg. *Fab.* 157). Even such late sources as scholiasts on the *Iliad* still connected Boiotos to Poseidon: one scholiast even makes Boiotos the founder of the sanctuary of Poseidon at Onchestos (Schol. B(L) ad *Il.* 2.506).

significant, then, that Arne's presence in the *stemmata* and Boiotos' Aiolid connections to southern Thessaly relate to the tradition of Boiotian migration, a story in which Boiotos may have been involved, as I discuss in the following Chapter. These points of similarity suggest that both the genealogy of Boiotos and the migration stories emphasized Boiotian links to southern Thessaly. Notably, then, each of the two main criteria of Boiotian ethnicity – claims of descent and claims of territory – recall and reinforce each other.

CHAPTER 2
EPIC HEROES: TRADITIONS OF BOIOTIAN MIGRATION
AND HABITATION

A second main criterion of ancient collective identity is a shared tradition of habitation and claim to territory.[1] This claim to land is a part of a shared history, and, as is clear from the multitude of contemporary political crises associated with such claims, the salience of such traditions depends little on where the community in question actually resides: the link between a people and their putative homeland is difficult if not impossible to challenge.[2] In addition to the well-known traditions of autochthony in Athens and elsewhere, the importance that various ancient Greek communities placed upon this category of collective definition has recently been demonstrated for Arkadia and Messenia, among others;[3] the tradition of the Herakleidai and the Lakonians provides perhaps the most famous example of the link between territory and an ancient *ethnos*.[4]

Traditions of territory were no less significant for the Boiotians. In what follows I examine the traditions of Boiotian migration and habitation diachronically in an attempt to establish a relative chronology. Thucydides is our most detailed non-Boiotian source (1.12.3). Yet elements of the migration tradition appear already in the panhellenic *Iliad* and *Ehoiai*, as well as the pseudo-Hesiodic *Aspis*. That many details from these panhellenic and archaic Boiotian sources also occur in Thucydides' later account indicates that by the middle of the fifth century the tradition of Boiotian migration had assumed a standard form, both inside and outside Boiotia, with a focus on several key points. The stories seem to have solidified during the Archaic period, the very time which provides a multiplicity of other evidence for collective Boiotian cohesion.

This study differs from earlier work by focusing on how the tradition of Boiotian migration and habitation concerns the development of collective identity in Boiotia. Nineteenth-century scholars sought to identify an historical point of migration and to define a precise genetic relationship between the Boiotians and Thessalians.[5] Wilamowitz wrote extensively on the topic and, following Thucydides (1.12.2), set the Boiotians in Boiotia before the putative Dorian invasion with Thebes as leader. Wilamowitz also speculated about areas in Boiotia which maintained pockets of earlier inhabitants. On the basis of Thucydides 3.61.2 and Herodotus 5.79 he suggested that "original Boiotians" remained in Plataia, Tana-

---

[1] Hall 1997, 25.

[2] See A. Smith 1986, 28–29.

[3] See Nielsen 2002 (Arkadia); Siapkas 2003 (Messenia); Morgan 2003, 187–205.

[4] Hall 1997, 56–65.

[5] E.g., Meyer's claim that the Boiotians and the Thessalians were of the "ursprünglicher Stammesgemeinschaft" (*RE* III, 1899, col. 642, s.v. *Boiotia*, quoted by F. Cauer).

gra, Thespiai and Koroneia: cities which were consistently hostile to Thebes and which preserved their independence until the sixth century, according to his view.[6]

Many of these earlier approaches are problematic for a number of reasons. Wilamowitz took much of his information about early Boiotia and Thebes from Thucydides' Theban speeches, for example, suspect as later exaggerations and fabrications.[7] Moreover, as McInerney notes, many early scholars concerned with migrations concentrated on proving the existence of Dorian influence on early Greek institutions as well as the superiority of a Dorian *Volksgeist*.[8] Scholars likewise emphasized race by focusing on "pure" Boiotian and "impure" non-native populations. The most serious flaw in much of the early work on the Boiotian migration, however, lies in its often synchronic approach to disparate sources from different time periods and an acceptance of them *in toto* as objectively true. While part of the tradition surrounding the Boiotian migration may indeed have arisen as a reflection of some historical activity, attempting to trace the tradition back to these hypothetical moments is methodologically untenable.[9]

In the following chapter, then, I instead trace the chronological development of the tradition of Boiotian migration and habitation of the region, suggest a general historical context into which we can set the development of this tradition's core, and discuss its significance in that context. I first treat the early sources and then discuss Thucydides' version in greater detail.

THE *ILIAD*

A. The Catalogue of Ships (*Il.* 2.494–511)

Our earliest source for traditions of Boiotian migration and habitation is the *Iliad's* Catalogue of Ships, where the poem lists numerous communities occupied by the Βοιωτοί. As we will see, the Catalogue successfully depicts the communality of the Boiotians by focusing in great detail on Boiotian geography; many other groups in the Catalogue do not receive similarly extensive treatment. The Boiotians also appear as a large and wealthy group, often associated with their central Greek neighbors. Although two of the Boiotian leaders from the Catalogue are visible elsewhere in the poem, only one is particularly noteworthy (Peneleos); even so he is identified only as a Boiotian and not distinguished by any other term; his fellow Boiotian leaders from the catalogue and elsewhere remain simply generic figures. The epic's overall portrait of the Boiotians is one of a heavily populated, wealthy regional communality that supports and in some sense subsumes its individual members.

---

[6] Wilamowitz-Möllendorff 1895, vol. 1, 264.

[7] E.g., Thuc. 3.61.2; see Chapter Six for more specifics on these speeches.

[8] E.g., Curtius, see McInerney 1999, 12–20, esp. 19–20.

[9] For similar warnings, see Morgan 2003, 188. For modern attempts to construct a narrative of Boiotian history from a variety of chronological sources, see R. Buck 1979, esp. 55–105, and Salmon 1978, esp. 15–17.

This characterization conveys the image of the Boiotians that was acceptable and familiar to both Boiotians and non-Boiotians alike at the time of the textualization of epic in transcript form, a process which, after Nagy, I set in the sixth century after the gradual consolidation of epic through oral tradition during the seventh century.[10] The Catalogue itself has been successfully defended as an integral part of the poem by Kirk and Visser; like other sections of the epic the Catalogue is highly formulaic, and its subjects are too integral to the rest of the poem to be separate additions later than epic's panhellenic period of fixity.[11] The Catalogue's portrayal of the Boiotians should thus be set in the Mid- to Late Archaic period. Certainly the Catalogue's core or parts of it could have derived from earlier tradition, as would seem natural for a catalogue, but in assessing its date, we must carefully focus on this main period of textual fixity; we cannot extrapolate backwards from this time to select an earlier period of creation.[12]

The Catalogue spends more time on the Boiotians than any other group and gives them primacy in the list. They have the greatest number of leaders, men, and communities. On this basis Kirk calls their entry "unique" and refers to the "Boeotian colouring" of the first few contingents of the Catalogue.[13] Anderson has even posited an eighth-century Boiotian poet for the Catalogue as a whole.[14] Whether or not the Catalogue was Boiotian in origin, the outstanding characteristics of the Boiotian entry, which have occasioned such speculation by modern scholars, would undoubtedly have also been of great significance to Boiotians throughout antiquity but especially during the Archaic period when other aspects of their collective identity were solidifying. As McInerney notes, the Catalogue as a whole marks an already present and strong collective consciousness of the

---

[10] Nagy 2004, 1–39, esp. 27. On the seventh century for the formulation of the *Iliad* and the following stage of crystallization/textualization in the mid-sixth century, see also E. Cook 2004, 49–50; S. Larson 2002, 219–222; van Wees 1998, 333–378; Osborne 1996; E. Cook 1995, esp. 3–5; Crielaard 1995, 201–288; M. West 1995, 203–219; Seaford 1994, 144–154; Stanley 1993, 279–293; Lowenstan 1992, 165–198; Nagy 1992, 17–60, esp. 51–52; Ballabriga 1990, 16–29; Burkert 1976, 5–21.

[11] See Kirk 1985, 169–171; Visser 1997, 53–77, 742–745; *contra* J. Anderson, whose assertions are unsubstantiated and based on Page 1959 (J. Anderson 1995, 188).

[12] Page argues for a Mycenaean origin (Page 1959, 124–125, 132, 134); J. Anderson posits a Geometric core (J. Anderson 1995, 183–189, esp. 188); Lang suggests an *Ur*-catalogue with later additions (Lang 1995, 149–150). Kirk also discusses the possibilities that the Catalogue originally derived from a putative muster list from Aulis, or was a natural offshoot of the geography of the land and the tradition's attempt to preserve it (Kirk 1985, 178, 183–186; J. Anderson 1995, 188; Visser 1997, 16–17; for a less likely possibility, see Giovannini 1969, 51–52). In the end however, Kirk refuses to push the Catalogue back before the time of "Homer and Hesiod themselves" (Kirk 1985, 179).

[13] Kirk 1985, 178.

[14] J. Anderson 1995, 188; see also Willcock 1978, 205. Although I am sympathetic to the idea of a Boiotian provenance for the Catalogue of Ships, that Thessalian Arne is not included in the Catalogue's Thessalian entry weakens the case for an exclusively Boiotian origin for the entire Catalogue, since Thessalian Arne was likely considered the mother city for Boiotian Arne, a significant locus in Boiotian tradition of territory and migration (see below in this chapter). For the Catalogue's Thessalian entry, see Morgan 2003, 102–105.

groups which it describes on a panhellenic level;[15] the import of the Catalogue's entries for the groups themselves thus almost goes without saying.

I consider the statistics of the Boiotian entry first and thus begin with the final two lines of the Boiotian contingent:

τῶν μὲν πεντήκοντα νέες κίον, ἐν δὲ ἑκάστῃ
κοῦροι Βοιωτῶν ἑκατὸν καὶ εἴκοσι βαῖνον.

From these [communities] went fifty ships, and in each one
went one hundred and twenty young Boiotian men (*Il.* 2.509–510).

It is unusual to find such an explicit account of the number of men assigned to each vessel in the Catalogue. In the descriptions of the other regional fleets immediately following the Boiotian entry, for example, the poem does not provide the number of Minyans (2.516), Phokians (2.524), Lokrians (2.534–5), Abantes (2.545), or men from Attica (2.556). Of the Greeks the only other contingent counted by number is that of Philoctetes (2.719–720). As Kirk remarks, the Boiotian entry seems to depart deliberately and remarkably from the more formulaic syntax of the usual catalogue entry to include the detail of the number of Boiotian men on each ship.[16] Together with the appearance of the collective regional ethnic Βοιωτοί in the final line of the entry, then, this counting of unnamed Boiotian men emphasizes the undifferentiated number of Boiotians involved in the expedition and brings the audience back to the mention of the collective at the opening of the Boiotian list (2.494). This large number also stands at the end of what we will find to be a strikingly geographically-oriented list. The implication: the numerous men specified at the end of the entry, the κοῦροι Βοιωτῶν, hail from all over the region and form a collective mass.

In support of this reading is the general tendency of the Catalogue to assign a larger number of ships to the contingents considered most important, although there is also some conventionality involved in assigning numbers to contingents.[17] In the case of the Boiotian entry, which receives a fairly high number of ships (50), this emphasis on importance can be extended, since the Catalogue also counts the men aboard the Boiotian vessels. The audience is thus left with an image of a great multitude of soldiers from a primary contingent in the war.

The Catalogue's emphasis on Boiotian communality is also generally evident in the named Boiotian leaders, most of whom do not exhibit defining characteristics or play major roles in the remainder of the epic or epic tradition (2.494–5):

Βοιωτῶν μὲν Πηνέλεως καὶ Λήϊτος ἦρχον
Ἀρκεσίλαός τε Προθοήνωρ τε Κλονίος τε ...

Peneleos and Leitos and Arkesilaos and Prothoenor
and Klonios led the Boiotians ...

[15] McInerney 1999, 8–9.
[16] Kirk 1985, 190.
[17] Kirk 1985, 171.

These men appear here without characterizing epithets; their names are generic and suitable for formulaic warriors. Leitos means "booty-man," for example; the names Arkesilaos, Prothoenor, and Klonios carry similar associations appropriate to any leader of a warrior contingent ("army-captain, front-runner, and havoc-man"). Arkesilaos, Prothoenor, and Klonios meet their ends perfunctorily and appear nowhere else.[18] Peneleos and Leitos are somewhat more active, although they also appear as a relatively unindividuated pair twice elsewhere, a tendency which may indicate that the two figures were not always imagined separately in the tradition and were somehow connected by virtue of being from Boiotia.[19] Outside these appearances, Leitos, the son of Alektryon (*Il.* 17.602), is shown at the kill in a relatively generic battle scene alongside a number of more well-known Greeks.[20] Notably, a sixth Boiotian warrior, Πρόμαχος, identified by the individual regional ethnic Βοιώτιος but not included in the Catalogue's original Boiotian entry, also appears, but only at his own death.[2] Since this Promachos occurs nowhere else in the poem, it is difficult to draw any conclusions about his specific relation to the Boiotian leaders of the Catalogue. Moreover, it is possible for Πρόμαχος Βοιώτιος simply to signify "a Boiotian fighting in the front ranks;" his inclusion may thus denote a formulaic epic expression included because of the already well-known numbers of Boiotian warriors from the Catalogue. On the whole, then, as generic and undescribed figures, these Boiotian characters do not contribute to knowledge of specific individuals or families in the Boiotian entry and therefore as a group provide a relatively bland introduction and characterization of the Boiotian contingent.

The exception is Peneleos who, although often appearing at the side of his Boiotian comrade Leitos, gives quite an individual show at *Il.* 14.487–507. Here Peneleos not only kills his opponent by stabbing him through the eye, but he also beheads him, displaying the head with sword still protruding, "like the head of a poppy:" ὃ δὲ φὴ κώδειαν ἀνασχών (14.500). With this trophy Peneleos rebukes and terrifies the watching Trojans.[22] Not only is his display significant in offering the sole characterization of a Boiotian leader from the Catalogue, but Peneleos' performance is also occasioned by the death of the generic Promachos, just discussed, a warrior described only as the Boiotian son of an Alegenor. Promachos thus functions as a dispensable Boiotian character who introduces the more developed Peneleos. That Promachos' brief and generic death stirs Peneleos to perform a mini-*aristeia* suggests that the Boiotians were meant to be characterized in epic as a community which fought partially in revenge for the loss of one

---

[18] *Il.* 14.450 (Prothoenor); *Il.* 15.329–342 (Arkesilaos and Klonios); Kirk 1985, 190.

[19] At *Il.* 13.91, where Poseidon encourages the two men, and at *Il.* 17.597–604, where both are wounded.

[20] E.g., Odysseus, Antilochos, and Agamemnon (*Il.* 6.30–35). For later traditions about Leitos, see Paus. 9.4.3 and 9.39.3.

[21] *Il.* 14.476: ἔνθ᾽ Ἀκάμας Πρόμαχον Βοιώτιον οὔτασε δουρί.

[22] It may not be coincidental that the first Achaean warrior to be spurred on by Peneleos' angry display is Telamonian Ajax. As we will see in the following chapter, Thebes and Aigina were intricately linked via genealogical traditions.

of their own, no matter how unknown the figure happened to be in the rest of epic tradition. That neither the generic Promachos or nor the more identifiable Peneleos are specified by civic community but are rather designated by collective regional ethnics breaks down any possible status or civic difference between the two in this passage and also reinforces the regional and communal designation by which the poem groups Boiotian men in general.

Analysis of the wounding-scene of Peneleos and his Boiotian comrade Leitos supports this interpretation by indirectly recalling the Boiotian entry from the Catalogue of Ships. The scene begins with Hektor grieving over his friend Podes' death. A typical depiction of payback for the death of a great warrior's comrade follows; two Boiotians fall in Hektor's killing spree, and the Greeks are routed. The first to fall is Peneleos: πρῶτος Πηνέλεως Βοιώτιος ἦρχε φόβοιο. | βλῆτο γὰρ ... (Il. 17.597). Through verbal correspondences the description of Peneleos' death here directly recalls the line of the Catalogue where the Boiotian contingent is introduced: Βοιωτῶν μὲν Πηνέλεως καὶ Λήϊτος ἦρχον. There Peneleos led (ἦρχον) the Boiotians (Βοιωτῶν); here Peneleos the Boiotian (Βοιώτιος) rules only over fear (ἦρχε φόβοιο). Hektor next attacks Peneleos' co-commander Leitos:

Λήϊτον αὖθ᾽ Ἕκτωρ σχεδὸν οὔτασε χεῖρ᾽ ἐπὶ καρπῷ,
υἱὸν Ἀλεκτρυόνος μεγαθύμου, παῦσε δὲ χάρμης·
τρέσσε δὲ παπτήνας, ἐπεὶ οὐκέτι ἔλπετο θυμῷ
ἔγχος ἔχων ἐν χειρὶ μαχήσεσθαι Τρώεσσιν.

Again Hektor wounded Leitos at close range, son of great-hearted Alektryon, on the hand at the wrist, and he stopped him from fighting. Leitos looked around sharply and withdrew, since he no longer hoped in his heart to battle the Trojans with a spear in his hand (Il. 17.601–604).[23]

Although Leitos is not identified with the adjectival ethnic Βοιώτιος (unlike Peneleos), his presence here continues to emphasize wounded Boiotians in the passage, since the audience knows him from the Catalogue's Boiotian entry. Ironically then, the Boiotians are thus again placed first in an epic list, only this time it is not a list of illustrious places and contingents like the Catalogue: it is rather a list of Greeks who fail to defend themselves against Hektor's wrath. But what exactly does the adjectival ethnic signify in these two passages? Given the verbal connections between the Catalogue of Ships and this passage from Book 17, it seems reasonable to suggest that the personal adjective used to describe Peneleos in Book 17 (Βοιώτιος) also recalls the primary association of the term Βοιωτοί in Book 2 — namely, geography. With no indications to the contrary, we may thus assume that the personal adjectival ethnic at Iliad 14.476 also carries such a geographical connotation and thereby likewise emphasizes Peneleos' and Leitos' association with their home region.

---

[23] Accordingly, in some sources Leitos is the only Boiotian thought to have survived Troy: τῶν δὲ ἡγεμόνων, οἳ Βοιωτοὺς ἐς Τροίαν ἤγαγον, μόνος ἀνέστρεψεν οἴκαδε οὗτος ὁ Λήϊτος (Paus. 9.4.3). Pausanias records a μνῆμα attributed to Leitos at Plataia.

It is worth noting that in later Boiotian tradition Peneleos seems to have been a figure of great local importance. He was considered a Theban by some, from what Pausanias records about his putative son Philotas, colonist and co-founder of Priene.[24] Peneleos may have had a shrine at Tanagra, if Plutarch's mention of it can be trusted;[25] pseudo-Aristotle even includes an epigram from Peneleos' tomb.[26] Notably, Diodoros gives a genealogy for Peneleos in which he appears as a grandson to Boiotos; here Peneleos' four brothers are conveniently identified as the remaining four Boiotian leaders from the *Iliad's* Catalogue.[27] Peneleos' later reputation thus seems an assortment of attempts to claim heroic involvement in the Trojan war for various Boiotian communities at various times; what they indicate about Peneleos in the Archaic period is simply his status an epic hero. Peneleos' early status as a relatively noteworthy Boiotian epic figure and his later significance to a variety of Boiotian communities nonetheless indicates the general import that epic heroism must have held in the region during this early time.

Since we cannot extrapolate back from these later sources to the earlier specific significance of Peneleos, however, I interpret the *Iliad's* representation of the hero on its own. Peneleos' portrayal as a distinct warrior with a brief episode of glory adds an individual note to his nondescript inclusion at the beginning of the Catalogue's Boiotian entry. Nonetheless, it is important to re-emphasize that despite Peneleos' speaking role, he is never identified by family or civic community; he is always marked as one of the Βοιωτοί. While his distinguished performance lends an air of individual heroism to the Boiotian contingent as a whole, then, the focus of the Boiotian entry in the Catalogue remains with the collective.

Although this interpretation contradicts Visser's argument for the primacy of the men named at the beginning of each contingent, in support of this reading we find a markedly different pattern of emphasis on distinct individuals in many other Greek entries in the Catalogue.[28] The Minyan contingent, for example, which immediately follows the Boiotian entry, comprises a mere six lines, four of which are devoted to descriptive stories of their leaders: Askalaphos and Ialmenos, sons of Ares (2.512–515). Emphasis on individual men is also apparent in the Phokian Catalogue (2.517–526), where the leaders are identified as υἷες Ἰφίτου μεγαθύμου Ναυβολίδαο (2.518) and are shown marshaling the ranks of soldiers at the end of the section (οἱ μὲν Φωκήων στίχας ἵστασαν ἀμφιέποντες, 2.525). The Lokrian section even mentions the linen corselet of the lesser Ajax

---

[24] Paus. 7.2.3 (Philotas as part of the Ionian expedition and descendant of Theban Peneleos); 7.2.10 (Philotas as co-founder of Priene and descendant of Peneleos).

[25] Plut. *Greek Questions* 37 (Halliday 1928, 159–164).

[26] Aristotle fr. 640.21 (Rose 1886, 400):
ἐπὶ Πηνέλεω κειμένου ἐν Βοιωτίᾳ·
τόνδ᾽ ἐπὶ Κηφισσῷ ποταμῷ θέσαν ὠκὺ ῥέοντι
παῖδες Βοιωτῶν σώφρονα Πηνέλεων.

[27] Diod. Sic. 4.67.7; see also Halliday 1928, 163.

[28] See Visser 1997, 742–750.

(λινοθώρηξ, 2.529). Subsequent descriptions of other contingents continue to emphasize famous leaders over civic or ethnic communities: e.g., Elephenor, leader of the Euboian Abantes; the Athenian Menesthios; the Peloponnesians Diomedes, Sthenelos, and Euryalos. The poem also describes Agamemnon's armor and Menelaos' matrimonial troubles (2.578–9; 2.589–590). Notably, the Catalogue likewise details the family tree and even the good looks of Nireus, the relatively obscure leader from Syme who leads only three ships to Troy (2.671–675). Such descriptions differ markedly from the Boiotian catalogue with its relatively perfunctory mention of leaders and, as we will see, its emphasis on the collective inhabitants of the region.

Following the Boiotian leaders, the Boiotian entry moves to a relatively more descriptive list of specific Boiotian communities. For example, Medeon appears as ἐϋκτίμενον πτολίεθρον (2.501); Thisbe receives the epithet πολυτρήρων (2.502). As Kirk argues, these characterizations should not be understood to reflect specific qualities of the settlements, for the same formulaic descriptions appear in reference to other towns from other regions and often appear in the second half of the line.[29] For example, the phrase ἐϋκτίμενον πτολίεθρον is also used to describe the community Ὑποθήβαι slightly later in the Boiotian entry; the Catalogue also repeats the epithet used for Thisbe for the Lakonian settlement Messe (πολυτρήρωνά; 2.582).

That one site mentioned in the Boiotian entry is described more specifically is thus all the more remarkable. The poem reserves an entire line for Onchestos, the revered sanctuary to Poseidon in central Boiotia which, as we have seen, played a significant role in the contemporaneous genealogical tradition of the Boiotian eponymous hero: Ὀγχηστόν θ᾽ ἱερόν, Ποσιδήϊον ἀγλαὸν ἄλσος (Il. 2.506).[30] Given the prominence of Onchestos in Boiotos' archaic family tree, its elaboration in the Catalogue's Boiotian entry can be no coincidence; clearly Onchestos' status as a premier Boiotian sanctuary was in no doubt even outside Boiotia in panhellenic tradition.

Although most of its descriptions are formulaic, however, the Boiotian entry emphasizes the whole of Boiotia as a geographic unit dotted with civic communities, for the Boiotian contingent includes *poleis* from every corner of the region. From far eastern and northeastern Boiotia we find Aulis (2.496) and Anthedon (2.508); from inland eastern Boiotia, Mykalessos (2.498); from the southeast central area come Harma and Eleon (2.499–500). From the north we have Kopai (2.502) and near the far southern Boiotian border sits Plataia (2.504). The catalogue includes west central Boiotia with Onchestos (2.506), Haliartos, and Koroneia (2.503), as well as the fertile Boiotian southwest with Thespiai and Thisbe (2.498; 2.502). Such wide topographical coverage grounds the Catalogue in physical Boiotia and maps the area's general extent. The inclusion of communities from all over the region also helps to mitigate some of the entry's more noticeable omissions: e.g., Tanagra, Chaironeia, Lebadeia, Thebes (specifically,

---

[29] Kirk 1985, 175–177, where he illustrates this conclusion with the Boiotian contingent; see also J. Anderson 1995, 186; *contra* Page 1959, 159.

as opposed to Ὑποθήβαι). It seems probable, then, that in its focus on widespread communities rather than only on the most influential Boiotian places the Catalogue is a rather "hit-or-miss affair," as Kirk has noted, perhaps meant to stimulate consideration of the vastness of the region.[31] Useful for comparison is the Attic contingent which comes from Athens alone, thereby emphasizing the definition of Attica as one political unit as opposed to a multitude of diverse, widespread and identified communities, as with Boiotia (*Il.* 2.546–556).[32]

In its geographic and regional focus the Boiotian entry resembles a number of the Catalogue's other descriptions of central Greek contingents. The Phokians provide a useful parallel: they appear as inhabitants of various civic communities but also of outlying rural territories: e.g., Krisa, Panopeus, Hyampolis, but also the area along the Kephisos river (2.519–522). The Lokrians seem to be listed according to *polis* (2.530–533). The Achaians are identified by civic communities too, but also by area inhabited, e.g. the island of Aigina (2.562). The Abantes, residents of Euboia, are both linked to various *poleis* and to the territory of the entire island itself (2.536). In these examples, when the Catalogue specifies non-*polis* areas, the designation seems to be geographic, most obviously in the case of the Phokians living along the Kephisos river, but also perhaps in the case of large islands where no unified political organization is thought to have existed in the Archaic period (e.g., Euboia).

The Catalogue of Ships often reinforces these necessarily geographic overtones by using the verbs ἔχω and νέμω to indicate how communities and areas were settled and/or inhabited, as we find in the Boiotian entry. These are the only verbs which describe the Βοιωτοί in their smaller communities, in fact.[33] Ἔχω sometimes connotes possession, especially of property, but the verb can and does often mean "to inhabit," especially when used with the accusative of place, as here.[34] The verb νέμω too can signify ownership of land (e.g., *Il.* 12.313) but also frequently connotes habitation, most notably when used with place-names.[35] Through the exclusive use of these two rather colorless verbs, the Boiotian entry thus further describes the people and the communities in relation to the land. In the end, then, the Catalogue's Boiotian contingent repeatedly evokes a relatively formulaic image of multitudinous and mostly undifferentiated Boiotians inhabiting and using a vast region dotted with varied communities as well as a specific sanctuary. The main focus of the entry lies in size and numbers; generic depictions of both cities and men, together with a more detailed mention of a specific regional cult center, imply that it is the regional community and its collective power that is most important in the Boiotian catalogue; the specific leaders and settlements are far less a focus.

[30] The community of Eteonos is also called by a *hapax legomenon* (πολύκνημον, 497), although, as Kirk notes, this designation could apply to many other sites in Boiotia (Kirk 1985, 191).

[31] Kirk 1985, 195.

[32] For the Attic contingent, see Seaford 1994, 144–154; Kirk 1985, 205–207.

[33] ἔχω: lines 500, 504, 505 and 507; νέμω: lines 496, 499, and 504.

[34] For similar use in epic, see *Il.* 5.890; 21.267; *Od.* 6.177, 195.

[35] See e.g., *Od.* 2.167.

That this portrayal appears in a panhellenic source indicates that this characterization of the Boiotians was palatable both inside and outside Boiotia at the time of the archaic transcription of the epic. Given the primacy as well as the power in numbers and geography represented in the Boiotian entry, it is hard to believe that the Boiotian catalogue was not wholeheartedly embraced within Boiotia in the Archaic period, and surely also later, as an accurate reflection of the heroic Boiotian past. Through repeated and widespread performances of epic, the Boiotians could hope that outsiders might believe, as the Boiotians themselves must have, that the Boiotian community had waned in strength little, if at all, since the heroic time of the Trojan expedition. We will shortly see that this was the case at least for Thucydides' audience in late fifth-century Athens.

B. Arne

Before turning to Thucydides' account of the Boiotian migration, however, I briefly discuss Arne, one of the communities mentioned in the Boiotian entry: οἱ τε πολυστάφυλον Ἄρνην ἔχον ... (*Il.* 2.507). While this line does not explicitly concern the Boiotian migration, we will shortly see that Arne is important in other sources for the tradition, including the Hesiodic *Ehoiai* and Thucydides. I thus consider its inclusion in the Boiotian contigent here.

The Arne of the *Iliad's* Catalogue is almost certainly a Boiotian settlement, based on its appearance in the Boiotian entry, although Thessalian Arne is also attested in the Archaic period.[36] In support of identifying the *Iliad's* Arne as a Boiotian location is the fact that the majority of place names mentioned in the Boiotian contingent correspond to identified sites in Boiotia. Boiotian Arne itself has not yet been located, although various sites have been proposed since antiquity. Zenodotus read Askre for Arne, and Pausanias identified Arne as an older name for Chaironeia;[37] since Chaironeia does not appear in the Catalogue, however, Pausanias' sources for this identification likely reflect a later Chaironeian attempt at inclusion in the famed epic list.[38] At any rate, the site seems to have been situated near Lake Kopais, since Strabo comments upon Arne's chronic flooding by the lake waters, quite a real danger for many Boiotian villages of the Kopaic basin until its draining in the nineteenth century.[39] If Arne was not another name for Chaironeia, and instead lay in or near lake Kopais, flood damage to the site may forever prevent its location. On the basis of Arne's place in the Boiotian entry, Visser suggests that Arne was centrally located, near Thebes, Onchestos and Mideia.[40] This thesis is attractive, for the Catalogue often lists

[36] For more details on archaic Thessalian Arne, see discussion of the *Aspis* below in this chapter.

[37] See Kirk 1985, 197; Paus. 9.40.5: ἐκαλεῖτο δὲ ἡ πόλις καὶ τούτοις Ἄρνη τὸ ἀρχαῖον.

[38] Simpson and Lazenby 1970, 31; Kirk 1985, 194, 197. For the other "conspicuous absentees" from the Catalogue who later identified themselves with unknown sites mentioned in the list, see Kirk 1985, 191, 194.

[39] Strabo 9.413.

[40] *Il.* 2.505–507; Visser 1997, 278; see also Fossey 1988, 382–383. The old identification of

Boiotian sites in roughly topographical order (e.g., Κορώνεια and Ἁλίαρτος, line 503). Regardless of Arne's current topographical anonymity, however, it is sufficient here to mark the existence of a Boiotian Arne in panhellenic epic tradition of the Mid- to Late Archaic period, during the *Iliad's* transcript phase. That Boiotian Arne was included in the Catalogue indicates its importance for the inhabitants of Boiotia at and after this time.[41]

BETWEEN THE *ILIAD* AND *EHOIAI*: ARNE AND BOIOTOS

With Boiotian Arne's presence in the Catalogue established, I consider its appearance in three other archaic sources which help corroborate Arne's significance in archaic panhellenic and Boiotian tradition. After presenting evidence from Hesiod, the *Iliad* and a scholiast on the epic, I suggest a possible rereading of the *Iliad's* passage which ties the eponymous Boiotos to the tradition of Boiotian migration.

Hesiodic fragment 218, embedded in a scholiast on the *Iliad*, discusses Boiotian Arne. The fragment is traditionally read:

ὁ γὰρ τοῦ Μενεσθίου πατὴρ Ἀρηΐθοος Βοιωτὸς ἦν κατοικῶν Ἄρνην· ἔστι δὲ αὕτη Βοιωτίας, ὡς καὶ Ἡσίοδός φησιν.

For Areithoos, the father of Menesthios, was Boiotian, an organizer/administrator of Arne. This is the Arne of Boiotia, as Hesiod also says.[42]

Without ἦν the last half of the first line roughly scans in dactylic hexameter (Ἀρηΐθοος Βοιωτὸς κατοικῶν Ἄρνην) and thus likely reflects its quoted source, at least in specific subject matter, if not more. Merkelbach and West attribute this fragment to the Ἠοῖαι;[43] from its subject matter West infers that the fragment comes from Arne's own *Ehoie*.[44] This Hesiodic citation is especially important in

Boiotian Arne as Gla is no longer tenable because of Gla's identification as a fortress and barracks (Simpson and Lazenby 1970, 31). For Gla as a Late Helladic citadel and administrative strongpoint of the Mycenaean drainage project, see e.g., Iakovidis 2001; Iakovidis 1992; McConnell 1978–1979, 73–103; Fossey 1973–1974, 7–21.

[41] It is difficult to accept Hornblower's suggestion that Arne in the Catalogue of Ships was merely a "phantom" settlement, mentioned out of deference to myth (Hornblower 1991, on 1.12.3); there are simply too many correspondences between Boiotian settlements of the Catalogue and identified communities in Boiotia to make this theory tenable. Simpson and Lazenby conclude that the Catalogue's currently unknown communities are "not fictitious" (1970, 153).

[42] Fr. 218 MW (= Schol. T. Hom. *Il.* 7.8–9, v. 234. 3 Maass), from the *Ehoiai*. This translation reflects traditional commentaries on the epic passage (for which see below).

[43] Merkelbach and West 1967, 110. The specific term κατοικέω may in fact also be Hesiodic and is attested by the Late Archaic period (see further below).

[44] Arne's *Ehoie* was possibly included under the family of Asopos, the Boiotian river god, as opposed to Arne's other common position in myth as a descendant of Aiolos, the predominantly Thessalian patriarch. On West's reasons for excluding Arne from the Aiolidai in Hesiod's catalogue, see M. West 1985, 60–63 and 102. For Arne as Aiolos' daughter, see Chapter One. As also mentioned there, because of Arne's appearance in other versions of Boiotos' genealogy, West speculates that Arne may have been related to Βοιωτός in the Hesiodic *Ehoiai* (M. West 1985, 102).

assembling the tradition of Boiotian Arne in the Archaic period, since it attests to a Boiotian settlement named Arne and thereby corroborates the Boiotian Arne of the *Iliad's* Catalogue.

The fragment gains further significance upon analysis of the epic passage on which the scholiast comments. I discuss the passage fully here, for conclusions drawn from its analysis will support a new reading of the Hesiodic fragment which bears significant implications for understanding the eponymous Boiotos' role in the Boiotian migration. The passage and a translation based on standard commentaries run as follows:

ἔνθ᾽ ἑλέτην ὁ μὲν [Ἀλέξανδρος] υἱὸν Ἀρηιθόοιο ἄνακτος,
Ἄρνῃ ναιετάοντα Μενέσθιον, ὃν κορυνήτης
γείνατ᾽ Ἀρηίθοος καὶ Φυλομέδουσα βοῶπις.

Then Paris killed the son of king Areithoos, Menesthios, who lived in Arne, whom Areithoos the mace-bearer and cow-eyed Phylomedousa bore (*Il.* 7.8–10).

Another Areithoos, also a mace-bearer, appears slightly later in the same book as a character in a story of Nestor's youthful exploits. Here, however, Areithoos seems to be an Arkadian. Nestor reminisces:

αἲ γάρ, Ζεῦ τε πάτερ καὶ Ἀθηναίη καὶ Ἄπολλον,
ἡβῷμ᾽, ὡς ὅτ᾽ ἐπ᾽ ὠκυρόῳ Κελάδοντι μάχοντο
ἀγρόμενοι Πύλιοί τε καὶ Ἀρκάδες ἐγχεσίμωροι,
Φειᾶς πὰρ τείχεσσιν, Ἰαρδάνου ἀμφὶ ῥέεθρα.   135
τοῖσι δ᾽ Ἐρευθαλίων πρόμος ἵστατο, ἰσόθεος φώς,
τεύχε᾽ ἔχων ὤμοισιν Ἀρηιθόοιο ἄνακτος,
δίου Ἀρηιθόου, τὸν ἐπίκλησιν κορυνήτην
ἄνδρες κίκλησκον καλλίζωνοί τε γυναῖκες
οὕνεκ᾽ ἄρ᾽ οὐ τόξοισι μαχέσκετο δουρί τε μακρῷ,   140
ἀλλὰ σιδηρείῃ κορύνῃ ῥήγνυσκε φάλαγγας.
τὸν Λυκόοργος ἔπεφνε δόλῳ ...

O father Zeus and Athena and Apollo, I long for the time
when the savage Pylians and the spear-fighting Arkadians gathered and
fought near the quick-flowing Keladon, by the walls of Pheia around the
streams of the Iardanos. Preeminent among them stood Ereuthalion, a god-
like mortal, holding on his shoulders the armor of king Areithoos, glorious
Areithoos, whom men and fair-girdled women called by
the name of mace-bearer because he was used to fighting
not with bows or a long spear, but he shattered phalanxes
with an iron mace. Lykourgos killed him with a trick . . . (*Il.* 7.132–142).

These two figures named Areithoos, the first a Boiotian, the father of Paris' victim in the first passage, and the second the Arkadian from Nestor's youth in this passage, seem to raise a serious chronological difficulty which commentators on *Iliad* 7 have long tried to reconcile.[45] According to Nestor's story, the second figure, king Areithoos of Arkadia, would have died when Nestor was about twenty years old. At the dramatic time of the telling of his story in the *Iliad*, Nestor was supposed to have been around seventy years of age. This implies that the Arkadian Areithoos had been killed fifty years earlier. Yet in the first passage, Areithoos has a son, Menesthios, who fights and dies at Troy. If the father Areithoos had died fifty years earlier, then his son Menesthios must have been conceived before that time. This puts the son Menesthios' age at least at an improbable sixty in the tenth year of the Trojan war.

Aristarchos originally suggested that the two passages referred to two separate men named Areithoos from the same family: one, a mace-bearing father from Arkadia (*Il.* 7.132–142), and the other, his son from Boiotia and father to Menesthios from the first passage (*Il.* 7.8–10).[46] Leaf later reviewed Aristarchos' thesis and in the end, as Kirk after him, rejected it as "forced," because it implied that the "author" of the second passage (7.132–142) "was as vague about his legendary history as about his geography."[47] In Aristarchos' defense, however, such word order is not entirely impossible, as Leaf himself noted, although Aristarchos' solution necessitates that the ὂν in 7.9 refers to Ἀρηιθόοιο ἄνακτος. Furthermore, mythic connections between Arkadia and Boiotia are perfectly reasonable, given the many significant and well-known cultic and topographic links between the two regions.[48] Given these possibilities and the fact that Aristarchos was closer to Greek antiquity by over two-thousand years than Leaf (and Kirk), I thus provisionally accept part of Aristarchos' original conclusion: namely, that these two passages from the *Iliad* refer to two different men, each of a different generation and ἄναξ in a different region.

It might be objected that traditional stories are full of similar chronological difficulties which result from constant oral adaptation. As members of an oral culture, the *Iliad's* audience might be unconcerned with inconsistencies in geography or chronology concerning a minor character named Areithoos.[49] Yet the passages which mention the two seemingly different Ἀρηιθόοι were performed in such close proximity to one another (a mere 123 lines apart) that the details of each man's story would have been fresh in the minds of the audience and thus easily recollected. Moreover, that the epic had taken a more fixed form by the Late Archaic period signifies that these specific stories about two seemingly different Ἀρηιθόοι were considered important enough for inclusion, out of all the possible combinations of characters, myth, formulae, and plot available for the textualization of the poem during its transcript phase. Incorporation of the two figures and the apparent contradictions in the details of their stories thus demand further investigation and explanation.

[45] E.g., Kirk 1990, 232.

[46] Kirk 1990, 233.

[47] Leaf 1886, 239.

[48] E.g., the cult of Demeter Erinyes in Arkadia and the cults of Telphousa in Boiotia and of Athena Onka in Thebes; see Breglia-Pulci Doria 1986, 107–126; Fontenrose 1959, 367–370; Nielson and Roy 1998, 5–44.

[49] For the problematic term 'oral culture,' see Finnegan 1977.

In reconciling these stories, I propose a further modification to the reading of the first passage from the *Iliad* based on the fragment from the Hesiodic *Ehoiai*. To recall the latter:

ὁ γὰρ τοῦ Μενεσθίου πατὴρ Ἀρηῖθοος Βοιωτὸς ἦν κατοικῶν Ἄρνην· ἔστι δὲ αὕτη Βοιωτίας, ὡς καὶ Ἡσίοδός φησιν.

For Areithoos, the father of Menesthios, was Boiotian, an organizer/administrator of Arne. This is the Arne of Boiotia, as Hesiod also says.

As translated earlier, the Hesiodic fragment has consistently been read as if Ἀρηῖθοος must be a proper name, yet the word occurs as an adjective twice in the *Iliad* in formulaic descriptions of young men "swift in war" (ἀρηῖθοοι αἰζηοί, *Il.* 8.298; 15.315). It thus seems plausible to read Hesiod's term (which itself refers to the *Iliad*) also as an epic adjective and the term Βοιωτός as a proper name, instead of the adjectival regional ethnic, "Boiotian." The line would then read: "the father of Menesthios, Βοιωτός, swift in war, was an organizer/administrator of Arne."[50] The absence of adjectival regional ethnics from the Hesiodic corpus supports this interpretation; only the personal and singular ethnic names Φῶκος and Λοκρός occur in identifying mythic figureheads of groups.[51] Use of these personal and mythical names and the absence of adjectival ethnic forms in Hesiod support the proposed interpretation of the term Βοιωτός in the Hesiodic fragment. I thus propose reading the term Βοιωτός here as a proper name and not as a regional ethnic:

ὁ γὰρ τοῦ Μενεσθίου πατὴρ ἀρηῖθοος Βοιωτὸς ἦν κατοικῶν Ἄρνην· ἔστι δὲ αὕτη Βοιωτίας, ὡς καὶ Ἡσίοδός φησιν.

The father of Menesthios, Boiotos swift in war, was an organizer/administrator of Arne. This is Boiotian Arne, as Hesiod says.

If one accepts this reading of the Hesiodic fragment, one ought also to consider its effect on the passage from the *Iliad* to which the scholiast originally referred. Here is the epic passage with the new reading:

Ἔνθ᾽ ἑλέτην ὁ μὲν [Ἀλέξανδρος] υἱὸν ἀρηιθόοιο ἄνακτος,
Ἄρνῃ ναιετάοντα Μενέσθιον, ὃν κορυνήτης
γείνατ᾽ Ἀρηίθοος καὶ Φυλομέδουσα βοῶπις.

Then Paris killed Menesthios who lived in Arne, the son of the king, swift in war, whom Areithoos the mace-bearer and cow-eyed Phylomedousa bore (*Il.* 7.8–10).

The implications of this new reading solve the original problem of the two Ἀρηιθόοι, as originally raised by Aristarchus. It is now easy to accept a single Arkadian Areithoos for both epic passages. He is now the grandfather at *Iliad* 7.10 whose age is thus no longer incompatible with the Arkadian Areithoos

---

[50] I observe this translation in the previous chapter on Boiotos' genealogy.
[51] Φῶκος: *Theog.* 1004 and fr. 58.8 MW (restored); Λοκρός: fr. 234.1 MW.

described by Nestor at *Iliad* 7.132–142.[52] The remaining difficulty in accepting this reading of the Hesiodic fragment in conjunction with the passages from the *Iliad* lies in explaining the absence of the proper name of Menesthios' father, the middle generation, now Βοιωτός, from *Iliad* 7.8–10. Why might the epic omit this figure?

A clue may lie in the epithet βοῶπις of line 10. Kirk finds this epithet curious, since the term is most often associated with Hera in epic. On different grounds, Kirk rejects an earlier line of the *Iliad* containing the epithet βοῶπις as an Athenian interpolation (3.144).[53] Since it is perhaps more plausible to suggest influence than interpolation, I thus propose that the adjective βοῶπις reflects Athenian influence here as well.

It is possible that in the mid-sixth-century Athenian environment in which the epic reached its transcript form of fixity, the figure Βοιωτός, the eponymous hero of one of Athens' main sixth-century rivals, was purposefully omitted from the poem in a spirit of hostile competition and as a subtle slight against the collective which bore his name. A clever and noticeable punning clue to the identity of this unnamed ἄναξ – Boiotos, eponym of the Βοιωτοί – would have been the epithet for his mother, βοῶπις, of line 10. This pun recalls the similar and well-recognized word play involved in late archaic Boiotian use of the Boiotian shield, a weapon made of oxhide (βοῦς), to mark the group's shared coinage.[54] Also notably, the figure Μενέσθιος, Boiotos' son, was retained in the same passage. Menesthios' inclusion here might likewise have been useful for sixth-century Athenian interests, as the death of a son of Boiotos at the hands of the infamous cowardly Trojan Ἀλέξανδρος would have further denigrated the mythic family of Βοιωτός and, by extension, those claiming descent from him in sixth-century Boiotia.

As if adding insult to injury, then, *Iliad* 7.8–10 gives a different genealogy for Boiotos from any other extant source. Recall Boiotos' usual descent from a Thessalian Aiolid and Poseidon.[55] The *Iliad* destroys the relationship between Βοιωτός and Thessaly by cutting Poseidon from the *stemma*, thereby making Βοιωτός the offspring of the otherwise minor Arkadian character Areithoos and

---

[52] The grammar and placement of the noun-epithet phrase ἀρηιθόοιο ἄνακτος at the end of a line is acceptable epic usage: e.g., the end of *Il.* 1.75: μῆνιν Ἀπόλλωνος ἑκατηβελέταο ἄνακτος. See also *Il.* 23.302; *Il.* 14.376; 14.450; *Od.* 14.7–8 and *Od.* 14.40, where the ἄναξ remains unnamed, as in the proposed reading of *Il.* 7.8 above; *Od.* 17.255; 17.296. The best parallel for *Il.* 7.8 comes from the Catalogue of Ships where the poem mentions the leaders of contingents from Nisyros, Karpathos, Kasos, and Kos: Θεσσαλοῦ υἷε δύω Ἡρακλεῖδαο ἄνακτος (*Il.* 2.679). Not only does this line place the noun ἄναξ in final position in the line and in the genitive case, as proposed for *Il.* 7.8, but the ἄναξ, Thessalos, is also a personal name formed from the collective regional ethnic, as Βοιωτός from Βοιωτοί. The line from the Catalogue thus provides an archaic parallel for the use of a personal regional name, analogous to the proposed reading of Βοιωτός in Hesiodic fragment 218.

[53] Kirk 1985, 282. For issues of Athenian influence on the *Odyssey*, see S. Larson 2002; Cook 1995.

[54] For Boiotian coinage, see Chapter Three.

[55] See Chapter One.

the mortal Phylomedousa. Poseidon's removal from Boiotos' family tree would have been a highly effective manipulation of myth for Athenian interests, for Poseidon was, of course, one of the primary deities worshipped on the Athenian acropolis alongside Athena. Altering Boiotos' genealogy in this way also nullifies Boiotos' connection to the collective Boiotian cult of Poseidon Onchestos. This new reading of *Iliad* 7.8–10, then, may be read as a clever Athenian slight leveled at the Boiotians through both omission of a name and inclusion of an alternate genealogy for the Boiotian figurehead. Evidence for anti-Boiotian Athenian sentiment will crop up again, as we will see in the next chapter, in the alteration of Attic iconography in the wake of Boiotian-Athenian hostility in the Late Archaic period.

In this new reading, however, not all of the details of Boiotos' biography present in other early versions are changed: the *Iliad* preserves Boiotos' link to an Arne, for example. Here, however, Arne is the Boiotian town of the same name as the southern Thessalian community commonly mentioned in the tradition of migration. I discuss these two communities in more detail below. It is sufficient now to note only that the two Arnes belong to the same tradition: the Thessalian community was understood as the mother city of Boiotia Arne. The *Iliad* observes a second consistency with other archaic tradition by naming Boiotos as a Ϝάναξ (*Iliad* 7.8). As noted in the previous chapter, this term is significant in a Homeric context; its use here indicates the importance and the perceived antiquity of the figure Boiotos. That Ϝάναξ is the same term which Korinna later applies to Boiotos ties her early fifth-century characterization of the eponymous figurehead back to this passage from the *Iliad*.

Aside from the possible relationship between Boiotia and Athens reflected in these passages, however, this reading of the Hesiodic fragment and the *Iliad's* passages has a further and more important ramification, for now in Hesiod Boiotos is linked to Boiotian Arne as an "administrator/organizer," κατοικῶν, if not oikist.[56] In classical sources, κατοικέω often means "to be installed, to be established" or " to inhabit, to occupy a territory" (with a personal subject); it can also specifically signify "to administrate/organize." Κατοικέω often appears particularly associated with those who have been exiled and take up new residence.[57] While the term can signify administration over an already existing community of which one is not a native, it can indicate colonization of entirely new settlements, as in Euripides' famous passage concerning the Athenian migration to and colonization of Ionia.[58]

---

[56] For κατοικέω, see Casevitz 1985, 161–163. Casevitz does not discuss use of the term before Herodotus.

[57] Casevitz 1985, 161–162. This meaning is especially apparent in Thucydides; as Casevitz notes, six of Thucydides' eight uses of the term fall into this category: 2.99.5; 3.34; 3.34.2; 5.83.3; 8.6; 8.104.4.

[58] Eur. *Ion* 1586. Other examples for the meaning "colonize" include Hdt. 7.164, on Kadmos and Zankle (although Casevitz argues against this meaning here; see Casevitz 1985, 162) and Eur. *Med.* 10. It may also significant that the term οἱ κατοικοῦντες often indicates Athenian kleruchs (Casevitz 1985, 163).

Both κατοικέω and related terms seem to have occured in archaic and early classical sources. Strabo uses the term κατοικία, for example, in paraphrasing a story from the late archaic/early classical logographer Hekataios:

Ἑκαταῖος μὲν οὖν ὁ Μιλήσιος περὶ τῆς Πελοποννήσου φησίν, διότι πρὸ τῶν Ἑλλήνων ὤικησαν αὐτὴν βάρβαροι. σχεδὸν δέ τι καὶ ἡ σύμπασα Ἑλλὰς κατοικία βαρβάρων ὑπῆρξε τὸ παλαιόν, ἀπ᾽ αὐτῶν λογιζομένοις τῶν μνημονευομένων·

About the Peloponnese Hekataios the Milesian says that barbarians inhabited it before the Greeks. Nearly all of Greece was a colony of barbarians back then, from the things remembered by the logographers.[59]

The term here may reflect its use in Strabo's earlier source. More convincing is the appearance of a related term in a fragment of the Old Comedy playwright Eupolis: νεοκάτοικος.[60] Use of this word in comedy may indicate that related vocabulary was in use by the Early Classical period. Also indicative of early classical familiarity with terms related to κατοικέω is line 725 of Aeschylos' *Prometheus Bound* where the Amazons are characterized as women who once colonized (κατοικιοῦσιν) a land called Themiskyra. Given the appearance of related terms in late archaic and early classical sources, then, it is not inconceivable that the term κατοικῶν in Hesiod fragment 218 reflects original usage. That the final part of the Hesiodic fragment scans in dactylic hexameter, including κατοικῶν, supports this possibility.

I thus consider the ramifications of the meaning of κατοικῶν in the fragment. As κατοικῶν, Boiotos is an inhabitant of Boiotian Arne, but in light of the other meanings for κατοικῶν discussed above, he may also be an organizer, an exile, and/or an oikist. Hesiodic fragment 218 thus potentially magnifies Boiotos' role in the tradition of Boiotian migration. The fragment also underscores a link between Boiotos and Boiotian Arne which is significant because of the important part settlements named Arne play in expanded versions of the tradition of Boiotian migration (e.g. Thucydides). I turn to Thucydides shortly. For now, however, we need only note that ca. 580 the *Ehoiai* links Boiotos to Boiotian Arne, its organization, and settlement.

By the Late Archaic period, then, both the *Iliad* and *Ehoiai* offer evidence for Boiotian Arne, a community of sufficient regional importance to be included in the Catalogue of Ships and to be connected to the eponymous hero of the group, Boiotos, an organizer of the settlement, and perhaps even its oikist. Given Boiotos' presence in these sources as a leader associated with migration, and given the genealogical link between Poseidon Onchestos and Boiotos in the other Hesiodic fragment (fr. 219, discussed in the previous chapter), it seems probable that Boiotos' other primary associations were on their way to becoming established at this time: namely, his links to the southern Thessalian Aiolidai, his direct descent from Poseidon, and his relationship to Itonia. In other words, these

[59] Hekataios *FGrHist* 1 F 119.3 (ap. Strabo 7.7.1).
[60] Eupolis fr. 300 (Kock 1880).

epic and Hesiodic passages about Boiotos' son Menesthios and Boiotos' connections to Arne suggest that the entire tradition about Boiotos began to gain prominence ca. 700–580. Accordingly, by this time the group which called itself after him and claimed descent from him had begun developing group consciousness which partially centered around traditions of migration and territory.

ADDITIONAL EPIC REPRESENTATIONS OF BOIOTIANS IN THE *ILIAD*

We find two additional representations of the Boiotians in epic, both of which concentrate on geography and thus corroborate the general tendency of the *Iliad* to characterize the area through population and resources.

Iliad 5.706–710 concerns the death of Oresbios, a Boiotian fighter linked to topography partly via his name, "Mr. mountain-life." Before the collective regional ethnic Βοιωτοί appears at line 710, the poem identifies two additional specifics about this Boiotian warrior. He is μέγα πλούτοιο μεμηλώς, greatly concerned with wealth (5.707). Furthermore, and appropriately for his name, Oresbios hails from Hyle, a settlement which the poem places in Boiotia in the following line (λίμνη κεκλιμένος Κηφισίδι, bordering the Kephisian lake, 5.709).[61] The poem continues this geographical focus by further describing Hyle's topographical setting and by associating this context with the collective regional ethnic: πὰρ δέ οἱ ἄλλοι, ναῖον Βοιωτοὶ μάλα πίονα δῆμον ἔχοντες (nearby lived the other Boiotians with very rich farmland, 5.709–710). The geographical associations of the epic Boiotians are thus marked in this passage. Not only is the verb of the passage, ναίω, one of the most common terms for habitation, but the group as a collective is depicted as living on the πίονα δῆμον, "rich farmland." The Boiotians are thus not described in terms of their major occupations or settlements but rather of their collective habitation of a fertile and rich geographic area.[62] That the community of Hyle had already been noted in the *Iliad's* Catalogue of Ships would have only added to the prestigious overtone of this community and thus of the group associated with it in this passage. I return to the town of Hyle and its more specific associations with shields in the next chapter.

[61] The *Iliad* had already mentioned Hyle in the Catalogue of Ships (*Il.* 2.500) and also notably specifies the locale as the home of another famous Boiotian, Tychios, the craftsman of Ajax's glorious shield (*Il.* 7.219, see Chapter Three). The town was clearly in Boiotia, but unlike so many of the other communities of the *Iliad's* catalogue, Hyle's precise location is unknown. On the basis of similarity in name, Simpson and Lazenby suggest that Hyle may have been located near lake Hylike in northeast Boiotia, an appropriately "hilly" region of Boiotia. Given the passage under discussion here, Hyle must have been a settlement near the shore of lake Kopais. These two options are not mutually exclusive, and it is quite possible that Hyle sat both near the edge of the Kopais and also near lake Hylike. Such a combination would in fact put the town somewhere in the hills near Akraiphia, as Simpson and Lazenby suggest (Simpson and Lazenby 1970, 25. Hyle is correctly placed on the most recent map of Boiotia in the Barrington Atlas; see Talbert 2000).

[62] It is interesting that the connection between the Βοιωτοί, land, and wealth in line 710 implies that the concern the now-deceased Boiotian Oresbios had shown for his wealth in line 707 was also an interest in productive Boiotian land.

The remaining instances of the collective regional ethnic from the *Iliad* likewise associate the Boiotians with geography. Two examples occur in Book 13, where the Greeks fight Hektor at the ships. In both instances the Boiotians appear alongside other groups from central Greece who defend the beach:

ἔνθα δὲ Βοιωτοὶ καὶ Ἰάονες ἑλκεχίτωνες,
Λοκροὶ καὶ Φθῖοι καὶ φαιδιμόεντες Ἐπειοί ...

There the Boiotians and the Ionians with long tunics,
And the Lokrians and Phthians and radiant Epeians ... (*Il*. 13.685–686).

The predominantly east-central Greek area covered by these groups is noteworthy: Boiotia, Lokris and Phthiotic Thessaly; the Ἰάονες are probably Athenians, and the Epeians here are the inhabitants of the Elian islands opposite Elis.[63] Janko suggests that the concentration on central Greece may reflect the perceived arrangement of the naval contingents according to region.[64] Later in this same passage the collective ethnic appears again; its use suggests that geography indirectly affected which groups were positioned together in the scene:

οἱ μὲν πρὸ Φθίων μεγαθύμων θωρηχθέντες
ναῦφιν ἀμυνόμενοι μετὰ Βοιωτῶν ἐμάχοντο·

In front of the great-hearted Phthians, these two, wearing the breastplate, defended the ships and fought together with the Boiotians (*Il*. 13.699–700).

The lines depict Medon and Podarces, two leaders of the central Greek Phthian contingent just mentioned; these men fight together with the Boiotians, surely not out of any perceived military alliance, but because the groups were imagined to have been situated near one another on the beach in army formation. It seems reasonable to assume that the common geographic region which these central Greeks inhabited provides the rationale for this affiliation.

The geographical connotations of these collective regional ethnics are corroborated by the final appearance of the term Βοιωτοί in the poem (*Il*. 15.330). The term occurs in a generic and brief battle scene in which some of the most illustrious Trojan warriors kill numerous Greeks in rapid succession (e.g. Hektor, Aeneas, and Paris; *Il*. 15.328–342). Hand-to-hand combat is not described in full; rather, Greeks are simply listed in a quick series as they perish, thereby illustrating the brute skill of the Trojans.

Most notably, most of the Greeks in this brief passage come from the same central Greek contingents involved in the defense of the ships in *Iliad* 13. The identifiable geographic associations of the dead warriors are as follows (in order): Stichios is Athenian; Arkesilaos is a Boiotian mentioned in Book 2 (15.329);[65] Medon is the same Phthian leader encountered in Book 13; Iasos is Athenian (15.332). Klonios, another Boiotian from Book 2, is killed by Agenor

---

[63] Janko 1992, 132–133. For these Epeians, see *Il*. 2. 627–630.
[64] Janko 1992, 131, where he plots battle positions based in part on this scene.
[65] See 2.495 for Arkesilaos.

(15.340).[66] Although the other Greeks in this list are not identifiable in terms of regional affiliation, it is sufficient here to note the similarity between the passages in books 13 and 15 (and book 2 for that matter). On this basis Janko has postulated that there existed a traditional catalogue involving these central Greek contingents; he calls this hypothetical work the "mainland catalogue."[67]

The similarities between the passages invite further comparison. First, in the battle scene of Book 13 the named warriors are certainly understood as leaders of the greater number of men designated by collective regional ethnics. That is, Medon and Podarkes are leaders of the Φθῖοι and fight on their behalf (see Il. 13.686; 13.699–700 above). The same can be said for the collective central Greek warriors killed in book 15. The passage which incorporates the collective regional ethnic Βοιωτοί makes this point quite clear:

Ἕκτωρ μὲν Στιχίον τε καὶ Ἀρκεσίλαον ἔπεφνε,
τὸν μὲν Βοιωτῶν ἡγήτορα χαλκοχιτώνων ...

Hektor killed Stichios and Arkesilaos,
the leader of the bronze-clad Boiotians ... (Il. 15.329–330).

All of these passages together project an image of single combat together with collective participation: the men from central Greece are never far from each other or their leaders, and the poem concentrates on depicting this geographic unity. Together with the geographic and numeric focus of the Boiotian entry in the *Iliad's* Catalogue of Ships, then, we may conclude that the collective regional ethnic Βοιωτοί in the epic consistently refers to a group of people understood as inhabitants of the central Greek region Boiotia. Archaic epic neither implies nor directly states anything else about this group.

THE *ASPIS*

The next relevant source for the tradition of Boiotian migration and habitation is the *Aspis*, a work which as a whole is generally dated ca. 570–520.[68] The numerous Attic vase paintings that depict the *Aspis'* battle between Herakles and Kyknos support this date, beginning ca. 565 and tapering off after 480.[69] The

[66] See 2.495 for Klonios.

[67] Janko 1992, 263.

[68] M. West 1985, 136 and n. 28 (this date is not without controversy; see Hirschberger 2004, 32–41). Janko once proposed a similar date in the "opening decades of the sixth century" (Janko 1982, 93, 127–128) but later specified a date for composition of the *Aspis* between 591 and 570. For this date Janko relies in part on one of Plutarch's two different dates for the Battle of Keressos, a battle which, as we will see in Chapter Six, cannot be securely dated (Janko 1986, 47 and n. 52). Nonetheless, Janko generally agrees with West's 570 as a *terminus ante quem* for the poem (Janko 1986, 42). Previous scholars had proposed dates which matched West's earliest: early sixth century (Russo 1965, 29, 34); ca. 570 (R. Cook 1937, 204–214, esp. 213), ca. 575 (Myres 1941, 17). On the *Aspis'* authorship, see Janko 1986, 38–39 and n. 2.

[69] Shapiro calls an amphora in Taranto "our earliest Kyknos scene" (after Paribeni), dating it ca. 570 (Shapiro 1984, 524). The other early depictions of this myth fall around 565–560 (Shapiro 1984, 527). Janko accepts a date ca. 565 as the earliest for these vases (Janko 1986, 41).

Aspis is traditionally attributed to a general post-Hesiodic tradition and is thus most often described as pseudo-Hesiodic, although Martin has recently and reasonably proposed Hesiod as author for both the *Ehoiai* and the much-maligned *Aspis*. In this context this controversy is noteworthy although it does not alter the general date of either text. More important, Martin's hypothesis places the *Aspis* in Boiotia, as does Janko's previous and more plausible argument that the poem as a whole is likely Theban in origin.[70] Either way, we situate the *Aspis* as an archaic Boiotian literary production and thus as a potentially important source for the Boiotian collective during this period.

Like the *Iliad*, the *Aspis* attests to an archaic community named Arne, only this Arne is probably Thessalian, not Boiotian. Arne appears twice in the poem:

πᾶσα δὲ Μυρμιδόνων τε πόλις κλείτη τ᾽ Ἰαωλκὸς
Ἄρνη τ᾽ ἠδ᾽ Ἑλίκη Ἄνθειά τε ποιήεσσα
φωνῇ ὕπ᾽ ἀμφοτέρων μεγάλ᾽ ἴαχον· ...

The entire *polis* of the Myrmidons and famous Iolkos and Arne
and Helike and grassy Antheia echoed greatly with the voice of the two
(*Aspis* 380–382).

Κύκνον δ᾽ αὖ Κῆυξ θάπτεν καὶ λαὸς ἀπείρων,
οἵ ῥ᾽ ἐγγὺς ναῖον πόλιας κλειτοῦ βασιλῆος
Ἄνθην Μυρμιδόνων τε πόλιν κλειτήν τ᾽ Ἰαωλκὸν
Ἄρνην τ᾽ ἠδ᾽ Ἑλίκην ...

Keyx buried Kyknos and countless people, those who lived near
the *polis* of the famous king, Anthe and the *polis* of the Myrmidons and the
famous Iolkos and Arne and Helike ... (*Aspis* 471–475).

In both passages Arne's Thessalian pedigree is indicated by its inclusion in a list consisting primarily of other important Thessalian towns.[71] Differentiating only in case endings, each passage repeats Μυρμιδόνων τε πόλις κλείτη τ᾽ Ἰαωλκὸς | Ἄρνη τ᾽ ἠδ᾽ Ἑλίκη. While the ancient site of Helike was situated in Achaia,[72] the πόλις Μυρμιδόνων (presumably Phthia) and Ἰαωλκὸς (*Il.* 2.712) were Thessalian sites renowned in archaic myth.

As the site of Thessalian Arne some scholars accept Kiérion, a low hill whose remains date to the end of the seventh century. Kiérion was the main community of Thessaliotis (south-central Thessaly); it is this site which Helly considers the oldest inhabited place in the region.[73] Associated with Kiérion was Philia, another candidate for Thessalian Arne, most famous for its sanctuary of Athena Itonia, a highly significant regional cult site active from the mid- to late Geometric

---

[70] R. Martin 2005, 173–175; Janko 1986, 47–48.

[71] Early commentators on the *Aspis* considered both these passages interpolations, esp. 474–475 (e. g. Goettling, mentioned by Paley 1883, *ad loc.*).

[72] See Paus. 7.24–25 for a description of Helike and the earthquake which submerged it; also see Frazer 1898 *ad. loc.* and Simpson and Lazenby 1970, 70–72.

[73] Helly 1991, 36.

period onward.[74] Whichever location one prefers, Thessalian Arne seems to have been of no small importance materially, and it seems reasonable to accept its inclusion in the *Aspis'* short formulaic list focused upon other celebrated Thessalian places. Furthermore, as we have seen, in Hesiodic fragment 218 it was certainly felt necessary to distinguish Boiotian Arne from another community of the same name, presumably its Thessalian counterpart. In light of Thessaly's predominance in the genealogy of the eponymous Boiotos, and as we shall see, also in the tradition of Boiotian migration, that the Thessalian community of Arne figures in the *Aspis* comes as no surprise, given the likely origin of the poem in Boiotian Thebes for a Theban festival.

CONCLUSIONS: THE ARCHAIC SOURCES

Given the readings proposed in this chapter, it seems that ca. 700–580 there were thought to have existed two distinct Arnes, both a Thessalian (*Aspis*; Kiérion; Philia) and a Boiotian one (*Iliad*; Hes. fr. 218). The Hesiodic fragment also indicates that Boiotos, eponym of the Boiotians, was thought to have played some sort of leading role in the organization and/or settlement of Boiotian Arne. Through various descriptions but especially through the Catalogue of Ships, the *Iliad* also portrays Boiotos' descendants, the Boiotian collective, as a numerous, powerful, and widespread population which contributed greatly to the Trojan expedition. Thus, by the Archaic period both a tradition of two Arnes existed as well as a vision of the heroic past which situated the Boiotians as prime participants in epic.

THUCYDIDES ON BOIOTIAN MIGRATION AND HABITATION

I now turn to Thucydides' late fifth-century version of the Boiotian migration (1.12). I discuss his account in relative detail, but I focus on its comparison with earlier aspects of the tradition analyzed above. Because Thucydides' aims as an author and as an Athenian are not my main pursuit, in what follows I raise only those aspects of his narrative relevant to the life of the tradition of Boiotian migration and its understanding outside Boiotia. A consistent picture emerges which suggests that the traditions of the Boiotian migrations which had formed ca. 700–580 had become canonical – even outside Boiotia – by the Late Archaic and Early Classical periods. This consistency is significant in emphasizing the unification of the Boiotians through myths of origins during the Archaic period and the effect such unity had on subsequent generations.

---

[74] Inscriptions firmly identify this site as the Thessalian Itonion. See Theokharis 1963, 135–139; 1964, 244–249; 1965, 311–313; 1967, 295–296. For the link between Kiérion and the Philian Itonion, see Helly 1991, 36; Leekley and Efstratiou 1980, 151. For Philia and Arne, see Morgan 1997, 171, 173, 194, and n. 31.

A. The Text

Thucydides includes the Boiotian migrations in his famous passage about the unrest in Greece following the Trojan war (1.12):

ἐπεὶ καὶ μετὰ τὰ Τρωικὰ ἡ Ἑλλὰς ἔτι μετανίστατό   1.12.1
τε καὶ κατῳκίζετο, ὥστε μὴ ἡσυχάσασαν αὐξηθῆναι.

ἥ τε γὰρ ἀναχώρησις τῶν Ἑλλήνων ἐξ Ἰλίου χρονία   1.12.2
γενομένη πολλὰ ἐνεόχμωσε, καὶ στάσεις ἐν ταῖς πόλεσιν
ὡς ἐπὶ πολὺ ἐγίγνοντο, ἀφ᾽ ὧν ἐκπίπτοντες τὰς πόλεις ἔκτιζον.

Βοιωτοί τε γὰρ οἱ νῦν ἑξηκοστῷ ἔτει μετὰ Ἰλίου ἅλωσιν   1.12.3
ἐξ Ἄρνης ἀναστάντες ὑπὸ Θεσσαλῶν τὴν νῦν μὲν Βοιωτίαν,
πρότερον δὲ Καδμηίδα γῆν καλουμένην ᾤκισαν (ἦν δὲ αὐτῶν
καὶ ἀποδασμὸς πρότερον ἐν τῇ γῇ ταύτῃ, ἀφ᾽ ὧν καὶ ἐς Ἴλιον
ἐστράτευσαν), Δωριῆς τε ὀγδοηκοστῷ ἔτει ξὺν Ἡρακλείδαις
Πελοπόννησον ἔσχον.

μόλις τε ἐν πολλῷ χρόνῳ ἡσυχάσασα ἡ Ἑλλὰς βεβαίως καὶ   1.12.4
οὐκέτι ἀνισταμένη ἀποικίας ἐξέπεμψε, καὶ Ἴωνας μὲν Ἀθηναῖοι
καὶ νησιωτῶν τοὺς πολλοὺς ᾤκισαν, Ἰταλίας δὲ καὶ Σικελίας τὸ
πλεῖστον Πελοποννήσιοι τῆς τε ἄλλης Ἑλλάδος ἔστιν ἃ χωρία.
πάντα δὲ ταῦτα ὕστερον τῶν Τρωικῶν ἐκτίσθη.

(1.12.1)
Then even after the Trojan War Greece was still continuously in the process of forced migration and settlement, so that she had no peace in which to grow.

(1.12.2)
For the return of the Greeks from Troy, a process which proved to be slow, caused many political changes, and for the most part civil strife occurred in the cities, with the result that exiles were constantly founding new cities.

(1.12.3)
For example, in the sixtieth year after the capture of Troy the present Boiotoi were pushed out of Arne by the Thessalians and they settled the land now called Boiotia, formerly called Kadmeia (earlier on in this same land there also lived a portion of these people, as a result of which they also took part in the expedition against Troy),[75] and in the eightieth year, the Dorians with the Herakleidai occupied the Peloponnese.

---

[75] Thucydides' date for the Trojan War likely derives from the early historians, perhaps Hellanikos, as has often been suggested, e.g., by Jacoby on Ephoros, *FGrHist* 70 F 223; see Gomme 1945, 72, on Thuc. 1.12.3. Hornblower is skeptical about Hellanikan influence (Hornblower 1991, 38).

Herodotus 7.176.4 is often raised in discussions of the Boiotian migrations and in the context of Thucydides 1.12.3. Yet the Herodotean passage says nothing specific about the Boiotians and rather concerns the wall at Thermopylai built by the Phokians to ward off the Thessalians. On the basis of Thucydides' passage, early commentators dated the Phokian wall to sixty

(1.12.4)
With difficulty and after a long period Greece attained secure peace and, no longer subject to forced migration, began to send out colonies; the Athenians settled Ionia and most of the islands, and the Peloponnesians settled most of Italy and Sicily and parts of the rest of Greece. All these places were settled after the Trojan War.

Although I refrain from discussing this chapter in entirety, the passage merits some initial comment as a unit, since its structure and grammar illuminate Thucydides' own and thus his audience's possible understanding of the Boiotian migration. The beginning of the chapter picks up Thucydides' narrative from 1.7 by re-introducing the theme of continuous unrest in Greece after the Trojan war (12.1). The upheaval is marked here by forced migrations (μετανίστατο) and settlement (κατῳκίζετο) which prevented Greece from growing in strength.[76] In a succession of parallel conjunctions which look to each other, balanced clauses, and coordinating vocabulary in this series of sentences, Thucydides gives prominent and somewhat parallel examples of exiled collectives who founded cities during this tumultuous period: the Boiotians and the Dorians.[77] The passage as a whole seems a straightforward account linked paratactically as we might expect in such a vast Thucydidean survey of post-Mycenaean history.

A number of modern commentators, however, have attempted to disconnect the chapter's middle sentence about the Boiotian and Dorian migrations (1.12.3) from Thucydides' opening statements (1.12.1–2), primarily on the basis of an understanding of Greek pre-history which accepts traditions like the Dorian invasion as historical events.[78] Stein was the first to excise the γάρ which introduces the account of the migrations; he reasoned that Thucydides' description of the movement of the Boiotians says nothing explicit about the στάσεις mentioned in the preceding section which were clearly a vital part of Thucydides' conception of post-Trojan war events.[79] For Stein the tradition of the Boiotian migration thus cannot serve as an example of the ἐκπίπτοντες that resulted from *staseis*. Steup follows Stein's lead on the bracketing, basing the excision on his understanding that the Trojan war and the Boiotian and Dorian migrations were historical events

years after the Trojan War (e.g., Rawlinson 1875, 145 and n. 9). McInerney now dates the wall to the years preceding 480 (McInerney 1999, 79–80, 174–175).

[76] This concentration on migration, upheaval and their prevention of healthy growth (αὔξησις) also ties the beginning of this chapter back to 1.2.2 where Thucydides treats the problems early communities faced in development and growth (for a discussion of this and related issues, see Kallet-Marx 1993, 23; Hornblower 1991, 37).

[77] See Casevitz 1985, 80. For grammatical exegesis of various aspects of this chapter, see the following commentators on the specified topics: γὰρ (Denniston 1954, 67; Smyth § 2810); τε (Morris 1888, 80); parallel use of οἰκέω and κτίζω (Casevitz 1985, 80; cf. Thuc. 6.4.1–2).

[78] For brief review of theories concerning the veracity of the Dorian invasion, see Malkin 1994, 43–45.

[79] *Non vidi;* these conclusions are an amalgamation of Steup's, Marchant's, and Gomme's later reflections on Stein's original idea. I have been unable to locate a copy of Stein's commentary.

belonging to different chronological periods.[80] Marchant, also concerned with "how Βοιωτοί τε γὰρ is connected with what precedes," offers a solution to the text as it stands. He proposes keeping the γάρ, explaining the particle as a reference not to what immediately precedes, but to the section before the mention of στάσεις, the passage describing "general unrest that continued" after the war (μὴ ἡσυχάσασαν).[81] Simply put, however, the problem with the passage lies not in any illogic of Thucydides' text, but in a modern refusal to understand its coherence as it stands. I thus retain Thucydides' γάρ and shortly consider the implications that both the Boiotians and the Dorians serve as *exempla* of the ἐκπίπτοντες and the στάσεις of 1.12.2.

Thucydides' fourth main comment (1.12.4) wraps up the entire section by artfully recalling the beginnings of the chapter through precise verbal echoes and parallel phrases, particularly to the opening statement.[82] Thucydides' short concluding remark – πάντα δὲ ταῦτα ὕστερον τῶν Τρωικῶν ἐκτίσθη – likewise recalls the chapter's first sentence by repeating its chronological parameters (μετὰ τὰ Τρωικὰ ...).[83] This last comment also evokes the chapter as a whole by focusing on *auxesis*, migration and colonization (πάντα δὲ ταῦτα ... ἐκτίσθη). Thucydides thus implies that the examples he provides throughout this chapter concern movement and foundation, from the first two instances – the Boiotians and Dorians – to the concluding examples of Athenian colonization of Ionia and Peloponnesian foundations in Italy and Sicily.[84] While Thucydides thus distinguishes between two periods of migration/colonization (one before *Hellas* calms down and one after), his overriding concern is with growth, migration, and colo-

---

[80] Steup 1897, 37. Steup also speculates that the γάρ could have been inserted into the text from a scribe's marginal note. Gomme, too, maintains that the Boiotian and Dorian invasions were not connected historically with the return of the Greeks from Troy (Gomme 1945, vol. 1, 117).

[81] Marchant 1905, 155.

[82] The subject of at least part of each sentence is ἡ Ἑλλάς, and in each sentence we find the verb ἡσυχάζω· μὴ ἡσυχάσασαν αὐξηθῆναι (sentence 1); ἡσυχάσασα ἡ Ἑλλάς (sentence 4; noted also by Hornblower 1991, 37 and 40). These verbs correspond through antithesis and emphasize Thucydides' constant concern with *auxesis*. Verbal corresponsion between sentences one and four involve two verbs used in Thucydides' first sentence: μετανίστημι and κατῴκιζω. The fourth sentence recalls these verbs by incorporating slightly different forms of the root verb and accompanying adverbs, e.g., ἡ Ἑλλάς is οὐκέτι ἀνισταμένη, a phrase which recalls ἔτι μετανίστατο of sentence 1. Sentence 4 also describes both Athenians and Peloponnesian settlement (ᾤκισαν) in different areas. These activities bring to mind κατῴκιζετο of the first sentence. Specific links to the second sentence of the chapter include: the τε of μόλις τε ... καί with the τε of the second sentence; descriptions of time (χρονία γενομένη of the second sentence with Thucydides' emphasis on time in this fourth sentence: μόλις τε ἐν πολλῷ χρόνῳ ἡσυχάσασα ἡ Ἑλλὰς βεβαίως).

[83] As de Wever and van Compernolle remark (1967, 490).

[84] Ellis has analyzed Thucydides' use of ring composition in the Archaeology (1.1–23.4; Ellis 1991, 344–375). While the parallels proposed above for Thucydides' chapter 12 do not correspond exactly to those which Ellis suggests, our interpretations are not mutually exclusive. My brief analysis of chapter 12 and its subsections corresponds to Ellis' larger frame (see Ellis 1991, 368–369 and tables 1 and 4). My discussion, however, concentrates more on the internal unity of chapter 1.12 and less on its relationship to the larger structure of Thucydides' Archaeology.

nization. That he chooses to illustrate these themes with the tradition of Boiotian migration indicates the importance of the tradition outside Boiotia as one of the most relevant and widely-recognized examples of population movement.

B. Interpreting Thucydides 1.12

I now consider Thucydides 1.12 more thematically by focusing on the relationship between his account of the early Boiotians in this chapter and his earlier statements in the Archaeology at 1.2. I also distinguish between two visible traditions in Thucydides' report of 1.12 and suggest that the historian's presentation of these two strands together further confirms the solidity of the tradition of Boiotian participation in the Trojan war.

I have argued above that both the Boiotians and the Dorians serve as examples of parallel examples of migrating ἐκπίπτοντες in Thucydides 1.12. This parallel also holds in Thucydides' introduction to the Archaeology at 1.2, a chapter which mirrors 1.12, as Thucydidean commentators have repeatedly noted. In delineating the tripartite structure of the entire Archaeology, Ellis in fact places chapters 1.2 and 1.12 at the beginning of two of his three main sections.[85] The likeness in detail between the two chapters is indeed remarkable: in both Thucydides describes the weakness of Greece in general in terms of constant upheaval (1.2.1; 1.12.1); *stasis* runs rampant (1.2.4; 1.12.2). In both passages Thucydides emphasizes the negative effect of *staseis* and migrations on *auxesis*. Parallelism between chapters 1.2 and 1.12 also includes direct verbal echoes (e.g., στάσεις, μὴ ... αὐξηθῆναι).

In determining possible interpretations of these links one might focus on the implied weakness of the groups mentioned, which the historian identifies specifically at 1.2.3 as Thessaly, Boiotia, and the Peloponnese (excepting Arkadia), regions constantly troubled by the kinds of population movement also identified at 1.12.[86] Thucydides attributes such lack of strength in early Greece to the problems involved in such population upheaval, since a large number of leaders vied for control and thus caused internal disunity in these regions (1.2.4). On this basis we might argue that both chapters 1.2 and 1.12 paint a weak and ineffectual picture of Boiotian and Peloponnesian history, thereby indirectly highlighting Athenian strength in the current conflict which is Thucydides' main interest.[87]

However, at 1.2.3 and the beginning of 1.2.4, Thucydides himself claims outright his reason for including these particular groups in his exegesis of early

---

[85] Taübler 1927, 58–61; Hunter 1980, 205; Hunter 1982, 24–25 and n. 12 (see Hunter for more bibliography on this issue); Ellis 1991, 368–369 and n. 30 (where he cites Taübler), 351 and 365, n. 28 (for 1.12 as the beginning of Thucydides' "intermediate period" of Greek history, from the Trojan to the Persian War); Bowie 1993, 141.

[86] See Thuc. 1.2.2: δι' αὐτὸ οὔτε μεγέθει πόλεων ἴσχυον οὔτε τῇ ἄλλῃ παρασκευῇ; 1.2.6: οὐκ ἐλάχιστόν ἐστι διὰ τὰς μετοικήσεις τὰ ἄλλα μὴ ὁμοίως αὐξηθῆναι.

[87] After Connor, who suggests that one of the major themes developed in Book 1 is the prominence, power, and possibility for ultimate victory of Athens over Sparta (see esp. Connor 1984, 40–41, 48–50, but chapter 1 as a whole).

Greek history. As he acknowledges, his choice simply hinges on the superiority of the soil in these areas:[88]

μάλιστα δὲ τῆς γῆς ἡ ἀρίστη αἰεὶ τὰς μεταβολὰς τῶν οἰκητόρων εἶχεν, ἥ τε νῦν Θεσσαλία καλουμένη καὶ Βοιωτία Πελοποννήσου τε τὰ πολλὰ πλὴν Ἀρκαδίας, τῆς τε ἄλλης ὅσα ἦν κράτιστα. διὰ γὰρ ἀρετὴν γῆς αἵ τε δυνάμεις τισὶ μείζους ἐγγιγνόμεναι στάσεις ἐνεποίουν ἐξ ὧν ἐφθείροντο ...

The continuous excellence of the soil particularly contributed to the changes in population, in what is now called Thessaly, and Boiotia, and the majority of the Peloponnese except Arkadia, and in many other areas as were most powerful. Because of the quality of the soil greater powers acquired by some led to internal problems which were destructive ...

Also notably, the Boiotians, the Peloponnesians and the Thessalians merely provide examples of what happened in other parts of Greece as well, as Thucydides implies at the end of 1.2.3 with the phrase τῆς τε ἄλλης ὅσα ἦν κράτιστα. That there were other areas which Thucydides could have named here implies that the specified regions were not singled out because they illustrated to a high degree the weakness of early Greece; given the context, the historian rather suggests that because of their most fertile soils these regions thus serve as the best *exempla* of his main point in this part of chapter 1.2. Moreover, that Thucydides includes Thessaly alongside Boiotia and the Peloponnese likewise implies that he does not name these regions on the basis of Athenian hostility toward them but rather for the more overt reason just noted.

This focus on fertility and richness of the soil in Thucydides' account of early Boiotia parallels the *Iliad's* repeated references to Boiotia's reputation for wealth of land populated by numerous inhabitants. Thucydides continues by contrasting Boiotian soil and that of the other naturally rich regions with the poverty of Athenian soil, which attracted exiles during the migration period simply because no one else wanted it. As Thucydides remarks, Attica was such a haven for exiles that it later had to send out colonies to cull its population, an activity in which Boiotian *poleis* took little part throughout history (excepting Herakleia Pontica), presumably because of Boiotia's vast and fertile land which could continuously support a large population. In the end, then, the parallels between chapters 1.2 and 1.12 do not highlight the weaknesses of Athens' traditional enemies as much as they emphasize the natural resources and strengths of the areas specified. Notably for Boiotia, Thucydides stresses the already canonical epic attributes of the region: its wealth in both land and population.

I now return to the section of Thucydides' account which is most crucial in examining the traditions of Boiotian migration: the first portion of 1.12.3, from Βοιωτοί to ἐστράτευσαν. The historian presents two seemingly independent and competing traditions of Boiotian history:

Βοιωτοί τε γὰρ οἱ νῦν ἑξηκοστῷ ἔτει μετὰ Ἰλίου ἅλωσιν
ἐξ Ἄρνης ἀναστάντες ὑπὸ Θεσσαλῶν τὴν νῦν μὲν Βοιωτίαν,

---

[88] Compare Hdt. 4.198.2 on the fertility of Libya (Steup).

πρότερον δὲ Καδμηίδα γῆν καλουμένην ᾤκισαν (ἦν δὲ αὐτῶν καὶ ἀποδασμὸς πρότερον ἐν τῇ γῇ ταύτῃ, ἀφ᾽ ὧν καὶ ἐς Ἴλιον ἐστράτευσαν).

For example, in the sixtieth year after the capture of Troy the present Boiotoi were pushed out of Arne by the Thessalians and they settled the land now called Boiotia, formerly called Kadmeia (earlier on in this same land there also lived a portion of these people, as a result of which they also took part in the expedition against Troy).

Here Thucydides raises a group of ἐκπίπτοντες exiled from Thessalian Arne by the Thessalians. Who exactly are these ἐκπίπτοντες? By calling them Βοιωτοί ... οἱ νῦν Thucydides implies that they had been known by a different name before their exile and were only later called Boiotians. On the basis of the eponymous Boiotos' links to Thessaly, we may assume that these ἐκπίπτοντες were originally considered Thessalians, but from Thucydides' account it is simultaneously possible that they were also known as Καδμεῖοι, since upon their expulsion from Thessaly, the οἱ νῦν Βοιωτοί settled in the land τὴν νῦν Βοιωτίαν, formerly called Kadmeia (πρότερον δὲ Καδμηίδα γῆν).[89] At any rate, this group is forced to migrate into Boiotia and settle there during the upheaval after the Trojan war. As we have seen, they provide a clear example of the nomadic groups which floated about Greece during those tumultuous years.

Thucydides' next statement thus seems surprising: ἦν δὲ αὐτῶν καὶ ἀποδασμὸς πρότερον ἐν τῇ γῇ ταύτῃ, ἀφ᾽ ὧν καὶ ἐς Ἴλιον ἐστράτευσαν.[90] The historian adds this remark parenthetically, since it seems to contradict the details of his account so far. If the οἱ νῦν Βοιωτοί were thought to have been exiled from Thessalian Arne after the war, then how could they have previously sent a contingent of two hundred ships to Troy from Boiotia? This parenthesis undoubtedly refers to epic tradition, specifically to the Catalogue of Ships, and its inclusion here provides a remarkably clear acknowledgment of the strength of the *Iliad's* tradition surrounding Boiotian participation in the Trojan War. Its presence in Thucydides' split-second account of early Boiotian history implies that the historian simply could not have omitted reference to the Catalogue: its hold was too strong in the tradition and thus also in the minds of his audience.

By acknowledging the *Iliad's* tradition in which Boiotians populated the entire region of Boiotia at the time of the war, Thucydides moreover suggests that large numbers of Boiotians had inhabited the region before the advent of the Boiotians from Thessaly. This implication affirms the Catalogue's familiar indications that the Boiotian contingent to Troy was one of the largest contributions. As discussed at the beginning of this chapter, the *Iliad* mentions fifty Boiotian ships of one hundred twenty men each, a large entry compared to the ships and men supplied by the majority of other contingents. Some commentators have thus considered Thucydides' term ἀποδασμός an inappropriately diminutive refer-

---

[89] For a tangential but interesting interpretation of Thucydides' statement about Boiotian settlement of the Kadmeian land as a response to Hellanikos (*FGrHist* 4 F 51), see Hornblower 1995, 671.

[90] Larsen 1968, 27, n. 2.

ence to the large number of Boiotians included in the Catalogue of Ships.[91] Yet ancient usage of ἀποδασμός suggests that the term was not used exclusively of small groups. Herodotus, for example, refers to a group of Phokian colonists of Ionia as ἀποδάσμιοι: he places them at the center of a list of other large groups, such as the Minyans from Orchomenos.[92] Further, the verb ἀποδατέομαι does not seem to indicate size or quantity, merely the division of a whole. The Boiotians of Thucydides' parenthetical acknowledgement of epic tradition may thus have been understood as part of a large group spread across the entire region, as the Catalogue of Ships itself had already indicated.

At any rate, Thucydides seems to have included two strands of the tradition of Boiotian migration, one which placed Boiotians in Boiotia sixty years after the Trojan war (after their residence at Thessalian Arne), and one from epic tradition which set them in Boiotia prior to and during the war as participants (the result of the ἀποδασμός).

Thucydides' use of Homer has occasioned a veritable library of commentary; Kallet nicely summarizes his general tendencies: "it is clear that Homer and Troy are present in the narrative on various levels. Thucydides' use of Homer, like his use of Herodotus, is highly complex: he will compare, contrast, show reversals, and, above all, stress ironies as he guides the reader toward the lessons he wants to be drawn."[93] Kallet reads Thucydides' presentation of the Trojan expedition through the lens of his contemporary disappointment in the failed Athenian Sicilian expedition. In the famous passage in which Thucydides comments on epic's numbers for the Greek fleet at Troy (1.10.5–1.11), then, Thucydides is less interested in discrediting the numbers than he is in expressing regret at the failure of Athens to support the expedition with proper resources;[94] the historian still acknowledges the size and power of the Greek fleet at Troy. Hunter similarly concludes that although Thucydides questions and points out ironies or inconsistencies in epic tradition, the historian ultimately relies on epic for his conclusions: "no matter how much he understood that caution was necessary in the face of poetic exaggeration, he nonetheless accepted both the poets and oral tradition as his factual basis."[95]

Given these views, there are a number of possible interpretations of Thucydides' double account of the Boiotian migration, in the first of which Thucydides plays the role of biased judge. His introduction of the post-Troy migration from Thessaly prior to the epic account of the Boiotian contingent to Troy may indicate

---

[91] E.g., Morris 1888, 80; Gomme 1945, vol. 1, 118.

[92] Hdt. 1.146.1: Μινύαι δὲ Ὀρχομένιοί σφιν ἀναμεμίχαται καὶ Καδμεῖοι καὶ Δρύοπες καὶ Φωκέες ἀποδάσμιοι καὶ Μολοσσοὶ καὶ Ἀρκάδες Πελασγοὶ καὶ Δωριέες Ἐπιδαύριοι, ἄλλα τε ἔθνεα πολλὰ ἀναμεμίχαται.

[93] Kallet 2001, 98, also 118–119; Howie 1998; see also Allison 1997, 449–515, who argues for specific literary and terminological parallels between Thucydides and Homer in the Sicilian narrative; Mackie 1996, 103–113 (on direct intertextuality between Thucydides and Homer in the Sicilian expedition); C. Smith 1900, 69–81 (for verbal parallels).

[94] Kallet 2001, 99–114, esp. 100–102.

[95] Hunter 1980, 201, also 194, 197–199; Howie later concludes similarly (Howie 1998, 95, 116–118).

that he favors the former story and desires to undermine the *Iliad's* account. Further, in describing the exiles from Thessaly Thucydides uses νῦν twice to emphasize names current in his own day. His parenthetical treatment of the epic version of Boiotian history thus may contrast with his emphasis on the contemporary relevance of the alternative story of forced migration from Thessaly. That Thucydides chooses to illustrate the upheaval after Troy with stories of the Boiotians and the Dorians might further support this view. The Dorians, like the Boiotians from Thessaly, are invaders from the north, not autochthons of their current regions. By singling out these two *ethne* as examples here, Thucydides calls attention to this similarity and thereby may implicitly support the version of Boiotian migration which includes forced exile from Thessaly, as opposed to the *Iliad's* account which emphasizes the wealth and strength of the Boiotian population already existing in Boiotia.

Alternatively and to my mind more plausibly, Thucydides may instead be trying to reconcile two traditions of Boiotian migration, as numerous scholars have suggested after Grote.[96] I propose a refinement of this view in which Thucydides does not set one strand of the tradition against the other or present Athens' current enemies as necessarily weak. Rather, I suggest that the two strands of the tradition of Boiotian habitation which Thucydides reports are not incompatible, since the historian presents the migration of Boiotians from Thessaly as having occurred sixty years after Troy. As noted earlier, in this passage Thucydides emphasizes the continuity of migrations after Troy over quite a long period (e.g., ἔτι μετανίστατό τε καὶ κατῳκίζετὸ χρονία γενομένη πολλά, 1.12.1–2). If movement of the οἱ νῦν Βοιωτοί from Thessaly was considered a second wave of migration during this protracted time of upheaval, then it is likely that the Thessalian Boiotians were understood to be joining their fellow Boiotians who already inhabited Boiotia before the Trojan war. Since Thucydides is concerned only in explicating migrations following the war, he does not mention the previous settlement of Boiotians in Boiotia. Realistically, there would have been no need to mention their previous habitation more explicitly, since the epic tradition of the Catalogue of Ships, which Thucydides himself includes, had already established their presence in Boiotia well before the war. To my mind, then, it is preferable to view Thucydides' account of the habitation of Boiotia as a unified and wholly reconcilable account which relies on his audience's understanding of widely accepted and thus easily omitted detail.

In this reading, the Boiotians and Peloponnesians escape any implicit criticism involved in a pro-Athenian interpretation of the Archaeology; these two groups instead serve as select examples of the historian's point about earlier migrations. This interpretation of 1.12.3 accords with Allison's reading of the Archaeology in which an unbiased Thucydides presents the two sides of the war as equally prepared.[97] In the end, however, what Thucydides himself thought about the Boiotians or the traditions of their history is not the essential point; the

---

[96] Bowie 1993; Sakellariou 1990, 182; R. Buck 1979, 76; Beloch 1912–1927, vol. 1.2, 84; Grote 1865–1870, vol. 2, 15–16.

[97] Allison 1989, 15; see also Howie 1998, 121.

most significant issues, as we have seen, involve identifying the existing traditions, their apparent strengths, their ability to be reconciled, and above all, what
Thucydides' audience might have understood from his account of them.[98]

That Thucydides' audience was a panhellenic one seems relatively clear from
his explanations of various Athenian practices and historical events which no
Athenian would require, as well as his attention to the history and culture of non-
Athenian communities, even the Spartans, Athens' enemy; Ridley suggests that
Thucydides includes such detail because his non-Athenian audience would have
required it.[99] It seems reasonable to posit, then, that Thucydides included the two
traditional strands of Boiotian habitation both because they were accepted in
many parts of the Greek world and also because their brief mention would thus
recall well-known and associated detail which did not need to be explicitly
discussed. That Thucydides openly nods to the Catalogue in his account of
Boiotian habitation indicates the pride of place that the Catalogue of Ships (not to
mention epic tradition in general) had come to hold in the minds of his panhellenic audience, especially to those of Boiotian or north-central Greek extraction.[100]
Thucydides' use of the Catalogue in his portrait of early Boiotia was thus a move
required by the solidity of panhellenic tradition, including the *Iliad's* lengthy
Boiotian entry which focuses, as we have seen, on numerical and geographic
strength, a facet of early Boiotia which Thucydides himself thus emphasizes at
1.2.

As I argue in the following two Chapters, the Boiotians were concerned to
link themselves to epic tradition through the shield-symbol stamped on their
coinage and through preservation of epicizing usage in Boiotian dialect. The
apparent potency of the tradition of Boiotian power from the Catalogue of Ships
both outside Boiotia and in Thucydides' account of early Boiotian history attests
to the fame of this putative Boiotian-epic relationship and suggests that the
Boiotians had begun promulgating their communal links to epic well before the
fifth century.

C. Thucydides and the *Ehoiai*

While certain elements of Thucydides' account clearly rely on earlier tradition,
especially epic, other aspects of his presentation deserve brief discussion with
reference to the Hesiodic passage discussed earlier in this chapter (*Ehoiai*, fr.
218). Recall that part of the earlier tradition about Boiotian Arne concerned
Boiotos, the ἄναξ and eponym of the group. There Boiotos was a community
leader, perhaps even oikist (κατοικῶν). Interestingly, Thucydides' passage may

---

[98] On Thucydides' audience, see Howie 1998, 78–88, 101, 118–121; Momigliano 1978, 60–
66.

[99] Ridley 1981, 25–46.

[100] See Howie for a similar view toward Thucydides' inclusion of traditions in the Archaeology which would have appealed to various groups in his audience (Howie 1998, 82, 84, 118–
121).

recall this term from the Hesiodic fragment, for as we have seen, Thucydides describes the οἱ νῦν Βοιωτοί as settlers in Boiotia (ᾤκισαν). In addition, Thucydides identifies the Boiotians as ἐκπίπτοντες. Naturally, the Boiotians are connected to their eponym Boiotos, a figure whom the Hesiodic fragment may connect to organization, leadership, and possible exile (κατοικῶν). That Thucydides often uses the term κατοικέω to indicate exiled leaders suggests that familiarity with Boiotos' Hesiodic role of κατοικῶν may have colored later accounts of the story and Thucydides' later characterization of Boiotos' followers as ἐκπίπτοντες. In other words, Thucydides' passage may bolster the argument for the existence of the term κατοικῶν (or at least a related term) in Hesiod's fragment 218. If so, then Thucydides' characterization of the Boiotians as ἐκπίπτοντες, much like his epic characterization of them as wealthy and populous, may also have an antecedent in earlier tradition, ca. 580.

D. Implications of Thucydides' Account

The tradition of Boiotian migration as a whole, including the versions of migration and habitation in Thucydides, bears wide-ranging implications about the Boiotian collective in the Late Archaic and Classical periods.

First, the tradition of Boiotian migration from Thessaly, which may have been understood more as an invasion of people from the north rather than simply a population movement, would have positively defined the claim of the Boiotians to Boiotia in the Archaic period, much as the tradition of the Dorian invasion did for the Dorians, as Thucydides' presentation of the two groups together suggests. Such territorial definition would have been particularly vital for the sixth-century Boiotians as they witnessed the rapid territorial expansion of Thessaly to the north, the rise of panhellenic Delphi to the west, and the development, power and influence of Athens under the Peisistratids to the south. Further, asserting rights to Boiotia as a territory would have been of great significance at this time in light of the chronic territorial rivalries between Attica and Boiotia during this period.[101] Also, as we have seen, Thucydides himself remarks upon the early attraction which Boiotia held as a territory because of the fertility of its land; it was to the late sixth-century Boiotians' advantage, then, to advertise their putative relationship to this land as its final occupiers.

Second, the status of Boiotian Arne also suggests that the story of migration from Thessaly could simultaneously be understood to emphasize a positive relationship between the two communities and thus by extension their surrounding territories. As we have seen, Boiotian and Thessalian Arne play consistently significant roles in the earliest sources connected to the Boiotian migration (*Iliad*; Hes. fr. 218; *Aspis*; Thucydides). We are left wondering exactly how these two communities were associated, for no early source is explicit on this point. Indirect

---

[101] E.g., the Athenian alliance with Plataia in 519 or 509; the attack of the Boiotians and Chalkidians against Athens in 507/6; Peisistratid alliance with Thessaly in the sixth century.

evidence suggests that the communities were strongly linked and that Boiotian Arne may have been considered a colony of Thessalian Arne. For the sake of interest, I briefly discuss this evidence here, noting however that any suggestions based on it necessarily remain speculative.

Our first clue in defining the link between the Thessalian and Boiotian communities of Arne lies in their mutual name, since archaic mother-cities are known to have given their own names to their colonies.[102] Most examples concern migration from the mainland overseas, but Pausanias provides a noteworthy parallel for migration from the mainland to another mainland site (notably, led by an exile) in discussing the legendary tradition about Phokian Stiris. In Pausanias' time inhabitants of Stiris claimed descent from the early Athenian kings:

οἱ δὲ ἐνταῦθά φασιν οὐ Φωκεῖς, Ἀθηναῖοι δὲ εἶναι τὰ ἄνωθεν, καὶ ἐκ τῆς Ἀττικῆς ὁμοῦ Πετεῷ τῷ Ὀρνέως ἀφικέσθαι διωχθέντι ὑπὸ Αἰγέως ἐξ Ἀθηνῶν· ὅτι δὲ τῷ Πετεῷ τὸ πολὺ ἐκ τοῦ δήμου τοῦ Στιρέων ἠκολούθησεν, ἐπὶ τούτῳ κληθῆναι τὴν πόλιν Στῖριν.

(The Stirians) say that they are not Phokian but Athenian in descent, and that they came (to Phokis) from Attika together with Peteos the son of Orneos when he was pursued from Athens by Aigeos; and they say that since the majority followed Peteos from the deme of Stirea, the polis Stiris got its name from this (Paus. 10.35.8).

Given the family tree of Peteos, grandson to Erechtheos and father to Menesthios, the legendary king and leader of the Athenian contingent to Troy, it seems that the tradition of Peteos' exile and migration with the inhabitants of Stiria was thought to have happened around the time of the Trojan war. This is relatively close in mythic time to the Boiotian migration as Thucydides describes it. The Steirian case thus provides a perceived contemporary paradigm for the leadership of mainland-to-mainland migration by an exile. Moreover, the names of the two communities in this tradition are very similar (Steiria, Stiris) and were understood to mark the relationship between the mother-city and the second settlement.[103] It thus seems reasonable to suggest that a similar pattern of mainland to mainland migration could have been perceived in the case of the two Arnes.

Together, Boiotos' status as Hesiodic κατοικῶν and Thucydides' characterization of the Boiotian settlers of Thessalian Arne as ἐκπίπτοντες (1.12.3) provide a second clue about the two Arnes. Oikists and their colonists were often remembered as having been originally forced from their home cities. For exam-

---

[102] E.g., Naxos, the eighth-century colony of the Naxians and the Chalkidians on Sicily; the seventh-century colony of the Opountian Lokrians in south Italy, Lokri Epizephyrii; the eighth-century Megarian colony of Megara Hyblaia on Sicily (for which see Malkin 1987, 164–174).

[103] For Phokian Stiris and its claims of Athenian descent, see McInerney 1999, 132 and 189; for its location, see McInerney 1999, 68–69 and esp. 319–320; see Camp and Vanderpool for a connection between the tradition of Athenian migration to Stiris and a second-century BCE Athenian decree found on the ancient site (Camp 1994, 8; Vanderpool 1971, 439–443); see Camp for additional links between Athens and Phokis (Camp 1994, 7–8); on Steiria, a relatively small Athenian deme set on Attika's east coast, see Whitehead 1986, 370 with map on p. xxiii.

ple, the oikist of Syracuse, Archias of Corinth, was thought to have brought natural disasters to his native city; he and a group of followers were then expelled
and moved on to Sicily.[104] Another useful case comes from a foundation oracle
for Kyrene, commonly understood to imply that Battos and his group were sent
away Thera to found the colony.[105] The foundation story for eighth-century Taras
also provides an instructive example of a group of exiled founders: Phalanthos,
the oikist, led a group of those who were not integrated into Lakonian society to
Sicily.[106] Boiotos, considered a leading figure in Boiotian Arne in the Hesiodic
Ehoiai (κατοικῶν), fits well into this pattern as a possible leader of the exiled
population of Thucydides (ἐκπίπτοντες).

Together, then, the identical name of the communities, the potential exiled
status of the characters involved (ἐκπίπτοντες; κατοικῶν), and the legend from
Steiris of mainland-to-mainland colonization strengthen the possibility that Boiotian Arne was considered a colony of Thessalian Arne. In fact, in the final sentence of his chapter on the Boiotian migration, Thucydides implies that all the
activities described in the passage should be considered foundation stories:
πάντα δὲ ταῦτα ὕστερον τῶν Τρωικῶν ἐκτίσθη (1.12.4).[107] Certainly from a
Boiotian point of view, the tradition of invasion from Thessalian Arne would
have been useful, not only in terms of claims to territory, but also as a foundation
story for Boiotian Arne, a community of sufficient importance to have been included in the *Iliad's* Catalogue of Ships as well as in some versions of the eponymous Boiotos' genealogy. Given the continued importance of Thessalian place
names and cults of Thessalian origins in Boiotia, it does not seem likely that the
Boiotians considered their putative origins in Thessaly a source of any later
embarrassment. The name and tradition surrounding Boiotian Arne may indeed
provide evidence for Boiotian pride in such descent.

RECAPITULATION

Our earliest sources for the Boiotian migration concern: Boiotian Arne, Thessalian Arne, the Boiotians and Thessalians, Boiotian expulsion from Thessaly, and
Boiotos' role in this migration and in the foundation of Boiotian Arne. Thucydides' version confirms many elements of earlier tradition. This consistency
suggests that the main strands of the migration story had emerged by the Archaic
period. This date roughly coincides with the appearance of other evidence for
Boiotian collective identity.

[104] Plut. *Mor.* 772d–773b; see Malkin 1987, 41–43. Examples of colonists leaving their
mother-city because of natural disasters are so numerous that I note here only the example of
Herakleia Pontica (see Justin XVI.3.4–7; Malkin 1987, 74).

[105] Hdt. 4.156.1–2; Defradas interpreted the oracle as such: see Malkin 1987, 64–65.

[106] For questions on the precise status of the groups called *Partheniai* or *Eupeunaktai*, see
Vidal-Naquet 1981, 187–200; see Malkin 1987, 216–221 for a full discussion of the cult of the
founder Phalanthos; Malkin, 1994, 115–142.

[107] This understanding of the sentence is implied by the comments of de Wever and van
Compernolle 1967, 490.

As a *terminus post quem* for the traditions, we have the brief passages from the *Iliad*, the *Ehoiai*, and also the archaeological evidence from Thessalian Kiérion, all of which date roughly in the form we have them from ca. 700 to 580 BCE. Notably, given these early dates, it is clearly not possible for the original tradition of Boiotian migration and habitation to have concerned a Boiotian military and political federation, for even in following the canonical interpretation of its genesis, the earliest date for a military federation is 519.[108]

As noted, Thucydides records two reconcilable strands in the tradition of Boiotian migration one of which explicitly connects the Boiotians to the Βοιωτοί of the Catalogue of Ships. Boiotian concern to link their collective to epic tradition is also apparent in a variety of additional sources, as we will see in the following chapters. Thucydides also portrays the Boiotians as migrants, perhaps even exiles, from Thessaly; within Boiotia this story could have conveniently served to lay claim to territory through invasion.

That Boiotos played a leading role in the migration and the foundation of Boiotian Arne indicates the importance of this aspect of the invasion story for the collective Boiotians by the time of its source, the *Ehoiai* (Hes. fr. 218). As we saw in Chapter One, by the mid-fifth century Boiotos is linked to Arne through genealogy, for Hellanikos records Boiotos as a son of a nymph Arne.[109] This *stemma* thus makes the eponymous hero of the Boiotian collective a direct descendant of the communities which were involved in its tradition of migration, thereby further indicating the collective importance of the migration story. The relationship between the Thessalian and Boiotian communities named Arne of the migration tradition also reaffirms Boiotos' genealogical Thessalian ties, as attested in the Archaic and Early Classical periods.

Finally and notably, the accounts of Boiotian migration connect the Boiotians to famous mythological groups. Not only are the historical Boiotians linked to the Βοιωτοί of the Catalogue of Ships, but Thucydides likens the Boiotians to one of the most respected groups of post-Troy invaders: the Dorians. It thus may be significant that during the late sixth and early fifth centuries other putative kinship groups also focused on bolstering collective identity through territorial claims: the Spartans through traditions of the Dorians, and the Ionians and Athenians through the story of the Ionian migration. Via portrayal as a group of conquering invaders like the Dorians, the Boiotians could further and respectably bolster their claims for territorial control throughout Boiotia.

A second facet to late archaic Boiotian collective identity thus emerges: by the late sixth century, the Boiotians had clearly constructed a complex tradition about ancestral origins which served as an important criterion for their collective. Such tradition comprises a significant aspect of ethnicity as defined by Smith and Malkin, for it provides group "memories" of mythic beginnings in time, places of origin, migration and exile, all tied to a collective eponymous ancestor.[110] The

---

[108] See Chapter Six for further discussion.

[109] Hellanikos *FGrHist* 4 F 51 (= Schol. ad *Il.* B 494).

[110] A. Smith 1986, 192; Malkin 1998, 57; also see Kearns 1989, 103, for the importance of correlations between fictitious ancestral groups and present day groups in the construction of the identity of the present day group.

tradition of migration and habitation of the Boiotians thus highlights the process
by which the Boiotians reaffirmed their ideas about themselves in the late sixth
century, just as traditions of the Dorian invasion did for Peloponnesians and the
return of the Herakleidai did for the Spartan elite.

CHAPTER 3
BOIOTIAN COINAGE AND THE SHARED SYMBOL
OF THE "BOIOTIAN" SHIELD

I now turn to the iconographic significance of the shield appearing on Boiotian coinage from its inception in the late sixth century. Traditional proposals for the advent of a late sixth-century Boiotian military federation rest upon the stamping of this shield on coins from different Boiotian *poleis* in this period; as Larsen remarks, "the chief evidence for the existence of a confederacy is the coinage."[1] Many have even understood the shared coin types as markers of federal membership. Recent work suggests, however, that shared coin types can signify a number of alternative underlying group affiliations, e.g., cultic, as in the case of the Λέσβιοι, or economic and imitative, as in the case of the south Italian *poleis* Sybaris, Kroton, Kaulonia, Metapontum, and Poseidonia in the late sixth century.[2] In what follows I offer complementary explanations of the shared shield symbol as a marker of genealogical, economic and putative historical ties underpinning late archaic and early classical Boiotian collective identity. Throughout this discussion I refer to the shield symbol as a "cutout" shield, as opposed to the more commonly used term, "Boiotian" shield, since this specific shield shape is in fact not at all exclusive to the iconography of Boiotia during any period of Greek history.

I begin with a numismatic discussion of Boiotian coinage, since the material is not widely familiar and many related assumptions require reassessment, particularly the connection between the coins and a federal military body. I then offer complementary alternative readings for the coinage. I first raise the simple function of the coins as a pun on the name of the Boiotians. I then analyze the shield symbol as a marker of the genealogical relationship between Boiotia and Aigina, as well as the related connection between Aigina, its Aiakid heroes, and Boiotian weaponry. This discussion involves an iconographic survey of the cutout shield in late archaic and early classical media; the evidence reveals an association between the cutout shield and the epic and Aiakid heroes Aiginetan Ajax and Achilles. The nexus of genealogical and symbolic relationships between Boiotia, Aigina and the heroic will be seen to reinforce the punning function of the shield coinage as well as Boiotian links to epic tradition, as established in the first two chapters. Discussion of the Boiotian provenience of Ajax's shield in the *Iliad* strongly reinforces this picture, as does analysis of the Boiotians in the Theban *Aspis*. I last raise a secondary meaning for the cutout shield as a possible marker of manufacture of raw materials and perhaps even weaponry. I

---

[1] Larsen 1968, 32. See also Head 1911, 343; Ducat 1973, 62.
[2] See further below.

conclude by briefly speculating about possible reasons for the decline in use of the cutout shield symbol in Attic vase painting of the early fifth century; this change may mark an adjustment in Athenian perceptions of the Boiotians brought about by souring relations between the two communities in the late sixth and early fifth centuries.

A NUMISMATIC HISTORY AND A RECONSIDERATION OF BOIOTIAN COINAGE

Boiotian coinage first appears in the very late sixth century.[3] The earliest issues display on the obverse the oval shield with semi-circular cutouts on either side; the reverse is stamped with an Aiginetan mill sail design in an incuse square. A few of these coins also have a capital *theta* stamped on the reverse. These issues have been used as evidence for Thebes at the head of an incipient military federation, although the Θ could refer to either Thespiai or, less plausibly, to Thisbe.[4]

By the turn of the century many Boiotian *poleis* appear to have issued coins with city-abbreviations on the reverse and the cutout shield on the obverse. The interval between the minting of these issues and the earlier ones which were uninscribed or inscribed with the Θ does not appear to have been great. All early Boiotian issues may in fact have been roughly contemporaneous.[5] The earliest of these so-called later issues hail from Tanagra and Hyettos and resemble the preceding coins with a shield on the obverse, a mill-sail on the reverse and a *polis*-abbreviation (T for Tanagra; closed H for Hyettos). Thereafter but still near the turn of the century issues of this same type appear from various *poleis*, including Thebes, Akraiphia, Koroneia, and Mykalessos, although a number of such coins have been reattributed to different communities. Nonetheless, these coins are often used as evidence for membership in a new late sixth-century military federation of Boiotian *poleis*.[6]

---

[3] Current chronology relies on Kraay's 1976 redating of Head's 1881 catalogue of Boiotian issues (Kraay 1976, 109; see also Schachter 1989, 85, n. 44). Perhaps in deference to previous scholarship on the issue, Kraay admits that coinage from Boiotia depicting a shield could have been struck "at any time after about 550, but there is little evidence from which to determine the actual date" (Kraay 1976, 109). The presence of four Boiotian coins in the Asyut Hoard (ca. 475) confirms that Boiotian coinage began "well before 480" (Price and Waggoner 1975, 53; see also Mackil 2003, 68 and n. 110); on the Asyut hoard see further below.

[4] Fossey 1988, 472; for the attribution of the coins to Thebes see, e.g., Mackil 2003, 68. Knoepfler argues that archaic Boiotian coins stamped with *phi* belong to Thespiai, as opposed to Pharai, in which case the early coins stamped with *theta* would most likely have come from Thebes. However, Knoepfler's hypothesis problematically requires Thespiai to have changed its *polis* abbreviation from *phi* to *phi-alpha* in the late fifth or fourth century (see Knoepfler 1981, 147).

[5] J. Kroll (pers. comm.); see S. Larson 2001, 57; Mackil 2003, 69.

[6] E.g., *RE* III, 1899, col. 643, s.v. Boiotia (F. Cauer); Salmon 1978, 18. For additional arguments about the reattributions of coins, particularly those of Hyettos, Pharai, Haliartos, and

Shared coin types have often bolstered arguments for political and military federal systems in other regions of Greece. One of the most recent discussions concerns the Arkadian silver coins stamped APKAΔIKON, which have long been thought to mark mid-fifth-century Arkadian federalism.[7] Psoma subtly argues that an Arkadian *symmachia* struck the coins, mostly triobols, for daily payment of soldiers following the Persian Wars.[8] Partly on the basis of evidence for civic rivalry, however, Nielsen suggests that fifth-century Arkadia was mostly disunited politically and militarily.[9] After reviewing the coinage and other evidence commonly adduced for the federal nature of the group,[10] Nielsen convincingly places the genesis of the Arkadian federation only in the fourth century and connects the APKAΔIKON issues to the pan-Arkadian festival and games for Zeus Lykaios.[11] According to this argument, fifth-century unity in Arkadia is thus founded on cultural grounds. Other shared coinage series have been interpreted as denoting *ad hoc* alliances between various communities, such as the issues from various Macedonian and Thracian tribes in the late sixth and early fifth centuries; Kraay suggests that such series represent temporary economic unity in the face of outside pressure, perhaps a quick means of paying tribute to the Persians preceding the Persian wars.[12]

Later federal organizations, of course, do indeed share coin types, the Boiotians and Arkadians being good examples. But as Nielsen remarks, most "uncontroversial examples of federal coinage are later than the fifth century."[13] We must therefore examine each individual series of early coins and the additional contextual evidence for the communities that issued them in order to conclude the precise nature of the issuing body. I thus return to Boiotian coinage.

In terms of Boiotian mints, no die study of Boiotian coinage has been conducted. We thus have no way of knowing for certain if the same obverse die was

Akraiphia, see Ashton 1995, 1–20; 1997, 188–189; 2000, 93–97; Knoepfler 1981, 146–147; Étienne and Knoepfler 1976, 219, 221–226. On Hyettos' importance in the Archaic period, see also Kunze 1967a, 98–100, plate 47.

[7] The series consists of silver triobols and obols, marked on the obverse with Zeus Lykaios and the reverse with Despoina/Artemis and an abbreviated collective regional ethnic; see Nielsen 1996, 39, and n. 1.

[8] Psoma 1999, 81–96; see also Nielsen 2002, 142–145.

[9] E.g., epigraphic evidence for regional and city-ethnics from dedications (some even from inter-*polis* wars, Nielsen 1996, 47–48), evidence from Thucydides and Herodotus (Nielsen 1996, 48–50). In a later article, Nielson further distinguishes various subgroups and *poleis* within Arkadia (Nielsen 1999, 51–59); he reviews and expands upon this evidence in his book (Nielsen 2002, 130–157, esp. 145–152 on the coinage).

[10] Nielsen 1996, 42–47, 50–56; Nielsen 2002, 121–130, 134–141.

[11] Nielsen 1996, 40–42, 50–56, 61; Nielsen 1999, 57, 59; Nielsen 2002, 145–157. For agreement with Nielsen and for a brief recapitulation of earlier scholarship on the topic, see Morgan 1999, 386, 407–408. See Morgan 2003, 84, for review of Nielsen's and Psoma's general arguments.

[12] Kraay 1976, 138–141. For another coin possibly minted in response to Persian demands for tribute, see Kraay 1976, 149.517 (western Thrace).

[13] Nielsen 1996, 40, where he cites the Boiotian, Aetolian, and Achaian League coinages of the fourth through second centuries.

used to stamp all the coins, thereby indicating a central mint. A glance at the obverse of issues attributed to the same periods suggests that different *poleis* used different dies, however. Moreover, it is the *polis* that the coins emphasize through the use of abbreviated civic ethnics. All definite federal coinages give the name of the *koinon* or the *koinon* and *poleis* involved, not the *poleis* alone, as we see in the earliest Boiotian coinage.

Polis-centered issues with a similar shield on the obverse continue into the fifth century, but by the second quarter of the century the marking of polity on the coins transforms. Attributed to the period following the Athenian victory at Oinophyta in 457, Boiotian coins begin involving specifically local types along with the city abbreviations: e.g., Akraiphian coins picture a kantharos and laurel, probable markers of local worship of the Akraiphian civic hero Ptoios and Apollo Ptoios, respectively; Koroneian issues depict a gorgon head, likely connected to the nearby sanctuary of Athena Itonia and perhaps also to Athena Alalkomenia.

To the beginning of this period (ca. 480–456) Kraay dates a group of interesting Tanagran issues which depict not only the shield and the city abbreviation, but also an abbreviation of the collective regional ethnic, B, BO or BOI, on the obverse. Although dates proposed for these coins formerly ranged from the 550's to the 450's, Kraay's post-480 to mid-fifth-century date is now generally accepted.[14] These coins are thus contemporaneous with other Tanagran issues marked with T/TA. I will return to these Tanagran issues shortly.

According to the current chronology, the next phase of Boiotian coinage begins after the battle of Koroneia in 447/6, when the Boiotians drove the Athenians out of Boiotia. For a period of about sixty years Thebes then operates the only active mint in Boiotia. It is only after this point that our first secure literary evidence for the existence of the Boiotian federation surfaces: the Oxyrhynchus historian's description of the military federal organization and the regional districts of Boiotia, a work dated to 386–356 but describing the years from 447/6–387/6.[15]

The fourth century saw many developments in Boiotian coinage, but most of this later activity is not relevant to the present discussion. It is noteworthy, however, that in the late fifth century and continuing through the dissolution of the Boiotian federation by the King's Peace in 387/6, various Boiotian *poleis* begin again to mint coins.[16] These coins are remarkably similar to the early fifth-century Boiotian issues with shields on the obverse and abbreviated city ethnics with local symbols on the reverse. The similarity between these fourth-century coins

---

[14] See Kraay 1976, 110 and n. 1 for others' proposed dates; to Kraay's note add Head 1884, 60 and Mackil 2003, p. 70, n. 117, who speculatively suggests linking the Tanagran issues with the problematic earlier Chalkidian shield coinage. For similar suggestions see, e.g., Schachter 2003, 65–66; Babelon 1907, 974.

[15] These are Bruce's dates for the composition and the period which the Oxyrhynchus historian describes (Bruce 1967, 4–5, 103, 157); his view is partially and problematically based on the numismatic evidence (Bruce 1967, 103). These dates are generally accepted by scholars concerned with Boiotia, however (e.g., Larsen 1960, 9, n. 1, and 11; Cartledge 2000, 401).

[16] Kraay 1976, 112–114; see Mackil 2003, 69 for brief discussion of this series.

and the earlier ones illustrates just one of the problems in the chronology of Boiotian coins and the arguments based on it: while the fourth-century coins from these twelve Boiotian *poleis* are said to reflect political independence during a period in which the federation did not exist, the earlier and similar coins are called federal and supposedly mark membership in an early military league. All further trends in fourth-century Boiotian coinage are documented by Head and can finally be called truly federal, since, as Nielsen notes, for this period "we have explicit evidence of the existence of the confederacy in the description of the constitution in the Oxyrhynchus historian 19.2–4."[17]

PROBLEMS IN ASSESSING BOIOTIAN COINAGE

There are further difficulties with this portrait of Boiotian coinage. First, it almost goes without saying that frustratingly few excavations and hoards provide evidence; analysis is still vital, but speculation is all one can expect from such paltry remains. Second and more problematically, alterations in the accepted chronology of Boiotian coinage appear to reflect political shifts in Boiotian organization. For example, after the battle of Oinophyta and during the Athenian hegemony over Boiotia of 457–446, no Boiotian coins are stamped with the abbreviation of the collective regional ethnic, BOI. Kraay places the Tanagran issues which display the abbreviation BOI before this battle, as noted above. The regional ethnic of the Tanagran coins is then used as proof for some sort of early-to mid-fifth-century federal and military consciousness, squelched by the Athenians after Oinophyta.[18] Lack of the abbreviated ethnic BOI in the post-Oinophyta series is then understood to reflect successful democracies set up by the Athenians in Boiotian *poleis* over the following decade.[19]

It is thus obvious that Boiotian coins, including other examples, have been dated partially on the basis of such historical events, even when there is no outside evidence that the event had any influence on coinage. As Howgego notes, documented battles in particular often become lynchpins on which scholars hang coinages whose chronologies are unknown: the historical event is then used to date the coin; the coin in turn reinforces the date for the historical event.[20] As Hansen remarks, as groups of Boiotian issues are redated or reassigned, alter-

---

[17] Nielsen 1996, 40. For similar brief histories of early Boiotian coinage, see S. Larson 2001, 61–77; Mackil 2003, 68–80. After 379 and apparently in accordance with the re-establishment of a federation, Boiotian coinage changes to a series "not bearing the name of any one city in particular" but abbreviating officials' personal names (Head 1884, 62; see Hepworth 1998, 61–96). After the battle of Chaironeia in 338 coinages stamped with the abbreviation BOIΩ or BOIΩTΩN and city ethnics again appear. For problems with reconstructions of these later Boiotian coinages, see Martin 1985, 166–170, 178–179.

[18] See e.g., Sordi 1968, 66; Fowler 1957, 164–170.

[19] The post-Oinophyta series also bears civic markers, e.g., a kantharos from Akraiphia; for this series and the supposed influence of Athenian democracies on it, see Head 1888, xxxviii–xxxix; Gardner 1918, 357; Kraay 1976, 110–111.

[20] Howgego 1995, 37.

ations in the coins can no longer be presumed to reflect the chronology of major historical events.[21]

Adherents of the traditional chronology conclude that the first historical event marked by the advent of Boiotian coinage was the genesis of the Boiotian federation in the late sixth century.[22] Certainly the Aiginetan millsail pattern stamped on the earliest Boiotian coins, first dated to the third quarter of the sixth century and now downdated to 520–480, could support this view.[23] Although the earliest Boiotian coinage stamped with this millsail pattern in imitation of Aiginetan coins appears only in the final years of the sixth century at the earliest, this general date still corresponds with the traditional date for a military federation, proposed on the basis of the alliance between Plataia and Athens (best dated to 519 BCE).[24] Yet coinage fundamentally implies inter-*polis* trade and interdependence, not necessarily political or military organization.[25] As Schachter has remarked, "the introduction of coinage can no longer be considered relevant" to the question of the origins of the Boiotian political and military federation.[26]

In considering alternative explanations for the production of shared coin types, two aspects of the early Boiotian issues deserve further comment: the abbreviation BOI and the symbol of the shield. As noted, the collective regional ethnic BOI or BOIO on the Tanagran issues has been understood to mark a military or political component of the Boiotian *ethnos*. Yet even if these coins date before the mid-fifth century, which is not at all certain, the abbreviation BOI/BOIO does not provide definitive evidence for a military body, for shared regional abbreviations on coinage from other areas of Greece do not always indicate federal states. To this end Hansen discusses coins from two Lesbian cities stamped with the legend ΛΕΣ; these issues recall the Tanagran coins stamped with BOI yet date well before any federal organization of Lesbian *poleis*.[27] As Nielsen too remarks with regard to the Arkadian shared coinage discussed earlier: "we have coins of federal appearance which were definitely not coins of a confederacy, like the coins inscribed ΛΕΣ(ΒΙΩΝ); Lesbos was not a political

[21] M. Hansen 1995, 20–21. See also Hansen and Nielsen 2004, 432–433; Mackil 2003, 67; S. Larson 2001, 64.

[22] E.g., Ducat: "Le monnayage béotien a vraisemblablement été créé pour répondre aux besoins propres, principalement militaires sans doute, de la Confédération. Il est en même temps l'affirmation que la nouvelle entité politique apparue en Grèce donne de son existence" (Ducat 1973, 71–72).

[23] See Kroll and Waggoner for the date in the third quarter of the sixth century (Kroll and Waggoner 1984, 339) and Gjongecaj and Nicolet-Pierre for the redating, based on the archaeological contexts of hoards containing Aiginetan coins, particularly an almost exclusively Aiginetan coin hoard found in Albania (Gjongecaj and Nicolet-Pierre 1995, 288–290). Vickers' downdating of the Aiginetan wind-sail pattern to the first two decades of the fifth century is now generally discredited (Vickers 1985, 1–44, esp. 34–35).

[24] For this date see Chapter Six.

[25] On Hellenistic inter-*polis* trade and economy in Boiotia, see Mackil 2003, 39–84, esp. 58–66 (on Akraiphia and Anthedon, the Kopais, and Tanagra).

[26] Schachter 1989, 85.

[27] M. Hansen 1995, 31 and n. 93.

unit, but settled in five *poleis*."[28] A fragment of Alkaios is illuminating in this regard; the poet describes the ΛΕΣΒΙΟΙ acting collectively to build a sanctuary:

] .. ρά . α τόδε Λέσβιοι
...] .... εὔδειλον τέμενος μέγα
ξῦνον κά[τε]σσαν, ἐν δὲ βώμοις
ἀθανάτων μακάρων ἔθηκαν

—

κἀπωνύμασσαν ἀντίαον Δία
σὲ δ᾽ Αἰολήιαν [κ]υδαλίμαν θέον
πάντων γενέθλαν, τὸν δὲ τέρτον
τόνδε κεμήλιον ὠνύμασσ[α]ν

—

Ζόννυσσον ὠμήσταν.

The Lesbioi ... established this great conspicuous precinct to be held in common, and put in it altars of the blessed immortals ... and they entitled Zeus God of Suppliants and you, the Aeolian, Glorious Goddess, Mother of all, and this third they named Kemelios, Dionysos, eater of raw flesh (Fr. 129.1–9 LP; trans., Campbell 1982).

It thus seems probable that the archaic ΛΕΣΒΙΟΙ identified with each other on cultural grounds and on this basis referred to themselves with the collective regional ethnic, which some of their *poleis* then stamped on coins. The same may hold true for the Arkadian festival coinage discussed earlier.

In light of such parallels, we should not rush to ascribe the Tanagran coins stamped with BOI to a military federation. The Lesbian and Arkadian correspondences suggest that the Tanagran issues might have been minted in honor of a festival, such as the Pamboiotia, the well-known regional Boiotian celebration for Athena, or more localized yet regionally significant events, perhaps for Tanagran Apollo or Hermes.[29] If the Tanagran coins date after the mid-fifth century, however, BOI might well reflect a military and political organization which may have solidified after the battle of Koroneia, a probability which I will discuss at length in Chapter Six. But even so, as Nielsen has suggested for Arkadia, the collective regional ethnic in Boiotia may not have signified a political group even in periods when a political and military federation is known to have existed.[30] Given such objections, the appearance of the collective regional ethnic on these few Tanagran coins cannot be used as proof of a military federation in the early fifth century.

---

[28] Nielsen 1996, 40.

[29] For Apollo at Delion, see Schachter 1981–1994, vol. 1, pp. 44–47; Pind. fr. 286; for a possible Theban dedication to Apollo Delios from the area, see Hdt. 6.118 and Schachter 1981–1994, vol. 1, p. 46. For Hermes at Tanagra, see Schachter 2003, 61; 1981–1994 vol. 2, 44–50.

[30] Nielsen 1999, 30. Salmon approaches this understanding of the abbreviation BOI in arguing that the Boiotian military federation had been temporarily dissolved during the period when Tanagra minted these coins (Salmon 1978, 27).

THE SYMBOL OF THE CUTOUT SHIELD

I thus turn to the cutout shield depicted on the obverse of most Boiotian coinage from ca. 500 onward and the main evidence used as proof for an early political and military federation in Boiotia.[31] In what follows I first argue briefly against this traditional view and then offer alternative readings of this symbol.

A. The Chalkidian Issues, the Asyut Hoard, and the Beginnings of Boiotian Coinage

Two late sixth-century coins from Chalkis have loomed large in arguing that the shield on Boiotian coinage marks a military federation of *poleis*. On their obverse the Chalkidian coins depict a shield notably similar to that of Boiotian issues of roughly the same period; the abbreviated civic-ethnic ΧΑΛ also appears on the obverse.[32] The reverse is stamped with the Chalkidian wheel in an incuse square.[33] Many scholars have linked these Chalkidian coins to Boiotian coinage and have understood them to reflect the joint military venture of the Boiotians and the Chalkidians against Athens in 507/6, as recorded in Herodotus and inscriptions from the Athenian Acropolis.[34]

Seltman, among others, has been a major proponent of this view.[35] He dates the Tanagran issues with the abbreviated ethnic BOI to the same year as the Chalkidian coins and on this basis argues that these issues represent a joint Boiotian-Chalkidian coinage minted in 507/6. His argument is unconvincing, particularly since the abbreviated ethnic BOI on the Tanagran coins may not even be a definitive marker of federal identity, as noted above. Most important, the chronology of both series of coins is insecure. Setting the Tanagran issues in a late sixth-century context and basing arguments for a military alliance on this chronology is thus untenable. Although Kraay too would like to connect the Chalkidian coins to the events of 506/7, he acknowledges that the two surviving examples cannot be dated precisely to that year, even though the hoard from Taranto in which one of the coins was found provides them a *terminus ante quem* of 500–490. He further adds: "the events of 507 do not self-evidently require an issue of coinage."[36] With the Chalkidian coins then, we find ourselves again with a

---

[31] *RE* III, 1899, col. 643, s.v. *Boiotia* (F. Cauer; on the shield as "Bundeswappen"); also Roesch 1965, 34–36, and Salmon 1978, 17. Notably, the shield cannot be dated by style or form as a class and shows no significant changes during its use on Boiotian coinage (Head 1911, 2).

[32] The ethnic appears as ΨΑΛ in Chalkidian script; see Jeffery 1990, 79–80, 82, 87.

[33] For the current locations of the coins, see Kraay 1976, 109, n. 4.

[34] Hdt. 5.74–82; *IG* I³ 501.

[35] Seltman 1955, 57; Price and Waggoner 1975, 19; W. Wallace (1962, 38, n. 2, where he posits a slightly different type of Boiotian-Chalkidian alliance); see also Kraay 1976, 90 and n. 4; Boardman 1983, 36, n. 129. Babelon was the first to propose the link (Babelon 1907, 975–976).

[36] Kraay 1976, 109. Price and Waggoner also acknowledge the weakness of the connection between the Chalkidian coins and the events of 507/6 (1975, 19 and n. 12). Schachter, citing Kraay, accepts the association as certain (Schachter 1989, 84, and n. 42). For the pre-500 date for

circularity problem. However, even if one persists in accepting circularity in this case by maintaining that the Chalkidian shield issues are tied to the events of 507/6, the five- to ten-year insecurity in their chronology destabilizes the connection between these coins and the joint attack on Attica.

Should one continue to accept a link between the Chalkidian shield-issues and late sixth-century Boiotian coinage, one must attempt to explain the relationship between the two; I thus briefly turn to the origin of Boiotian coinage itself. I propose a new, speculative, but equally plausible model for the appearance of shared Boiotian coin types. In my view it seems probable that the early shared Boiotian coins were imitative of an issue from one Boiotian *polis* which itself was minted in imitation of earlier sixth-century Aiginetan silver types.[37]

It is almost certain that Aiginetan coinage was used in Boiotia as a standard medium of exchange in the area for some time before Boiotian *poleis* minted their own coinage, a practice which was common in other regions of Greece during the century.[38] Boiotian coinage, like that of other areas in central Greece (Phokis and Thessaly, for example), later used the Aiginetan weight standard.[39] The windmill sail reverse on Boiotian coinage is almost certainly based on the Aiginetan type,[40] and the width and convexity of the shield on Boiotian coins even recalls the shape of the Aiginetan turtle obverse. It is thus arguable that the first shield-windsail coin struck in Boiotia was meant to recall the Aiginetan turtle-windsail issues.

Imitation of widely circulated and trusted coinage was certainly common in antiquity, especially in areas that yet had no coinage of their own. Imitation of Athenian owl coinage is a well-known phenomenon, for example, even in cities and regions known to have been politically hostile toward Athens.[41] Aiginetan coinage was copied too, especially early in the Kyklades and in Kydonia, Crete, in the late sixth century.[42] It is thus reasonable to imagine a Boiotian *polis* striking issues based on Aiginetan types at this same time.

The new Boiotian coin was almost certainly used for the same purpose as most early Greek coinage seems to have been: as a local all-purpose currency, for use within the *polis* as payment for cattle, state labor, taxes, fines, and not necessarily for military purposes. In Boiotia the shield-windsail type was imitated by other Boiotian *poleis* as they found the need for coinage and thus began to mint; such mimicry caused the type to take on a regional acceptability and a homogenous appearance. Inter-city trade could now occur with a new coinage which subsequently assumed a traditional character as the recognized legal tender used within and between Boiotian *poleis*. It might also be possible to characterize this sharing as an informal regional economic union, a recognition of what

the Taranto hoard, see Kraay 1976, 109; Price downdates the hoard to 500–490 (Price and Waggoner 1975, 13).

[37] I am grateful to J. Kroll for help with this interpretation.
[38] Kraay 1976, 44–45.
[39] See Nielsen 2002, 221.
[40] See Kraay 1976, 44, for a full description of the windsail pattern.
[41] See Kraay 1976, 73–74, for a brief list and description of such imitative issues.
[42] Stefanakis 1999, 250–253.

each city in the region accepts as approved money (*dokima chremata*), thereby easing inter-*polis* trade and payments.[43]

We find an archaic parallel for imitative regional coinage in southern Italy. There around 550 the *poleis* Sybaris, Kroton, Kaulonia, and Metapontum used coins which shared both weight standard and an unusual local production technique. The non-Achaian south Italian community of Poseidonia later minted similar issues. Kraay has proposed that either Sybaris or Metapontum first developed the coinage and that the other communities copied those originals soon afterward.[44] As far as is known, these south Italian cities were not associated in a military or even political alliance but may have enjoyed a certain economic unity.[45]

Developing a hypothesis for the advent of Boiotian coinage is not the main point of this chapter; nonetheless, I will briefly speculate on origins in the context of the two problematic late sixth-century Chalkidian shield coins discussed above. A first option: if one insists that the Chalkidian coins mark a military expedition involving more than one Boiotian *polis*, this campaign could have been an *ad hoc* military alliance formed under the special circumstances of central Greek and Athenian turmoil in the late sixth century BCE. To a similar end Schachter suggests that the Chalkidian and Tanagran BOI-issues could have been minted for payment of mercenary soldiers or even as collective ransom for the Chalkidian and Boiotian prisoners of 507/6.[46] Although this is an attractive suggestion, corroborating numismatic and material evidence beyond shared coin types is needed to associate the Chalkidian coins (not to mention the Tanagran issues) with any military event or alliance, even such an *ad hoc* group. While it is tempting to connect the newly discovered late archaic Theban column commemorating a collective ransom with the minting of the Chalkidian and Tanagran BOI-issues, this piece still does not provide a conclusive link to the coins; it is likewise not absolutely clear that the fragment should be linked unequivocally to the events of 507/6, since the piece will then have marked the ransoming of the 700 prisoners taken by the Athenians, an event which surely involved not a little embarrassment in Thebes and elsewhere in central Greece. However, it seems possible, as Aravantinos and Schachter note, that the column may attest to a Theban and Boiotian attempt at propaganda within Boiotia, with the intention of minimizing the humiliation caused by the events of 507/6.[47] Nonetheless, a link between this piece and the Chalkidian shield coins is not a foregone conclusion.

A second option for the Chalkidian coins: given the imitative nature of early Greek coinage in general, it is alternatively possible that the Chalkidian issues were stamped in imitation of the coinage of one Boiotian *polis* to mark an economic or perhaps military relationship with that particular Boiotian community.

[43] For complementary arguments, see S. Larson 2001; Mackil 2003.

[44] Kraay 1976, 162–163, 165–167.

[45] Le Rider proposes that the south Italian coinage may reflect an economic union, but this interpretation applies only to post-510 issues (Le Rider 1989, 167–171).

[46] Schachter 2003, 65–66 and n. 74; see also Babelon 1907, 967–970, 974.

[47] Whitley 2005, 46 (reported by Aravantinos); Schachter (pers. comm).

The most likely theory is an extension of this second possibility. The Chalkidian shield coins may have been stamped with the shield in order to acquire monetary acceptability in the larger area of Chalkis and southeastern Boiotia. It seems almost certain that, as in later periods, a great amount of commerce was conducted between Chalkis and various nearby Boiotian *poleis* in the sixth century (e.g., Mykalessos, Tanagra, Thebes); these communities thus required an easily recognizable and acceptable currency between them. That the Boiotian and Chalkidian coins were struck on different standards is problematic in interpreting the coins as markers of a strictly economic alliance; yet at the same time the Chalkidian coins could have kept the traditional Euboian standard as local convention while imitating the shield of the Boiotian type.[48]

Admittedly, the question of the Chalkidian coins may never be securely resolved given the state of the evidence. At least, however, the Chalkidian issues imply some kind of relationship between one or more Boiotian community and Chalkis. The suggestion that the Chalkidian types were meant to achieve regional economic acceptability in southeastern Boiotia is attractive, especially considering the proximity between the two areas and the likely economic exchange between them. This hypothesis is no weaker than the traditional explanation of the Chalkidian coins as markers of a military alliance between Chalkis and a military Boiotian federation in the late sixth century.

Most significant in establishing Boiotian economic activity are the four Boiotian coins from the Asyut hoard: two from Thebes (presumably), and two from Tanagra. In addition to situating the advent of Boiotian coinage before the hoard's burial, the presence of the four Boiotian issues confirms the travel of Boiotian coinage outside Boiotia ca. 475–465, at the lower end of the period under consideration.[49]

The first of the four issues requires comment, since Price and Waggoner indicate that abbreviation of a civic ethnic might appear on the coin between the cutout sides of the shield.[50] The photograph included in the publication of the hoard is too dark and blurred to shed light on this possibility, and the coin's whereabouts after the dispersal of the hoard are presently unknown. The specific attribution of this coin is thus unclear, although according to the usual reading, the coin may be assigned to Thebes, on the possibly mistaken assumption that Thebes alone minted the earliest coins with the cutout shield but without a civic ethnic. The possibility still exists, however, that the coin may have come from another Boiotian *polis*. The same can be said of the second Boiotian coin in the hoard which displays no civic abbreviation.[51] The remaining two Boiotian issues from the Asyut hoard are Tanagran.[52] That the four coins thus originated at three potential mints is an important aspect of this Boiotian assemblage.

[48] On the different standards, see Seltman 1955, 57.

[49] Price and Waggoner date the Asyut hoard ca. 475 (Price and Waggoner 1975, 117–125); Kraay downdated the hoard slightly to the 460's (Kraay 1976, 189–198).

[50] Price and Waggoner 1975, 53 (no. 246).

[51] Price and Waggoner 1975, 53 (no. 247).

[52] Price and Waggoner 1975, 53 (nos. 248–249).

While the Asyut hoard situates this grouping of Boiotian coins in a non-local Mediterranean context, one might still and reasonably object that so few Boiotian coins have been found outside Boiotia in other late archaic and even classical contexts that they do not seem to have been widely used outside the region.[53] Indeed, aside from the Asyut coins, only a few Boiotian issues from Thebes and Tanagra appear in hoards before or even close to 450: two Theban staters come from a fifth-century hoard in Elis, and one Tanagran stater appears in a similarly dated Aetolian group.[54] However, as Howgego notes, failure to travel, or at least failure to appear in hoards, does not necessarily indicate that coins were not used outside their community of origin.[55] Further, in terms of coin movement, appearance of coins does not always correlate with other evidence for trade of various sorts.[56] At any rate, the Asyut coins do indicate that Boiotian coins traveled outside the region to a certain extent. Our scanty evidence for archaic and early classical coin hoards in general limits additional speculation, but such has been the case for other coinages in the past, until discovery of additional hoards confirmed their presence abroad in certain areas and time periods.[57]

In sum, evidence from Boiotian coinage sheds little light on political and military Boiotian federalism in the late sixth century. An economic and imitative interpretation of the shared coinage is equally possible. And, although I have had to raise the question of the origin of Boiotian coinage here, I am not so much interested in determining exactly why Boiotian *poleis* minted coins in the first place, but rather why they chose to mark their common coinage with the symbol of the particularly distinctive cutout shield. What, then, did the cutout shield symbolize? In the following sections, I suggest that the cutout shield was chosen to emphasize multivalent communal associations that centered upon collective genealogy, community ties to epic saga and the Aiakid epic heroes, and possible regional manufacture of raw materials or weapons.

B. The Pun

After Lacroix, who first addressed the "Boiotian shield" methodically, numismatists generally accept that the image of a shield served to pun on the name of the issuing group, the Βοιωτοί, since a variety of shield-types were manufactured from wood and metal covered with layers of oxhide, the Greek word for which is βοῦς.[58] Epic poetry is explicit about the leather from which epic shields were

---

[53] Mackil 2003, 79.

[54] Thompson, Mørkholm, and Kraay 1973, hoard nos. 28 and 37.

[55] Howgego 1990, 3.

[56] Howgego 1995, 94.

[57] Corinthian coins, for example, were long thought to have been involved in the west through trade and as an influence on local Sicilian coinages, as indicated by the Taranto hoard. It was not until the discovery of the Selinos hoard in 1985 that the influence of Corinth was fully confirmed (see Arnold-Biucchi et al. 1988, 24–26, 28–35). For a skeptical view about the value of hoards as markers of coin circulation in antiquity, see Holloway 2000, 1–8.

[58] Lacroix 1958, 20–22; Kraay 1966, 336.

constructed, especially Ajax's magnificent shield, described in the *Iliad* four times as ἑπταβόειον (*Il.* 7.222, 245, 266; 11.545).[59] Lacroix lists other epic terms for shields which are even more directly connected to the word βοῦς: e.g. ῥινοῖσι βοῶν (*Il.* 12.263), ταλαύρινος (e.g. *Il.* 5.289, 7.239), βοάγρια (*Il.* 12.22), even βῶν (*Il.* 7.238), βόεσσι (*Il.* 12.105), βόας (*Il.* 12.137), βοῶν (*Il.* 16.636).

Although our first direct evidence for puns on the word βοῦς and the name of the eponymous hero of the Boiotians, Boiotos, comes from late fifth-century Athenian tragedy,[60] we can quite reasonably apply the punning interpretation to the earliest Boiotian coins, on analogy with other ancient coinages of a similar period. Well-known examples from other relatively contemporaneous local issues include the seal (φώκη) on sixth-century Phokaian coins, the quince (μῆλον) on Melian coins, and wild celery (σέλινον) on the important archaic issues from Selinos. Later examples include the Rhodian rose and the Klazomenian swan.[61] We also have useful parallels from Boiotia's neighbor Euboia, many of whose coinages depict cattle prominently, thereby illustrating the meaning of the name Euboia.[62] Similarly, from vase painting we have one black-figure example of the mythic antihero Kyknos bearing a shield with a swan (κύκνος) as its shield device.[63] There is no reason to believe that the symbol of the cutout shield played on the name of the Boiotians differently, although the adoption of the cutout shield instead of a bull's head or some other more obvious representation of an ox or cow is important and demonstrates that the pun was not the sole rationale behind the choice of symbol. The punning interpretation does not exclude other possibilities which could operate simultaneously, nor is the pun alone necessarily sufficient to account for the choice of the cutout shield. What then, of other additional meanings?

---

[59] See also Whallon 1966, 7–8.

[60] Euripides' two fragmentary *Melanippe* plays, dealing with the youthful exploits of Boiotos, refer to cattle sheds, cowherds, and Boiotos being raised and suckled by cows (see Webster 1967, 117, 147–157). The Rhodian comic poet Antagoras later parodied the Boiotians with the same pun well outside central Greece; the poet jokes that the Boiotians even have the ears of cows: βοῶν γὰρ ὦτα ἔχετε Βοιωτοί; (Antagoras *Paroemiograph* II, p. 333); see Vottéro 1998, 165.

[61] On fifth-century Melian issues, see Kraay 1976, 45–48. The Phokaian seal was especially consistent in the first half of the sixth century (Kraay 1976, 265; Howgego 1995, 3). For Selinos' celery, see Kraay 1976, 208 and Arnold-Biucchi 1992, 13–19; the Rhodian rose (Kraay 1976, 257–258); the Klazomenian swan (Kraay 1976, 208). To this list can be added the rooster on archaic Himeran issues (perhaps a personification of ἵμερος, desire, or the advent of day, ἡμέρα, both of which would pun on the name of the community; Kraay 1976, 208). Another possible parallel are the goat issues from late archaic and early classical Macedonia, often attributed to Aigai (αἴξ, Kraay 1976, 141) but now also tentatively ascribed to Mygdonia or possibly Krestonia (Lorber 2000, 130–133). See also Hind for a possible Thasian pun via depiction of a *thiasos* (Hind 2001, 281–282).

[62] Kraay 1976, 4; Ridgway 1992, 16; on punning types in general, see Kraay 1976, 3–4. Lacroix calls such issues "types parlants" (Lacroix 1958, 29; also Kraay 1976, 109).

[63] Spier 1990, 123–124.

C. Divine Significance

Earlier scholars interpreted the shield as a cultic attribute,[64] most often of Athena Itonia, the manifestation of the goddess worshipped at the Itonion, the pan-Boiotian sanctuary which later became a religious center for the Boiotian *koinon*.[65] This is a tempting suggestion but one which ultimately lacks support in iconography of other media. The best known black-figure Boiotian vase connected to the Pamboiotian festival, for example, depicts Athena brandishing a round shield.[66] Athena likewise exclusively holds a round shield on coinage of Thessaly, the region to which ancient sources connect her Itonian cult in Boiotia.[67]

A second hypothesis attributes the shield to Herakles. Lacroix argues against this view by relying on the *Aspis*, a work which to Lacroix pairs Herakles with a round shield (line 141).[68] Yet the *Aspis* consistently refers to Herakles' shield as a σάκος, a term which in epic chiefly seems to refer to an old type of body-shield, as opposed to ἀσπίς, a term seemingly reserved for all other shield types and which comes to be the standard designation for round shields in later literature (see below).[69] Herakles does often appear, in fact, in Attic black-figure vase painting holding a cutout shield, although as Lacroix notes, his depiction with this shield is not entirely consistent on the vases.[70] Nonetheless, associating the cutout shield with Herakles in the sixth century remains a possibility, particularly in light of the epic *ekphrasis* on his shield in the *Aspis*. I thus shall revisit this point at the end of the chapter.

D. Links Between the Shield and the Aiakids in Genealogy and Iconography

A more convincing meaning for the cutout shield lies its connections to the Aiginetan family of Aiakos. In iconography the cutout shield seems to have held a certain salience as a badge of the Aiakids; the symbol of the shield thus may have symbolically linked the Boiotian *ethnos* to this illustrious epic family tree. As we will see, this relationship comes as no surprise, since literary sources are

[64] Lippold 1909, 399–504.

[65] First by Head 1887, 291 (repeated in the second ed., 1911) and also by Seltman (1955, 55) and Roesch (1982, 224 and n. 103); see also Lacroix 1958, 7. Lacroix refutes Head's hypothesis that the shield symbolizes Ares (Lacroix 1958, 7; see Head 1911, 343–344). For scholars who hold this view, see Salmon 1978, 17, n. 2.

[66] On this vase and its series, see P. Ure 1927, 57; A. Ure 1929, 160–171; A. Ure 1935, 227–228; Sparkes 1967, 121; Maffre 1975, 432 (no. 1); Kilinski 1990, 45; Schachter 1981–1994 vol. 1, 117–121.

[67] Moustaka catalogues five types of Athena-depictions on Thessalian coins, three of which portray an armed Athena, always with a round or oval shield. In these three groups Moustaka lists ten coins depicting an armed Athena, nine of which show the shield (the tenth is not pictured; Moustaka 1983, 25); Lacroix includes one example (Lacroix 1958, 16, fig. 1, no. 6).

[68] Also see Myres' famous reconstruction of Herakles' shield, depicted as round (Myres 1941, 17–38).

[69] See Lacroix 1958, 15; Whallon 1966, 20–25.

[70] Lacroix 1958, 10.

virtually unanimous in tying the Boiotians to Aigina via genealogy. I thus begin this section by detailing literary evidence for Boiotian ties to Aigina and the Aiakids; I follow with the iconographic material.

In many of the earliest versions of their genealogies, both Achilles and Ajax descend from sons of Aiakos, the only son of Zeus and Aigina. Aigina herself was traditionally a daughter of Asopos, mythical eponym for a number of rivers in the Greek world, including the streamlet Asopos on Aigina as well as the larger river which ran through southeastern Boiotia.[71] Asopos also likely served as eponym for the Boiotian border community of Oropos whose port sat at the mouth of the river.[72]

The tradition of the daughters of Asopos was well known in Greek antiquity; we find our first extant lengthy account in Hesiod's *Ehoiai*, which builds on a tradition of inherited material.[73] In West's reconstructed genealogy, Aigina is most likely a sister to Arne, a figure of Boiotian importance who also appears as the toponym for the Thessalian cradle from which the Boiotians migrated to Boiotia, as we have seen;[74] with Arne as sister to Asopos, the Aiginetan Aiakos thus becomes cousin to Arne's son, the eponymous hero of the Boiotians, Boiotos. Boiotos' other descendants of regional prominence, for example, Onchestos, are thus related quite closely to the epic Aiakid descendants: Ajax, Achilles and Patroklos. The probable attestation of these ties at 580–520, West's general date for the Hesiodic Catalogue, gives us a nice start in dating the established tradition; the panhellenic nature of this tradition attests to its familiarity outside Boiotia and thus its almost certain importance inside the region as well.

We find more evidence for a Boiotian-Aiginetan link in Pindar's *Isthmian Eight*. Although the poem celebrates an Aiginetan victor, Pindar begins by recounting the genealogical link between Aigina and Thebe, the eponymous nymph of Thebes: both were daughters of Asopos, and Pindar even makes them

---

[71] See Pind. *Paian* 6. 123–183. There is also attested a Sikyonian Asopos to which West links the Peloponnesian daughters, as well as an Asopos in Thessaly. However, West rightly notes that the ancients, e.g., Bacchylides, had no trouble in treating Aigina and Thebe as daughters of the same river (M. West 1985, 100–101, see also 162–163). It is likely that all rivers named Asopos were thought to have a link to the famous mythical figure Asopos; the preponderance of the same name for different bodies merely attests to the popularity and fame of the figure and the relevance of his family and descendants for a variety of areas. It thus attests to the desire of various groups to coopt the mythology of the family of Asopos/Aiakos for their own purposes, much as West suggests that the Aiginetans themselves did (M. West 1985, 163–164). The adoption of the Aiakid stemma by various groups seems to have taken place by the late sixth century, if not far earlier, since most of the stemmata in the *Ehoiai* have been traced back to the eighth century (M. West 1985, 164–165).

[72] Knoepfler 2000, 91–98, but see the entire article (81–98) where he discusses the localized appearance of the name Oropodoros and the attribution of the name Oropos for the river; Mazarakis Ainian 2002, 152–154.

[73] See M. West 1985, 100–103, 162–164, 181. The *Ehoiai* detailed five daughters of Asopos (M. West 1985, 181); earlier mentions of the daughters occur in the *Odyssey* and Eumelos (M. West 1985, 100). See also Breglia 2005, 25.

[74] M. West 1985, 102–103.

twins![75] It is not just that Pindar needs to redeem himself for being Theban – the poem, after all, was performed in 478, in the aftermath of the Persian wars, unkind to Thebes and Boiotia in general – but the poet may also have included this genealogy to remind his Aiginetan relatives, grieving over so many men lost, that their family tree is shared with the whole city of Thebes; Thebes grieves with them, too, as it also celebrates Aigina's victor.[76] Significantly, Pindar continues by recounting the myth of the Aiakidai, particularly Achilles, whom he likens to the Aiginetan victor. Thus, by opening his poem with Aigina and Thebes and by continuing to discuss Achilles in detail, Pindar specifically ties one of the most powerful Boiotian *poleis*, if not the head of an early Boiotian collective, to Aigina, her son, Aiakos, and his sons, Ajax and Achilles.

Pindar's contemporary Bacchylides, although not himself a Boiotian, likewise links the city of Thebes to Aigina through Asopos. In his Ninth Ode, the poet lists both daughters back to back,[77] later including other daughters of Asopos as well. In his description of Aigina Bacchylides also briefly gives the story of the hero Aiakos, whose name would surely evoke those of his more famous descendants, Ajax, Achilles, perhaps even Patroklos.[78] This all in a poem for a victor from Peloponnesian Phlius, a *polis* which seems to have had a vested interest in the Asopides too, since, as Pausanias records, Phlius dedicated a statue of five Asopides at Olympia.[79]

Moving to strictly local Boiotian tradition, we find Korinna praising the Asopides; to them Korinna even attributes the entire race of heroes, ἡμιθέοι – the same term used in Hesiod. This fragment, as J. Larson remarks, "contains an audacious attempt to claim the prestige of the Aeacids and the other ἡμιθέοι for Boiotia."[80] Korinna's claim for the heroes' origin aside, the appearance of the Asopides in epichoric Boiotian tradition establishes their importance for Korinna's native *polis*, Tanagra, as well as for Boiotia at large, since she composed for local audiences, strictly in Boiotian dialect, relying exclusively on traditions of epichoric significance. The Asopides' appearance in Korinna, then, is an impressive indication of their significance in Boiotia by the early to mid-fifth century.[81] Although the names of the daughters cannot be reconstructed back into Korinna's fragment, it is extremely likely that she discussed Aigina, the most famous Asopid elsewhere, as well as Arne or Thebe, since these two figures both pertained to Boiotia and can be traced back into previous archaic genealogical tradition.[82]

---

[75] Pind. *Isthm*. 8.17.

[76] Pind. *Isthm*. 8.17–23.

[77] The poet has been using Theban mythology, so the leap to the tradition of Asopos seems reasonable.

[78] Bacchyl. 9.40–70.

[79] Paus. 5.22.6. According to the tradition, a watery figure named Asopos showed the first king of Phlius where the local river flowed, which was then called the Asopos after him (Paus. 2.12.4).

[80] J. Larson 2002, 53.

[81] See Chapter One for a discussion of Korinna's place in the early fifth century.

[82] For the five daughters whom Korinna discusses (Aigina, Thespiai, Corcyra, Sinope, and Thebe) see Gentili and Lomiento 2001, 7–20.

Other archaic and early classical literary accounts also show that Asopos was of importance in wider Boiotia. To Asopos are credited numerous additional Theban and Boiotian characters, including Antiope, mother of Amphion and Zethus (founders of Thebes), and Ismene, eponymous figure of the Theban Ismenion.[83] Through Asopos, then, the Aiakid genealogy is relevant both to Aigina and also to Thebes and wider Boiotia, especially the southeast, one of the most important areas of activity in Boiotia in the Late Archaic and Early Classical periods.

Herodotus later shows that Thebes, the Boiotians, and the Aiginetans were still thought to have strong genealogical links which dated back into the Archaic period, as far back as 507/6, immediately after the ignominious defeat of the Boiotians and Chalkidians by the Athenians.[84] Upon inquiring from Delphi how to get revenge, the Thebans are told to seek after their "nearest" (ἄγχιστα). Classical military historians have made much of this account in terms of who the Thebans are made to think are these "nearest:" the Thebans name the inhabitants of nearby and select Boiotian *poleis* who fight with them. However, the oracle actually suggests relying on putative blood relations: it is the Aiginetans who are the answer, Herodotus relates, not political or military allies, for Aigina and Thebe were sisters, daughters of Asopos, and thus family. So, after a request from the Thebans for aid, the Aiginetans, instead of giving military help via reinforcements, send the statues of the Aiakids to the Thebans as help in Theban revenge. When this fails, the Aiginetans send real men, but it is fascinating that the Aiginetan's first impulse was to send cultic representations of those heroes who were relatives of the Thebans. Whether this event actually happened or whether this story is a later Herodotean invention with a decidedly anti-Aiginetan slant, it was at least humorously believable to some in Herodotus' audience that the Aiginetans would have sent cult statues of the Aiakids to the Thebans before sending real military reinforcements. [85]

I now turn to the iconography of the cutout shield which will be seen to reinforce the literary connections adduced above. Even in a lengthy chapter, it is impossible to give a full account of the development of the cutout shield from the figure-eight Mycenaean shape through the Dipylon form. For details of the Mycenaean shields in particular as well as the development of shield iconography, I refer the reader to the relevant works of Lorimer, Lacroix, Snodgrass, Fortenberry, Borchhardt, Hurwit and others.[86]

---

[83] On Antiope, see *Od.* 11. 260; Asios fr. 1 (PEG); later traditions give Antiope a different genealogy, the first of which is found in Euripides' *Antiope* (Gantz 1993, 232; also see M. West 1985, 101–102 for a possible earlier version); on Antiope's sons as founders of Thebes, see Hes. fr. 182 MW and Pind. fr. 52k.44 (Snell). On Ismene, see Hes. fr. 294 MW; Apollod. *Bibl.* 2.5.

[84] Herodotus narrates the story at 5.79.1–5.81.3 (specific mention of the link between Thebes and the Aiginetans at Hdt. 5.80.1–2).

[85] See Burnett 2005, 27–28.

[86] Lorimer 1950, 134–135, 159–166; Lacroix 1958, esp. 17–18; Snodgrass 1964, 58–59; Snodgrass 1967, 19, 32, 45; Carter 1972, 57; Symeonoglou 1973, 89, n. 332; Borchhardt 1977, E16; Hurwit 1985, 122–125.

Before getting to particulars about the cutout shield, however, as background I briefly raise scholarly opinion on the association between the Geometric Dipylon shield form, general heroic scenes, and also the cutout shield shape itself. Such review is important because our first iconographic evidence for a possible link between the Aiakid Achilles and a specific shield shape comes in the form of a Geometric bronze figurine which sports a decidedly Dipylon shield form. I return to this figurine shortly.

Scholars debate whether or not the Dipylon shield was meant to convey epic/heroic connotations. While Snodgrass calls the Dipylon "a piece of heroic property," Borchhardt finds this association highly speculative.[87] Yet warriors holding Dipylon shields often appear driving chariots on late Geometric vases. Snodgrass demonstrates that such chariots were not actually used in warfare during the eighth or seventh centuries but were rather "heroic property" influenced by epic tradition.[88] That chariots may have been used as objects of ceremony in the Geometric period supports the claim that they were not in practical use but were instead symbolic objects of status.[89] The juxtaposition in Geometric war-scenes of two items of weaponry which were likely no longer used in war, the Dipylon shield and the chariot, is thus suggestive of a conscious attempt at recollecting the past, particularly the heroic past when these items were presumably thought to have been in use by one's ancestors.[90] Supporting the Dipylon shield's potential as an heroic image is the occasional use of the Dipylon shield as a distinguishing marker between one group of warriors and another,[91] perhaps even between victors and vanquished.[92]

This view has led some scholars to attempt to identify Geometric scenes which represent legends. The Dipylon shield appears in many of the most dis-

---

[87] Snodgrass 1964, 58 (see also Hurwit 1985, 125); Borchhardt 1977, E22.

[88] Snodgrass 1964, 160.

[89] *Contra* Boardman, who divorces the potential ceremonial function of the chariot from its antiquarian symbolism, while acknowledging that war chariots were "sung about" and perhaps even used as "status symbols" (Boardman 1983, 28–29). Boardman problematizes his belief in Geometric use of war-chariots by using Strabo's "surely Archaic account" of an Eretrian parade for Artemis which involved sixty chariots (Boardman 1983, 29). For an analysis of chariot use in the Near East, see Crouwel and Littauer 1979, 50–55, 62–64, 68–71, 74–81, 90–96, 101–110, 128–134, 144–148, 152–154.

[90] The Dipylon shield has also occasioned much debate over its material existence. On the basis of its archaeological absence, Snodgrass posits that the Dipylon never existed in reality; it was instead a romantic depiction of a long unused type, perhaps of the Mycenaean figure-eight shield (Snodgrass 1964, 59; Snodgrass 1967, 45; for similar evolutionary claims, see Webster 1958, 169–170; Lorimer 1950, 159–166; Borchhardt 1977, E16). For positive arguments for the Dipylon's existence, see Carter 1972, 57; Karusu 1976, 26; Boardman 1983, 27; Hurwit 1985, 122 (who argues for the shape as a misunderstood Minoan-Mycenaean double axe, turned on its side).

[91] E.g., on an Attic krater fragment discussed by Snodgrass 1998, 18–19.

[92] E.g., on an Attic oinochoe, ca. 730, which depicts warriors with the Dipylon shield vying with unshielded figures, some of whom are already dead, while others still seem to be defending themselves. Snodgrass provides an excellent discussion of this vase (Snodgrass 1998, 20–22, figs. 7 and 8).

cussed scenes, e.g., the famous Attic bowl in the British Museum depicting a man boarding a large ship, fitted out with two levels of rowers.[93] The man grasps the arm of a woman holding a garland; a Dipylon shield marks the prow of the ship. Identifications of this scene include the departures of Ariadne and Theseus, Medea and Jason, Helen and Paris. But the figures remain unnamed; we thus have no way of knowing which story the vase potentially represents, or if it alternatively depicts an otherwise unknown tradition or simply a generic scene. Indeed, Snodgrass suggests that if this scene depicts a legend, it is unknown to us and certainly not a specific one from the *Iliad* or *Odyssey*.[94] Although the inability to identify this scene on this particular vase exemplifies the problem one faces in interpreting Geometric vases in general, it is nonetheless possible to entertain Snodgrass' argument that the Dipylon shield type connotes generic heroism, on the basis of its likely evolution from the figure-eight shield as well as the Dipylon's portrayal alongside the obsolete chariot on Geometric vases.[95]

Scholars generally agree that we are generally on firmer ground with the cutout shield than with the Dipylon form in terms of heroic implications. For Snodgrass, Carpenter, Borchhardt and Hurwit the cutout shield imparts a heroic tone to any scene, and for Snodgrass, it "is usually a sign that the scene is taken from heroic saga."[96] In the sixth century the cutout shield often appears in generic scenes of combat between two unnamed warriors or in scenes depicting a solitary warrior, as well as in scenes with Amazons.[97] However, numerous unnamed warriors, Amazons, and even Giants on vases also hold the round *hoplon* shield, modeled on those actually in use from the Archaic period onward.[98] The most pressing question in this context, then, concerns how the cutout shield could impart a more heroic tone than the round shield.

[93] London BM 1899.2–19.1.

[94] Snodgrass 1998, 33–35, fig. 13. See this entire work for more analyses of this type. For review of the scholarship on this vase, see Ahlberg-Cornell 1992, 27–28.

[95] Kossatz-Deissmann, a scholar of Achillean iconography, supports this view (Kossatz-Deissmann 1981, 195). Notably, if late Geometric figural scenes represent the "leading edge" in Geometric art, as Snodgrass suggests, the heroic overtone of the Dipylon shield becomes even more significant and involves development in Geometric iconography of the hero (Snodgrass 1998, 49).

[96] Snodgrass 1967, 45, 55; Carpenter 1991, 199; Borchhardt 1977, E23 and n. 195; Hurwit 1985, 125. Also see Ahlberg-Cornell's comments (1992, 60), but note her acceptance of the existence of the Boiotian shield. Nonetheless, she still speculates that the Boiotian shield served "the same function as the Dipylon shield in Orientalizing art."

[97] Borchhardt 1977, E24. As examples I cite only a few black-figure pieces here from the Beazley archive (www.beazley.ox.ac.uk) and from Boardman 1974: hydria from Eleusis, attributed to the Polos painter, ca. 600–550 (arming warriors, Beazley 1956, 44.12); cup attributed to the C painter, ca. 600–550 (crouching warrior, Beazley 1956, 681.50BIS); neck-amphora, ca. 600–550 (fighting warrior, Beazley 1956, 583.51TER); neck-amphora from Cervetri, Camtar painter, ca. 600–550 (fighting warrior, Beazley 1971, 31.7); amphora B, painter of London B 76, ca. 600–550 (fighting warrior, Beazley 1971, 33.16BIS); neck-amphora, ca. 600–550 (fighting warrior, Beazley 1971, 40); Tyrrhenian amphora, ca. 565–550 (Boardman 1974, 63.1; Beazley 1956, 97.22); neck-amphora and name vase of the painter of Vatican 309 from Caere, ca. 560–540 (Boardman 1974, 73; Beazley 1956, 121.7); belly-amphora by Amasis from Vulci, ca. 560–525 (Boardman 1974, 87; Beazley 1956, 151.21).

Analysis of iconographical scenes in which the cutout appears provides our most tangible evidence for a connection between the cutout and the heroic, particularly when restricted to scenes which name the figures with the cutout shield or portray cutout shields in identifiable scenes from epic. Most scholars acknowledge that on black-figure vases depicting named characters the cutout shield most often appears as the property of Telamonian Ajax and Achilles, frequently in specific scenes from their epic traditions.[99] The majority of these scenes concern Achilles and include Achilles' ambush of Troilos,[100] his receiving armor from Thetis,[101] Achilles and Ajax at draughts, Ajax carrying Achilles' corpse,[102] and the battles between Achilles and Penthesileia, and Achilles and Memnon.[103] On the basis of this evidence Karusu associates the cutout shield primarily with Achilles, as do Hampe and Simon. Carpenter dissents, commenting that "the Boeotian shield ... is not the property of any one hero."[104] In light of this disagreement, I examine evidence for the identification of the cutout shield with Achilles and Ajax in the Late Archaic and Early Classical periods.

[98] E.g., on a black-figure belly amphora by the Munich painter, from Vulci, ca. mid-sixth century (Boardman 1974, 141; Beazley 1956, 311.2); lekythos of the Phanyllis group, end of the sixth century (arming scene, Boardman 1974, 237).

[99] Lippold 1909, 419–436 (where he catalogues some of the Achilles scenes); Lorimer 1950, 167; Lacroix 1958, 7–30; Snodgrass 1967, 45; Boardman 1983, 31.

[100] On the development of this and related scenes of Achilles' murder of Troilos, see Ahlberg-Cornell 1992, 53–57.

[101] In myth Achilles received two shields, one before leaving Phthia in preparation for the Trojan war, and the other from Thetis after Patroklos' death and the loss of his armor to Hektor. Carpenter finds it "often difficult to be certain which scene is being shown" in vase painting. When Peleus is identifiable in the scene, Carpenter argues that the armor is the first set, for Peleus would have been present when Achilles left his home before the war (Carpenter 1991, 200). However, it is unlikely that the individual artists always had one specific chronological frame in mind in every scene of Achilles' receipt of armor, as a plate by Lydos indicates. There, Peleus is present, but also named is Neoptolemus, Achilles' son "whose presence in the scene," if one were to follow a strictly temporal interpretation of the chronology of the tradition, "is, to say the least, puzzling," as Carpenter himself acknowledges (Carpenter 1991, 199). The natural inference from this chronological difficulty is that strict temporal narrative is not always followed in depictions of this scene (or in vase painting in general, for that matter); this artist has chosen to compress associated mythological characters together in one spot, not an uncommon practice in vase painting (see e.g., Carpenter 1991, no. 316). Karusu, pointing out that only a few arming scenes without doubt illustrate Phthia, concludes that the two scenes cannot be distinguished on the vases (Karusu 1976, 28 and n. 27). Thus, it is entirely unproven that before 550 black-figure representations of Achilles' arming depict his Phthian reception of weapons and that red-figure vases commonly portray his second arming, as Carpenter suggests (Carpenter 1991, 200). For our purposes it is important to note only that Achilles is often depicted in scenes where he receives armor, and that the shield which he receives often has cutout sides.

[102] For the view that even the unnamed versions of these scenes represent Ajax carrying Achilles corpse, see Ahlberg-Cornell 1992, 35–38.

[103] See Lippold's catalogue and descriptions (Lippold 1909, 426–435); also Borchhardt 1977, E24; Lacroix 1958, 16.

[104] Karusu 1976, 29 (although there she does not accept the cutout shield as associated with Achilles after the last quarter of the sixth century); Hampe and Simon 1964, 55; Carpenter 1991, 199.

I thus offer the following analysis, based on images of Achilles and Ajax included in *LIMC*, Boardman, Carpenter and the Beazley archive database.[105] This survey does not pretend to be a complete overview of depictions of Achilles and Ajax in archaic art, but it is large enough to be representative of trends in archaic iconography. As will become clear, percentages suggest that in the Archaic period, Achilles and Ajax were associated with the cutout shield far more often than other epic heroes. The cutout shape was thus associated in people's minds with at least these two major epic heroes, both Aiakids. After reviewing the iconographical evidence, I will turn to evidence for Ajax's epic shield in particular which the *Iliad* records as having been of Boiotian manufacture. The link between Ajax, the cutout shield shape, and the Boiotian provenience of his epic shield is enough to explain why the Boiotians chose to mark their shared coinage with this symbol.

Because of the possible evolutionary relationship between the Dipylon shield and the cutout shield forms, I begin my examination of the iconographical evidence with an early seventh-century Thessalian bronze figurine.[106] The male figure stands looking forward, his broken left arm bent downward, his complete right arm raised up and the hand pierced, presumably to hold a spear. The body is muscular with highly emphasized calves and neck; the genitals are large in proportion to the body, and for a bronze figurine, the warrior is tall (27.6 cm). He wears a wide belt and a small crested helmet. Most notable is his shield, a nearly circular piece of metal with a deep oval cutout on each side, attached to the figure's neck by a *telamon* and hanging across its back. Many parallels exist for the stance and body type of this figurine, often called the "Pferdeführer," especially from Olympia.[107] Because of the figure's seventh-century date, Karusu describes the shield attached to the figure as "anachronistic;" she mistakenly calls it a Boiotian shield, however, and not a Dipylon shield with which its shape is most closely allied.[108]

The figurine's findspot has excited much speculation, since it came to light near modern Kharditsa, a central Thessalian site (near ancient Metropolis and Kiérion) which later boasted a famous Achilleion. Kharditsa lies rather near classical and modern Pharsalos and within the area of ancient Phthia, Achilles'

---

[105] *LIMC* I, 1981 (Achilles and Aias); Boardman 1974; Carpenter 1991; Beazley archive database: www.beazley.ox.ac.uk. An appendix of pieces used in the survey is found at the end of this book.

[106] Athens NM 12831; *LIMC* Achilles 1.902. Karusu convincingly dates the figurine to the first years of the seventh century on the basis of parallels from Olympia (Karusu 1976, 24 and n. 9, followed by *LIMC*). Snodgrass dates the piece less specifically to the Archaic period (Snodgrass 1964, 59); Rolley advocates the end of the eighth century (Rolley 1986, 70). Error on the conservative and slightly later side seems best. For a good photograph, see Rolley 1986, 71.

[107] E.g., "Pferdeführer" B5600 from Olympia (Kunze 1967b, 224–236, and pls. 108–109).

[108] Karusu 1976, 25; also Rolley 1986, 70. Karusu seems to reject this shield as Dipylon because round shields already appear on vases at the time of the statue's production; this problem seems imaginary, however, for it is entirely possible that two or more distinct shield types could be used in iconography simultaneously, one indicating a shield in material use, another a shield never attested in the material record.

epic home. Near Pharsalos lay a Thetideion. Found at the site of a candidate for Old Pharsalos, a few kilometers east of the classical walled city, were inscriptions to Thetis and archaic vase fragments which depict Patroklos' corpse and his funeral games, including the famous Sophilos fragment.[109] I do not follow Karusu in saying that the figurine's Dipylon shield type thus "regularly" indicates Achilles at this time in Greek iconography.[110] However, in light of its findspot near Achilles' home territory, the shape of the shield and its use in a dedication of a warrior figure are suggestive. Rolley is willing to speculate on the Achillean identity of the figurine; Thomas seems convinced of it.[111] To my mind, given the likely heroic overtone of the Dipylon shield on vases in general and the findspot of this figurine in particular, the figurine can tentatively although not conclusively be identified as Achilles. If correct, the Dipylon type of shield may be linked to the tradition of this specific epic hero in the early seventh century, at least in Thessaly.

The true cutout shield appears in mid-seventh-century iconography. It is not commonly depicted until the late seventh century, becoming very widely used in sixth-century Attic black-figure vase painting. Like the Dipylon, the cutout shield has two side curves, but they are much smaller and less extreme. The shield as a whole is generally ovular but is occasionally depicted as rather round. Various shield emblems decorate its exterior face, and on the inside appear various mechanisms for holding and wielding it.[112]

A number of art historians have proposed models for the evolution of the cutout shield from the Dipylon shape. Hurwit calls attention to two important amphorai that depict round shields marked with blazons of the Dipylon-type shape: one, late Geometric, and the other, proto-Attic.[113] It is easy to see how these "Dipylo-Boiotian" shields may represent an iconographical step between the pure Dipylon shield and the markedly different looking cutout shield. Alternatively, some scholars, in noting the existence of a similar cutout shape in earlier iconography, including early Minoan, have suggested that the cutout shield form had always existed as a variant way of representing the Mycenaean figure-eight shield.[114]

A third possibility for the cutout shield's evolution involves twelfth-century parallels. Following Snodgrass, Borchhardt links the cutout shape to shields depicted on a twelfth-century sherd from Iolkos. The piece shows warriors bearing

[109] For modern Kharditsa and the ancient Achilleion, see Karusu 1976, 28, and *LIMC* 1.902 (following Karusu). For a good map of the ancient and modern sites of southern Thessaly, see Doulgeri-Indzessiliglou 1991, 43. For the inscriptions and the archaic vase fragments from Old Pharsalos, see Karusu 1976, 27, and *LIMC* Achilles 1.491.

[110] Karusu 1976, 28.

[111] Rolley 1986, 70; Thomas 1992, 52.

[112] Snodgrass suggests that the portrayal of these mechanisms was influenced by grip of the hoplite shield (Snodgrass 1967, 55; see Boardman 1983, 30, 32; van Wees 2000, 134–135 (where he illustrates the hand-grip of the cutout shield).

[113] Hurwit 1985, 126.

[114] Most notably Higgins 1957, 33. For a full review of Higgin's thesis, see Borchhardt 1977, E15–E16.

shields with slightly cutout edges; both scholars consider this image the most convincing evidence for the iconographic evolution of the later cutout shield shape.[115] In support of this evolutionary view, one might also adduce the iconography of the unique shields found on the Mycenaean warrior vase and also a real shield remnant from twelfth-century Cyprus thought to be similar to a cutout shape.[116] Although the exact evolution of the cutout shield may never be satisfactorily traced, Snodgrass' interpretation of the cutout shield as a variant or evolutionary iconographical step from the Dipylon shield-shape seems generally plausible. The early seventh-century Thessalian figurine with the Dipylon shield, then, takes on added meaning in this discussion of the cutout shield shape, particularly in light of the figure's common identification as Achilles.[117]

The earliest example of Achilles with a true cutout shield appears ca. 670 on a Melian neck-amphora from Delos, which depicts a scene that has been identified as Achilles' receipt of armor from Thetis.[118] On a second piece, a bronze relief strip for a shield from the first half of the sixth century, Achilles, bearing a cutout shield, kills Penthesileia.[119] The iconography of Achilles with the cutout shield was also known in Boiotia in this early period, as three works of Boiotian provenience attest. The first, a relief pithos from Thebes, ca. 625, has been accepted as depicting Achilles' theft of Aeneas' cattle.[120] The second and third pieces from Boiotia both date to the second half of the sixth century. An Attic column-krater shows Achilles receiving Hephaistos' arms from Thetis, and on an Attic lekythos from Thespiai, Ajax carries Achilles' corpse.[121] On all three pieces of Boiotian provenience, Achilles bears a cutout shield. We can accept, then, that

[115] Borchhardt 1977, E17; Snodgrass 1964, 58–59; also van Wees 2000, 134.

[116] Alternatively, as Fortenberry suggests, these twelfth-century "cutout" shields may simply be called variants of the figure-eight, as opposed to predecessors of the archaic cutout shape. The Cypriot shield remains and the unique shields on the Mycenaean warrior vase remind Fortenberry of twelfth-century Hittite shields, which she speculates may have led to experimentation with a new type of shield in Greece at this time (see Fortenberry 1990, 31, and notes 93 and 94 for additional interpretations of variant figure-eight types). For the Mycenaean warrior vase, the shield remnant from Cyprus, and Hittite influence, see Fortenberry 1990, 30–33.

[117] The material existence of the cutout shield is not crucial to my argument, although scholars have taken various stances on its reality. For arguments against the use of real cutout shields, see Snodgrass 1964, 60 and plate 15a–b; Snodgrass 1967, 55; Carter 1972, 55–57 (who argues for the material existence of the Dipylon shield); Borchhardt 1977, E23 and n. 195; Hurwit 1985, 125 and n. 16; Carpenter 1991, 199. For positive arguments for their existence and use, see Boardman 1983, 31, 33; van Wees 2000, 134.

[118] *LIMC* Achilles 1.506; Schefold 1966, no. 24c; Kemp-Lindemann 1975, 157.

[119] From Perachora; *LIMC* 721; Schefold 1992, no. 77 (Delphi mus. inv. no. 4479).

[120] *LIMC* 389; see Ahlberg-Cornell 1992, 53. Although the provenience of pieces from the Tenian-Boiotian group of relief pithoi is suspect as information from dealers, scholars generally accept that pieces from this group belong to the "larger regional *koine* of *pithos* potters" (Ebbinghaus 2005, 53).

[121] Attic column-krater: Beazley archive, attributed to the painter of London B 76, ca. 575–525 (Beazley 1956, 87.17; Carpenter, Mannack, and Mendonça 1989, 24; Beazley 1971, 32); Attic lekythos from Thespiai: Beazley archive, ca. 550–500 (Athens NM CC939, 429; Beazley 1956, 379.281).

the cutout shape and its association with the Aiakid Achilles was familiar inside the region. The image of Achilles with the cutout shield on the relief pithos would likely have been particularly public, given that decorations on such storage containers served not only to display the scene but also to draw attention to the wealth and status of the piece's (Theban) owner.[122]

By far the most numerous iconographical representations of Achilles with a cutout shield occur in Attic black-figure vase painting of the second half of the sixth century, as the above examples of Boiotian provenience reflect. Black-figure vases depicting the hero with this specific shield-type total 115. Ten of these date before 550; from 550–ca. 510 come our greatest number (98). Only seven date ca. 510–500. [123] Also from the second half of the sixth century come two bronze shield reliefs from Olympia: one, depicting Thetis giving armor to Achilles and the other, Penthesileia's death at his hands.[124] In both scenes Achilles is associated with the cutout shield. The bulk of archaic artistic representation of Achilles with the cutout shield thus dates to the second half of the sixth century.[125]

Achilles is not exclusively depicted with the cutout shield at this time, of course; he also bears a round hoplite shield in black-figure iconography. However, he appears with this type of shield far less frequently (36 times); these pieces are also spread over a much wider chronological period, from ca. 700 (an early Proto-Corinthian aryballos) to ca. 480 (an Attic lekythos).[126] Thirteen of the thirty-six pieces fall before 550, twenty in the second half of the sixth century, and three after the turn of the century.[127]

Telamonian Ajax, too, often carries a cutout shield in sixth-century black-figure painting, and here again, the contrast between black-figure depictions of Ajax with a cutout shield and those with a round shield is telling. I find thirty-one secure black-figure illustrations of Ajax with the cutout shield, ranging in date from 575 to the early part of the fifth century. Only four of these pieces date before 550; twenty of them come from the second half of the sixth century. Six of the remaining seven depictions date from 525–475; only one portrayal of Ajax

---

[122] See Ebbinghaus 2005, 53–58.

[123] See Appendix section A for information on these vases.

[124] Two bronze reliefs on Argive shields: Bol 1989, 69–70 (pl. 60) and 67 (pl. 64). See Appendix section B.

[125] Notably, the great majority of these episodes comes from epic tradition outside the *Iliad*: Achilles' pursuit of Troilos and Polyxena, Ajax carrying Achilles' corpse, and one scene in particular not from epic tradition as we know it but of extreme popularity in archaic vase painting, Ajax and Achilles playing *krotala*. Only nineteen of the 115 black-figure depictions of Achilles with the cutout shield are from the *Iliad*.

[126] See Appendix section C.

[127] Over half of the scenes depict Achilles' ambush of Troilos and Polyxena; only six come from the *Iliad*. The total figures: Achilles pursues Troilos/Polyxena (including the death of Troilos, 18; Achilles and Ajax gaming, 3; Achilles and Penthesileia, 3; Achilles and Memnon, 3; Achilles arming, 2; Achilles drags Hektor, 2; dead Achilles (body or *eidolon*), 2; Ransom of Hektor, 1; Ajax carries Achilles corpse, 1; Achilles fights Hektor, 1.

with the cutout shield dates securely after 500.[128] In contrast, Ajax appears only eight times in black-figure with a round shield. As was the case with black-figure depictions of Achilles, the few examples depicting Ajax with a round shield are scattered over the sixth century as opposed to clustered between 550 and 500.[129]

It thus seems that in archaic iconography, especially in sixth-century Attic black-figure vase painting, Achilles and Ajax are depicted in similar proportions with the cutout shield and with the round shield. In black-figure Achilles appears with a cutout shield at least three times more often than with a round one (3.14:1), as does Ajax (3.875:1). Although these heroes are not exclusively linked to the cutout shield in archaic iconography, then, the high ratio of their appearances with it as opposed to the round *hoplon* shield is striking, especially in the second half of the sixth century. These ratios suggest that while the cutout shield was associated with heroism in general, it was particularly associated with these two figures from epic tradition during this time.

The iconographical link between these two epic heroes and the cutout shield is further supported by the fact that other epic heroes popular in Attic vase painting do not carry the cutout shield nearly as often, if at all. Of sixty-four black-figure vases in the Beazley archive depicting Menelaos, for example, only two show him bearing a cutout shield (3%); most of the time he is without a shield at all.[130] One might argue that this absence depends on the scene depicted, for the reunion between Helen and Menelaos is this hero's most popularly illustrated tale; Menelaos would have had little need for a shield of any type in this situation. However, that Menelaos carries a cutout shield on both vases that depict his reunion with Helen speaks against this objection.

In the end, then, black-figure evidence demonstrates that the correlation between cutout shields, Achilles, and Ajax predominates during the very period in which Boiotian *poleis* start producing and stamping coins with this same shield type. It is also notable that the depictions of the two heroes with cutout shields reflect episodes from epic tradition outside the *Iliad* in a ratio of almost four to one, especially Achilles' pursuit of Troilos (*Kypria*), and Achilles' death and the bearing of his corpse off the battlefield (*Aithiopis*).

Since the Late Archaic and Early Classical periods also witnessed the shift from black- to red-figure vase painting, I turn to portrayals of Achilles and Ajax with shields in that technique. The change in iconography between the two styles is marked. A mere ten red-figure examples of Achilles with a cutout shield are identifiable; these vases range in date from roughly 550 to 450, a span which

---

[128] As was the case with the Achillean episodes, Ajax's most popular scene with this shield type also shows him carrying Achilles' corpse from battle (19 total, 61.3%); the frequency of other scenes is less, with the game between Ajax and Achilles running a distant second (5 total, 16.1%). Notably, neither of these scenes is from the *Iliad*. See Appendix section D.

[129] See Appendix section E.

[130] It is also notable that on eight of these sixty-four black-figure vases depicting a scene involving Menelaos (12%), the hero does not carry a cutout shield himself, but a generic warrior elsewhere on the vase does; see Appendix section J.

makes red-figure portrayal of Achilles with a cutout shield quite rare.[131] In contrast, red-figure vases depicting Achilles with the round shield number forty-four and begin in the last quarter of the sixth century; twenty-nine of the forty-four examples date to the first half of the fifth century (66%).[132] In the new red-figure technique, then, artists seem to have moved away from the popular black-figure depiction of Achilles with cutout shield. In the last quarter of the sixth century and especially in the first quarter of the fifth, Achilles is rather increasingly shown with the contemporary round shield. This trend took hold, for after the mid-fifth century Achilles was almost uniformly shown with a red-figure *hoplon* shield. Interestingly, in these red-figure pieces, a greater proportion of the scenes concern episodes from the *Iliad* than in the black-figure pieces.[133]

Fewer red-figure vases portray Ajax with any type of shield. Only one secure example from ca. 520–500 depicts him with a cutout shield; six later pieces portray him with a round type. Five of these images date after the turn of the fifth century. It is striking that four of these six scenes portray an episode from the *Iliad* not attested in the earlier period: Ajax and Hektor's battle from *Iliad* 7. Although the examples are few, these red-figure pieces may nonetheless indicate that in fifth-century iconography, Ajax was disconnected from his most popular episodes in black-figure (e.g., carrying Achilles' corpse). He instead became associated with one of his most memorable battles of the *Iliad*. Most notable for our purposes, the paucity of depictions of Ajax with any type of shield in red-figure vase painting of the first half of the fifth century may indicate a lack of interest in presenting Ajax's renowned strength as a warrior on the part of Athenian vase painting workshops.

To summarize: in black-figure vase painting and other media of the second half of the sixth century, Achilles and Ajax are depicted with the cutout shield over three times more often than with a round shield. A connection to the cutout shape through its iconographic predecessor, the Dipylon form, may have begun for Achilles as early as the early seventh century, marked by the bronze figurine from Thessaly. In red-figure iconography, especially of the first half of the fifth century, the ratio of cutout shield to round shield is dramatically inverted, Achilles now being shown with the round shield over the cutout shield 4.5 times to 1. Representation of Ajax with any type of shield in red-figure is rare. I speculate on the possible reasons for this shift in iconography at the end of this chapter. For now it is important to mark the predominantly sixth-century connotations of the cutout shield in the visual arts: the shield is heroizing in general but is also strongly linked to the heroes Ajax and Achilles and their epic exploits outside the *Iliad*. The variety of findspots for Attic vases that depict such scenes

---

[131] I use the date 550 because of the tendency of the Beazley archive to date pieces to broad fifty-year periods. There are few examples of red-figure painting from the mid-sixth century; most of the examples adduced in this chapter date to the end of the century or the beginning of the fifth. These scenes are still the same familiar episodes from black-figure Achillean iconography outside the *Iliad* (the ambush of Troilos, gaming with Ajax, battle with Memnon, etc.). See Appendix section F.

[132] See Appendix section G.

[133] Nineteen of forty-four (43.2%).

indicates that their iconography would have been familiar in many different regions, including Boiotia, where three examples were found; other proveniences include Delos, Athens, Rhodes, Etruria, and southern Italy. Non-ceramic depictions of Achilles with the cutout shield also come from Thessaly, Boiotia, Perachora, Olympia, and Delos. It is in this panhellenic iconographical context that Boiotian *poleis* begin stamping their shared coinage with the symbol of the cutout shield. It seems reasonable to suggest, then, that by choosing this shield to individuate their coinage, the Boiotians were associating themselves with the epic traditions of Achilles and Ajax.

E. The Boiotian Provenience of Ajax's Shield

That the Boiotians were associating themselves with the Aiginetan epic heroes via shield imagery finds its most definitive literary support at *Iliad* 7.219–225, the passage which describes Telamonian Ajax's famed shield. The passage attests to a panhellenically recognized link between the Boiotians and an older type of shield with specific heroic connotations:

Αἴας δ᾽ ἐγγύθεν ἦλθε φέρων σάκος ἠΰτε πύργον,
χάλκεον ἑπταβόειον, ὅ οἱ Τυχίος κάμε τεύχων,
σκυτοτόμων ὄχ᾽ ἄριστος, Ὕλῃ ἔνι οἰκία ναίων,
ὅς οἱ ἐποίησεν σάκος αἰόλον ἑπταβόειον
ταύρων ζατρεφέων, ἐπὶ δ᾽ ὄγδοον ἤλασε χαλκόν.
τὸ πρόσθε στέρνοιο φέρων Τελαμώνιος Αἴας
στῆ ῥα μάλ᾽ Ἕκτορος ἐγγύς ...

And Ajax drew near, bearing a shield like a tower,
bronze, made of seven oxhides, which Tychios laboring made for him,
he was by far the best leather cutter, living in his home at Hyle,
who for him made the gleaming shield of seven oxhides
from well-fed bulls, and on it he hammered an eighth layer of bronze.
Carrying this shield before his chest Telamonian Ajax
Stood very close to Hektor ...

One of the many fascinating aspects of this passage is the care with which the poem describes the craftsman of Ajax's tower-like shield: Tychios, the master leather-cutter and metal-worker. That such a skilled craftsman manufactured Ajax's famed weapon is no surprise, but that the poem includes the name and particularly the origin of the craftsman seems a bit peculiar – its incorporation here indicates its larger significance in the presumably formulaic tale of the weapon's origin. Notably, twice elsewhere the *Iliad* publicizes the same provincial community: Hyle is mentioned as home to the wealthy Boiotian fighter Oresbios (*Il.* 5.706–710) and is also included in the Boiotian section of the Catalogue of Ships (*Il.* 2.500).[134] Hyle seems to have been a rather remote

---

[134] See Simpson and Lazenby 1970, 25. That the scansion of Hyle differs in the various passages does not indicate more than one community with the same name.

Boiotian community in the hills near Akraiphia slightly to the east and south of the border of lake Kopais, perhaps even between the other two smaller lake areas south of Akraiphia. Τυχίος is thus Boiotian and from a remote but nonetheless well-known Boiotian community in epic.

That the craftsman's name reflects his work (Τυχίος/τεύχων) is no surprise.[135] That his obscure Boiotian community is identified is more remarkable, for it is on Tychios' superior craftsmanship that the passage concentrates. He is second to none as a leather-cutter (σκυτοτόμων ὄχ᾽ ἄριστος); he toils laboriously (τεύχων), and he has produced an extraordinary product for a human shield-maker: a shield with seven oxhides and an eighth layer of bronze. With only a mere four layers of leather, not even Odysseus' shield in the *mnesterphonia* is such an impressive piece of work.[136] In fact, it is only its seventh layer of leather that prevents Hektor from killing Ajax in the *Iliad*; and it is only the shield of Ajax that Achilles considers a worthy replacement for the one he loses to Hektor (*Il.* 18.192–193). It may not be a stretch to suggest that numerically the seven layers indicate the magical uniqueness, strength and superlative completeness of Ajax's powerful and Boiotian-made weapon.

While epic often marks the provenience of important artifacts, other items are usually mentioned in association with specific figures, not necessarily places: Zeus' *skeptron* in *Iliad* 1, and Hephaistos' shield in *Iliad* 17, for example. Yet here the poem categorizes Ajax's shield according to its relatively remote Boiotian provenience. That this description occurs in a panhellenic poem suggests that the association between shield workmanship, Boiotian craftsmen and the community of Hyle was somehow recognizable to a wide Greek audience and was important enough to be included in the transcription of the epic. But the link is more particular than this: through this Boiotian community the *Iliad* itself connects the region of Boiotia to the specific shield of Telamonian Ajax, the very figure to whom, as we have seen, the Boiotians are also repeatedly tied genealogically in a number of other archaic and early classical accounts.

The epithet ἑπταβόειον provides a further link between Ajax and the Boiotians that corroborates this genealogical and geographical nexus of symbolic relations. The epithet ἑπταβόειον is used exclusively of Ajax's shield in epic; this exclusivity becomes more interesting when one considers that the term is metrically formulaic enough to have been used in descriptions of other shields in epic, but is not.[137] An epic singer would have had ample opportunity to use the term, for of all armor in extant epic, the shield is the most commonly mentioned and described piece, ca. 25% more than the helmet, the next most commonly

---

[135] See Kirk 1990, 264, where he calls Τυχίος a "speaking name;" also Kirk 1985, 283.

[136] *Od.* 22.122. Compare also Teukros' shield (*Il.* 15.479, made of four layers). Achilles metal shield of *Iliad* 18 may have been considered superior to these human-made oxhide shields, partially on the basis of its divine craftmanship, but also because of its greater value as a metal object. However, Achilles' shield is made of fewer layers of metal than is Ajax's of leather. Leather layers may in fact have been as strong as if not stronger than thin layers of metal, as Jarva suggests; leather had the added practical benefit of being lighter (Jarva 1995, 138–143).

[137] Whallon 1966, 8–20, 35.

included type of weaponry.[138] Because of its exclusive pattern of use, the epithet
ἑπταβόειον thus signifies more than other standard epic adjectives (e.g., rosy-
fingered). Given the connections between this specific leather-layered shield and
Boiotian craftsmanship, it seems probable that the epithet subtly emphasizes the
link between Ajax's weapon and the term βοῦς, thus cleverly recapitulating the
pun on the name of the Βοιωτοί that the symbol of the shield itself marked on
Boiotian coinage.

F. Ajax's Shield Type

Before turning to additional literary representations of the Boiotians and shields
as well as to possible secondary meanings behind the cutout shield on Boiotian
coinage, I present evidence which suggests that Ajax's epic shield was meant to
be understood as an older type of weapon and of a cutout shape.

Evidence from the *Iliad* suggests that the kind of shield Ajax was understood
to have carried was an archaistic type, a Mycenaean body shield, perhaps even a
figure-eight form. The *Iliad* refers to Ajax's shield exclusively as a σάκος:
twenty-two times in ten books, in fact.[139] The term σάκος stems originally from
Indo-European, as indicated by Sanskrit *tvák: hide, skin* (also Hittite *tuekka*,
body).[140] It is generally agreed that in a great majority of cases σάκος designates
a large Mycenaean body shield.[141] In epic σάκος is to be differentiated from
ἀσπίς, a term denoting a smaller, round shield often described "πάντοσ᾽ ἐΐση;"
the term ἀσπίς comes to be used most commonly of shields in later literature.[142]
Epic sometimes uses the terms σάκος and ἀσπίς loosely to denote the same
shield of a particular warrior, e.g. Paris' shield, a σάκος at 3.335, is called an
ἀσπίς later in the same scene (3.356). The consistency with which the poem
refers to Ajax's shield as a σάκος is thus notable.[143]

It is possible to classify Ajax's Mycenaean σάκος more specifically. In epic
the term σάκος can connote either a rectangular shield or a figure-eight type.[144] It
is tempting to identify Ajax's σάκος as a rectangular "tower-shield" on the basis
of its formulaic modifying phrase ἠΰτε πύργον, found three times in the *Iliad*,

---

[138] Jarva 1995, 113.

[139] Kirk 1990, 263; Whallon 1966, 13–16; For the construction of the shield, see Borchhardt
1977, E3–4.

[140] Chantraine 1999, 985; Borchhardt 1977, E3; Lorimer 1950, 187.

[141] Chantraine 1999, 985; Lippold 1909, 420; Kirk 1990, 169–170.

[142] See Lacroix 1958, 14–15, on the distinction between the two terms.

[143] Lorimer notes that a σάκος is once likened to the moon (*Il.* 19.374), a comparison which
signifies its roundness (Lorimer 1950, 187). This link is not the only possibility for the simile,
however; if the shield were envisaged as a Dipylon or cutout shape, likening it to waning or
waxing moon could equally indicate its concave sides. Moreover, even if the simile does indicate
roundness, the outline of the Dipylon shield and the Boiotian shield, two representations of the
figure-eight shield, is often depicted as round in iconography (as opposed to ovular).

[144] Kirk 1985, 315; Kirk 1990, 169.

solely in association with Ajax's shield (*Il.* 7.219, 11.485, 17.128).[145] While the phrase could signify the tower-like quality of the σάκος, it is not clear what this means exactly, for as Kirk notes, ἠΰτε πύργον could equally "connote function, or visual aspect (e.g., size and/or shape, or both)."[146] In other words, it is possible for a tower-like shield to have been imagined either as being carried like a protective battlement or as resembling one.[147] Fundamentally, then, the real problem in scholarly discussions of Ajax's shield is the modern term "tower-shield." In origin it was likely adopted from this epic phrase and then applied to the rectangular shield in Mycenaean iconography (e.g., the lion-hunt dagger). The rectangular shape was then projected back on the shield of Ajax, even though this is not necessarily what the Greek ἠΰτε πύργον signifies.[148] Thus, Ajax may be erroneously associated with the Mycenaean rectangular body shield. With one exception the term σάκος is also used of Achilles' famous shield in the *Iliad*, yet no commentator has tried to suggest that Achilles' carried a rectangular "tower-shield," in part because his shield is never described ἠΰτε πύργον.[149]

Archaic iconography supports this position. I am unaware of any representation of Ajax (or any other identifiable hero for that matter) with a rectangular shield from the Archaic period. If the archaic Greeks knew or even fantasized about a tower-like shield, then we would fairly expect to see them depicted. In other words, Ajax's shield should naturally be understood in terms of shield-types with which the Greeks were familiar as attested in contemporary Athenian vase painting. The phrase ἠΰτε πύργον thus likely connotes the enormous size or fortress-like impenetrability of Ajax's shield, and not necessarily its shape.

As we have seen, Ajax is often pictorially depicted with the cutout shield by the late sixth century, the period following the mid-sixth-century phase of the *Iliad's* crystallization. This cutout shape is closer to the Mycenaean figure-eight type than the rectangular tower shield. Although late, evidence from fourth-century Salaminian coins may also be helpful in determining with which shield shape Ajax should be associated. This series, dated 350–318 and stamped on the reverse with a cutout shield remarkably similar to the type found on Boiotian coinage, is thought to recall earlier iconography of the cutout shield.[150] Head equates the shield on the Salaminian coins with the shield of Telamonian Ajax, worshipped on the island.[151] In considering all these factors together, then, it

---

[145] See Whallon 1966, 7–8.

[146] Kirk 1990, 263–264.

[147] The phrase might also indicate in part that Ajax was "regarded as a πύργος among his comrades" (Whallon 1966, 7).

[148] See, e.g., Whallon 1966, 21.

[149] The exception is *Il.* 18.458, where Thetis begs Hephaistos to craft new armor for her son. It may be indicative that this is the only reference to Achilles' shield as an ἀσπίς, for in this episode the armor does not yet exist. The passage thus does not necessarily require a specific term reflecting a Mycenaean body shield. Later illustrations of Achilles shield may have solidified the identification of it as a rounded, non-"tower shield."

[150] See Evans 1892–1893, 214.

[151] Head 1888, lxi–lxii, 116, and plate XX; see Paus. 1.35.3. Also see Lacroix 1958 (pl. 4.3) for a picture of one of these Salaminian issues.

seems reasonable to accept Stubbings' and Wace's suggestion that the epic term σάκος ultimately refers to the Mycenaean figure-eight shield shape through its evolution from the Dipylon.[152] That the *Iliad* repeatedly emphasizes the oxhide material of Ajax's σάκος may also be significant,[153] for in Mycenaean iconography, the "tower-shield" was less often explicitly depicted as made of leather (although presumably it was conceived of as partially leather). Pictorially, it was rather the figure-eight type which was painstakingly shown as dappled oxhide. This phenomenon may thus recall one of the original Indo-European meanings of σάκος: "hide," as mentioned above. Together, then, these factors, including the *Iliad's* formula ἠΰτε πύργον, suggest that Ajax's σάκος was envisaged as a cutout shield which recalled the figure-eight Mycenaean shape.[154]

In sum, in the Archaic period in general and even later specifically on Salaminian coins, Ajax's quasi-Mycenaean σάκος was imagined as an oxhide cutout shield. This shield was reputed to have been painstakingly made by the Boiotian craftsman, Τυχίος, who hailed from the remote but yet well-publicized epic Boiotian community which thus may have symbolically represented the entire region of central and eastern Boiotia in the *Iliad*. The epic seems to link the region both to shield-craftsmanship and more specifically to the shield type of the Aiginetan hero Ajax, a figure to whom the Boiotians were also closely connected through genealogy. The Boiotians chose to mark this relationship on their coinage with the image of Ajax's famed cutout shield.[155] Thus, as in both the traditions of Boiotian migration and the Boiotian eponymous hero, the Βοιωτοί are tied to epic tradition, this time in the mid-sixth century at the point of the transcript phase of panhellenic epic. Each of these categories of identification – symbol, traditions of migration and descent – thus reinforces the others.

G. Boiotian Links to Shields in the *Aspis*

The Boiotian link to epic shields is reiterated in the pseudo-Hesiodic *Aspis* and projected onto the Boiotian figure Herakles. As we have seen, West dates the *Aspis* to 570–520, and Attic vase paintings of Herakles and Kyknos from ca. 565 to 480 support this date.[156] The proem, a Hesiodic fragment taken from Alkmene's *Ehoie* (lines 1–56),[157] dates slightly earlier than the standard date for the

---

[152] Stubbings and Wace 1962, 510.

[153] *Il.* 7.220, 7.222, 7.245, 7.266, 11.545.

[154] Telamonian Ajax is to be distinguished from Ajax "the Lesser," son of the Lokrian Oileus. On Lokrian coins, the shield of Lokrian Ajax is often depicted, but the shape of his weaponry does not bear on the iconography associated with the more famous Telamonian Ajax from Salamis.

[155] Ajax's ties to shields in general may be accentuated by the epithet Τελαμώνιος, which may have originally indicated a shield strap (*telamon*) and only later became the patronymic (Whallon 1966, 27–35).

[156] M. West 1985, 136 and n. 28; Shapiro 1984, 524–527.

[157] Janko 1986, 39, and 42, after Wilamowitz 1905, 122 (also R. Cook 1937, 207). M. West earlier disagreed with this view, claiming that "the two texts were juxtaposed by a later redactor"

rest of the *Aspis*, ca. 580.[158] As a Theban and possibly even Hesiodic work, the *Aspis* thus offers an early sixth-century portrait of the Boiotians generated within the region for consumption by members of the group.[159]

The proem lists the Boiotians together with two of their nearest central Greek neighbors, all identified by collective regional ethnics: the Boiotians (Βοιωτοί), the Lokrians (Λοκροί), and the Phokians (Φωκῆες). The passage briefly describes the character of the Boiotians in the context of Amphitryon's military quest for purification:

τῷ δ' ἄμα ἱέμενοι πολέμοιό τε φυλόπιδός τε
Βοιωτοὶ πλήξιπποι, ὑπὲρ σακέων πνείοντες,
Λοκροί τ' ἀγχέμαχοι καὶ Φωκῆες μεγάθυμοι ἕσποντ' ·

with him went the Boiotians, strikers of horses, eager for battle and the battle cry, breathing above their shields, and the Lokrians, fighting hand to hand, and the great hearted Phokians (*Aspis* 23–25).

At first glance, the characterization of the Boiotians seems relatively bland. They yearn for battle and are identified as πλήξιπποι as they breathe above their shields (ὑπὲρ σακέων πνείοντες). The epithet πλήξιππος is not reserved for the Boiotians in the *Iliad*; Menesthios, the leader of the Athenian contingent, is πλήξιππος for example, as is Orestes, an otherwise unknown Greek victim of Hektor.[160] Nor are the Βοιωτοί alone in being characterized as a martial group in the passage; the Lokrians too are depicted similarly as "fighting hand to hand" (ἀγχέμαχοι, 25). At first glance, then, nothing in these generic depictions seems unusual in an epic poem about war.

One detail stands out in the *Aspis'* portrayal of the Boiotians, however, and the generic attributes in the descriptions of the other two Greek groups mentioned accentuates this detail. In a single line the poem describes both the Phokians and the Lokrians with nonspecific epic epithets: ἀγχέμαχοι (Lokrians, 25) and μεγάθυμοι (Phokians, 25).[161] In contrast the poem devotes two solid lines to the Boiotians and uses a relatively specific and individualized phrase to describe them (ὑπὲρ σακέων πνείοντες). The poem thus associates the Boiotians particularly with shields, and the relative number of lines dedicated to describing the

(M. West 1985, 136). Given evidence for the sixth-century composition of the *Homeric Hymn to Delian Apollo*, it is preferable to accept that the poet of the *Aspis* performed similar literary surgery (for the *Hymn. Hom. Ap.*, see Janko 1982, 109–114). West seems to have accepted the *Aspis'* proem as Hesiodic in his essay on Hesiodic tradition in the *OCD*[3].

[158] For 580 as the earliest date for the *Ehoiai*, see M. West 1985, 130–137 (esp. 136), 164 and 137–164 (for the different chronological layers of the poem); also R. Fowler 1998, 1 and n. 4.

[159] Janko 1986, 43, 47–48; R. Martin 2005, 173–175.

[160] Menesthios: 4.327; Orestes: 5.705. In the context of the Βοιωτοί πλήξιπποι, however, it is interesting that Pindar later uses the same epithet to characterize Θήβα, his "mother" and the font of his poetic inspiration at *Ol.* 6.85.

[161] ἀγχέμαχοι: *Il.* 13.5, 16.248, 16.272, 17.165; occurrences of μεγάθυμος in the *Iliad* are too numerous to mention.

group in even this short passage indicates the depiction's importance, particularly since it originates in a Boiotian source. A second phrase in the *Aspis'* proem corroborates this characterization: at line 13 the Thebans are described as φερεσ-σακέας Καδμείους (13).[162]

In light of the connection between Boiotia and Ajax's Boiotian-crafted shield in the *Iliad*, what the *Aspis* signifies about the Boiotians here becomes clearer. The shield the Boiotians carry in these passages is a σάκος, the epic term for the heroic shield in general and also the term for Ajax's epic shield to which the Boiotians are connected in epic through its maker, the Boiotian craftsman from Hyle. The *Aspis'* characterization of the Boiotians as ὑπὲρ σακέων πνείοντες may thus recall the *Iliad's* entire story of the creation of Ajax's σάκος. Thus, an archaic Boiotian source may explicitly tie the Boiotians and specifically the Thebans to an old shield type and may also implicitly allude to Ajax's Boiotian epic σάκος. This is a strikingly appropriate way to begin an epicizing poem that centers on an *ekphrasis* of the local Theban Herakles' shield. Both the panhellenic *Iliad*, then, as well as the *Aspis*, a Boiotian work which takes the *Iliad* as its model, record a recognized connection between the Boiotians and epic shields by the Mid-Archaic period.

The *Aspis'* portrait of Herakles, the consummate club-wielding archer, as a σάκος-bearer is thus rather important (*Aspis* 139–321). In its depiction the poem follows the epic tradition of *ekphrases* on heroic weaponry, most obviously Achilles' famous shield in the *Iliad*, a passage which the *Aspis* is thought to have imitated,[163] but also and most appropriately, the *Iliad's* shorter description of Aiginetan Ajax's Boiotian shield. Forty percent of the *Aspis* is in fact dedicated to the *ekphrasis* on the face of Herakles' epic shield (lines 57–480). Janko seems correct in identifying the poem's occasion as the Theban Herakleia for many reasons, most notably in this context because of the πόλις pictured on the front of Herakles' σάκος: a seven-gated city which in Greek tradition can only have been Greek Thebes.[164] In the mid-sixth century, then, Herakles, portrayed in Boiotian tradition as having originated in Thebes, appears in a Boiotian epicizing poem carrying an epic σάκος instead of his customary club, and on this σάκος is pictured the city of Thebes. Boiotian Herakles is thus transformed into the epic hero, particularly through the specific epic shield type of Achilles and Ajax.

Yet it is not just the *Aspis* which connects Herakles and epic shield-types at this time. Trends in Attic black-figure iconography also bear again on this issue. Shapiro demonstrates that in the second half of the sixth century scenes of Herakles and Kyknos became widely popular in Athenian vase workshops. The frequency of these scenes trails off ca. 500, and the latest depiction dates slightly after 480.[165] Shapiro convincingly argues that the *Aspis* influenced these Attic

---

[162] Wilamowitz considered this formula older than the poem although not as old as the Catalogue of Ships (1905, 116).

[163] Janko 1986, 42; see R. Cook 1937, 210–214, esp. 212 for a table of the imitated sections of Achilles' shield.

[164] Line 272; Janko 1986, 43.

[165] Shapiro 1984, 523 and n. 6.

depictions. On these vases Herakles, wearing his lion skin, often holds a sword and a shield, according to the requirements of the literary source and in contrast to his customary iconography. While the shield-types vary, it is of interest that Herakles is sometimes depicted with the cutout shield.[166] Of course, it is possible that the cutout shield on these vases may only reflect a concern to place Herakles in a generic epic context. Yet in light of the *Aspis'* imitation of *Iliad* 18 and the concomitant trend in sixth-century black-figure vase-painting to portray Achilles and Ajax with cutout shields, Herakles' occasional and contemporaneous appearance with this same shield-type in *Aspis*-influenced Attic iconography is noteworthy.[167]

I return, then, to the chronology of the sources adduced in this chapter. The *Aspis*, with its treatment of Herakles as an epic hero complete with σάκος, was composed in Thebes the mid-sixth century, the very period which saw Achilles and Ajax predominantly depicted with cutout shields in black-figure iconography. These years just preceded the advent of Boiotian coinage stamped with this same shield-type. Boiotian material and literary output in the second half of the sixth century thus seems complementary: the Boiotians maintain their earlier epic and Hesiodic characterization by producing both literature and coins which mark their association with epic tradition.[168]

H. Boiotian Manufacture of Raw Materials and Weaponry

Epic sets the creation of Ajax's remarkable shield in Boiotia and thus links Boiotia to craftsmanship.[169] I thus now turn to a possible secondary nexus of meanings behind the choice of the cutout shield on Boiotian coinage: as a marker of manufacture of raw materials used in weaponry, particularly leather and iron, and possibly of weaponry itself.

Oxhide will have been one of Boiotia's major products in all periods, since Boiotia was one of those rare regions whose plains and plateaus could support raising of cattle and livestock in general.[170] In the manufacture of ancient shields,

[166] For three examples, two of which Shapiro includes in his plates, see: Shapiro 1984, plate 68.3; Vian 1945, no. 3; black-figure amphora by Priam painter, Munich coll. Loeb 460, first quarter of fifth century. Vian 1945, no. 33; lekythos, Castellani 570, first quarter of fifth century. Shapiro 1984, plate 69.9; Vian 1945, no. 36; Boardman 1975.65; Beazley 1963, 63.88; red-figure cup by Oltos, *BM* E8, fourth quarter of the sixth century.

[167] Earlier scholars concentrated on connecting the *Aspis* to archaic art in general. R. Cook drew parallels between the groupings of characters on Herakles' shield and those in sixth-century iconography (e.g., Lapiths/Centaurs), as well as the sixth-century *kommos* (R. Cook 1937, 208–211). Myres dated the *Aspis* slightly earlier (ca. 575) but also on the basis of iconography (Myres 1941, 17–38, esp. 37–38).

[168] The association between Boiotians and shields in literature continued past this point, of course, as it also continued to be marked on coins (see, e.g., Aesch. *Septem* 19; Snodgrass 1967, 45).

[169] See Lacroix 1958, 13 and n. 4.

[170] Vottéro 1998, vol. 1, 33–38 (where he lists Boiotian *poleis* recognized for their produc-

leather was often preferred to metal as a less expensive layer offering both equal protection and less weight.[171] Such availability of leather and its utility in weaponry may help explain why Ajax's Boiotian-made epic shield was thick with seven layers of oxhide. It is not insignificant that the Boiotian craftsman responsible for Ajax's shield is characterized as a leather-cutter (σκυτότομος), not exclusively a shield-maker; σκυτότομος is a relatively rare word until late fifth-century Athenian comedy, in fact, and a *hapax* in the *Iliad*. Leather was also used in the production of breastplates and corselets, as well as other types of weaponry (probably even helmets), but it was perhaps the shield that was the most well known and recognizable partially leather weapon in antiquity. Oxhide will thus have been an important Boiotia product inside the region for outfitting the Boiotians themselves, but also perhaps as export material meant to be transformed elsewhere.

Evidence suggests that certain areas of mainland Boiotia may also have been involved in manufacture and trade, perhaps in iron and iron ores, with Chalkis and Euboian colonies to the west by the Early Archaic period.[172] Our best evidence now comes from Oropos, a geographically Boiotian frontier site.[173]

Oropos is now known to have been highly active in the eighth and seventh centuries in metallurgy and "in the forming of complex economic associations" with Euboian *poleis* and far-flung parts of the Mediterranean.[174] Many Geometric and archaic buildings associated with metalworking, reminiscent of the contemporaneous metal workshops at the Eretrian sanctuary of Apollo Daphnephoros

tion of cattle in antiquity: Haliartos, Koroneia, Lebadeia, Chaironeia, Orchomenos, Hyettos, Kopai, Akraiphia, Thebes, Anthedon, Tanagra, Plataia, Thespiai, Thisbe, Siphai, Chorsiai, and Oropos). As evidence for Boiotian (or at least Theban) interest in cattle, one might also adduce the hundreds of archaic votive bulls from the Theban Kabeirion.

[171] Jarva 1995, 139–143.

[172] Evidence from Kommos suggests that Boiotian traders were active in the Archaic period (see Csapo 1991, 211–215; 1993, 235–236). As for trade in metal, a variety of raw metals is now thought to have been transported widely in the Geometric and Archaic periods (Triester 1996, 166), often from east to west to be worked into goods at their final destination. This likely happened, for example, at Pithekoussai, a colony of Chalkis and Eretria; it has even been argued that most raw metal had to be brought to Pithekoussai from abroad (Ridgway 1992, 99, 147; for Pithekoussai, see Coldstream 1994, 56; Ridgway 1992, 32, 100–101, 107–108). Although no extant examples have been found, Chalkis was especially well known by the Archaic period for its production of iron swords (Bakhuizen 1976, 43–44; Snodgrass 1967, 70; see Alkaios fr. 54 Diehl; central Euboia as a whole is known for its ancient mining, metal production capabilities, and weapons manufacture, including its access to iron ores and its mining of them (Forbes 1964, 262; Bakhuizen 1976, 48, 51; Ridgway 1992, 16–17; Higgins and Higgins 1996, 85). As with Chalkis, few material examples of Euboian weapons survive, but the literary tradition linking Euboian warriors to spears, swords, and swordfighting has traditionally been considered strong enough to warrant belief in the material existence of such Euboian weaponry (Snodgrass 1967, 71; see e.g., Archil. fr. 3 Campbell; *Il.* 2.543–544; Alk. fr. 357 Lobel and Page; Aesch. fr. 703 Mette).

[173] Oropos may have originally been an Eretrian colony, but on the basis of inscriptional evidence pre-classical Oropos was likely only partially populated by Eretrians in the Iron Age (Mazarakis Ainian 2002, 157; see also Knoepfler 2000).

[174] Horden and Purcell 2000, 128.

and at Pithekoussai,[175] have now been excavated at Oropos.[176] Building A in Oropos, in use in during the second half of the seventh century, contained extensive metalworking remains which can only be associated with iron production, including hammerscale, microscopic particles leftover from iron-smithing.[177] From Oropos also come many intact iron implements (tools and knives) which are, as Mazarakis Ainian remarks, "unique and [which] complement our knowledge of the procedures in metalworking."[178]

Cosmopoulos suggests that Oropos as *polis* emerged because of the prosperity of the earlier Geometric and archaic settlement in terms of access to land and resources, technological knowledge, and the importance of the site as a port on the Euboian gulf.[179] Oropos' location quite clearly could not have been better in terms of trade routes by sea between north and south; Thucydides later mentions Oropos' continued importance for Athens in the grain trade.[180] In all likelihood by the late sixth and fifth centuries, Oropos had become an important trading port for a variety of other goods, including manufactured products and even raw metal.

There is additional evidence for Boiotian production of metal goods and possible involvement in metal trade which supports the possibility that eastern Boiotia as a whole was involved in iron and metal export by the Late Archaic and Early Classical periods, perhaps in tandem with Chalkis. Thebes itself is known to have been an iron trading center, and iron weapons from Boiotia were reputed in antiquity, albeit in late sources such as Plutarch, Stephanos, and Eustathios.[181] More significantly, together with the Lakonian coast, Boiotia is considered by modern scholars of ancient metallurgy to have been one of the primary iron mining and smelting areas of the mainland by the fifth century.[182] Although

[175] Mazarakis Ainian 1997, 104 (Building C, fig. 105, Eretria); Mazarakis Ainian 2002, 151, 161.

[176] Mazarakis Ainian 1997, 47, 100–101 (buildings A, B-G), 115 (perhaps the circular buildings ST).

[177] Mazarakis Ainian 2002, 154 (also possibly involved in metalworking at this time is building E, although the remaining contents of the building are too slim to allow secure conclusions, as Mazarakis Ainian notes at 157).

[178] Mazarakis Ainian 2002, 151. Enough were found to warrant describing them as a hoard (Mazarakis Ainian 2002, 157, 159, figs. 5a–b). Metalsmithing at the site was of course not restricted to iron and the material evidence indicates that craftsmen at the site worked a variety of crafts and were thus not highly specialized, at least in production and manufacture of specific metals (e.g., copper vs. iron; Mazarakis Ainian 2002, 164).

[179] See Cosmopoulos 2001, 42 for the contrast between habitation of the site and the relative dearth of habitation of the Oropia during the Geometric and Archaic periods. Cosmopoulos acknowledges the uniqueness of this kind of nucleated settlement pattern in comparison with other regions of Greece at this time, even in other areas of Boiotia (Cosmopoulos 2001, 73).

[180] Thuc. 7.28.1; see also Cosmopoulos 2001, 6.

[181] Pleiner 1969, 24, citing Blümmner 1886 (*Technologie und Terminologie der Gewerbe und Künste bei Griechen und Römern*); Vottéro 1998, 26. Boiotian iron weapons do not seem to have been as well known as their Chalkidian counterparts, but it is significant that ancient sources mention Boiotian iron weapons at all.

[182] Forbes 1964, 261–262; Pleiner 1969, 23, again citing Blümmner 1886; Bakhuizen 1976, 51–52 with map (after Petrascheck 1953); Healy 1978, 62.

ancient literary sources are few and are generally late, Boiotian iron ores were known in antiquity; Pliny's detailed knowledge of the kind of iron found in northeast Boiotia and its difference from other types of ores indicates a definite recognition of the area as iron-bearing which does not seem to have been a new-found discovery.[183]

There are in fact a number of iron ore deposits in north and northeast Boiotia in the hilly and relatively mountainous areas: northeast of Orchomenos, and north and northeast of Lake Kopais, the area near the sanctuaries of Apollo Ptoios and the Akraiphian civic hero Ptoios, sites which, as we shall see in Chapter Five, not incidentally seem to have served as repositories for collective Boiotian dedications. Iron deposits have also been located north and immediately south of Tanagra and east of Thebes.[184] Austrian geologists have mapped and tested these deposits in two separate investigations; the high nickel content of the ores indicates of their relatively high percentage of iron.[185] Even today there is a nickel factory built over part of ancient Larymna near the Euripos straits. In this area of Boiotia, including the region of the Ptoion but particularly the approach to Larymna from the Ptoion which follows an ancient road, the soil is a dark red hue. Olivier Davies, a mid-twentieth-century traveler to Boiotia, noticed the remains of ancient mines in the northwestern vicinity of the Ptoion near Hyettos, a community also mentioned by Pliny in this context and which sits in the immediate vicinity of some of the geologically located iron ore deposits.[186] These ores are of the same laterite iron deposits as found on Euboia northeast of Chalkis.[187]

The combination of these factors, but especially the possibility of archaic metalworking and trade from Boiotian Oropos, suggests that by the Late Archaic period northern and eastern Boiotia may have been involved in metal mining, smelting, and possible export, in a lesser role but in conjunction with Chalkis and Eretria.[188] As is well known, by this time trade in metals was widespread and advanced throughout the Mediterranean; much of it involved copper, tin, lead ores, and especially iron.[189] Demand was high for many reasons: iron bullion and *obeloi* had become popular dedications by the period;[190] iron spits and other metal products, such as tripods, seem to have had proto-monetary value in some

---

[183] Pliny *NH* 36.128; Bakhuizen 1979, 19.

[184] See Vottéro 1998, 26.

[185] See Bakhuizen 1979, 19 and n. 9 for bibliography.

[186] See Bakhuizen 1979, 19; Étienne and Knoepfler 1976, 14. For a geologic discussion of these deposits and other geologic zones in Boiotia, see Higgins and Higgins 1996, 74–78, esp. 76. It may be significant that the *Theogony*, a panhellenic poem with possible Boiotian roots, depicts iron bloomeries operating in mountain glens, and as Pleiner has characterized them: "far from habitation sites, ... close to supplies of ore and fuel" (Pleiner 1969, 14; Hes. *Theog.* 864–865).

[187] Higgins and Higgins 1996, 85.

[188] *Contra* Bintliff, who attributes a low rate of export of metal ores to Boiotia (without supporting evidence; Bintliff 2005, 9).

[189] Treister 1996, 103 (quoting I. Hahn 1983), 121; Snodgrass 1980, 49–50; see also *Od.* 1.184.

[190] Horden and Purcell 2000, 349–350.

areas of the Mediterranean well before the introduction of coinage.[191] A number of weapons were crafted of iron;[192] iron had certainly superseded bronze as the metal for spearheads and swords by the Archaic period.[193] The variety of iron objects common from the Geometric and Archaic periods onward include but are not limited to brooches, pins, fibulae, finger rings, sickles, axeheads, arrowheads, lanceheads, picks, chains, nails, cauldrons, and statues.[194] The Lydian or Persian iron helmet from Sardis raises the issue of the quantity of iron needed outside the Greek world and its sources.[195] In epic, some of the most interesting iron objects include the iron axeheads from the contest between Odysseus and the suitors and the iron mass and the twenty iron axeheads that Achilles offers as a prizes at Patroklos' funeral. Of course, not all iron remains can be specifically identified with these or other objects, but it is often underestimated that we have so many extant types of iron products from these early periods of Greek history, including large quantities of weaponry.

Metals from Boiotia would certainly have been easy of transport, moving from Boiotian ports on the eastern coast to Euboia and then perhaps even further abroad. In his description of Boiotian topography, the fourth century Herakleides Kreticos discusses the types of exports and proximity of the Boiotian communities of Anthedon and Salganeus to Chalkis on Euboia and the Euboian straits.[196] In the context of sea routes Strabo later describes the Boiotian east coast similarly, adding the comment that by his time Euboia had virtually become part of Boiotia.[197] The natural geography of the area and the reputation in trade of the southern Euboian coastal cities prohibits us from thinking that shipping and trade routes would not have passed through the Euripos straits well before Herakleides and Strabo. Transport from Euboia and northeastern Boiotia through the center of Boiotia south to the economic hub of the Corinthian gulf would also have been relatively simple via well-studied ancient roads and perhaps even, at least during rare wet seasons, across lake Kopais.[198] Ridgway has acknowledged the possibility of utilitarian trans-Boiotian travel from Euboia westward in early Euboian

[191] Howgego 1995, 15 after Kraay 1976, 213–215; Strøm 1992, 41–51 (where she details additional functions of iron *obeloi* in sanctuaries); Kroll 2001, 84–88; Pleiner 1969, 15–17. Trade in metals continued to be strong after the advent of coinage, however; silver-bearing lead ores were moved from origin to be coined elsewhere, for example, as we now know happened to Siphnian and Attic silver at Aigina (Howgego 1995, 24–25; Kim 2001, 16).

[192] Such as the famed sword and spear with which the Lefkandi male was buried; see, e.g., Ridgway 1992, 17.

[193] Healy 1978, 251; see also Jarva 1995, 123.

[194] For some excellent examples, see Kilian 1983, 135–136, 138–144 (mostly small iron objects and *obeloi* from Philia in Thessaly); Blinkenberg 1931, 186, 190–196, 206 (iron weapons from Lindos, including swords [nos. 591–593], lanceheads [nos. 596–597], arrowheads [no. 611], the tip of a scepter or lance [no. 662], and an iron Corinthian helmet [no. 569]); Snodgrass 1967, 35–88.

[195] Mellink 1989, 127–128 and fig. 13; Jarva 1995, 9.

[196] Herakleides Kreticos 1.22–27, 29 (Pfister).

[197] Strabo 9.2.2.

[198] Higgins and Higgins 1996, 76. For the possibility of ancient travel across the lake, see Paus. 9.24.1.

pursuits abroad.[199] In this context is thus striking that the supposedly haphazard survival of early Boiotian coins consists almost exclusively in issues from northern and eastern Boiotian *poleis*, cities situated either in the metal bearing area or quite near along the trade routes through the region.[200] Perhaps, then, our collection of early Boiotian coins from within Boiotia is not a result from coincidental finds and illegal excavation after all, as has sometimes been assumed, but rather reflects early economic interactions between a number of Boiotian *poleis* and a resulting sense of regional interdependence.

I thus recall the evidence adduced earlier in this chapter for the movement of Boiotian coins outside the region. Although the dearth of recorded findspots within Boiotia prevents us from reaching definitive conclusions about intra-Boiotian trade, analysis of Boiotian and related issues in archaic and early classical coin hoards outside Boiotia tentatively supports the hypothesis of involvement of Boiotian *poleis* in some sort of international trade by ca. 475 at the latest.

In sum, given Boiotian access to both leather and metals, particularly iron, which would have been useful not only in manufacturing daggers and swords, but also pins and other smaller pieces for shields, it is conceivable that the cutout shield on Boiotian coinage marked Boiotian involvement in the production not only of raw materials, but also of weaponry itself, perhaps even whole shields. Despite possible Boiotian links to other kinds of weaponry, such as leather and boar's tusks helmets, one of which is described in the *Iliad* as a Boiotian product (*Il.* 10.260–271), in this context it would nonetheless make sense to mark Boiotian coinage with the cutout shield shape, since the Boiotian link to the Aiakid Ajax and his epic shield was already so well-defined through genealogy and panhellenic poetry. Given Boiotian proximity to major trade routes, as well as the evidence from hoards for the movement of Boiotian coins outside Boiotia, it seems reasonable to suggest that the cutout shield on Boiotian coinage also marked in part Boiotian involvement in manufacture and trade of raw materials and perhaps even weaponry itself. These observations complement Morgan's observations about the disposal of real weaponry in the eighth to sixth centuries; she argues that during this time weapons disposal and movement should "primarily be considered in the context of attitudes to metal as a commodity."[201]

Similar marking of local products occurs in other coinages from the same period. Between ca. 510 and 480, for example, Kyrene minted silver issues which on the obverse depicted the silphium fruit or the entire silphium plant, a medicinal and culinary herb famous in antiquity for its origin at Kyrenaean silphium plantations.[202] The plant continued to be shown on Kyrenaean coins, along with

[199] Ridgway 1992, 14, 60. This is not to suggest that other iron and metal rich areas of the ancient Mediterranean did not participate in regional trade in metals; many areas certainly superseded Boiotia in both chronology and importance as sources of iron and manufactured goods, e.g., Sardinia, Elba, Tuscany, northern Etruria (see Ridgway 1992, 28–29, 91, 99–100).

[200] Our sole exception is a single coin from Koroneia, the existence of which is not odd considering Koroneia's close link to the panboiotian sanctuary of Athena Itonia and thus to the Boiotian collective.

[201] Morgan 2001, 21.

[202] Wartenburg 1995, 12, and no. 121; Kraay 1976, 3 and 296, nos. 1065, 1066. For a brief

other new themes, throughout the fifth and fourth centuries.[203] The Chalkidian city Mende also marked production of its famed wine by stamping grapes on the obverse of some of its coins near the turn of the sixth century.[204] Other wine-exporting cities stamped new sixth-century silver issues with Dionysiac imagery.[205] Also well known are the Metapontan issues which showed an ear of corn, a symbol of the lucrative grain trade in which the city was engaged for centuries. The corn ear and the silphium plant, in fact, became widely recognized symbols of Metapontum and Kyrene, respectively, just as the turtle symbol on Aiginetan coinage came to symbolize that entire island. It thus does not seem fanciful to suggest that the cutout shield on Boiotian coinage may have acted similarly: it marked a popular product linked to the production of raw materials, possible manufacture of weapons, as well as to the epic tradition of a specific hero with a Boiotian weapon to which the group was linked in a wider Greek context.[206] In addition to its punning function, then, the multivalent symbol of the cutout shield on Boiotian coinage seems a very clever choice.

RECAPITULATION AND SPECULATION
ON AN ICONOGRAPHIC SHIFT

Evidence adduced in this chapter for the connections between Boiotians and shields in the Archaic period comprises a network of independent details. Each individual detail is suggestive yet on its own fails to explain the link between Boiotia and shields. In combination, however, these features comprise the cultural context into which we can reasonably place the symbol of the cutout shield.

The material suggests that by the end of the sixth century Boiotia was specifically associated with Ajax's shield from the *Iliad* and that the Boiotians were linked to shields and shield-making in general; in a Boiotian context the Boiotians even portray themselves and their hero Herakles as bearers of epicizing shield-types (*Aspis*). Southeastern Boiotia and Thebes were also linked to the Aiakid epic heroes through genealogies recorded in Hesiod, Pindar, Bacchylides and Korinna. It is at this time that some Boiotian *poleis* begin stamping coins with the shape of the cutout shield, an already iconographically established heroicizing symbol which appeared in scenes from both the *Iliad* and the epic cycle, predominantly in conjunction with Telamonian Ajax and Achilles.[207] Use of the

history of Kyrene's silphium industry, see Tatman 2000, 8, 12–14. On the modern existence of the once-thought extinct silphium plant, see Wright 2001, 23–24.

[203] Kraay 1976, 297.

[204] Kraay 1976, 136.

[205] Spier 1990, 119 mentions the two Naxoses as examples. Also see Kraay 1976, 206–207.

[206] These examples concern primarily agricultural products, but inanimate metal objects are known to have appeared on coinage earlier than our Boiotian examples: the shield device of a fibula, for example, depicted on a shield around 600; see Spier 1990, 111 and note 46.

[207] As noted in the Introduction, we should thus no longer refer to this shield as the "Boiotian" shield, since it clearly held meaning in archaic art before the minting of Boiotian coins (see also Boardman 1983, 32).

cutout shield symbol on Boiotian coins thus reifies these Boiotian ties to epic tradition in general and to Ajax and Achilles and their family in particular. Thought to have been made from oxhide (βοῦς), the cutout shield also cleverly plays on the name of the group. At the same time but secondarily, the shield symbol may also mark actual Boiotian production of raw materials used in manufacturing weapons or perhaps even production of weaponry itself.[208]

These links to epic tradition, heroes, and weaponry thus complement the tradition of Boiotian habitation of Boiotia at the time of the Trojan war as well as links to their eponymous hero through this habitation, as discussed in Chapters One and Two. Accordingly, the shield may also have served, as Lacroix suggests, to mark the significance of the Boiotian contingent in the Catalogue of Ships and thus in the Trojan expedition.[209]

That these Boiotian connections to shields and epic were recognized outside Boiotia is suggested by the shifts in archaic and early classical Attic iconography outlined above. As we have seen, the frequency with which Achilles and Ajax are shown with the cutout shield changes radically from black-figure to red-figure vase painting. Moreover, around 480 Attic vase workshops also stop producing representations of the Herakles and Kyknos scene influenced by the Theban *Aspis*. The period ca. 480–450 thus marks a transformation in Attic production of scenes and shapes associated with Boiotia through literature (*Aspis*, ca. 570–520) and through the symbol stamped on early Boiotian coinage (ca. 510–500).

Lorimer once attributed this change in Attic iconography to a loss of real Dipylon shield models in the Persian sack of Athens, but it seems more likely that the shift was influenced by a combination of the following historical events.[210] First, around the time that Boiotian *poleis* begin minting coins stamped with the cutout symbol, Athens soundly defeats the group of Boiotians and Chalkidians who marched against Attica in 507/6. This collective victory of the newly democratic *polis* was considered of such importance that it was memorialized on the Athenian Akropolis by a commemorative inscription and bronze *quadriga*. The inscription's placement testifies to the significance of the battle for Athens, for the trophy was erected near the statue of Athena and would have been immediately visible from the entrance to the Akropolis. At this same time vases produced in the relatively new technique of Attic red-figure mark a striking shift in the use of the cutout shield in connection with the epic heroes Telamonian Ajax and Achilles. The chronological relationship between the minting of Boiotian coins, the joint Boiotian and Chalkidian attack on Attica, and the change in Attic representation of the cutout shield is so close that it seems possible that the Athenian victory over the Boiotian *ethnos* in 507/6 may have influenced the subsequent and near virtual abandonment of the Boiotian-linked cutout symbol from Attic vase-painting.

[208] Other groups in antiquity were marked through their association with unique types of shields: the Thracians through the *pelte*, for example (see Eur. *Alk.* 498: ζαχρύσου Θρηκίας πέλτης ἄναξ).

[209] Lacroix 1958, 12.

[210] Lorimer 1950, 167.

Also at this same time Plataia's relationship with Athens must have served to alienate Athens from the rest of Boiotia. As we learn from Herodotus and Thucydides, at some date in the late sixth century Plataia entered into some sort of relationship with Athens, partly on the basis of Theban hostility in Boiotia at the time.[211] Whether the Plataians were δοῦλοι of Athens or equal partners in a συμμαχία, whatever complaints the Plataians had against their fellow Boiotians were enough to cause Athens to take this bold step.[212] Surely this move indicates a certain hostility toward Boiotia on the part of Athens which could have been reflected in changes in Attic iconography.

Inter-regional competition between Boiotia and Athens likely played its part in this animosity and is most apparent in the regions' mutual appropriation of the hero Ajax. A Boiotian claim to Aiakid connections in the Late Archaic period might very well have been viewed as an aggressive propagandistic move by Athens, since the Aiakidai were also considered heroes of Salamis, a territory that Athens was concerned to conquer and maintain.[213] Kleisthenic reforms instituted Aiginetan Ajax as a hero in the Athenian Agora, for example, an almost certain result of recent Athenian acquisition of Salamis.[214] Also in the Archaic period Athens co-opted the Salaminian heroes Periphemos and Kychreos and allowed a new *genos*, the *Salaminioi*, to oversee cult activity at some significant sanctuaries on the Akropolis and in Attica.[215] Most important, between the reforms of Kleisthenes and the Ionian revolt, Athens established an Aiakeion, modeled on the Aiginetan example, in the Athenian agora.[216] The building of this sanctuary has also been interpreted as a response to Athenian acquisition of Salamis.[217] Boiotian links to the Aiakids through genealogy and symbol thus may express subtle aggression toward Attica. It seems apposite in this political context to envision a concurrent Athenian undermining of Boiotian symbol that associated the Boiotians with the illustrious and coveted Salaminian hero.

Events of the first half of the fifth century may also have reinforced changes in Attic use of the cutout image. Victory over the Persians in 480–479 affected many well-documented aspects of Greek culture, of course, from production of Athenian tragedy to a further interest in defining "Greekness." It is thus possible that the victory also influenced iconographic portrayal of weaponry. Now that living Greeks could boast about the courage and heroism of those who fought the Persians, it was no longer urgent to represent epic heroes with archaizing cutout shields. In Attic iconography of the first half of the fifth century, then, Achilles'

[211] On dating the Plataian-Athenian alliance, see Chapter 6.

[212] Badian argues that the Plataians were somehow δοῦλοι of Athens on the basis of Herodotean terminology and the fact that the Plataian dead were buried together with Athenian slaves after Marathon (Badian 1989, 104–108; 1993, 116–123). For the view of some scholars of the relationship as a military alliance, primarily based on Thucydides' term for it (συμμαχία), see Badian 1989, 110–111; 1993, 219–220, n. 21, and the work of Raaflaub mentioned there.

[213] See e.g., Hdt. 8.64; Paus. 1.36.1; Taylor 1997.

[214] Garland 1992, 44.

[215] Garland 1992, 37–38.

[216] Hdt. 5.89–90; Stroud 1998, 84–104, esp. 85–86.

[217] Stroud 1998, 88; Kearns 1989, 47.

and Ajax's shields thus more often reflect the round shield used so effectively against the Persians, thereby linking heroes of the epic past to those of most recent memory.

However, that Attic depictions of *Aspis*-influenced Herakles scenes literally disappear from the material record at the same time indicates that Athenian painters may also have been reacting against images linked to Boiotia. The Boiotians' already low reputation in Athens was now further tarnished by the Medism of certain Boiotian *poleis*: a much reviled choice, well-publicized in Athenian sources from the mid-fifth century on. Boiotian Medism must have further strengthened the negative Athenian view of the Boiotians manifest in the Athenian victory inscription of 507/6. Thus, by the end of the Persian Wars, not only did Attic workshops stop depicting the cutout shield particularly in its association with Ajax, but they also stopped portraying scenes influenced by the Boiotian *Aspis*.

In this chapter I have delineated a plausible context into which we can situate this alternate reading of the cutout shield on Boiotian coinage. The multivalent symbol encapsulated much of concern to the late archaic and early classical Boiotian *ethnos*: like other coinage, the cutout played on the name of the issuing group, thereby emphasizing the collective *ethnos*; the shield may also have marked regional participation in manufacture and export. In its shape and weight the shield coinage was modeled on Aiginetan coinage and thus quickly assumed acceptability as currency. But most important, the cutout shield symbolized the already panhellenically recognized Boiotian genealogical links to Aigina and Ajax, the Aiakid known for his Boiotian-made shield. Through this symbol the Boiotians reinforced their additional links to epic tradition, already well known from the *Iliad's* Catalogue of Ships and the tradition of the expedition's departure from Aulis. The decision to stamp Boiotian coinage with this image can thus be read as a defining moment in Boiotian collective history; it was through this mark that the Boiotians tied together many of the indications of their collective identity: a common name, shared trade and manufacture, traditions of descent, and a shared history of ties to the Trojan expedition. The late sixth- and early fifth-century changes in Attic iconography discussed above suggest that the symbol of the cutout shield had become quickly established as a Boiotian mark and had thus suffered iconographic consequences in Athens by the middle of the fifth century BCE.[218]

[218] That other traditionally archaic and classical Boiotian shapes, the black-glazed kantharos for example, were not changed in Attic iconography is significant. The relative stability of the archaic kantharos image may indicate that in the wake of the Persian wars only symbols strongly associated with the Boiotian *ethnos* were altered, such as the cutout shield, but not vase shapes or religious objects traditionally attributed to a divinity associated with the region. Of course, the attribution of the kantharos shape to Boiotia is open to some discussion (see *CVA* Thebes 1 [Greece 6], 15; Kilinski 2005, 184–185), but Kilinski argues convincingly for the Boiotian origin of the carinated kantharos (Kilinski 2005, 185–212; Kilinski 1992, 262; Kilinski 1990, 58–59), calling it "an especially intriguing artifact in terms of its significance to the people of this region of Greece" (Kilinski 2005, 183). This is not to suggest that Boiotia controlled exclusive production of the shape (see Kilinski 2005). For kantharoi in general and as associated with the Kabeirion, see Daumas 1998, 93–104.

CHAPTER 4
THE BOIOTIAN DIALECT:
MAINTENANCE OF AN EPIC PAST

Like shared symbolism and religion, language is a secondary indicium of ethnicity that can be used to reinforce identities that have previously been constructed through other means. Language and dialect are now thought to play an active role in the maintenance of difference between ethnic and social groups.[1] Ancient historians previously considered only innovation linguistically significant in marking identity, "on the assumption that retention of linguistic idioms requires little or no conscious effort."[2] However, from an ethnolinguistic standpoint, the maintenance of archaistic dialect forms in ancient Greek dialects may be as important as the invention of new forms, particularly since ancient Greek regional identities seem so persistently tied to the past via claims of descent and migration.[3] As Colvin remarks, "language is perhaps the most easily manipulated and flexible tool of social self-identification."[4] These ideas hold true in analysis of late sixth- and early fifth-century Boiotian dialect, for many of the more conservative aspects of Boiotian dialect seem to have evoked an epic register and thus served as a whole to reinforce the various epic connections apparent in the genealogy of Boiotos, the traditions surrounding Boiotian habitation of the region, and the epic ramifications of the shared symbol of the cutout shield.

That distinct dialects were associated with different communities is clear from the comedies of Aristophanes who represents Lakonian, Megarian, and Boiotian dialects with a reasonable degree of accuracy.[5] In his *Phoinissai* Aristophanes' contemporary Strattis likewise lampoons the Thebans for a number of specific lexical peculiarities.[6] Given epigraphic and literary evidence for dialect forms well before this time, it seems reasonable to believe that members of various Greek-speaking communities recognized and characterized each other and themselves as dialectically distinct far earlier than Aristophanes' day.

[1] See, e.g., Colvin 2004, 95.

[2] Hall 1995, 90 (this seminal article serves as a foundation for much of what follows). For the more traditional view of the insignificance of retaining archaisms in dialect, see, e.g., Palmer 1980, 71.

[3] Hall 1995, 90. See Horrocks 1997, 195–196, for a discussion of the difficulty in determining earlier dialect forms from retained archaisms.

[4] Colvin 1999, 3; see also Colvin 2000, 285.

[5] Colvin 2000, 292; Colvin 1999, 297–298; Hainsworth 1967, 66, 71. Aristophanes does not render the Boiotian dialect with as much accuracy as he does Lakonian or Megarian, but nonetheless, as Colvin remarks, his divergence from the epigraphic record "is not considerable." Colvin attributes Aristophanes' imperfect representation of the Boiotian dialect to its eccentricity and difficulty (Colvin 1999, 297–299).

[6] Strattis fr. 49 (Kassel-Austin); Ath. XIV.621.

The Boiotian dialect is statistically unique in that it contained a great proportion of features which might have seemed peculiar to speakers of Attic Greek.[7]
Nevertheless, that the various Greek dialects, including Boiotian, were portrayed
with care and a reasonable degree of accuracy by Athenian comic poets indicates
that it was not the dialect forms of others *per se* that were generally the main point
of ridicule; rather, it was the collective itself that was satirized along with its perceived social oddities.[8] Dialect was only a factor which helped to indicate collective affiliation, both from within and also from outside the group.

Certain communities of the southern Peloponnese provide useful examples of
seemingly purposeful maintenance of distinctive dialect forms in an attempt to
mark communal boundaries. For instance, both the Dorian Lakonian and Messe-
nian communities retained certain conservative dialect features as other groups
were changing and innovating around them. As Hall remarks, one might "understand the retention of archaisms as a [more] conscious and deliberate policy
which was actually designed to preserve Lakonian distinctiveness and to mark
out the Spartans as the true Dorians of the Peloponnese."[9] Arkadian *poleis* likewise shared a number of dialect characteristics, and, although Nielsen has recently argued that the Arkadian dialect was not integral to the creation of Arkadian
ethnicity,[10] it is nevertheless important to note that most of the Arkadian *poleis*,
with the fourth-century exception of the Triphylians, stick to Arkado-Kypriot
dialect characteristics, although the area was surrounded entirely by Doric speakers.[11] While part of this conservatism may be explained by the general geographical inaccessibility of Arkadia, the Arkadians did not live in complete isolation;
despite interaction, even they thus be understood to have observed a certain
dialectical uniqueness that helped mark an Arkadian distinctiveness from other
surrounding regional communities.

There is also further evidence for local pride, or, as Colvin calls it, "prestige
variety," in the use and thus presumably the maintenance of dialect in ancient
Greece. Colvin has discussed the influence of Boiotian dialect on a variety of
Attic which, because of its link to Boiotian, would have been stigmatized in
Attica.[12] From this evidence it seems reasonable to speculate that those using a

---

[7] Colvin 2000, 292.

[8] Colvin 2000, 289, 296.

[9] Hall 1995, 90. *Contra* Morpurgo-Davies, who has argued that the Lakonians "showed few
or no signs of pride in their dialect," and even "an absence of interest in language" (Morpurgo-
Davies 1993, 269).

[10] Nielsen 2002, 74. Nielsen does not discount the cultivation of dialect as an indicium of
ethnicity *per se*; he rather objects primarily to the attribution of dialect innovation in the creation
of an Arkadian community. Nielsen unnecessarily complicates the issue by arguing that the later
Arkadians did not use dialect to disassociate themselves from other Peloponnesian communities
with whom they allied; here he confuses a military/political alliance with ethnic cooperation: it
is clear from the record that the Arkadians, while observing their own ethnic dialect, were able to
make military/political alliances with other communities as needed (Nielsen 1999, 20).

[11] Nielsen 2002, 50–51; Palmer 1980, 58.

[12] Colvin 2004, 95–108, esp. 101–106. For general Athenian scorn for Boiotia onstage, see
Colvin 2000, 289.

regional dialect denigrated by neighbors in such close proximity would attempt to counter this portrayal by promulgating the differences and possible superiority of their own dialect.[13]

Indeed, as Morpurgo-Davies demonstrates, at least from the fifth century onward, the Boiotians were nothing if not interested in documenting their way of speaking, even as it evolved; through all later periods, despite inter-*polis* rivalries, wars, and differing foreign allegiances, the various Boiotian *poleis* deliberately observed a high degree of homogeneity in recording their dialect.[14] As she suggests, that the Boiotians were interested in this kind of detailed recording "at all is significant;"[15] that they were not always on friendly terms with each other while observing such relative homogeneity in linguistics and spelling is even more remarkable.[16] There must have been some other foundation for such correspondence. I suggest that the other categories of collective identity upon which the Boiotians cohered served to fuel a Boiotian "linguistic pride;" this use of dialect in the maintenance of the Boiotian *ethnos* can be traced from the sixth century onward.

It is not the purpose of this chapter to discuss the possible origins of the dialect itself; Hall has thoroughly treated the history of Greek dialects and the problems with various theories of its development.[17] Instead, in what follows I present select aspects of sixth- and early fifth-century Boiotian dialect which bear particular relevance to the issue of the uniqueness of the dialect and its possible effect in relation to the epic register.

SOURCES

Given the dearth of evidence for archaic Boiotia in general, we have a surprising variety of sources for late archaic and early classical Boiotian dialect. Particularly rich are Boiotian inscriptions, which have been exhaustively studied by grammarians and epigraphists for well over a century and a half, with a high mark

---

[13] That the third-century Boiotian federation observed a certain open-mindedness toward the Oropian use of the Attic dialect at the Ptoion does not negate this general point (for the case of Oropos and the inscription from the Ptoion which attests to Boiotian attitudes toward other dialect usage, see Morpurgo-Davies 1993, 277–278; also Vottéro 1998, vol. 1, 18, 130, 132–133).

[14] Morpurgo-Davies 1993, 270–273. For possible exceptions to this general linguistic homogeneity, see Vottéro 1998, vol. 1, 21, 130, 143; however, elsewhere Vottéro generally agrees with this interpretation (see, e.g., Vottéro 1998, vol. 1, 105, 107).

[15] Morpurgo-Davies 1993, 273.

[16] Vottéro has attempted to identify certain sub-dialects within Boiotia, but in his treatment of the archaic and early classical inscriptions, he fails to take into account dialectical demands of genre. In the end, his distinctions between subdialects is unconvincing because of numerous contradictions and his assumption that the geography of Boiotia favored disunity (Vottéro 1996, esp. 47–48, 84–86).

[17] See Hall 1997, 153–170; M. West 1988, 162–172; Householder and Nagy 1972; for this topic with regard to Boiotian dialect in particular, see also R. Buck 1968, 268–280; Janko 1992, 15–16.

beginning with Dittenberger's publication of *IG* VII in 1892.[18] It has been this corpus of inscriptions, with the additional Boiotian epigraphic material that has come to light since its publication, that has served as the foundation for the various treatments of the Boiotian dialect published since Buck's still useful epigraphically-based *Greek Dialects* in 1955. In what follows I rely heavily on these and other works on Boiotian dialect and epigraphy, most recently augmented by Vottéro's research on the Boiotian dialect (1996, 1998) and Wachter's work on non-Attic vase inscriptions (2001). The important inscriptions for the present study consist mainly of dedications, for as Vottéro remarks, for this period civic texts are essentially nonexistent, and funerary inscriptions consist in a mere name without patronymic.[19]

A second and often overlooked source for the Boiotian dialect is the work of Korinna, the Tanagran poetess who used certain forms of the Boiotian vernacular.[20] As argued in Chapter One, I accept the early date for Korinna and thus include her work here in elucidating early fifth-century Boiotian dialect.

A third source is the pseudo-Hesiodic *Aspis*, a work which, as noted in Chapter Two, dates to 570–520. Although likely Theban in origin, the *Aspis* can, like the Tanagran Korinna's work, be used as evidence for the contemporary usage of Boiotian dialect in performance around the late sixth and early fifth centuries.[21] Interestingly, however, the Theban *Aspis* contains few Boiotian dialect forms of note, with two important exceptions: the digamma and the demonstrative pronouns τοί and ταί (used alongside οἱ and αἱ).[22] The Theban origin for the work and its relative absence of many other Boiotian dialectical forms thus may attest to a Theban attempt to assimilate as much as possible to the partially Ionic sound of the more panhellenic hexameter tradition, especially the *Iliad*.[23] However, that the epic forms used in the *Aspis*, in particular the poem's obsessively visible digamma, also appear in contemporaneous Boiotian dialect supports including the *Aspis* as a source here, despite the poem's tendency to assimilate to the epic genre.

To these sources I add the sixth-century *Homeric Hymn to Pythian Apollo*, since the poem is thought to have originated in central Greece.[24] Although the precise area of its origin is disputed (Phokis or western Boiotia),[25] the *Hymn*, much like the Theban *Aspis*, observes the digamma throughout, together with other older forms.[26] Most importantly, Janko has suggested that the *Hymn* marks

---

[18] Dittenberger 1892 (reprinted in 1992 and with a concordance).

[19] Vottéro 1996, 45.

[20] It is even said that Korinna criticized Pindar for his use of Atticisms (*PMG* 688).

[21] For the Theban context of the *Aspis*, see Janko 1986, 47–48.

[22] See Janko 1986, 43 and n. 33; Russo 1965, 34. For the possible Boioticism ἐπικυρτώοντε at *Aspis* 234, see Edwards 1971, 118 with bibliography there.

[23] Edwards 1971, 27–29. On these dialectical grounds, in fact, the *Aspis* was attributed to Hesiod for decades. See West for the most cogent discussion of the various Aeolic, West Greek and possibly Boiotians elements of Hesiodic diction (M. West 1966, 82–89).

[24] For the sixth-century date, see Janko 1982, 120–121.

[25] Janko 1982, 10, 128–129, 198, after Guillon 1963.

[26] E.g., dative plurals and genitives in -οιο which occur "with suspicious frequency" (Janko 1982, 77).

a newfound development in traditional epic diction, namely the purposeful and intense use of false archaism.[27] I will remark again on the significance of this purposeful archaism below in discussing particular aspects of the Boiotian vernacular.

These sources thus provide a wide foundation of evidence from various media and genres on which I base my conclusions about the effect of the Boiotian dialect. This range is important, since I am attempting to define the standard late archaic and early classical Boiotian register as recorded in the extant epigraphic and literary evidence. Dickey defines the term register as "the use of different types of language in different situations."[28] Because the evidence we have from the period appears mostly in public dedications and literary works, I am concerned with what I will call a "high register" of Boiotian vernacular. In what follows, then, I am not attempting to reconstruct everyday or conversational speech. I rather focus on a higher level of dialect likely used between speakers of aristocratic status: e.g., those who made such dedications and who formed audiences for relatively highbrow performances and festivals. In this endeavor the orality of Greek culture is on my side, since much of what we call literary was also oral, especially at this early period, including the epigraphic verse tradition.[29]

I turn, then, to an examination of maintained archaisms and other conservative features in this register of Boiotian dialect.

SELECT DETAILS OF BOIOTIAN DIALECT

I begin by briefly assessing the Aeolic categorization of the Boiotian dialect. By the Late Archaic period, one might reasonably expect Boiotian dialect to show even more influence from its West Greek neighbors than it does, given its location in central Greece and its proximity and shared border with the West Greek Phokians, Lokrians, and Aetolians. To be sure, Boiotian dialect does show more West Greek dialectical characteristics than does Thessalian, such as the refusal to assibilate, for example, a decidedly non-epic feature.[30] Boiotian, like West Greek, Thessalian, and Pamphylian, also features the form Ϝίκατι or ἴκατι for εἴκοσι.[31] In West Greek and in Boiotian, as in Homeric epic, we find the nominative plural articles in τοί and ταί, as evident in the *Aspis*, noted above.[32] Boiotian also features some epic-Ionic forms. I mention in particular a few select isoglosses that Boiotian shared with epic-Ionic, such as Buck has collected: the use of νυ as an independent particle; -αν used as a third plural secondary ending of athematic verbs; and the use of the genitive θέμιτος.[33]

---

[27] Janko 1982, 132.

[28] Dickey 1996, 12; see 12–14 for a full discussion of register.

[29] See Dickey 1996, 30–32.

[30] C. Buck 1973, 5, 57–58, 152–153.

[31] C. Buck 1973, 57.

[32] C. Buck 1973, 100.

[33] R. Buck 1968, 268–280; see also Vottéro 1998, vol. 1, 139, for brief mention of an early Boiotian, Attic and Euboian isogloss.

However, conservative adherence to aspects of Aeolic is marked in Boiotian, despite the fact that Boiotia did not share border territory with Aeolic Thessaly. Many of the Aeolic features in Boiotian also appear in epic. Boiotia's Aeolic tendency is evident in the morphological use of Aeolic ἴα for numeral μία, for example, as in Korinna and in epic.[34] Also attested in Boiotian and epic is the rare oblique case ending -φι and dative plural endings in -εσσι, as also found in Korinna.[35] Another noteworthy form, often called Homeric and shared by Aeolic Thessalian (Pelasgiotian) is the infinitive of thematic and athematic forms in -μεν/-μεναι.[36] Moreover, as in Thessalian, the Boiotian dialect uses the thematic and Aeolic inflection of the perfect active participle, e.g., ϝεϝοκονομειόντων, as in the epic form κεκλήγοντες.[37] With regard to this term Palmer remarks that although κεκλήγοντες is the only example of the Aeolic perfect participle in epic, there exist "also certain artificial forms in -ῶτες which are suspected of concealing earlier -οντες."[38]

There are a number of additional similarities between epic Aeolic and the Boiotian dialect. Like the other Aeolic dialects, for example, the Boiotian dialect uses the patronymic adjective instead of the genitive singular of the father's name in prose. This epigraphic habit was still in force in the fourth century in fact, when other aspects of Boiotian dialect were being influenced by Attic practice.[39] Buck cites a fascinating Akraiphnian example from the late fourth century in which the patronymic adjective identifies nine official representatives from various Boiotian *poleis*, with the exception of the Plataian delegate, who is specified with the genitive singular of his father's name, as in Attic practice, which conceivably influenced Plataian epigraphic trends from the time of its alliance with Athens in the late sixth century.[40]

---

[34] C. Buck 1973, 94, 147; Korinna fr. 654.iii.17 Campbell (the daughters of Asopos fragment; col. iii.17); Page 1953, 57. Hall identifies this feature of Aeolic as a primary characteristic (Hall 1995, 176).

[35] The attestation of -φι appears as ἐπιπατρόφιον on a late Tanagran inscription (3rd century BCE; see Solmsen and Fraenkel 1930, 25–27, no. 17.30); however, the form is also attested by Hesychios, who cites the Boiotians as using this ending ("ὁ δὲ σχηματισμὸς Βοιώτιος" at *Il.* 24.268, Hesych. P 1070; "Βοιωτοί" at Hesych. I.89 for Ἴδηφι; see Chantraine 1948, 236). On -φι in epic, see Chantraine 1948, 324–242. Interestingly, the form also appears in Linear B. On -φι in general, see Palmer 1980, 45, 89–90; on its appearance in Linear B, see Chadwick 1958, 120, and Horrocks 1997, 197. For the dative ending -εσσι, see Page 1953, 51–52, 55; Korinna frs. 1.34, 4.2 (Page). The form appears also in Phokis and Lokris: see C. Buck 1973, 5, 89, 147; Palmer 1980, 84. See Horrocks 1997, 205, for the introduction of this dative form to Aeolic; also Horrocks 1997, 213; Chantraine 1948, 204 for the forms in epic.

[36] C. Buck 1973, 122, 148; Palmer 1980, 61, 72, 84; Horrocks 1997, 212. The form appears in Korinna fr. 1.20 (see Page 1953, 56). See Chantraine 1948, 485–489 for these Aeolic forms in epic, used alongside Ionian infinitives (with examples).

[37] C. Buck 1973, 117–118, 147; Palmer 1980, 72, 84; Horrocks 1997, 212–213.

[38] Palmer 1980, 84; also Horrocks 1997, 212–213.

[39] For the fourth-century transition period in Boiotian epigraphy, see, e.g., C. Buck 1973, 228–229, nos. 39–40.

[40] C. Buck 1973, 230, no. 41, 312–304 BCE.

Use of the patronymic adjective instead of the genitive singular of the father's name also occurs in epic, perhaps most notably in our context, in the phrase Τελαμώνιος Αἴας, the example which Buck coincidentally selects to illustrate this occurrence.[41] The Boiotian relevance of the *Iliad's* story of Ajax's shield, as discussed in the previous chapter, may thus have marked the use of the patronymic adjective in epic with an added significance for Boiotian listeners, particularly but perhaps not exclusively in reference to Ajax's story. At the same time, everyday use of the patronymic adjective in Boiotia may have recalled its use in epic with particular emphasis on its repeated appearance in the *Iliad's* descriptions of the Aiakid hero.

Another major feature that epic shares with Boiotian, as well as most other dialects except Attic/Ionic and Arkadian, is the use of the potential particle κε/κα instead of ἄν (κε is the Lesbian, Cypriot and Thessalian form; κα the Boiotian and West Greek form).[42] In Boiotian and West Greek this form persisted until the latest phase of Attic influence in these dialects.[43] Epic uses both ἄν and κε, and κε appears about 25% more than ἄν. While epic does not use κα *per se*, the similarity in sound between κα in Boiotian and epic κε is certainly more close than that between κα and ἄν; moreover, κε and κα would be indistinguishable when elided, as was common in epic and would have also been common in everyday speech. It thus seems reasonable to suggest that the use of κα, in addition to the other dialectical features just described, would have imparted another non-Ionic yet epicizing sound to the resonance of Boiotian dialect.

More noteworthy are the normal long genitive endings of α-stem nouns in Boiotian, a feature which Janko calls: "a crucial and characteristic part of the epic diction *in toto*."[44] These endings appear in conservative literary contexts, but much more in Homeric epic as a whole than in later traditions in dactylic hexameter.[45] In the *Aspis* the genitive singular of these masculine α-stems appears exclusively with the long ending -αο (as opposed to the Ionic -εω/-ω), although the number of occurrences is small (three).[46] Nonetheless, the *Aspis* also uses the long plural ending -αων in equal proportion to the long Ionic ending and furthermore often places the Ionic ending in the same spot of the line as epic;[47] the poem can thus be said to favor the Boiotian genitive forms somewhat over the Ionic and in Ionic usage to show the influence of epic.

The phonological trend toward Aeolicism and distinctiveness in the Boiotian dialect is particularly evident in the long-lived Boiotian use of the digamma. The digamma dropped out of use in Attic-Ionic, the other main dialectical strand of

---

[41] C. Buck 1973, 134, 147; see also C. Buck 1973, 135 for genitives used in apposition to a noun implied by an adjective, as in epic.

[42] C. Buck 1973, 105–106; Palmer 1980, 61.

[43] C. Buck 1973, 106.

[44] Janko 1982, 90.

[45] Janko 1982, 48–50, 89–90; Edwards 1971, 123–126 [gen. sg.], 126–130 [gen. pl.]).

[46] *Aspis* 100, 112, 134; Edwards 1971, 123–125, table on p. 124.

[47] *Aspis* 4, 6, 7, 10, 19, 128, 178, 260, 338; Edwards 1971, 126–130, table on p. 127 (who might disagree with the reading proposed here).

epic, quite early in the Archaic period,[48] perhaps even before alphabetic inscriptions began.[49] Boiotian dialect, in contrast, retained the digamma, both intervocalic and initial, until the end of the third century, a very late date indeed for the recording of the sound in inscriptions from any region in Greece.[50]

Examples of this early Boiotian digamma come from a variety of media and venues. On a dedication from the Ptoion (below) we find fine attestations of the use of both the initial and intervocalic digamma. The digammas of line 1 are all rather archaizing; as Wachter remarks, the inclusion of the digamma in line 2 also appears to be so: "its purpose must have been to make clear to the reader the {Homeric} scansion of the verb:"

καλϝὸν ἄγαλμα ϝάνακτι ϝ[εκαβόλοι Ἀ:πόλονι :]
[ca. 3]ορίδας ποίϝεσέ μ᾿ Ἐχέστροτίος· αὐτὰρ ἔπεμφσαν :
[ca. 16, 2.5 dactylic feet; ; ca. 11, 1.5 feet]ον Πτοιἐϝι, :
τὸς τύ, ϝάναχ|ς, φεφύλαχσο, δίδοι δ᾿ ἀρ<ε>τάν [τε καὶ ὄλβον].

A beautiful agalma for lord far-shooter Apollo, Echestrotos, son of [?]-or, made me. But [at least two names] sent [? (it) as a gift] to (Apollo) Ptoios. May you, lord, watch over them and grant [both] excellence [and prosperity].[51]

We find the digamma in numerous archaic and late archaic Boiotian vase inscriptions as well, including in personal names (e.g., Εὐϝάρχα).[52] The sound appears written even in simple incised signatures from the middle of the sixth century onwards (e g., Γρύτον ἐποίϝεσε) and is included in *abecedaria* into the late fifth century.[53] Although there are a few noteworthy absences of the digamma in the papyrus of Korinna, the initial digamma and internal digamma between ρ and a vowel appear quite regularly.[54]

---

[48] Janko 1982, 42 (initial digamma); Edwards 1971, 132; C. Buck 1973, 46, 142; Chantraine 1948, 116. The Lesbian dialect, although Aeolic, provides an interesting contrast to Boiotian retention of the digamma; like Attic and also island Doric, Lesbian dialect stopped using the sound quite early (Janko 1982, 91, after C. Buck 1973, 46).

[49] Horrocks 204; see also Palmer 1980, 71.

[50] C. Buck 1973, 152; M. West 1966, 91; Page 1953, 48.

[51] Wachter 2001, 237; P. Hansen 1983, no. 334; translation J. Day. The end of the final verse is missing because of a break at the bottom of the piece (C. Buck 1909, 77).

[52] See Wachter 2001, 18–19, no. 10. He notes that the retention of digamma in both personal names and in hexametrical inscriptions is common. For more examples of the digamma on other archaic media from Boiotia, see *LSAG* 94.4 (late seventh century, base for kore); 94.7 (early sixth century, phiale); 94.9 (c. 550, lebes).

[53] Wachter 2001, 9, no. 1 (potter's signature). For more makers' and writers' signatures, see Wachter 2001, 10–11, nos. 2A–D; 14–15, nos. 5A–B. For *abecedaria*, see Wachter 2001, 20–21, no. 14.

[54] Page 1953, 46–49, 65. On reviewing the Berlin papyrus of Korinna for himself, in fact, West remarks: "it is delightful to read a neatly-written papyrus containing real digammas" (M. West 1996, 22). For examples, see Korinna fr. 4 (Page; ϝέροια, possibly the title of her collected works, as ascribed by Antoninus Liberalis 25; see Page 1953, 30, 33–34: Clayman 1978, 396–397; O. Hansen 1989, 70–71).

A notable spelling correction of a digamma appears on a Boiotian vase from Thebes from the first half of the sixth century.[55] Here, according to Wachter's reading, the writer wrote an epsilon for a digamma in the verb ποιέω (ἐποίεεσε), but later corrected his spelling, after realizing that he pronounced and usually recorded the word with a Ϝ sound (ἐποίϜεσε).[56] Wachter attributes this to a trend toward "archaizing spelling," but it might be best, as he implies, to see this not only as a preference for spelling but also, and more important in this context, a reflection of the sound of the Boiotian digamma, still prevalent in the spoken dialect.

Of course, the digamma is not always recorded in Boiotian vase inscriptions, even in the verb ποιέω which often used the sound; the digamma must therefore not always have been pronounced in Boiotia.[57] This difference in recording of the same sound in the same dialect both points to a possible difference in register between Boiotian speakers and thus also the likely inclusion of the digamma by particular Boiotians interested in imparting a certain tone to their speech. The occasional non-use of the digamma in Boiotian vase inscriptions does not negate its persistent presence and usefulness in this upper register of the Boiotian dialect from the Late Archaic and Early Classical periods and later.

In turning to epic tradition, it is clear that epic presupposed the presence of the initial digamma for metrical reasons, although it is not indicated in the text: over two thousand cases of hiatus of a short final vowel in epic can be resolved by beginning the following word with a digamma.[58] Janko gives percentages for epic retention of the initial digamma for meter. The *Iliad* shows an 84% rate of retention; the Odyssey 83%; the *Theogony* 66%; the *Erga* 62%; the relatively early *Homeric Hymn to Demeter* 54%.[59] Interestingly, the diction of the *Aspis* maintains the effect of the digamma 72% of the time; in such a Boiotian (and likely Theban) authored work, this is a striking correspondence to the Homeric epic figures, as late as 570 BCE.[60] Janko attributes the retention of the digamma in both the *Aspis* as well as the *Homeric Hymn to Pythian Apollo* to the continued existence of the digamma in the Boiotian vernacular, in addition to the *Hymn's* reliance on the *Iliad's* Catalogue of Ships and the *Odyssey*.[61] If this is the case, which seems reasonable, then we may likewise view the continued use of the digamma in the Boiotian dialect similarly: as a purposeful retention of archaism meant to recall the epic register.

Palmer attributes the retention of the digamma in epic to conservatism involved in the transmission of the tradition, despite the loss of digamma in the

---

[55] Wachter 2001, no.2A.

[56] Wachter 2001, 10–11, 209.

[57] Wachter 2001, 11, 237. See also Wachter 2001, 15–18, nos. 6A-E, 7A-C, 9.

[58] Palmer 1980, 86; see also Kirk 1985, 7; for the digamma in epic, see Hoekstra 1999 (1964), 237–250; Chantraine 1948, 116–164.

[59] Janko 1992, 13–14.

[60] Janko 1992, 14; see also Edwards for the high retention of the digamma in the *Aspis* (1971, 132, 196).

[61] Janko 1982, 78, 129–131; for the influence of Boiotian dialect on the diction of the *Aspis* in particular, see Janko 1986, 43. *Contra* Edwards 1971, 39 and n. 17, 135–139, 138.

Ionic vernacular.[62] However, in terms of the sound of the various literary works transmitted in epic style, Janko has shown that the digamma was "less frequently introduced in non-Homeric (and therefore often innovative) contexts" than was the neglect of the sound.[63] The digamma thus serves as a useful criterion in determining the progression of epic diction. Upon applying this conclusion to the persistent use of the digamma in Boiotian speech, it seems quite likely that the sound of the digamma imparted an old and epicizing tone to the dialects which retained it, such as Boiotian, Thessalian and Lakonian.

For the sake of argument, I here include additional but minor Boiotian dialectical features which also correspond to epic usage. Boiotian uses the independent particle νυ, as do epic and Cyprian only.[64] Other forms of note include the reflexives ἑέ, ἑοῖ which appear exclusively in Korinna and epic.[65] Like many other dialects, Boiotian also uses the dual often, as does epic.[66] Boiotian πέτταρες seems a remarkable cross between Homeric πίσυρες and pure Aeolic Lesbian πέσσυρες.[67] In epic the form τέτρατος for τέταρτος occurs; Boiotian πέτρατος appears similar.[68] Finally, in Boiotian we also find the pronoun ὅττω which is much like epic ὅττεο.[69]

It thus seems that in the late sixth and early fifth centuries Boiotian dialect employed a variety of Aeolic archaisms and epicizing forms which neighboring west Greek regions did not. Moreover, as Buck has remarked, Boiotian as a whole was a relatively homogenous dialect across the region in the sixth and fifth centuries, at least as far as can be deduced from the available evidence. As one might expect, then, any differences arise late and between the areas of northern and southern Boiotia.[70] The maintenance of such regional dialectical conservatism seems quite important in a community which, as we have seen with the Boiotians at this time, shows itself interested in using "other, non-linguistic symbols in a boundary-marking function."[71]

This is not to say that Boiotian dialect of Aeolic was not at all laterally influenced by certain aspects of neighboring dialects, not only West Greek, as noted above, but also Attic-Ionic and even Doric;[72] some of these shared forms also appear in epic. West in fact briefly discusses certain West Greek forms which occur in both Boiotian dialect and epic:[73] the second person pronominal

---

[62] Palmer 1980, 103; Hainsworth 1988, 28 (for the loss of digamma in Ionic).

[63] Janko 1982, 45–46.

[64] C. Buck 1973, 100, 106.

[65] M. West 1988, 167–168.

[66] C. Buck 1973, 87; see Korinna fr. 654.col. iii.15 (Campbell); Page 1953, 56.

[67] For Attic τέτταρες/Ionic τέσσερες (C. Buck 1973, 95).

[68] See C. Buck 1973, 95.

[69] See C. Buck 1973, 101.

[70] R. Buck 1968, 270.

[71] Hall 1997, 179.

[72] See Hall 1997, 165 and note 97 for features.

[73] He attributes these similarities to the partial crystallization of epic in central Greece and Euboia.

forms of epic τύνη, τεοῖο, τεῖν, for example, as also found in Korinna.[74] The -νη suffix in τύνη, in fact, is found only in Boiotian and Lakonian.[75] Interestingly, in terms of percentages, Boiotian employed statistically similar ratios of Lakonian forms as it does Aeolic Thessalian forms.[76] On the basis of its varied influences, in fact, Buck calls Boiotian a "mixed" dialect, alongside Thessalian.[77] In the end, however, through its conservative Aeolic and West Greek morphology and phonology, I suggest that this Boiotian concoction of forms created a rather distinctive sounding dialect which may have been understood as reminiscent of epic, since these and other Aeolic characteristics of Boiotian seem to be widely recognized as epic traits.

I do not mean to suggest that the Boiotian dialect mimicked epic exactly. Rather, given the number of similar forms attested in both Boiotian and epic, Boiotian may have been highly evocative of many of the sounds associated with the important Aeolic stratum of epic.[78] Of course, epic's diction as a whole was still artificial and panhellenic in its amalgamation of forms; it is the "language of the ἀοιδή."[79] The strongest strand in epic was predominantly East-Ionic, which makes sense given the well-known traditions about the Athenian milieu in which the epic was supposedly at least partially fixed as well as the possible influence of culture from the Ionian seaboard on the formation of part of the oral tradition.[80] However, the strength of the Aeolic thread that winds through epic is unmistakable, despite its frequent inclusion for metrical reasons.[81] This Aeolic substratum helped give epic its "generally archaic feel," to quote Horrocks;[82] Hainsworth has even described epic speaking as "a tradition that evoked the heroic world by its exotic language."[83]

However much this older tone to the Boiotian dialect may have been related to an earlier Mycenaean form of the language is impossible to say, although it is quite reasonable to speculate, given earlier traditions about migrations and naval contingents, that the late sixth-century Boiotians were trying to connect themselves to putative forebears through the maintenance of an archaistic way of speech thought to evoke that epic world in general.[84] Scholars have identified

[74] Fr. 654.iv.20 (Campbell); see Page 1953, 54.

[75] M. West 1988, 167–168, where he adds a few additional forms. For my purposes, the conclusion of West's argument is not altogether relevant. Wherever the epic may have crystallized, it is the forms involved that are pertinent here.

[76] Hall 1995, 87, and 1995, 175.

[77] C. Buck 1973, 7, 9.

[78] For specific Lesbian features of epic Aeolic, see M. West 1988, 163–165.

[79] Hainsworth 1988, 24.

[80] Palmer 1980, 83–84 (on Athens). For Ionian influence, see Janko 1992, 16–18 (where he argues for discontinuity in such influence); Kirk 1985, 5–6; Horrocks 1997, 212, where he lists many of the common Ionic features of epic; *contra* M. West 1988, 165–166.

[81] See Horrocks 1997, 212–213; Janko 1992, 16; Hainsworth 1988, 24; Kirk 1985, 6; Janko 1982, 89, 196 (where he posits a link between the Aeolic phase of epic and Lesbos); Chantraine 1948, 509.

[82] Horrocks 1997, 194.

[83] Hainsworth 1988, 25.

[84] See Horrocks 1997, 196–199, 201–203 for brief discussions of the relationship between Mycenaean and epic language.

such nostalgia as inherent in the epic register itself, which is thought to have evoked the past through its amalgamation of dialects not in everyday use together, thereby "placing it more plausibly in the remote past and creating a suitably heroic tone."[85] With regard to the Lesbian Aeolians, Janko remarks: "if anyone had good cause to glorify a panhellenic military enterprise in that area [Lesbos], it was the Aeolians. It cannot be coincidental that analysis of the epic diction points in the same direction."[86] I would argue that the Boiotians, as putative relations of Aeolic speakers elsewhere in the Greek world, could and would have made similar claims, with particular relevance to their part in the *Iliad's* Catalogue of Ships, which "gives Boiotia first place."[87] It is most definitely the *Iliad* and the *Odyssey* which the archaistic tone of the Boiotian dialect would have recalled, if one trusts, as I do, the qualifications and proportions of archaic style adduced by Janko, to whom the *Iliad* and the *Odyssey* are most archaic in diction.[88]

I do not mean to suggest that other *ethne* did not share dialectical forms with epic; certainly all other Greek dialects shared some forms which appear there: e.g., Corinthian and Lakonian, which also preserve the digamma.[89] However, given the variety of lexical, morphological, and phonological evidence adduced above, late sixth- and early fifth-century Boiotian dialect seems to have been more epic "sounding" than some others, e.g., Arkado-Cypriot, which shared mainly vocabulary items with epic, but not morphology.[90] In the end, Boiotian dialect is distinguished both in its amalgamation of a variety of dialectical forms and in some of these specific forms themselves, many of which are remarkably like those of epic.

These aspects of Boiotian dialect were likely difficult to maintain. Retaining linguistic features when surrounding communities evolve linguistically requires effort, if not diligence.[91] Boiotia was bordered by Attica, of course, and also the strictly West Greek speaking Phokis and Lokris. That Boiotian clung to many of its Aeolic elements amid this sea of dialectical neighbors is thus remarkable indeed, particularly given the major north-south and east-west roads and other networks that linked the region to others (e.g., the Euripos straits); the late sixth-century Boiotians simply did not live in isolation from any of their neighbors nor from areas further afield. It thus required a concerted effort and a palpable drive toward cohesiveness for the Boiotians to have maintained such a distinctive linguistic identity.

Notably, in terms of Boiotian collective identity, Boiotian ties to the Aeolic dialect are not restricted to characteristics shared only with epic. Boiotian dialect also exhibits some noteworthy Aeolic traits also visible in the Thessalian dialect,

---

[85] Janko 1992, 9.

[86] Janko 1992, 19.

[87] Janko 1992, 19; *Il.* 2.494–511.

[88] Janko 1982, 46; Hainsworth 1988, 27–29.

[89] See Wachter 2001, 120–121, 236–237 for examples and discussion.

[90] Householder and Nagy 1972, 63 (who also discuss the "rare instance of a morphological innovation shared by epic and Arkado-Cypriot"); Palmer 1980, 85; see also Kirk 1985, 6.

[91] Hall 1997, 179.

such as the third plural active ending -νθι for -μι verbs and use of -θ in the third plural middle.[92] It is also remarkable that Thessalian dialect, like Boiotian, retained the digamma until about 400 BCE while the Lesbian dialect, the other generally Aeolic dialect, did not.[93] As noted above, also found in Thessalian are the infinitive in -μεν and the genitive singular in -οιο.[94] Boiotian dialect, then, was both epicizing in an Aeolic manner and shared a few distinct characteristics with Thessalian dialect both inside and outside the epic register. Like its epic traits, the relationship of Boiotian dialect to specific Thessalian features suggests their purposeful retention. Given Boiotian ties to Thessaly through the eponymous Boiotos' Aiolid genealogy and through the tradition of Boiotian migration, it is not difficult to see why the Boiotians would have chosen to emphasize their dialectical relationship to Thessaly as well.

In sum, then, although the Boiotian dialect alone does not qualify the Boiotians as an ethnic group,[95] together with other Boiotian links to panhellenic epic tradition and the other Boiotian criteria and indicia of ethnicity, the Boiotian dialectical features shared with epic and with Aeolic Thessalian take on added significance as markers and reinforcers of difference, descent, affiliation, and boundaries based on a putative past.

A FEW EPICIZING EXAMPLES

It is noteworthy, then, that nearly all extant Boiotian inscriptions of any length as well as fragments of epichoric literature are highly reminiscent of epic in style and meter. I thus present in more detail a few of the more illustrative pieces.

The hexameter piece from the Ptoion, adduced above for its frequent use of initial and intervocalic digamma, is obviously epicizing in rhythm and sound. Again, here is the text:

καλϝὸν ἄγαλμα ϝάνακτι ϝ[εκαβόλοι Ἀπόλονι :]
[c. 3]ορίδας ποίϝεσέ μ' Ἐχέστροτος· αὐτὰρ ἔπεμφσαν :
[c. 16, 2.5 dactylic feet; c. 11, 1.5 feet]ον Πτοιϝι, :
τὸς τύ, ϝάναχις, φεφύλαχσο, δίδοι δ' ἀρ<ε>τάν [τε καὶ ὄλβον].

A beautiful agalma for lord far-shooter Apollo, Echestrotos, son of [?]-or, made me. But [at least two names] sent [? (it) as a gift] to (Apollo) Ptoios. May you, lord, watch over them and grant [both] excellence [and prosperity].[96]

In addition to the prevalence of the digamma in the verse, one might also adduce the term ϝάναχς, whose usage here parallels epic tradition, where the term is

---

[92] C. Buck 1973, 112, 152 (-νθι); C. Buck 1973, 113, 152 (θ).
[93] C. Buck 1973, 150; Horrocks 1997, 205, after Janko 1982.
[94] C. Buck 1973, 88, 150.
[95] Hall 1997, 169.
[96] P. Hansen 1983, no. 334; translation J. Day (as above).

often attributed both to gods and heroes, particularly Apollo, Zeus, and Agamemnon.[97] The term remains linked primarily to gods and epic heroes in later Greek literature, especially tragedy.[98] As we saw in Chapter One, Korinna also uses Ϝάναχς in a context of epic tone and collective identity to address the Boiotian eponymous figure, Boiotos: Ϝάναξ Βοιωτέ (fr. 6 Page). The term thus may have carried certain connotations of regional relevance, in addition to its reminiscence of epic gods and heroes. Further, the second epithet of the Ptoion dedication, Ϝ[εκαβόλοι, seems significant; even though the term is only a restoration by Buck, few other alternatives would fit the sense and meter of the remainder of the hexameter line. Other such epic epithets occur in Boiotian inscriptions, for example ἀργυροτόχσοι, ca. 500 BCE.[99] Buck's restoration of Ϝ[εκαβόλοι with a term directly borrowed from epic thus seems reasonable, and we should accept it as an accurate reflection of an absent epic epithet (see also below).[100] The final hemistich, although likewise a restoration, seems a common epic formula, as seen in the *Homeric Hymns* 15.9 (Herakles) and 20.8 (Hephaistos). Surely something similar, if not this exact formulaic and thus relatively common phrase, appeared here in the text. And finally, even some of the simplest vocabulary of the Ptoion piece mimics epic vocabulary, as in the conjunction αὐτάρ of line 2.[101]

Most significantly, in the Ptoion piece we find the present imperative δίδοι (line 4) which also appears in line 2 of the famous early archaic dedication of Mantiklos from Thebes (700–675 BCE):

Μάντικλός μ' ἀνέθεκε Ϝεκαβόλοι ἀργυροτόξσοι
τᾶς {δ}δεικάτας· τὺ δέ, Φοῖβε, δίδοι χαρίϜετταν ἀμοιβ[άν].

Mantiklos set me up for the far-shooting, silver-bowed (god), out of the tithe. As for you, Phoibos, may you grant a charis-filled return.[102]

The native Boiotian Pindar, who did not compose in Boiotian vernacular, nonetheless often allows this form creep into his *epinikia*.[103] In other words, then, in these two Boiotian inscriptions we find a rather arcane and poetic way of ad-

---

[97] Apollo: e.g., *Il*. 1.390, *Aspis* 100, *Hymn. Hom. Ap.* 526; Zeus: e.g., *Il*. 3.351, Hes. *Th.* 660, *Op.* 69; Agamemnon: *Il*. 1.442 (and subsequently, over forty times in the epic).

[98] E.g., Zeus: Aesch. *Pers*. 762, *Supp*. 524; Apollo: Soph. *OT* 80. In Euripides the term is used of mortal kings with power and, as Lenfent notes, can also connote less positive associations (Lenfent 1993, 30).

[99] P. Hansen 1983, no. 337.

[100] C. Buck 1909, 76–80; Vottéro 1996, 46.

[101] Vottéro 1996, 46.

[102] P. Hansen 1983, no. 326; Jeffery 1990, 94.1; translation J. Day. Jeffery remarks only that the Mantiklos piece is said to have originated in Thebes and thus attributes it to the Ismenion; its real provenience in Boiotia thus remains unknown (Jeffery 1990, 90). P. Hansen includes a restoration of δίδοι on an early sixth-century Corinthian inscription (P. Hansen 1983, 191, no. 358) and suggests another for an early fifth-century Spartan piece (P. Hansen 1983, 202, no. 377). I do not include these examples here. It has been suggested that the Mantiklos piece was a tripod attachment, in which case the inscription would have also had divinatory overtones (Papalexandrou 1999, 345–346).

[103] Pind. *Ol*. 1.85; 6.104; 7.89; 13.115; *Nem*. 5.50; see P. Hansen 1983, 191–192, no. 358.

dressing the divinity, attested primarily by Boiotian inscriptions and the Theban Pindar. Although the imperative δίδοι does not appear in epic *per se*, Wachter has convincingly argued for its origin in very early traditional poetry in Aeolic hexameter which spread across the Aegean and in essence became virtually indistinguishable from the Ionic dactylic tradition.[104]

Returning to extant epic, the more common form of the imperative, δίδου, appears at *Od.* 3.58 in a request from Athena to Poseidon on Nestor's behalf. Notably, here the epic verb introduces the same formulaic phrase with which the writer of the Mantiklos inscription ends his verse: δίδου χαρίεσσαν ἀμοιβὴν. A clearer epic parallel would be difficult to find.[105] The Mantiklos dedication sports other epic forms as well: for example, the epic epithets for Apollo Ϝεκαβόλοι and ἀργυροτόχσοι in line 1.[106] When taken together as a whole, then, juxtaposition of the digamma, the imperative δίδοι, the term Ϝάναχς, other divine epithets, lesser epic vocabulary, and the fluency of the hexameter creates a resoundingly epic style for the Ptoion dedication, as we also find in the Mantiklos dedication, a piece which even contains an epic formula paralleled in the *Odyssey*.[107] The early archaic date for the Mantiklos piece suggests that this trend began early in Boiotia and contemporaneously as epic was crystallizing into a more fixed form.

Given the proximity between the Ptoion piece and epic verse, the medium of the Ptoion dedication is worth pondering. The verse appears on a flat clay tile, perhaps a rooftile.[108] I. Raubitschek suggested that the piece was "the upper part of a ladle or strainer," although its presence at the Ptoion would thus seem rather odd, since to my knowledge none of the other contemporaneous dedications from this sanctuary qualify as kitchenware.[109] Jeffery tentatively remarked that the tile may have been the draft of an inscription, "sent with the ἄγαλμα for a local mason at the Ptoion to copy on the base." This possibility seems likewise unlikely, however, since after incising the stone base the draft-tile would then presumably have been discarded. Jeffery's second suggestion seems most likely, that the tile was meant to be inserted in some larger object, perhaps a column or a statue base.[110] Since the precise use of this piece is not decisively understood, then, we must leave open the possibility that this epicizing hexameter may have appeared on a relatively small and somewhat odd dedication, a piece quite unlike common types of Ptoion dedications, such as fine local or imported *kouroi*. In other words, the Ptoion hexameter tile may provide an example of skilled epic style verse written on a smaller and perhaps rather minor type of gift; the piece may thus reflect a slightly more everyday use of the epic register in Boiotia at this time.

---

[104] Wachter 2001, 341.

[105] On this parallel see also Day 2000, 46–47.

[106] See Vottéro 1996, 46.

[107] These are not the only dedications which pertain to the discussion; for further epicizing inscriptions from Boiotia, see Vottéro 1996, 45, nos. 2, 4, 6. For the audience as reader and thus as continual re-enactor of the original context of these kinds of epigrams, see Day 2000, 37–57.

[108] For a photo see C. Buck 1909, 79.

[109] Raubitschek and Raubitschek 1966, 162. For other archaic dedications from the Ptoion (statuary, bronzes, weaponry, fine ceramics), see Ducat 1971.

[110] Jeffery 1990, 92–93, n. 4, presumably on the analogy of similarly used bronze plaques.

Since the Ptoion and Mantiklos dedications were erected in a public setting, it is not entirely surprising that they exhibit archaic and epic-sounding language of a high register (although, again, the medium of the Ptoion piece may be remarkable). In turning to a less public medium, however, we find a similarly Boiotian epicizing inscription painted on a Boiotian ring aryballos apparently meant as a private gift around the middle of the sixth century.[111] As Wachter suggests, the second metrical line was likely added some time after the potter's signature on the same vase:

Μνασάλκες π[οίεσε *vac.*] Ἐμπεδιόνδαι.
Αὐτ[ὰ]ρ *ho* δõκε φέρον φιλοτάσιον Αἰσχύλοι αὐτό.

Mnasalkes made (me) for Empediondas.
But the latter took and gave the same love-gift to Aischylos.

Wachter lists the numerous epic qualities of the line: "the metre, the construction φέρων + Verb, demonstrative ὁ (without -δε), and the lack of augment in δõκε."[112] Additionally, the line is roughly paralleled at *Od.* 21.366, as first noted by Raubitschek.[113] The epic register of the line does not itself require an exact verbal parallel, however; its epic tone itself has led Wachter to query: "were there still people (in Boiotia) in the second half of the sixth century whose experience embraced a wider and perhaps still partly epic tradition?" He even attributes the line to Empediondas' skill at composing verse.[114] It is indeed noteworthy that such an epic-style line appears on such a personal gift which would have seen only limited exposure between friends. Its presence thus not only testifies to the donor's skill as a poet but simultaneously attests to use of an epic register between people in a relatively private setting in Boiotia.

In toto, these inscriptions also display a few standard phonetic and morphological forms of the Boiotian dialect, as Vottéro has discussed. For instance, in the Mantiklos dedication we find the characteristic long α of Boiotian in ϝεκαβόλοι and τᾶς {δ}δε|κάτας; the epithets ϝεκαβόλοι and ἀργυροτόχσοι also show endings proper to Boiotian.[115] However, in the end it is the epic register that predominates in these earliest Boiotian inscriptions, and, as Vottéro has remarked, the "Homeric oeuvre" seems to have been wholly adapted into the local dialect.[116]

On a more thematic note, in this epic context we may again adduce evidence from Korinna, who, contrary to previously held opinions of her work, is beginning to be appreciated as a poetess in her own right. As discussed in Chapter One, Stewart and Larson have resuscitated the fifth-century Korinna; Snyder and

[111] The piece is said to have come from Thebes (see Wachter 2001, 12 and n. 35); for the date see Wachter 2001, 12 and n. 38 with bibliography.
[112] Wachter 2001, 13–14.
[113] *Od.* 21.366: ὣς φάσαν, αὐτὰρ, ὁ θῆκε φέρων αὐτῇ ἐνὶ χώρῃ.
[114] Wachter 2001, 14; for the parallel, see also Vottéro 1996, 46.
[115] See Vottéro 1996, 46, 48 for more examples and additional inscriptions.
[116] Vottéro 1996, 46–47.

Collins too would place Korinna into the same poetic milieu as Pindar and Bacchylides. To Snyder Korinna's use of epic epithets and her interest in the genealogies of founding Boiotian heroes situate the poetess in a poetic tradition whose foundations go back to hexameter tradition.[117] To the epic-style Hesiodic *Ehoiai* Larson cogently compares Korinna's genealogical focus, evident particularly in Korinna's treatment of the daughters of Asopos and also in her Terpsichore fragment. Korinna, like Hesiodic tradition, is concerned to explicate the origins of heroes; although Korinna's heroes and heroines are Boiotian, the urge to document their divine births and thus their present importance is notably similar.[118] In Korinna, then, who writes in the Boiotian vernacular, we find an epichoric expression of hexameter structures and themes.[119] Given Boiotian emphasis on collective genealogy, traditions of migration, epic symbolism and epicizing dialect, Korinna's focus on themes similar to panhellenic hexameter tradition seems natural and reinforces these collective concerns.

In sum, the material adduced in this chapter for an epic register to the Boiotian dialect, attested through various literary and material evidence, suggests that by the Late Archaic and Early Classical periods the Boiotians had promulgated a form of linguistic pride in their dialect through which they simultaneously reified and buttressed their collective links to one another, particularly those which concerned ties to epic tradition, such as the tradition of Boiotian migration, the *Iliad's* portrayal of the heroic Boiotian past, and also Boiotian genealogical ties to the Aikaid hero Ajax. This tendency toward epic dialect may have been in use, as the Mantiklos dedication suggests, as early as 700–675 BCE.

---

[117] Snyder 1984, 132–133; Collins 2004.
[118] J. Larson 2002, 49–53.
[119] See also Collins 2004.

CHAPTER 5
A COMMON NAME:
THE REGIONAL ETHNICS Βοιωτοί AND Βοιώτιος

One of the most significant indicia of a plural community in antiquity – not to mention in modern eras – is the use of a common name, or *ethnikon*, as a marker of the collective. As used by members inside the group, a common name calls to mind the core of the community in all its parts; to outsiders the name will hold an entirely different meaning, perhaps even an antithetical one, than the totality which it signifies to its own members. As Smith nicely summarizes: "a collective name 'evokes' an atmosphere and drama that has power and meaning for those whom it includes, and none at all (or a quite different resonance) for outsiders." He further remarks that "part of any study of ethnicity is to discover and grasp these different images of community which names evoke."[1] It is important to state at the outset, then, that ancient ethnics do not automatically indicate a political group, although they are commonly and thus often erroneously assumed to do so, especially in textual analyses.[2]

The following chapter thus concerns late archaic and early classical use of the collective regional ethnic (Βοιωτός, singular and Βοιωτοί, plural) and the collective regional adjective (Βοιώτιος, Βοιώτιοι). These terms comprise two related categories of naming which were demonstrably significant for self and group definition in all periods of Greek history. While Greek names commonly included the *onoma* plus patronymic, names could also include a third term which signified involvement in a group outside the immediate family, such as a *genos*, *phyle*, state (i.e. *polis*), or even an entire region.[3] This third element was sometimes a regional ethnic like Βοιωτός. That Greeks cared to add such indications to their personal names signifies their importance in discussing non-*polis* communities.[4]

From one category of ethnics, of which Βοιωτοί and Βοιώτιος are part, are derived certain toponyms (e.g., Βοιωτία from Βοιωτός; Ἀχαία from Ἀχαιός). It is often assumed that the regions indicated by such topographical terms were first "loosely organized" political groups that later divided into *poleis* and still later formed federal states.[5] What follows thus centers on this category of ethnic identification.[6]

---

[1] A. Smith 1986, 23.

[2] See Morgan 2003, 7, 207. See the following chapter for specific discussion of *ethnika* in the fifth-century Athenian historians.

[3] See M. Hansen 1996b, 170, 181, and 194.

[4] M. Hansen 1996b, 190.

[5] See M. Hansen 1996b, 187–188.

[6] For the two categories of regional ethnics, see Dittenberger 1906, 167–168. The second

Evidence suggests that although Greek ethnics often signified political affiliation (e.g., membership in some sort of organized political group), this was not
always the case, particularly in the Archaic period but also in later centuries.
Hansen raises the fourth-century use of the regional ethnic Ἀρκάς as a case in
point. This same term was used before the formulation of the Arkadian federation, during the existence of the federation, and after its dissolution. This continuity of usage thus demonstrates discontinuity of meaning: while the ethnic Ἀρκάς
may have indicated membership in the Arkadian federation during its fourth-
century existence, the term did not continuously indicate membership in a federal
body.[7] In other words, then, regional ethnics "designating a people ... may signal
a feeling of national identity, but not necessarily membership of a political community. The political connotation became prominent only if the region formed a
federation and if the ethnic was used to signify federal citizenship, which was far
from always the case."[8] Since the specific group these terms specify is not consistent, each occurrence of a regional ethnic must be examined in its historic context in order to define the community which the term designates at that time.

Below I present the late sixth- and early to mid-fifth-century evidence for the
use of the collective regional ethnic Βοιωτός/Βοιωτοί and the regional adjective
Βοιώτιος/Βοιώτιοι, referring the reader to previous chapters when necessary. I
begin with use of ethnics from inside Boiotia, since these internal examples attest
to the group's self-perception and self-representation to its members. I then compare this treatment with non-Boiotian use of the same terms. This division will
distinguish Boiotian from non-Boiotian comprehension of the collective.

I reach a number of conclusions from the evidence. In addition to affirming
the relationship between Boiotians and shields discussed in Chapter Three, a concentration on collective cultic links to Athena is evident in internal collective use
of the ethnics in late archaic and early classical sources. Internal individual use of
the ethnic does not occur until after the middle of the fifth century; this new
appearance may signify a change on an individual level in the internal perception
of the group, although the precise meaning of the ethnic in this later context is
still debatable.

Contemporaneous evidence for external use of Boiotian ethnics reveals a
different approach to the collective from outsiders. As we saw in Chapter Two,
epic depicts the Boiotians as a wealthy and populous group inhabiting a specific
geographic region. In the sixth and early fifth centuries, Athenian sources either

category of ethnics are an exact inverse of the first: that is, they are derived from names of
places, e.g., Εὐβοιεύς from Εὔβοια. According to M. Hansen, most ethnics which fall into this
second category do not signify a political unit; they are "primarily topographical" although they
may occasionally connote a "feeling of belonging to the same people" (M. Hansen 1996b, 187).

[7] M. Hansen 1996b, 189 (based on Nielsen 1996, 39–61, esp. 61); also Nielsen 1999, 57,
59).

[8] M. Hansen 1996b, 190; see also M. Hansen 1995, 45, where he allows the adjectival ethnic
to denote a person's regional and/or federal affiliation. See Roesch for the use of the Boiotian
adjectival ethnic as a federal designation in the fourth century and Hellenistic periods (Roesch
1982, 415–420, 451).

perpetuate this geographic characterization or refer to the Boiotians with the vague term, *ethnos*. Near the first quarter of the century, Pindar shows that the reputation of the collective Βοιωτοί as gluttons was commonplace both inside Athens and in a wider panhellenic context. Notably, a change in external use of the regional ethnics occurs only in the middle of the fifth century BCE; this shift parallels the mid-fifth-century transformation of the internal usage of the terms. Corroborating this fifth-century shift in the use and meaning of Boiotian *ethnika* is also the fifth-century historians' use of the collective term, which I take up in the next chapter.

BOIOTIAN USE OF REGIONAL ETHNICS (INTERNAL USE)

A. The Sixth Century

The first internal attestation of the collective regional ethnic occurs, as discussed in Chapter Three, in the early sixth-century proem to the Theban *Aspis*. There the Boiotians are described at relative length as bearers of epic style shields (σάκος); this characterization parallels the Boiotian link to Ajax's σάκος from the *Iliad* and also reinforces an epic connection to shield manufacture in general. The Herakles of the *Aspis*, too, is depicted as an epic hero reminiscent of Ajax and Achilles.

A different but complementary focus emerges in Boiotian use of their collective name from epigraphic evidence later in the sixth century. At this time, the plural ethnic appears primarily in association with Athena at Apolline sanctuaries. As we will see, epigraphic use of the collective regional ethnic outside Boiotia from the same period corroborates this picture.

Inside Boiotia, our evidence comes from three dedicatory inscriptions from two sanctuaries in northeastern Boiotia: the sanctuary of Apollo Ptoios and the nearby sanctuary of the Akraiphian civic hero Ptoios. These dedications offer an intimate view of the internal self-representation of the group, since the Boiotians erected them at popular Boiotian sanctuaries where their own Boiotian colleagues will have encountered them on numerous occasions. It is not surprising, then, that these inscriptions present a consistent picture of the Boiotians as a collective concerned to promote itself through cult.

Our best preserved and most important example in this context comes from the sanctuary of Apollo Ptoios, an oracular cult associated with the *polis* Akraiphia in northeastern Boiotia.[9] The piece consists in a small stone base with dowels for

---

[9] Akraiphia's status as a *polis* in the Archaic period is attested by the numerous examples of the city-ethnic found on dedications to Apollo and to the hero Ptoios, as well as on coins and *horoi*. Our earliest example of the city's ethnic appears on a tripod dedication from the sanctuary of Ptoios, ca. 525–500 (Jeffery 1990, 95 no. 13). Akraiphian coins display the abbreviated ethnic A from c. 500 BCE (Head 1884, 13–14; Kraay 1976, 109–110). On a fragmentary *horos* of the Late Archaic period appears [Α]κραι[φ], convincingly restored by Lauffer and dated to the sixth or fifth century (Lauffer 1980, 161–162; *SEG* XXX 440; see also Roesch 1980, 2, no. 1). For Akraiphia's status as a *polis*, see Hansen and Nielsen 2004, 437–438; M. Hansen 1996, 73–116.

supporting two feet of a statuette. The brief inscription, which consists simply in the name of the collective and the recipient divinity in the dative case (Βοιοτοί | Προναίαι), was marked on two sides of the small base, one word on a side.[10] From the forms of the *nu* and the *alpha*, Ducat dates the stone ca. 500–470 BCE.[11] The dedication is to Athena Pronaia, a divinity commonly worshipped in central Greece alongside Apollo. Judging from the position of its cuttings, the base probably supported a small bronze Athena in a warrior pose.[12] The Boiotian sanctuary of Apollo Ptoios and Athena Pronaia was of local and regional importance, as epigraphic and sculptural material suggests. In addition to attracting visitors from Akraiphia and other nearby Boiotian communities, the sanctuary received dedications from outside the region, the most famous of which were given by Alkmaion, son of Alkmaionides of Athens, and by Hipparchos, son of Peisistratos.[13] Many of the *kouroi* and *korai* from the Ptoion are of fine local craftsmanship, but also dedicated were a number of significant Naxian, Parian, and Athenian pieces.[14] Thus, the Boiotian dedication to Athena Pronaia from this sanctuary explicitly promotes the association of the collective Boiotians with Athena at a significant regional cult center.

A convincingly restored and comparative text from the same sanctuary of Apollo appears on the rim of a small bronze vase: Βο[ιοτοὶ ᾿Αθαναῖ τ]αῖ Προναίαι. As Ducat suggests, other restorations are possible, but none radically alters the text: Βο[ιοτοὶ ᾿Αθαναι]αι Προναίαι or Βο[ιοτοί τ᾿ Αθαναι]αι Προναίαι.[15] As Ducat did not publish a photograph or facsimile of the piece, one must rely on his firsthand view that the piece is clearly archaic.[16] If accepted, then here again, the Boiotians associate themselves with Athena in an Apolline context.

An additional inscription from the sanctuary deserves brief mention, although its poor preservation prevents its secure connection to the Boiotian collective. The piece, a column dated ca. 500, shows: [ἀνέ]θειαν τ᾿ ᾿Αθᾶναι.[17] In light of the other two dedications by the Boiotians to Athena from this sanctuary, the plural [ἀνέ]θειαν is suggestive, although the dedicators of this piece remain unknown.

From the sanctuary of the Akraiphian hero Ptoios comes a third dedication attributable to the Boiotians, unfortunately mentioned by Ducat only in a foot-

---

[10] Athens NM 7394; Ducat 1971, 409.257, plate CXLI. Dimensions: 4.95 x 5.5 cm; found in 1885 (Holleaux 1885, 523).

[11] Ducat 1971, 410.

[12] On the suggestion of Dr. Catherine M. Keesling (pers. comm.), after Ducat 1971, 409.

[13] For Akraiphian dedications, see Ducat 1971, 355, no. 202 and 411, no. 260; for Theban dedications, see Ducat 1971, 201, no. 124 and 379, nos. 232–233. For Alkmaion's dedication, see Ducat 1971, 242, no. 141; Schachter 1994, 291–306; S. Larson 2002, 209 and n. 66, 210–211. For Hipparchos' dedication, see *IG* I³ 1470; Ducat 1971, 251, no. 142 and 252–258; Jeffery 1990, 7,8 no. 38; Schachter 1994, 291–306, esp. 304; S. Larson 2002, 209 and n. 66, 210–214.

[14] See Ducat 1971; Schachter 1981–1994, vol. 1, 52–73.

[15] Ducat 1971, 419.269a.

[16] Ducat 1971, 419.

[17] Ducat 1971, 396.249.

note.[18] However, here Ducat likens the piece to the first inscription on the base for the statuette, although he does not give a reading of the text. Nonetheless, if we tentatively accept his comparison, we have a total of three relatively secure and one possible epigraphic connections between the Boiotians and Athena from the Boiotian sanctuaries of Apollo Ptoios and the local hero Ptoios, all of which date roughly to the Late Archaic and Early Classical periods.[19]

Because these pieces were composed and set up in a Boiotian environment by the group itself, they reflect Boiotian self-representation at the turn of the sixth century. The origin of these dedications in sanctuaries and their association with the goddess Athena reveals a collective which was perceived of internally as partially founded and publicized in cult.

Given these internal links between the Boiotians and Athena, evidence for archaic pan-Boiotian celebration at the sanctuary of Athena Itonia near Koroneia merits brief comment.[20] Although secure evidence for pan-Boiotian worship at the site does not appear until the late fourth century BCE, certain factors support identifying the Itonion as pan-Boiotian by the late sixth and early fifth centuries.[21] First, the sanctuary and festival appear to have been widely known by this time, as a fragment from Alkaios attests:

ἄνασσ᾽ Ἀθανάα πολε[. . . . . .]
ἄ ποι Κορωνήας † ἐπιδεω- †
ναύω πάροιθεν ἀμφι[. . . . . .]
Κωραλίω ποτάμω πὰρ ὄχθαις.

Goddess Athena, [. . . . . .]
who Koroneia . . .
Before the temple [. . . . . .]
On the banks of the Koralios river.[22]

The poet's detailed knowledge of the name of the river near Koroneia suggests widespread non-Boiotian familiarity with the sanctuary, a likely effect of large

[18] Ducat 1971, 448, n. 5 (no photograph). Guillon does not refer to this piece in his 1943 study of the hero Ptoios' sanctuary (Guillon 1943).

[19] That these types of Boiotian dedications have been found only at these two northeastern sanctuaries does not reflect a pattern in dedication or a particular interest by the Boiotians in these two religious sites alone. Surely more excavation in Boiotia would reveal further dedications by the group at other important archaic sanctuaries of Athena and Apollo, e.g., the Theban Ismenion, the Tilphossion, the Alalkomenion (for the possibility of a new collective Boiotian dedication from Thebes, see Whitley 2005, 46). Moreover, these dedications are not the only offerings to Athena Pronaia from our two sites: Holleaux found numerous inscribed archaic pottery and bronze fragments dedicated to Athena Pronaia at the sanctuary of Apollo (Holleaux 1887, 1–5 and plate 7).

[20] For a collection of the evidence, see Schachter 1981–1994, vol. 1, 117, 122–127.

[21] Most scholars generally accept this possibility, e.g., Farnell 1921, 301; Schachter 1981–1994, vol. 1, 119, 122–123; Schachter 1978, 81–107.

[22] Alk. fr. 324 Voigt (fr. 147 Page; fr. 325, Lobel and Page 1955, 264); Strabo quotes Alkaios (Strabo 9.2.29); for commentary, see Lobel and Page 1955, 268–269; Schachter 1981–1994, vol. 1, 119.

non-local celebrations there. Bacchylides too refers to Athena Itonia (in terms of musical performance), and Pindar mentions the Itonion alongside the famed sanctuaries of Onchestos and Olympia in praising the illustrious family of the Theban Agasikles:

τί-   41
μαθεν γὰρ τὰ πάλαι τὰ νῦν
τ᾽ ἀμφικτιόνεσσιν
ἵππων τ᾽ ὠκυπόδων πο[λυ-
γνώτοις ἐπὶ νίκαις,
αἷς ἐν ἀϊόνεσσιν Ὀγχη[στοῦ κλυ]τᾶς,   46
ταῖς δὲ ναὸν Ἰτωνίας α[. . . . . . .]α
χαίταν στεφάνοις ἐκό-
σμηθεν ἔν τε Πίσα περιπ[

For long ago and still today they have been honored
by their neighbors for famed victories of their swift horses
by which they decorated their hair with garlands
on the shores of famous Onchestos and at the
temple of Itonia and in Pisa ... [23]

Although Pindar celebrates a Theban family here, his juxtaposition of the Itonion with the renowned sites of Olympia and Onchestos reflects the fame of Athena's Koroneian cult. That Pindar includes the Itonion in an *epinikion* for a Theban family suggests that victories won there were considered of local importance for aristocrats of the region. Further, his use of τὰ πάλαι (42) implies that these contests were the kind which Agasikles' family had been winning for some time, perhaps for generations. Together, then, these fragments from Alkaios and Pindar indicate that the Itonion enjoyed wide popularity during the Archaic period, perhaps particularly among local aristocrats, but also outside Boiotia.

A series of mid-sixth-century black-figure Boiotian vases thought to have been produced by a single workshop further confirms the Itonion's local significance.[24] Many of the vases depict festival scenes, including boxers, chariot races, runners, horsemen, tripods, flute players, and figures bearing garlands and oinochoai. A lekane from the British Museum which most scholars accept as depicting a sacrificial procession for Athena Itonia has received much attention in this context.[25] Athena as a warrior goddess, brandishing a spear and a shield,

---

[23] Bacchyl. fr. 15 Snell; Pind. fr. 94b, 41–49 (an *epinikion* for performance at the *daphnephorikon* at the Theban Ismenion); see Schachter 1981–1994, vol. 1, 119.

[24] Lekanoi, skyphoi, tripod-pyxides, lekythoi, spout vases, and kantharoi. A. Ure argued that a single workshop produced these vases (based on fabric) and linked them to the Itonion (A. Ure 1929, 160–171, esp. 167–170 and plates 9–13); also see P. Ure 1927, 57; A. Ure 1935, 227–228; Sparkes 1967, 121; Maffre 1975, 432 (no. 1); Schachter 1981–1994, vol. 1, 119–120; Kilinski 1990, 45. For other vases connected to worship of Itonia, see Schachter 1981–1994, vol. 1, 117–118, esp. on four pieces from the Louvre (*CVA France* 26 *Louvre* 17).

[25] BM B80. For bibliography on this important vase, see T. Smith 2004, 18, n. 63 and Schmidt 2002, 51–63, esp. 51–54.

stands in front of a large snake, thought to represent her chthonic consort.[26] Behind the snake rises a tall column topped by a krater. A burning altar topped by a perching crow (κορώνη) stands before Athena. As A. Ure first discussed, the crow's presence strongly indicates that the vase depicts Athena Itonia from Koroneia.[27] A priestess carrying a tray bearing offerings approaches the altar followed by a man leading a sacrificial bull. The rest of the figures on the lekane comprise the festival procession. Men carrying garlands and oinochoai play flutes and drive wagons toward the altar.[28] To be sure, none of these details alone directly suggests that the revelers are celebrating a pan-Boiotian festival. The crow, however, likely marks the site as Koroneia, and the large number of Boiotian black-figure vases found elsewhere in Boiotia that are associated with this lekane by fabric, workshop, and design seem to indicate the widespread popularity and reputation of the site and its cult.[29] Moreover, the plentitude of pieces in this series contrasts with the relative dearth of other figural pottery from Boiotia, thereby further suggesting widespread regional familiarity with and popularity of the cult of Koroneian Athena.

That the Itonion became a cult center for the later *koinon* also recommends its identification as an earlier locus for pan-Boiotian activity. Our earliest evidence for the Itonion as a federal sanctuary is a Boiotian-Aetolian treaty of 301 BCE. It specifies that the treaty was to be displayed at shrines known to have been of religious and administrative importance for the Aetolians (Thermon and the sanctuary of Artemis Laphria) and at three Boiotian sanctuaries: the Itonion, the Alalkomenion, and the sanctuary of Poseidon at Onchestos.[30] By the late fourth century, as Roesch has shown, Onchestos had become the administrative center for the Boiotian *koinon*;[31] the Itonion remained a primary federal religious center, as did the Alalkomenion, as evident in this same inscription.[32] A sanctuary originally associated with one particular Boiotian community, as opposed to the whole region as well, would not have made a good candidate for a later federal cult center, since that community would then have held a privileged position

---

[26] Schachter 1981–1994, vol. 1, 120–121.

[27] A. Ure 1929, 170; citing Pausanias, Ure notes that κορώνη was associated with Athena by colonists from Koroneia (Paus. 4.34.4). On the associations between Athens and a variety of birds, see Bron 1992, 47–84, esp. 64–68.

[28] For similar descriptions of the scene, see A. Ure 1929, 167; Schachter 1981–1994, vol. 1, 122.

[29] See Schachter 1981–1994, vol. 1, 117–120, 122, for numerous additional vases associated with the site and cult.

[30] The treaty was also to be set up at Delphi in common (*IG* IX2 1.170). See Roesch 1982, 218 and 270; Schachter 1981–1994, vol. 1, 113, 123, 126–127. Schachter notes that other sanctuaries received federal proxeny decrees and other inscriptions as well, e.g., Oropos. However, since the Itonion, Alalkomenion, and Poseidonion all date earlier than the cult at Oropos and are grouped together on treaties such as this one, it seems best to accept them as an original group of religious sites chosen as federal religious centers (for decrees at Oropos, see Schachter 1981–1994, vol. 1, 127).

[31] Roesch 1982, 266–282; also see Schachter 1981–1994, vol. 1, 127.

[32] Schachter 1981–1994, vol. 1, 123, 126–127.

within the *koinon*. It is thus difficult to imagine the fourth-century Boiotian *koinon* choosing sites for federal festivals that had not previously played central cultic roles for the *ethnos*.

Whichever of the two candidates for the Itonion one prefers, the sanctuary would have been distinguished as a central cult site for the region through both geography and topography.[33] Its location at or near Koroneia would have made the site a convenient stopping point between *poleis* in western Boiotia. Set near the edge of what would have been lake Kopais, the Itonion would have been easy of access for those traveling east or west through the southern and central parts of the region. Most of all, the Itonion would have been located close to the main road from Thebes to Delphi, a factor which would have promoted wide access to the sanctuary.

It may be no coincidence that the Itonion was established at a locale so functional for intra-regional communication, much like centrally located cult sites in Achaia. As Morgan demonstrates, because early *ethne* were primarily organized around ideas of common kinship rather than control of territory, cult placement in Achaia focuses very little (if at all) on external regional borders. Regional cult places instead lie at central spots and "cultural junctions."[34] It seems reasonable to consider the archaic Boiotian Itonion a similar regional cult place by virtue of its location, later federal status, the festival depictions associated with the sanctuary, its fame outside Boiotia, its relevance in *epinikia* for Theban victors, and its perceived antiquity. As Schachter acknowledges, we cannot be absolutely certain of the antiquity of the sanctuary, but the evidence for the site discussed here complements the late sixth-century internal connection between the Boiotians and Athena evident in Boiotian inscriptions from the Ptoion sanctuaries.

[33] For the Itonion's location near Koroneia at the site of the modern Metamorphosis church see Foucart 1885, 428; Frazer 1898, 169–170; Pritchett 1969, 85–88; Buckler 1996, 62. The number of Hellenistic proxeny decrees of the later Boiotian *koinon* found in the immediate area of the Metamorphosis church support this identification (for these decrees, see Foucart 1885, 427–433; Fossey 1988, 326, 330–331, esp. 331; Pritchett 1969, 86; Feyel 1942, 16–18). For the alternate site, just north of Koroneia's acropolis, where brief excavations yielded a mid-sixth-century building and high quality pottery, see Spyropoulos 1973, 385–392, 394; Spyropoulos 1973b, 5–6; Spyropoulos 1972, 317–338; Roesch 1982, 221; Schachter 1981–1994, vol. 1, 119; Krentz 1989, 313–317. Despite the existence of a boundary stone and some inscribed rooftiles, one of which reads -ΘΑΝ-, the evidence is insufficient in determining the divinity to whom this sanctuary belonged (for these pieces, see Krentz 1989, 313–317, esp. 315; for the rooftiles and boundary stone, see also Schachter 1981–1994, vol. 1, 119 and n. 3; Fossey 1988, 331). For the few third-century public inscriptions found there, which are exclusively local in character, see Roesch 1982, 221; Schachter 1981–1994, vol. 1, 119; Lauffer 1976, 15–17, no. 8; Fossey 1988, 331. Wallace has put forward a third candidate for the sanctuary of Athena Itonia, but as Krentz notes, there is no physical evidence for Wallace's site and it thus must be discarded (Wallace 1979, 115–116; Krentz 1989, 314).

[34] Morgan 1991, 142–144. Morgan notes that while boundaries of material culture reflect the geographic and natural borders in Achaia, there are few or no markers of focus at external cultural borders. See also Morgan 1997, 174.

From Delphi, the earliest epigraphic attestation of the collective regional ethnic Βοιωτοί from outside the region corroborates this picture by testifying to Boiotian interest in linking the collective to the cult of Athena at a panhellenic location.[35] Since Marcadé's work on signatures (1953), this inscription has been grouped with a set of stones bearing artists' names, but a reassessment of the piece allows its recategorization and reinterpretation:

[——] καὶ Τριτο̣ [——]
[——] κἐποίεσαν [——]
[Β]οιοτοὶ χαλ[——]

The stone seems to have been a flat square or rectangular base with the dedication inscribed on the top face orthograde and in three concentric circles. The white marble measures from 0.055 m. to 0.076 m. in height, depending on the point at which one measures; despite this variation, the piece would have lain flat atop a smooth surface. Although Marcadé provides measurements of 24 cm. width and depth, it is difficult to determine the minimum original width or depth (thickness) of the stone, since, aside from the preservation of one corner, the piece was later reused and cut into a circular shape, as visible in Marcadé's original photograph. This later use destroyed most of three of the stone's four sides; only the bottom corner of the stone below the concentric inscription is relatively preserved. Furthermore, all three lines of the extant inscription are now incomplete. Despite this damage, the generally small measurements of the stone in terms of height and letter height (0.025 m) suggest that the piece would have been relatively small of stature, at least on its own.

Marcadé dates the inscription to the fifth century, but the letter forms as a group rather point toward a sixth-century date. The *E* here resembles earlier types, as do the *K* and *N*.[36] The four-barred *Σ* suggests an early date indeed, for in early Boiotian script, the three-barred *sigma* occurs only a few times before 550, becoming the standard form only after that date.[37] The tailless *P*, seen here in Τριτο̣-, is the more common form in Boiotia before ca. 525 and was "normal everywhere in the Archaic period."[38] Together these letter forms suggest a date in the mid- to late sixth century. Although not conclusive, the somewhat circular fashion in which the stone is inscribed may also support this date. Thus, while this collective dedication by the Boiotians at Delphi appears to predate the dedications from the two Ptoion sanctuaries by a slight margin, all these collective pieces seem to have been erected roughly in the second half of the sixth century.

[35] Marcadé 1953, vol. 1, 108; Delphi Museum inv. 3078. I should like to thank the Delphi Museum for allowing me to examine the stone.

[36] Jeffery 1990, 89. These forms also correspond with the early versions of these letters from other regions of central and northern Greece: Attika, Euboia, Lokris, Phokis, and Thessaly.

[37] Jeffery 1990, 89. The evolution from four- to three-barred *sigma* is also evident in two sixth-century inscriptions from Halai in Opountian Lokris (Jeffery 1990, 108.7 and 8).

[38] Jeffery 1990, 80. For the tailed *rho* which occasionally appears in the sixth century, see Wachter 2001, 227; Johnston 1979, 209–210.

Before turning to the text, I note a number of possibilities for the type of dedication attached or associated with this base. The probable small size of the original base and the concentric writing may suggest that the stone served as a base for a votive statuette or some other small metal object, much like the best-preserved Boiotian inscription from the Apolline Ptoion discussed above. Our best comparanda for inscribed bases for statuettes and small metal votives comes from the Athenian Acropolis, where small bronze late archaic votives often appear in the form of an armed Athena likened in name to Pheidias' fifth-century Athena Promachos.[39] These pieces are associated either with their own inscribed bronze plinths, uninscribed bronze plinths and inscribed stone bases, or inscribed stone bases with dowel marks for attaching the statuette.[40] Given the plentitude of such pieces, we may plausibly envision the Boiotian piece from Delphi as fitting into one of these latter two categories of dedications.

The inscription on the Boiotian piece from Delphi would presumably have appeared near or even have wrapped around the feet or plinth of the votive object, much like that of an early fifth-century dedicatory inscription to Athena from the Athenian Acropolis which likely carried a small bronze Athena Promachos.[41] Two additional inscriptions from the Acropolis also compare nicely to the Delphi inscription in terms of lettering wrapped around the feet of small votives: one, another early fifth-century example, whose lettering sits immediately adjacent to the dowel-holes for the feet of an Athena statuette and which curves directly around the hole for the front foot of the votive; the other, a late-sixth century bronze base for a statuette.[42] However, because neither a plinth cavity nor dowel holes are preserved on the piece from Delphi, it is impossible to tell exactly where a votive would have been placed in relation to the text. A deep depression near the beginning of the extant text, however, may indicate the general vicinity from which a votive was forcibly removed, comparable to the remainder of a dowel hole seen on a fragmentary base, also from the Athenian Acropolis and also with engraved lettering on its top.[43]

Many of the smaller dedications on the Athenian Acropolis, such as the votive statuettes, were placed inside buildings, as Raubitschek suggests for the Athenian pieces with lettering comparable to the Delphi inscription.[44] Alternatively, some were displayed outside and atop other larger votive dedications, such

---

[39] Keesling 2003, 81.

[40] For the variety in statuette bases, including many inscribed stone bases with uninscribed plinths which seem to have supported statuettes of Athena, see Keesling 2003, 84; de Ridder 1896, 209–218 (nos. 575–613). For more Athena statuettes, see de Ridder 1896, 297–314 (nos. 777–796).

[41] Raubitschek 1949, no. 313, pp. 334–335 (Athens EM 6419).

[42] For the first piece, see Raubitschek 1949, no. 314, p. 335 (with tracing); for the second, see Lazzarini 1976, 269, no. 658 and plate 2, fig. 3 (= IG I³ 533). Comparison with additional stone bases for votive statuettes is also possible: see, e.g., de Ridder 1896, 210, no. 581 (to be associated with statuette no. 781, of Athena) and de Ridder 1896, 212, no. 587.

[43] Raubitschek 1949, 335–336, no. 315.

[44] Raubitschek 1949, 334–335.

as larger bases or pillars.[45] Either situation can be envisioned for the Delphi piece. In the latter case, the piece would have likely been highly visible, given its findspot near the eastern terrace to the temple of Apollo and thus perhaps close to its original spot of erection near the entrance to the building.

That the Boiotians originally dedicated the base to a divinity is clear from a re-examination of the inscription. The first fragmentary line names a Τριτο-. The last part of the name is broken off, but the upper left arc of a round letter is legible, most prominently in Marcadé's photograph; today the stone is badly damaged in this spot but the arc remains slightly apparent. Together with the κέποίε-σαν of the second line, Marcadé originally viewed Τριτο- as the signature of the artist, but this reading seems unlikely for a number of reasons. First, there is no attested Greek name beginning with these letters until the late fifth century BCE; these names remain uncommon even after that point.[46] Second, it seems unlikely that a small statuette would have required more than one sculptor, as the plural κέποίεσαν implies. Further, the aorist plural of ποιέω only rarely appears in archaic and early classical inscriptions as a marker of plural artists and then in the unique early fifth-century context of identifying the acclaimed Athenian large-scale sculptors Kritios and Nesiotes (ἐποιεσάτεν).[47] The group of bases which bear their signatures, moreover, seems to have been inscribed by the same hand;[48] one stone-cutter at one workshop is thus responsible for the six uses of the plural term as a reference to plural sculptors.[49] This evidence casts the use of κέποίε-σαν as a marker of plural artists for the Delphic piece further into doubt and thus also the identification of Τριτο- as an artist's signature.

That Τριτο- specifies the divine epithet of the divinity to whom the Boiotians originally dedicated the base seems the most likely possibility. As a first candidate, Marcadé tentatively suggests Τριτοπάτωρ.[50] Although Τριτοπάτωρ does not occur in archaic literature, it is attested on numerous archaic inscriptions. The name refers to ancestors "of the third degree back," and was meant to recall the "indefinite remoteness" of a group's predecessors.[51] The term may not be restricted to Attica, as once thought, but rather a "zone of shared cult-practices that encompassed the central and western Aegean."[52] The possibility that the Boiotians made this dedication to Τριτοπάτωρες seems unlikely, however. First, we have no extant dedications to Τριτοπάτωρες; the term occurs solely on *horoi*,

---

[45] For placement of the small bronzes from the Athenian Acropolis see Keesling 2003, 84; for examples of such offerings see, e.g., Raubitschek 1949, 332–335 and no. 331.

[46] Τριτώ (see *IG* II² 12824; Osborne and Byrne 1994).

[47] See Lazzarini 1976, 211 (no. 235), 265 (no. 628), 269 (no. 661), and 282 (no. 746). Also relevant are Raubitschek's two restorations of the plural ἐποιεσάτεν for the same artists (see Raubitschek 1949, 129–130, no. 122, and 178–179, no. 161).

[48] Raubitschek 1949, 129. For more on Kritos and Nesiotes, see Raubitschek 1949, 513–517.

[49] For this same stone-cutter, see also Raubitschek 1949, 516, and nos. 114 and 119.

[50] Marcadé 1953, vol. 1, 108.

[51] Farnell 1921, 355.

[52] Jameson et al. 1993, 111; for a list of Athenian examples, see Malkin 1987, 210–212.

calendars, and sacred laws.[53] Second, the Boiotians made this dedication at Delphi, not in Boiotia, the region where one might more naturally expect the group to express an association with ancestral figures of regional and collective significance. Also and most important, to my knowledge the term Τριτοπάτωρες is not attested in Boiotian inscriptions or literature. Despite its occasional use elsewhere in Greece, the overriding connection between the term Τριτοπάτωρες and Athens or Athenian-influenced places is still strong.

A better prospect for the fragmentary epithet on the Boiotian inscription, and one which Marcadé also briefly suggested, is Τριτογένεια, an epithet of Athena attested in both archaic epic, Hesiod, an Athenian *scholion*, the pseudo-Hesiodic *Aspis*, and numerous archaic and early classical Athenian inscriptions.[54] Most significant in this context is the appearance of Τριτογένεια at *Aspis* 197 in describing Athena as depicted on Herakles' shield. Since the *Aspis* is thought to be a sixth-century Theban work, the poem thus reflects usage of the epithet concurrent with the collective Boiotian dedication from Delphi. Given the provenience of the inscription outside Boiotia at a panhellenic sanctuary where both Athena and Apollo were worshipped, and in light of well-known Boiotian connections to Athena from within the region, it thus seems reasonable to accept Τριτογένεια as the best reconstruction for the damaged epithet.[55]

The χαλ- of the final line probably indicates the material from which the dedicatory statue was manufactured. Marcadé suggests χαλϙ-, bronze, and thus clearly himself understood the first letter, which appears to be a Ψ on the stone, as a Χ instead, presumably the Boiotian and Chalcidian form of Χ. This interesting form of Χ, indicated on the stone by three lines reaching a common central point and then broken away, is indicated in Marcadé's text by a downward arrow, a symbol which does not indicate a shift in direction of the inscription but rather a problem in Marcadé's ability to print this form of the capital Χ. Today the stone is badly damaged in this spot but each of the three lines of the Boiotian/Chalcidian Χ is still visible on the stone.

The appearance of this type of Χ does not seem unusual, given the proximity between Euboia and Boiotia and the possible influences between the two regions

---

[53] See Jameson et al. 1993, 107–112.

[54] *Il.* 4.515, 8.39, 22.183 (identical with 8.39); *Od.* 3.378; Hes. *Theog.* 895 (where the epithet appears with one of Athena's better known epithets, *glaukopis*); Athenian *scholion* 884 (Campbell 1982); pseudo-Hesiodic *Aspis* 197. For the term on Athenian inscriptions, see, e.g., Lazzarini 1976, 183 (no. 24; Raubitschek 1949, no. 115), 184 (no. 32; Raubitschek 1949, no. 66), 186 (no. 49; Raubitschek 1949, no. 372), 263 (no. 619; Raubitschek 1949, no. 227), 272, (no. 682; Raubitschek 1949, no. 133).

[55] See Schachter 1981–1994, vol. 1, 111–124 (on Athena in general), 111–114 (Athena Alalkomeneia), 117–127 (Athena Itonia), 59–60 and 69 (Athena Pronaia at the Ptoion); see also the concluding remarks below. That the name Τριτογένεια continued to have salience within Boiotia is indicated by the existence of a stream called Triton near the sanctuary of Athena Alalkomeneia, which, as Pausanias records, was named so in order to explain the epithet (Paus. 9.33.7; see Schachter 1981–1994, vol. 1, 114 and n. 1). Although one can only speculate about the identity of any other divinities to whom the base from Delphi was dedicated, it is possible, if not likely, that the base included Apollo as well as Athena, for the Boiotians dedicated it to a plurality of figures, as evidenced by the καὶ of καὶ Τριτο-.

in script. Although it is fascinating to consider the possibility that the χαλ- of this line could mark the Chalcidians themselves as additional collective dedicators, this proposition seems unlikely. First, the dedication itself is rather small, contrary to what one might expect from a joint dedication by two relatively large communities. Second and more important, there is no known historical event from this time period in which both the Boiotians and the Chalcidians participated and from which one would expect a public offering to be dedicated at a panhellenic sanctuary. The only documented joint venture by these two parties from the late sixth century is their ignominious defeat at the hands of the Athenians in 507/6, an event which, as we have seen, was memorialized on the Athenian Acropolis with the first collective dedication by the Athenian *demos*;[56] it is impossible to accept that the Boiotians and the Chalcidians would have commemorated this disaster with a joint dedication outside their own regions. I thus understand Marcadé's χαλ- as a simple indication of the material from which the dedicatory statue was made.[57]

On this interpretation, the text mentions the divinities to whom the piece is dedicated first. It next describes the act of dedicating and concludes with the dedicators and the type of object dedicated.

[——] καὶ Τριτο̣ [——]
[——] κἐποίεσαν[——]
[Β]οιοτοὶ χαλ[——]

To ... and to Tritogeneia ...
.. dedicated ...
... the Boiotians bronze ..

It is not unreasonable for a late archaic dedication to exhibit such order. There are in fact a variety of similarities between this inscription and other dedications from the Late Archaic period. I raise again the late sixth-century piece from the Akropolis which separates the identities of the dedicators from the name of the divinities to whom the piece is given:[58]

[56] *IG* I³ 501; *SEG* 31.28; Meiggs and Lewis 1988, no. 15; see Hdt. 5.77; Keesling 2003, 53–54 and fig. 17.

[57] Specification of dedicatory material in bronze was often indicated in inscriptions, at least from the fourth century on (see *SEG* XXXVIII 143.14, 304/3 BCE; *SEG* XXVIII 60.96, 270/69 BCE; *SEG* XLII 138, second century BCE; *SEG* XLI 59, 186/5 BCE; *SEG* XLVII 357.9, late second/early first century BCE; *SEG* XXIX 752.4, first half of first century BCE). Bronze was so often specified that modern restorations often pair some form of χάλκεος/χαλκοῦς with εἰκών or στήλη (see, e.g., *SEG* XL 335, 375–350 BCE; *SEG* XXXI 84, end of fourth century; *SEG* XXXVIII 112.45, ca. 135 BCE).

[58] Lazzarini 1976, 285, no. 760. For other inscriptions with relevant word order, see Lazzarini 1976, nos. 713, 749, 669, 680–681. For public dedications by other collective groups, see e.g., Lazzarini 1976, nos. 885–921 (some of which come from *poleis* in Boiotia: Thebes, no. 903; Koroneia, no. 916; Akraiphia, nos. 917–919).

[- - :: Θα]ρελείδες :: Θοπείθες :: [ἐ]πόιον :: 'Α[θεναίαι :: τὸν βο]μόν

Thareleides ... Thopeithes ...made ... to Athena ... the altar

Given such variety, the proposed rereading of the Boiotian inscription from Delphi seems reasonable.

Together with the extant text, then, I suggest a brief and simple restoration of the inscription; line 2 follows Marcadé:

'Απόλλονι] καὶ Τριτο[γένειαι
ἀνέθεν] κἐποίεσαν[——]
[Β]οιωτοὶ χαλκ[ὸν δῶρον

With this reassessment, this piece corroborates the cultic portrait that the Boiotians promoted to each other during this same period, as documented both inside Boiotia at the Ptoion sanctuaries and also by the evidence associated with the sanctuary of Athena Itonia near Koroneia, as we have seen. That the Boiotians chose to emphasize this same relationship at panhellenic Delphi indicates the importance of this cultic aspect of the Boiotian collective, since dedications there were highly public and surely intended for more numerous and varied viewers than inscriptions from local sanctuaries inside Boiotia. Together, then, this evidence offers a glimpse of Boiotian cultic identity which complements other discussions of archaic group identity through cult in mainland Greece as well as previous scholarship on Boiotian cult.[59]

B. The Early to Mid-Fifth Century

Pindar

In the first half of the fifth century Pindar uses the collective regional ethnic and the adjectival ethnic four times: two of these examples buttress Boiotian internal use of the collective ethnic in a cultic context; in the other two instances the adjectival ethnic appears as part of a slanderous cliché against the Boiotians. Accordingly, I treat the latter two instances of the ethnic in my later discussion of external use, since in these examples Pindar reacts against outsiders' perceptions and characterizations of the Boiotians. Given the internal sources' concentration on Boiotian cult, I thus consider first the Boiotian ethnics which Pindar ties to religion. Together these two examples suggest that both the Boiotians and Pindar's panhellenic audience conceived of the group as a partially cultic entity by the second quarter of the fifth century BCE.

In *Olympian* 7 Pindar celebrates the boxing victory of Diagoras of Rhodes at the games of 464 BCE. In the middle of the fifth strophe, the poet describes the festive procession for Tlepolemos, the founder of Rhodes, as well as Tlepolemos' festival contests in which Diagoras has twice been victorious (lines 80–1: πομπᾷ

---

[59] Particularly Mackil 2003; Morgan 2002; Nielsen 2002; McInerney 1999; Nielsen and Roy 1999; Schachter 1981–1994.

... ἀέθλοις). Pindar continues by listing the numerous other games where Diagoras was victor: Isthmian, Nemean, Athenian, Argive, Arkadian. Diagoras' prolific victories force Pindar to introduce "some variety into this potentially wearisome list."[60] In doing so Pindar mentions the blossoms of victory crowns in reference to the Isthmian, Nemean, and Athenian games (80–82); he associates Argive games with their bronze victory prize (χαλκός, 83), as he does for the Theban and Arkadian festival games (τά τ᾽ ἐν Ἀρκαδίαι | ἔργα καὶ Θήβαις, 83–84).[61] Here Pindar also directly mentions festivals in Boiotia: ἀγῶνες τ᾽ ἔννομοι | Βοιωτίων (84–5). He concludes by referring to games in Pellana, Aigina, and Megara (86–87).

Notably, this passage mirrors some of the previous results seen in the *Iliad's* relatively extensive treatment of the Boiotians in comparison with other central Greek groups.[62] With the exception of the ἀγῶνες τ᾽ ἔννομοι Βοιωτίων, Pindar refers to all the festivals and associated prizes in the passage simply in terms of topography and region: τόθι (Rhodes, 77), ἐν Ἰσθμῷ (81), Νεμέᾳ (82), κρανααῖς ἐν Ἀθάναις (82), ἐν Ἄργει and ἐν Ἀρκαδίᾳ (83), Θήβαις (84), Πέλλανά τ᾽ Αἴγινα (86), ἐν Μεγάροισίν (86). In contrast, the ἀγῶνες τ᾽ ἔννομοι Βοιωτίων are not connected to a specific location; Pindar instead ties them to the Βοιώτιοι (Βοιωτίων), as indicated by the plural adjectival ethnic. Of all the agonistic festivals Pindar mentions, then, only these games are explicitly connected to a human collective; the contrast between this portrayal of Boiotian ἀγῶνες and the other geographically indicated festivals is thus notable.

But which Boiotian festivals is Pindar specifying? The poet's omission of topographical references indicates that his audience was expected to have automatically known where the ἀγῶνες τ᾽ ἔννομοι Βοιωτίων took place. It is improbable that the ἀγῶνες were Theban. Pindar mentions both games at Thebes as well as local Boiotian games; this separation distinguishes the ἀγῶνες ἔννομοι Βοιωτίων from the Theban festivals and suggests that the ἀγῶνες were well-known pan-Boiotian games.[63] A likely candidate, of course, is thus the Pamboiotia, a festival which celebrated the divinity to whom the Boiotians linked themselves in inscriptions both internally and externally, as we have seen. The multivalent meaning for the term ἔννομοι may also support identifying one of the ἀγῶνες ἔννομοι as the Pamboiotia. It is possible to derive ἔννομοι from νομός, "habitation" or "district," thereby signifying "regional festivals of the Boiotians" with the phrase ἀγῶνες τ᾽ ἔννομοι Βοιωτίων. At the same time, the term ἔννομοι raises associations with νόμος, "custom," thereby additionally suggesting "customary" and "calendrical."[64] The phrase ἀγῶνες τ᾽ ἔννομοι Βοιωτίων thus may

---

[60] Willcock 1995, 130.

[61] The ἔργα were probably bronze tripods or some sort of bronzework, as Willcock notes (Willcock 1995, 131); for ἔργα as a bronze lebes or tripod in Pindar, also see Rumpel 1883, 176; as simply a "work of art," see Slater 1969b, 195, meaning no. 2.

[62] See Chapter Two.

[63] Willcock 1995, 131.

[64] Willcock suggests this meaning on analogy with the use of the noun νομός in the same poem at line 32 (Willcock 1995). *LSJ* defines ἔννομοι primarily as a derivation from νόμος:

not only include the Pamboiotia but also other well-known regional festivals in Boiotia in which the Boiotians participated, e.g., the festivals of Poseidon Onchestios at Onchestos and the Greater Daidala at Plataia.[65] However, given the fame of the Pamboiotia outside Boiotia, it is likely that at least one of the festivals signified here was meant to be that celebration. At any rate, the adjectival ethnic in Pindar's phrase ἀγῶνες τ' ἔννομοι Βοιωτίων indicates a cultural community, identified on religious grounds. This link recalls and reaffirms the cultic affiliation between the Boiotian collective and Athena evident in their own use of the collective ethnic in epigraphic and cultic contexts from the late sixth century.

Pindar reinforces this connection again as he catalogues various myths about human origins; the first few lines of this fragmentary passage concern a Boiotian tale, linked to the collective by Pindar's only use of the collective regional ethnic (as opposed to its adjectival form):

εἴτε Βοιωτοῖσιν Ἀλαλκομενεὺς λίμ-
    νας ὑπὲρ Καφισίδος
πρῶτος ἀνθρώπων ἄνεσχεν.

Whether for the Βοιωτοί Alalkomeneus emerged
as the first man over lake Kopais.[66]

The characterization of the Boiotians here seems at first no more than a collective indication, since the poet does not qualify the ethnic term. However, further consideration of the story of Alalkomeneus reveals collective ties to the goddess Athena.

Pindar includes Alalkomeneus alongside other first men; in later versions of Alalkomeneus' story this categorization still holds. Pausanias reports that some people believed the *polis* Alalkomenai was named after Alalkomeneus,[67] but most notably, Alalkomeneus is associated with Athena. In this same passage, Pausanias reports that the autochthon Alalkomeneus was raised by the goddess herself (ὑπὸ τούτου δὲ Ἀθηνᾶν τραφῆναι λέγουσιν).[68] The small community of Alalkomenai was famous for its cult of Athena, in fact; testimonia for this link go back well into the Archaic period.[69] Stephanos of Byzantium later even attributed the founding of this cult of Athena to Alalkomeneus.[70] In light of the significance of Athena to the Boiotians attested in the inscriptions discussed above, Pindar's story of Alalkomeneus as a Boiotian first man points to a special relationship

---

"lawful, legal." However, *LSJ* allows room for a relationship between ἔννομοι and the verb νέμομαι; see also Chantraine for a connection between νόμος, νέμω, and νομός (Chantraine 1999, 742–743).

[65] For these festivals, see Schachter 1981–1994; Schmidt 2002, 39–49 (Daidala).

[66] Page, *PMG*, Lyrica Adespota, fr. 67b, 1–3.

[67] Paus. 9.33.5: γενέσθαι δὲ αὐτῇ τὸ ὄνομα οἱ μὲν ἀπὸ Ἀλαλκομενέως ἄνδρος αὐτόχθονος.

[68] Pausanias is not specific about his source and merely uses the plural λέγουσιν.

[69] See *Il.* 4.8 and 5.908 (where the reference may simply be topographic); Bacchyl. fr. 15a Snell; later ancient writers considered the cult a very old one (Paus. 9.33.5–7; Strabo 9.2.29).

[70] Steph. Byz. s.v. *Alalkomenion*.

between the collective Boiotians and a Boiotian figure closely associated with
Athena; this relationship strengthens the late archaic internal depiction of the
group as a collective partially centered on the goddess.

Epigraphic Evidence

Also from the first half of the fifth century, perhaps before the Persian Wars,
comes the second epigraphic attestation of the collective regional ethnic Βοιωτοί.
A small limestone *telamon* from Delphi bears the text: Βοιωτῶν Ι Λοϙρῶν.[71]
Immediately below the inscription lies an indented rectangular field for adhering
a now lost metal plaque.

Bousquet's suggested archaic date for the stone is problematic, since the
short inscription provides few diagnostic letters. Based on the forms of the B and
P it is possible, however, as Knoepfler suggests, that the stone dates before the
Persian Wars. The Λ, presumably a Phokian form of the later Phokian type, may
also indicate a date in the first quarter of the fifth century, although the letter is
not well-preserved on the highly picked and somewhat damaged surface of the
block.[72] Bousquet otherwise assigns the stone only generally to the fifth century,
however.

Both Bousquet and Knoepfler suggest that the collective term Λοκροί specifies either the Epiknemidian or Hypoknemidian Lokrians. Nielsen has shown,
however, that the collective Λοκροί does not always indicate East Lokrians,
especially when the collective ethnic "is used as a heading in lists of various
kinds." The plural ethnic, moreover, often designates the entirety of the Lokrian
ethnos and not its various subgroups.[73] In light of such usage and given the
absence of the metal plaque which would likely have revealed additional detail
about this commemoration, it is impossible to pinpoint which if any subgroup of
Lokrians the term designates on this Delphic inscription. It is preferable, then, to
read the term as a general designation of the Lokrian *ethnos*. In the absence of any
additional information for the collective ethnic Βοιωτοί, we probably should
conclude similarly about the Boiotians here.

The most that can be adduced from the ethnics on this particular stone, then,
is that the two groups observed some sort of relationship and that the ethnics
referred to the larger *ethne* as they were known outside Boiotia and Lokris in the
first half of the fifth century. That they were military or political groups is not a
foregone conclusion by any means. From the extant evidence for late archaic
internal use of the Boiotian collective regional ethnic discussed above and from
the findspot of this stone at Delphi, it seems more reasonable to suggest that the
Boiotians here were understood as a collective with cultic overtones. A *telamon*

---

[71] *SEG* XLI 506; Delphi mus. inv. no. 6753; Knoepfler 1992, 422, no. 15; Bousquet 1991,
167–168 (with photograph). For a discussion of the term *telamon*, see Stroud 1984, 208–209.

[72] For the letter forms, see Jeffery 1990, 89, 99–100, 104–105.

[73] Nielsen 2000, 96. Notably, many of the cases in which the collective ethnic indicates the
East Lokrians derive from literary accounts (see Nielsen 2000, 96, n. 40).

from the Argive Heraion, dated 460–450, which lists tribal *hieromnamones* may offer comparison, although we can only speculate that the Boiotian and Lokrian dedication may have concerned a topic similar to this contemporary Argive piece.[74]

In analyzing group affiliation, the regional ethnic takes on perhaps its greatest significance when used to denote an individual member of a larger collective; I thus now present Boiotian use of the regional adjectival ethnic as a personal marker of collective identity for single individuals from the early to mid-fifth century.

As one might expect, inside the geographic region of Boiotia the adjectival ethnic, Βοιώτιος, is not used in marking individuals, since Boiotians had no need to publicize similarity to their fellow inhabitants in this way. Such is the use of regional ethnics within other regions of Greece. Archaic gravestones from Boiotia identify the deceased by name only; in many areas of Boiotia this system continues through the Classical and Hellenistic periods.[75] Even where there was extra space on the stone, such as we see in the Tanagran epitaph of Dermis and Kitylos, ca. 600 BCE, the regional ethnic does not occur.[76] Only rarely does a patronymic occur.

Outside Boiotia, individuals from the region identify themselves exclusively through their city ethnics during the Archaic and Early Classical periods, as evidenced in the Olympic victor lists. No Boiotian victor is specified by the adjectival ethnic Βοιώτιος until the 121st games of 296 BCE;[77] the only other Βοιώτιος appears in the 146th games of 106 BCE.[78] Yet Boiotian athletes certainly won victories at Olympia during the Late Archaic and Early Classical periods. The first attested Boiotian victor is Pagondas, Theban winner of the quadriga race in 680 and illustrious ancestor of Agasikles, the *daphnephoros* for Apollo Ismenios celebrated by Pindar two centuries later.[79] The Olympian victor lists identify this archaic Pagondas only by his name and city ethnic.[80] Also identified by *polis* is Kleondas, Theban victor of the stadion at the 41st games in 616 BCE[81] and an unknown Theban victor of the quadriga at the 65th games in 520.[82] This pattern continues for non-Theban Boiotian victors. An aptly named Orchomenian, Asop-

---

[74] *SEG* XXXIV 289; see Richardson 1896, 42–48. Perhaps not incidentally, the collective Lokrian ethnic is also used in a late classical inscription denoting *hieromnamones* (see Nielsen 2000, 96 and n. 42).

[75] E.g., Thespiai, see Plassart 1958, 107–119; Tanagra, see Venencie 1960, 589–610.

[76] Venencie 1960, 609; on this stone, see also Richter 1949, 23.

[77] Nikon of Boiotia: Moretti 1957, 133, no. 517. It is interesting to note that the same Nikon won first place in the *pankration* in the previous Olympics of 300 BCE, but there he was identified only as being from Anthedon, a *polis* on the northeastern Boiotian coast (Moretti 1957, 132, no. 504).

[78] Mikion of Boiotia: Moretti 1957, 143, no. 604.

[79] Pind. fr. 94b, *Parthenion* 2; the poem is associated with the Theban Ismenion and the Daphnephorion by Proclus (Proclus in Photios *Bibl.* 321a 34 and 321b 23 [Bekker]).

[80] Moretti 1957, 63, no. 33.

[81] Moretti 1957, 67, no. 69.

[82] Moretti 1957, 76, no. 136.

ichos, won the stadion at the 73rd games in 488, for example;[83] the name Asopichos suggests that he was Boiotian, yet the text does not identify him as
Βοιώτιος. In fact, Asopichos' identification by *polis* here could lead to some
confusion between the Boiotian settlement Orchomenos and the Arkadian Orchomenos, yet the regional ethnic is still not included. A Thespian, Polynikos, a
victor in 448, is likewise specified only by his city-ethnic.[84] This evidence together points toward a pervasive lack of interest on the part of Boiotian victors in
identifying themselves to foreigners at Olympia in terms of their regional affiliation throughout the Archaic and Early Classical periods. To Boiotians at this
time, *polis* identity was the stronger personal association to be presented outside
the region.

I thus now consider the first internal attestation of the personal adjectival
ethnic Βοιώτιος, found on a dedication from Delphi.[85] The cuttings on its upper
surface suggest that the stone formed the base for a bronze statue.[86] The inscription on its front face reads:

['Ε]πίδαλλος τὀπό[λλονι]
Βοιότιος = ἐχς Ἐρχ[ομένο]
[h]υπατόδορος = Ἀρισστ[ογείτον]
ἐποιεσάταν Θεβαῖο.[87]

Here, Ἐπίδαλλος explicitly identifies himself as an individual Βοιότιος from
Orchomenos. This personal use indicates that by the time of this dedication, the
ethnic adjective helped in defining an individual's identity as a member of a
collective; the date of the stone is thus quite significant in establishing the time by
which the term had taken on this meaning.

---

[83] Moretti 1957, 84, no. 182,.

[84] Moretti 1957, 102, no. 302. Other Boiotian victors include a Thebaios of unknown name,
victor in quadriga, 520 BCE (Moretti no. 136); Arsilochos Thebaios, 480 BCE (Moretti no. 206);
Daitondas Thebaios, 480 BCE (Moretti no. 206); Lasthenes Thebaios, 404 BCE (Moretti no.
352); Agenor Thebaios, 360 BCE (Moretti no. 427); Dionysodoros Thebaios, 352 BCE (Moretti
no. 441); Aischylos Thespiaios, 348 BCE (Moretti no. 444); Nikon Anthedonios, 300 BCE
(Moretti no. 504); Kleitomachos Thebaios, 216 and 212 BCE (Moretti nos. 584 and 589);
Phorystas Tanagraios, unknown date (Moretti no. 1018).

[85] I omit the one earlier attestation of the adjectival ethnic from the Hesiodic *Ehoiai* where it
modifies the name of a Boiotian nymph Hyrie, most likely the local nymph who shared the name
of the *polis* Ὑρίη, as the nymph Thebe did with Thebes (Hesiod fr. 181 MW = Schol. A. *Il.*
2.496, who quotes the line out of an interest in spelling Ὑρίη). Although the use of the ethnic in
the *Ehoiai* can be technically categorized as individual use (since it appears with a personal
name), the phrase Ὑρίη Βοιωτίη does not help in determining a more specific connection
between the adjective and Boiotian collective identity, since we know nothing more about this
nymph in myth. The topographic associations of the name Hyrie also give the adjective an unmistakable geographic connotation, as we might expect within a catalogue. Give our ignorance
of Hyrie and its geographic connotations, I thus exclude this use of the regional adjective from
consideration.

[86] For a picture of what remains on top of the stone, see Marcadé 1953, vol. 1, 8.

[87] Lazzarini 1976, 228.374 (=*LSAG* 93.17; *FD* III.1, 388–389, no. 574, plate 12; Marcadé
1953, vol. 1, 8, plate 4.1).

Although in his original publication Bourguet remarked on the "archaic character" of the text and Jeffery dates the stone only tentatively to the second quarter of the fifth century, a strong argument can be made for dating the piece to the second half of the fifth century.[88] As Jeffery acknowledges, certain letter forms suggest a fifth-century date: the dotted *theta* and the late *heta* (*h*3), forms which became prevalent only after the turn of the sixth century in Boiotia.[89] The text also exhibits additional classical Boiotian forms, many of which point to a date in the second half of the fifth century. For example, the *pi*, especially the example in line four, resembles Jeffery's Π3, a type used only after the sixth century. *Beta* corresponds to Jeffery's later B2, not B1. The form of the *rho* is especially noteworthy, as it is tailed and resembles Jeffery's final rho (P4). Notably, tailed *rhos* of this type occur throughout the fifth century in Boiotia.[90] Together with the other letter forms, the existence of P4 in the second half of the fifth century suggests that Jeffery's tentative date of 470–450 is too early.[91] Marcadé's date of the second half of the fifth century is thus the most reasonable date yet proposed and should be accepted as the safest *terminus post quem* for the use of the adjectival ethnic as an individual marker of collective identity for a Boiotian.[92]

This specific use of Βοιότιος thus falls just outside the chronological scope of the present discussion; given the piece's proximity to the Late Archaic and Early Classical periods, however, it is worth briefly considering the possible meanings behind its use. Several interpretations come to mind, in light of evidence adduced in this and in previous chapters.

In this piece Βοιότιος could specify the region Boiotia as distinct from Orchomenian territory, which had been considered separate from Boiotia, as early as the Catalogue of Ships (*Il.* 2.511–516). It is noteworthy, then, that the coins of Boiotian Orchomenos did not conform to the minting and monetary practices of the other Boiotian *poleis*. Orchomenian coins depict an ear of corn, not the cutout shield, and are minted in smaller denominations than coins from the other Boiotian *poleis*, even during the second half of the fifth century, when we know from the Oxyrhynchus historian that Orchomenos was a member of the Boiotian *koinon*.[93] Orchomenian coins continue to differ until well into the fourth century.[94] The singular adjectival ethnic on this dedication may thus distinguish between the Orchomenian and the Boiotian identities of Ἐπίδαλλος, in part on regional grounds. In other words, Βοιότιος ἐχς Ἐρχ[ομένο] could indicate that

---

[88] Bourguet 1929, 388–389, no. 574 (based on use of the dual and aspiration).

[89] Jeffery 1990, 89.

[90] Jeffery 1990, 89. For the beginnings of the tailed *rho* in Boiotia, see Wachter 2001, 17–18, no. 8 and 227.

[91] Jeffery herself considers this stone of such a secure fifth-century date that she accepts its tailed *epsilons* as typical fifth-century Boiotian forms. The *chi*, since it resembles both the earliest and the latest forms in Boiotia, cannot be used to indicate a date for the text.

[92] Marcadé 1953, vol. 1, 8 (and plate 4.1).

[93] *Hell. Oxy.* 19.3 (Chambers).

[94] R. Buck 1979, 142; Head 1881, 18–19.

Ἐπίδαλλος was an inhabitant of Minyan Orchomenos but that he also claimed to be associated with those who lived in wider Boiotia. The stone would thus reflect the situation sometime before the incorporation of Orchomenian territory into Boiotia, an event which must happened after the crystallization of the *Iliad* but before the second half of the fifth century when we know Orchomenos was a member of the Boiotian federation. Given the probable date for the dedication in the second half of the fifth century, however, this reading seems less likely than some of the other possibilities.

In its use of the prepositional phrase ἐχς Ἐρχ[ομένο] the text may instead suggest that Ἐπίδαλλος was a citizen of a different *polis* in Boiotia who happened to live in Orchomenos. One would expect an actual citizen of Orchomenos to use the ethnic Ὀρχομένιος. The identification of individuals by toponym is paralleled later in lists of *theorodokoi* from the third century BCE: these hosts of ambassadors who announced festivals were listed according to where they lived, not by the *ethnika* of their home cities.[95] Although these comparanda date far later than the Ἐπίδαλλος inscription, it is worth speculating that Ἐπίδαλλος too may have served as some sort of Boiotian religious host for Minyan Orchomenos.

The simplest and most reasonable explanation for the term Βοιότιος, however, relates to the dedication's origin at Delphi. The regional ethnic was in all likelihood added to ἐχς Ἐρχ[ομένο] in order to identify Ἐπίδαλλος to the diverse panhellenic audience at the sanctuary. As a Boiotian, Ἐπίδαλλος would not have added the ethnic had he dedicated the *stele* inside Boiotia. The phrase Βοιότιος = ἐχς Ἐρχ[ομένο], then, simply indicates a citizen of Orchomenos and marks a distinction between Boiotian Orchomenos and Arkadian Orchomenos. Parallels for regional ethnics attached to personal names of Arkadians outside Arkadia and from panhellenic sanctuaries support this interpretation.[96]

At the same time, however, Epidallos' individual identification as Βοιότιος may extend beyond geographic associations and include a sense of solidarity with the Boiotian collective on additional grounds. Lazzarini has interpreted the term as an indicator of federal citizenship;[97] given the date of the piece in the second half of the fifth-century, this interpretation seems simultaneously likely. At this date, then, Ἐπίδαλλος marks himself both as a Boiotian from Orchomenos and a participant in the mid- to late fifth-century Boiotian *koinon*. This new and particular appearance of the ethnic may thus signify a change on an individual level in the internal perception of the group. At the same time, the date of the dedication prohibits us from retrojecting these or any other meanings for Βοιότιος back into the earlier decades of the fifth century. It is safe to remark, however, that this mid-fifth-century Βοιότιος Ἐπίδαλλος still seems to express a parallel interest with his late sixth-century Boiotian predecessors: a concern to display an association with the Boiotian collective through cult at Apolline sanctuaries.

---

[95] See Perlman 2000, 39.
[96] See Nielsen 1999, 24, where he cites four fifth-century examples.
[97] Lazzarini 1976, 67.

NON-BOIOTIAN USE OF REGIONAL ETHNICS (EXTERNAL USE)

Predictably, external sources using the collective regional ethnic and adjectival ethnic employ different criteria in defining the group; they do not characterize the Boiotians primarily in terms of cult. As discussed in Chapter Two, epic use of the regional ethnics, particularly in the Catalogue of Ships, suggests that outside Boiotia, the term "Boiotian," used either collectively or individually, could be understood simply to refer to inhabitants of the relatively fertile and populated geographic region, despite the relatively individuated appearance of the Boiotian Peneleos in the *Iliad*.[98] Outside this early geographic meaning, archaic and early classical external examples of the collective ethnics denote an established collective with few additional distinct characteristics, save stereotyped and humorous aspects, as attested by Pindar for panhellenic consumption.[99] I discuss these instances here chronologically.

After epic, external use of the collective regional ethnic is not attested until the final decade of the sixth century. I cite the famous Athenian dedicatory inscription erected on the Akropolis following Athens' victory over the Boiotians and Chalkidians in 507/6:

[δεσμοῖ ἐν ἀχνυόεντι (?) σιδερέοι ἔσβεσαν hύβ]ριν·
    παῖδε[ς Ἀθεναίον ἔργμασιν ἐμ πολέμο]
[ἔθνεα Βοιοτõν καὶ Χαλκιδέον δαμάσαντες]·
    τõν hίππος δ[εκάτεν Πάλλαδι τάσδ᾽ ἔθεσαν].

With iron bonds they vanquished their pride, the sons of the Athenians, by deeds in battle, when they defeated the Boiotians and Chalkidians, from whom these horses, as a tithe, they dedicated to Pallas Athena.[100]

---

[98] For these passages, see Chapter Two: 2.495; 2.510; 2.526 (this final instance of the collective ethnic in the Catalogue of Ships appears after the Phokian entry and indicates the physical proximity of the two contingents); 5.710 (the passage concerning Oresbios from Hyle); 13.685 and 13.700 (defense of the ships of the central Greek contingents); 15.330 (death of various Greek leaders at the hands of Trojans).

[99] In this section I include little about non-personal use of the adjectival ethnic Βοιώτιος, since such generic examples of the adjective do little to explicate external perceptions of the Boiotians, except perhaps to reinforce vague geographic associations. Bacchylides, for example, in a possible *skolion*, mentions Boiotian *skyphoi* full of sweet wine (Bacchyl. fr. 21; Ath. 11.500ab); a fragment from Kratinos addresses the spirits who inhabit the fertile Boiotian land of Lebadeia (Kratinos fr. 220.1; Kock 1880).

[100] *IG* I³ 501, probably destroyed by the Persians in 480 (=*SEG* XXXI 28; Meiggs and Lewis 1988, no. 15; Fornara 1977, no. 42; A. Raubitschek 1949, no. 168; translation after Fornara). The location of the monument near the statue of Athena Promachos is suggested by cuttings there which would fit the piece. As S. West, notes, however, this location does not square with Pausanias' account (Paus. 1.28.2). I am inclined to trust Herodotos on the issue, especially since he quotes the inscription *verbatim*, and to attribute Pausanias' account of the location to error. Pausanias places the monument near Pheidias' Athena. It would have been quite easy for Pausanias to incorrectly attribute the statues of Athena or even to conflate them. But the question remains open (see S. West 1985, 284–285). On ἀχνυόεντι, see S. West 1985, 283–284.

This heavily restored text depends in part on a later republication which likely commemorated Athenian victory over the Boiotians at Oinophyta in 457.[101] The restoration also relies on Herodotus' *verbatim* quotation of the republished inscription (Hdt. 5.77). These two consistent sources secure the restoration.

The dedication depicts the Boiotian collective differently from epic, our only previous external source, since the inscription defines the collective as an ἔθνος. It is thus tempting to ascribe to this piece a more specific characterization of the Boiotians. Nonetheless, the term ἔθνος does not help in determining a more precise signification behind non-Boiotian use of the ethnic. In archaic and early classical sources ἔθνος ranges in meaning from a band of friends, foreign nations, professional guilds, to even trade occupations; it often indicated nothing more than a band of comrades.[102] For example, in the *Iliad* ἔθνος designates a group of people, the λαοί, soldier-followers of Aineias and other Trojan leaders (*Il.* 13.495).[103] As late as the early fifth century the term seems no more specific. In three instances Pindar uses ἔθνος to refer generally to the entire race of mortals.[104] Even these few instances suggest that the term was a generic one which could refer to a variety of groups. Moreover, use of ἔθνος to mark a kinship group is not established until the mid-fifth century.[105] I thus observe caution in interpreting the term here.

The Athenian inscription uses the term broadly by referring to two distinct male collectives as ἔθνεα: Βοιωτοί and Χαλκιδεῖς. The Χαλκιδεῖς are members of a *polis* while the Boiotians are not. The term ἔθνος thus cannot specify the communities involved in terms of their political or military organization but rather seems to indicate inhabitants of the geographic areas specified: the *polis* Chalkis and the region Boiotia.[106] The term may also recall its use in epic where it stresses the number of people involved in an activity, thereby emphasizing the quantity of defeated Βοιωτοί and Χαλκιδεῖς and thus the notable Athenian victory. As was suggested in Chapter Three in discussing the Chalkidian staters with the cutout shield, it is possible that the Boiotians who attacked Athens consisted in an *ad hoc* mobilization of neighbors. It seems reasonable to suggest that the term ἔθνος on this inscription could refer to such a group. This inscription, then,

---

[101] See Meiggs and Lewis 1988, 29; S. West, 1985, 283; A. Raubitschek 1949, no. 173.

[102] Morgan has noted that *ethnos* often connoted no more than this and certainly did not always include the ethnic overtones modern scholars tend to associate with it; see esp. Morgan 1999, 385 and notes 15 and 16; Morgan 2003, 9–10; Siapkas 2003, 12 and n. 15; McInerney 2001, 55; also Cohen 2000, 22–30 for the term as vaguely applied to the Athenians; cf. modern Greek συγκρότημα, "group."

[103] At the same time, when applied to animals, the term implies something more than a voluntary social group – namely, an innate association as a distinct species.

[104] *Ol.* 1.66, of mortal men: τοὔνεκα προῆκαν υἱὸν ἀθάνατοί οἱ πάλιν / μετὰ τὸ ταχύποτμον αὖτις ἀνέρων ἔθνος. *Nem.* 3.73–74 , of mortals: μέρος ἕκαστον οἷον ἔχομεν / βρότεον ἔθνος. *Nem.* 11.42–43, again of mortals: καὶ θνατὸν οὕτως ἔθνος / ἄγει μοῖρα.

[105] Bakhuizen 1989, 67; also Nielsen 1999, 21.

[106] *Contra* Bakhuizen who, while acknowledging that ἔθνος connoted no "political organization, or even a cohesive union," interprets this epigram as indicating the political and military organization of a Boiotian *koinon* (Bakhuizen 1989, 67).

reveals little, if anything, about specific ethnic or federal organization in Boiotia but rather depicts the Boiotians as a populous geographic collective mobilized around the chance at acquiring new territory from Athens, in tandem with Sparta and the Chalkidians in 507/6.

In sum, then, during the Archaic period, external use of the collective region-al ethnic Βοιωτοί remains static; at the time of this Athenian inscription in 507/6, the term still seems to have been primarily a generic regional designation to those living outside Boiotia, as it had also been in the *Iliad*. Notably, in the Early Classical period Aeschylus continues to characterize the Boiotians similarly.[107]

The appearance of an Athenian stereotype of the Boiotians in Pindar, howev-er, points toward a change in external perception of the collective and thus suggests that the internal cohesion of the Boiotian collective had begun to effect their perception abroad by the Early Classical period.

This stereotype, together with the adjectival regional ethnic, first appears *Olympian* 6, an *epinikion* composed for Hagesias of Syracuse, victor in the mule race of either 472 or 468 BCE.[108] After detailing the divine ancestry of Hagesias and his connections to Arkadia (22–81), the poet begins a personal aside in which he carefully emphasizes his Boiotian pedigree:

ματρομάτωρ ἐμὰ Στυμφαλίς, εὐανθὴς Μετώπα,
πλάξιππον ἃ Θήβαν ἔτικτεν, τᾶς ἐρατεινὸν ὕδωρ
πίομαι, ἀνδράσιν αἰχματαῖσι πλέκων
ποικίλιον ὕμνον.

My grandmother was Stymphalian, the blooming Metope, who bore horse-driving Thebe, whose lovely water I drink, weaving for spear-bearing men my varied song (*Ol*. 6. 84–87).

Here Pindar focuses on the relationship between Arkadian Stymphalos and Thebes, thereby connecting himself to the *laudandus* and simultaneously praising his own Boiotian descent.[109]

Pindar continues to maintain his Boiotian character as he addresses the chorus leader, Αἰνέας. The poet first urges Αἰνέας to exhort his minstrel ἑταίρους and to praise Hera Partheneia; the chorus is then to judge whether they have evaded the reproach, "Boiotian pig:"

ὄτρυνον νῦν ἑταίρους,
Αἰνέα, πρῶτον μὲν Ἥραν Παρθενίαν κελαδῆσαι,
γνῶναί τ᾽ ἔπειτ᾽, ἀρχαῖον ὄνειδος ἀλαθέσιν
λόγοις εἰ φεύγομεν, Βοιωτίαν ὗν.

---

[107] See Aesch. *Pers*. where both uses of the regional ethnic modify the noun χθών; 482–483: στρατὸς δ᾽ ὁ λοιπὸς ἔν τε Βοιωτῶν χθονὶ/ διώλλυθ; 805–806: μίμνουσι δ᾽ ἔνθα πεδίον Ἀσωπὸς ῥοαῖς / ἄρδει, φίλον πίασμα Βοιωτῶν χθονί.

[108] The *epinikion* may have been performed in Arkadia, if the concentration on Hagesias' Stymphalian associations is any indication.

[109] Pindar claims a Boiotian pedigree in other poems performed in non-Boiotian settings: *Ol*. 10.85; *Pyth*. 2.3–4, 4.299; *Isthm*. 6.74–75, 8.16.

Urge on your comrades, Aineas,
first to praise Hera Parthenia,
and then to know if through truthful words
we escape the old slander "Boiotian pig" (*Ol.* 6. 87–90).

This exhortation has excited much debate over the performance of Pindar's *epinikia*, part of which concerns exactly whom the first person plural verb φεύγομεν specifies: the chorus, the poet, or the chorus, poet and audience together.[110] Whichever view one advocates, it is certain that a body of performers was present at the presentation of this ode, and it is partly to this group that the verb φεύγομεν refers.

It is the activity of this group that is the most significant aspect of the passage in this context: they are attempting to avoid the traditional criticism of Boiotians as piggish. This characterization implies that there were a number of Boiotians present to whom such slander will have been relevant, including Pindar himself, who has already advertised his own Theban pedigree. Whether the Boiotians number only Pindar and Αἰνέας or whether they include the rest of the performers (as well as any Boiotians present in the audience) is an interesting but ultimately tangential question. The main issue is the link between the adjectival ethnic of the slanderous cliché (Βοιωτίαν) and the plural "we" of φεύγομεν. The relationship between the ethnic and the plural verb suggests that by the time of the performance of this *epinikion* the Boiotians as a collective had become targets of this specific slander.

That such a characterization appears in a poem performed for a relatively panhellenic audience outside Boiotia suggests that the slander was well known outside the region and thus had likely been leveled against the Boiotians well before the composition of the poem. The wording ἀρχαῖον ὄνειδος ... Βοιωτίαν ὗν further implies that the specific stereotype of Boiotians as pigs had been in existence for some time. Pindar employs the term ἀρχαῖον on only one other occasion, as a reference to an undoubtedly old and highly traditional Theban tale, the myth of Herakles' youthful strangling of two snakes in his cradle.[111] Thus, although Pindar's reference to the ἀρχαῖον ὄνειδος, "Boiotian pig," can only give a *terminus ad quem* for the stereotype of 472 or 468, it is likely that this specific slander of the Boiotians was known before the composition of *Olympian* 6.[112]

[110] The verb has traditionally been understood to refer to a choral performance, as later scholiasts suggest (see Lefkowitz 1991, 196). Slater marks no distinction between a Pindaric first person singular and first person plural unless indicated by the poet. A first person verb, such as φεύγομεν, may thus indicate both the chorus and the poet collectively, the chorus alone, or simply the poet (Slater 1969, 90). Lefkowitz argues that φεύγομεν refers only to Pindar, thereby mirroring other commands in Pindar which refer to the poet himself (Lefkowitz 1991, 197). Kurke suggests that first person plural verbs include not only the poet and the chorus but also the audience (Kurke 1991, 139, n. 7).

[111] Pind. *Nem.* 1.33–36.

[112] Roller 1990, 140–141; Cartledge also posits a certain antiquity for the slander (Cartledge 2000, 402: "Already long before the time of Pindar ... the phrase 'Boiotian swine' had acquired a pejorative, anthropocentric application").

A scholiast on *Olympian* 6 comments on the history of the reproach and cites another instance of the adjectival ethnic from Pindar:

εἰ φεύγομεν, Βοιωτίαν ὗν· ὅτι διὰ τὴν ἀγροικίαν καὶ τὴν ἀναγωγίαν τὸ παλαιὸν οἱ Βοιωτοὶ ὕες ἐκαλοῦντο· καθάπερ καὶ αὐτὸς ἐν τοῖς διθυράμ-βοις· ἦν ὅτε σύας τὸ Βοιώτιον ἔθνος ἔλεγον.

"If we avoid (the reproach) Boiotian pig:" because the Boiotians were called pigs on account of their rusticity and their vulgarity of old: just as Pindar also says in his dithyrambs: "there was a time when they called the Boiotian *ethnos* swine."[113]

On the basis of this scholiast, Maehler has ascribed the final quotation of this passage to one of Pindar's dithyrambs composed for Athens.[114] The fragment is undated but given its content could tentatively be placed during the 470's around the time of *Olympian* 6.

In this context two aspects of this fragment are most significant. First, as in *Olympian* 6, the characterization of the Boiotians as pigs is taken as an old re-proach, as indicated by the adjective παλαιός with which the scholiast describes the condemnation's antiquity. The quotation from Pindar's dithyramb itself also emphasizes the stereotype's long life, since it begins with ἦν ὅτε, a phrase which immediately projects the audience back to a previous time when the cliché Βοιωτίαν ὗν was current. Pindar thus implies that the reproach existed before his time and also recalls the phrase ἀρχαῖον ὄνειδος from *Olympian* 6. Second, the Pindaric fragment is important in defining the Boiotian collective, for just as in *Olympian* 6, the adjectival ethnic is implicitly associated with the group. By mo-difying τὸ ἔθνος with the adjectival ethnic Βοιώτιον, Pindar signifies the collec-tive regional ethnic, Βοιωτοί. It is clear, then, that by the time of the dithyramb's composition, the Boiotians were considered a definite collective with enough coherence to have been recognized by outsiders as the butt of a humorous insult.

These Pindaric examples of the adjectival ethnic are significant for under-standing external perceptions of the Boiotians in several ways. They indicate that the Boiotian *ethnos* was seen as a cohesive unit by the second quarter of the fifth century at the latest, but likely earlier than *Olympian* 6 (472 or 468) if not before, as the dithyrambic fragment which hints at the age of the swine image may imply (ἦν ὅτε...). This collective was recognizable to Pindar's panhellenic audience, comprised on the relevant occasions of Rhodians, Stymphalians, and almost cer-tainly citizens from many other *poleis* and regions, including Athens. In present-ing his group to outsiders, then, Pindar utilizes a stereotype clearly accepted and promulgated by non-Boiotians and one which focuses on the gluttony and provin-cialism of the Boiotians.

Not incidentally, the Boiotian poet exonerates the Boiotian collective through brilliant use of irony. As noted above, by invoking his own Theban origins Pindar

---

[113] Schol. Vat. Pind. *Ol.* 6.90 (Drachmann 1903, 188). Also see Strabo 7.7.1, where this line of Pindar again appears.

[114] Pind. fr. 83; Maehler thus groups this fragment with fr. 75 (Maehler 1989, 83–84).

brings Boiotia into the poem; he then includes the chorus leader and chorus in this group with the plural "we" (φεύγομεν). He also links the *laudandus* and the Arkadian audience to the Thebans/Boiotians by connecting his own Boiotian pedigree to the genealogy of the Stymphalian nymph Μετώπα. It is in this setting that Pindar uses the adjectival ethnic to describe the Boiotians as pigs; the slander against them may thus now include the poet, the chorus, the *laudandus*, and the audience of the poem. With this sleight of hand Pindar does indeed escape the old slander against the Boiotians, in part because the implicated audience and the victor must also wish to avoid it. Pindar further evades accusations of piggishness by simply being a Boiotian composer and performer of *epinikia* of panhellenic reputation.

In the end, the collective Boiotians are recognizable to Pindar's panhellenic audience through a stereotyped cultural characteristic: piggishness, an image, likely coined in Athens, which connoted rustic provincialism, as additional contemporaneous sources attest.[115] In none of Pindar's examples does the adjectival ethnic indicate a political or military aspect to the group.

At this time Pindar's rival Bacchylides also adds literary tones to the collective ethnic, which he uses as an adjective at the end of his fifth *epinikion*. In urging his audience to put aside envy for the sake of truth, the poet closes the poem by referring to Hesiod:

---

[115] Plutarch, a native Chaironeian, tells us that the Athenians coined this specific cliché against the Boiotians (Plut. *De Esu Carnium*, orat. i. 6). Fifth-century sources corroborate his assertion, e.g., the Athenian comedian Kratinos, who, as noted in the Introduction, encapsulates the tradition in one word: καθάπερ ... Κρατῖνος· οὗτοι δ᾽ εἰσὶν Συοβοιωτοί, κρουπεζοφόρον γένος ἀνδρῶν ("just like Kratinos says: these men are Boiotian pigs, a group of men that wears wooden-shoes;" fr. 310 Kock 1880, 103 [= 225.153 Meineke]; see Wilkins 2000, 98). Photios' comments later clarify the link between Kratinos' term and the cliché Βοιωτίαν ὗν; Photios states: συοβοιωτοί· σύες γὰρ ἐκαλοῦντο οἱ παλαιοὶ Βοιωτοί. He also explains κρουπέζαι as ξύλινα ὑποδήματα, ἐν οἷς τὰς ἐλαίας ἐπάτουν. We thus find in Kratinos a parody of the Βοιωτοί as pigs and rustic provincials, similar to Pindar's portrayal of them in the songs performed in Arkadia and Athens. Achaios, a contemporary of Kratinos, depicts the Boiotians similarly as gluttons in his play ΑΘΛΟΙ (see fr. 3: Snell 1986, 116 [= Ath. 10.417]). By the early fourth century, this stereotype had taken on seemingly exclusive meanings of gluttony, as shown by a number of Athenian comic poets quoted by Athenaeus (see Ath. 10.417). Given the appearance of Boiotians as gluttons in Achaios, it seems possible that this characterization was common in the fifth century as well. For the contrast between the abstemious Athenian diet and the perceived self-indulgent diets of others in comedy, see Wilkins 2000, 97–98; for the differences between Old, Middle and New Comedy on this issue, see Gilula 1995, 386–387. On the Kopaic eel as a marker of licentiousness, see Wilkins 2000, 37–38 and Gilula 1995, 390–391. That the early fifth-century Boiotians were aware of this external stereotype is clear from the references to it in Pindar; that the late archaic and early classical Boiotians may have made fun of the joke may be indicated by the existence of a few outstanding pieces of Boiotian pottery which depict pigs. One example is a rather humorous one-handled kantharos/kyathos for which the potter has fashioned the missing handle into the tusked face of a boar (see Kilinski 1990, 17.2, plate 8.2; *CVA* Louvre 17, 27–28, plate 22.3–4). See also the figure vase in the shape of a boar in Berlin (Kilinski 1990, plate 11.2).

χρὴ] δ᾽ ἀλαθείας χάριν   187
αἰνεῖν, φθόνον ἀμφ[οτέραισιν
   χερσὶν ἀπωσάμενον,
εἰ τις εὖ πράσσοι βροτῶ[ν.   190

Βοιωτὸς ἀνὴρ τᾶδε φών[ησεν, γλυκειᾶν
   Ἡσίοδος πρόπολος
Μουσᾶν, ὃν <ἂν> ἀθάνατοι τι[μῶσι, τούτωι
   καὶ βροτῶν φήμαν ἕπ[εσθαι.   194

For the sake of truth it is necessary to praise,
With envy pushed away with both hands,
When a mortal man does well.
A Boiotian man said this,
Hesiod, the servant of the sweet Muses:
"The man whom immortals honor, to him
Reputation among men will follow" (Bacchyl. 5.187–194).

This reference to Hesiod as Βοιωτός is nothing unusual, since the traditional biographical connection between the *persona* of Hesiod and Boiotia was well-established by the second quarter of the fifth century. As the translation suggests, Bacchylides' quotation has even been read as an excerpt from a real Hesiodic work.[116] Bacchylides' passage certainly recalls the words of the Helikonian Muses in the *Theogony's* proem; there the poet discusses the persuasive language which empowers kings and brings them honor on earth. Bacchylides' passage also reminds the audience of Hesiod's Boiotian Muses by describing what it is necessary to do for the sake of ἀληθεία (187–190, cf. *Theogony* 27–34). Bacchylides' use of the term Βοιωτός here thus raises literary links with the traditional Hesiodic corpus; at the same time the poet evokes Hesiod's Boiotian Muses and thus, the sacred valley in which they were worshipped in the Archaic period, controlled by the *polis* Thespiai and near the hilltop settlement Askra, traditionally reputed to be Hesiod's hometown. It thus seems that it was possible to use the adjectival ethnic to denote a famous figure from Boiotian tradition, such as Hesiod, in this case, while also maintaining the canonical geographic connotations of the collective ethnic from earlier tradition.

Notably, the adjective Βοιωτός here in Bacchylides 5 may also be a personal and intertextual reference to Pindar himself. Bacchylides' fifth *epinikion* was performed in 476 in honor of Hieron's Olympic victory in the single-horse race; Pindar's first *Olympian* celebrates the same victor on the same occasion. It is entirely possible that both *epinikia* were performed at the same time, but if not, one presupposes the other. Certainly the final stanzas of Bacchylides' ode recall one of Pindar's best-known statements about truth and fiction from *Olympian* 1. There, at the beginning of his variant version of the Pelops myth, Pindar justifies its difference from previous accounts:

[116] Fr. 344 MW, accepted as a Hesiodic fragment on the basis of its similarity to *Theogony* 81–97 (Merkelbach and West 1967, note on 172).

ἦ θαύματα πολλά, καί πού τι καὶ βροτῶν
φάτις ὑπὲρ τὸν ἀλαθῆ λόγον
δεδαιδαλμένοι ψεύδεσι ποικίλοις
  ἐξαπατῶντι μῦθοι.

Indeed wonders are many, but somehow the talk of men deceives, stories
elaborated by a variety of lies beyond the true account (Pind. *Ol.* 1.28–29).

Pindar here concentrates on the φάτις βροτῶν which distort the true account
(ὑπὲρ τὸν ἀλαθης λόγον). Bacchylides raises the same issue in claiming that his
song praises mortals for the sake of truth: χρὴ] δ᾽ ἀλαθείας χάριν Ι αἰνεῖν ... εἰ
τις εὖ πράσσοι βροτῶ[ν. Bacchylides' phrase Βοιωτὸς ἀνὴρ may thus be more
than just an overt reference to Hesiod and truth; with it Bacchylides may also
point to Boiotian Pindar's statement about truth and falsehood. Nonetheless, in
the end, Bacchylides' use of the adjectival ethnic Βοιωτός as a personal marker
connotes only new personal and intertextual associations as well as the now
canonical geographic meaning for the term in the beginning of the second quarter
of the fifth century BCE.

In the middle of the century, a different use of the term Βοιωτοί appears in
non-Boiotian sources. This change may indicate that around this time, non-
Boiotians were beginning to comprehend the Boiotian collective not only as
inhabitants of a geographic region, as a group meriting derogatory humor, or as
individual Boiotian literary figures, but also as a collective that could act together
politically.

Perhaps the earliest attestation of this new use of the collective regional
ethnic occurs in an inscription on a small and relatively well-preserved bronze
plaque from Olympia.[117]

῎Αγαλμα Διός· Πύρρο(γ) γρ[α]φέας vac.
<u>v</u> καὶ Χαρίξενος καὶ τοὶ μαστροὶ vac.
τ]αὶρ δίκαις, ταὶρ κά(τ) τὸν Βοιοτὸν Μένανδρος
κ᾽] ᾿Αριστόλοχος τοῖρ᾽Αθαναίος ἐδικαξάταν, vac.
ἀ]πέγνον καὶ τοῖ(ρ) Θεσπιέσσιν καὶ τοῖρ σὺν αὐτὸς
μ]ὲ δικαίος δικαστάμεν, κάπὸ τὸν Θεσαλὸν
ἀ]πεδίκαξαν. vacat

A pleasing gift for Zeus. Pyrrhon was the scribe. Charixenos and the financial
officials have examined the judgments which Menandros and Aristolochos
made against the Boiotians in favor of the Athenians, and they have rendered
and judged justly in favor of the Thespians and their associates, and from the
Thessalians ... they have (freed them?).[118]

---

[117] *SEG* XXVI 475; Olympia museum inv. no. B6362.
[118] Translation partly after Siewert 1981, 229. The last line of the text is unclear, and Siewert's arguments for its meaning have left me unconvinced; I have thus rendered the translation
as literally yet as comprehensibly as possible.

Notably, here the term Βοιωτοί is no longer clearly associated with geography, unlike the other archaic and early classical instances of the regional ethnic considered thus far. Because of this potentially significant shift in meaning, I turn to Siewert's extensive analysis; although his reading of the stone is sound, his proposal of a general date in the first half of the fifth century, specifically between 476 and 472, is debatable.[119]

The inscription represents the revision of a previous judicial decision. Here the Elian *mastroi*, under the chairmanship of Charixenos, amend a previous judgment rendered by the *Hellenodikai* Menandros and Aristolochos.[120] Because the present text is only an amendment of an earlier decision, it mentions only those parts of the original decision which are relevant to the amended one. It is thus difficult to deduce much about what the original judgment involved. We do not know, for example, which *poleis* or groups were involved in the original conflict.[121] From the mention of the former *Hellenodikai* Menandros and Aristolochos, however, it is possible although not certain that the original matter was of panhellenic significance.

It is most useful to consider what the amended decision tells us about its own circumstances. We find a group of local Elian officials judging in favor of both Athens and Thespiai. This judgment quite literally happens at the expense of the Boiotian collective, according to Siewert, which from this point is required to pay a penalty to Athens (δίκαι, line 3). In its final lines the judgment may also demand that the Thessalians pay a fine to the Thespians, although this point is by no means certain.[122]

Considering the early fifth-century activities of the four groups named in the inscription (Athens, the Boiotians, Thespiai, and the Thessalians), Siewert has convincingly argued for a *terminus post quem* of 480 BCE when the Persians destroyed Thespiai and Attica with the support of many Boiotian and Thessalian medizers.[123] Siewert proposes a more specific date of 476–472 from five additional deductions for the decree's production, some of which invite reconsideration.[124]

That Thespiai was independent at the time of the original decree is reasonable to suggest, since Thespiai and Plataia's independent activities during the Persian war period are well documented. However, Siewert's claim that Thespiai and Plataia ought to be distinguished from *poleis* on the basis of the control they enjoyed over smaller communities in their respective *chorai* is now undermined

---

[119] Siewert 1981, 231 (for the middle decades of the first half of the fifth century) and 248 (between 476 and 472); cf. Siewert's original remarks on the text, where he more conservatively dates the piece only to the first half of the fifth century (Siewert 1977, 463).

[120] See Siewert 1981, 235 for Menandros and Aristolochos as *Hellenodikai*; for Menandros and Aristolochos as Elian, see 238.

[121] Siewert 1981, 243 and 247.

[122] Siewert 1981, 232 and 237; as a parallel for the use of δίκαι as a monetary payment, he cites Thucydides 5.49.1.

[123] Siewert 1981, 245.

[124] Siewert 1981, 245–247.

by M. Hansen's work on Boiotian *poleis* and the territorial expansionism of such communities in the Archaic and Early Classical periods.[125] In Boiotia even the communities that were set within the territory of another *polis* and had no independent territory of their own often enjoyed *polis*-status; the leading communities of these territories were also still considered *poleis*, e.g., Thespiai and Plataia.[126] Siewert's earlier understanding of the Boiotian *poleis* Thespiai and Plataia thus destabilizes his subsequent conclusions about the region as a whole during this period.

It is safe to conclude, however, as Siewert does, that the Boiotians of this inscription, as an aggregate body, were concerned with some infraction for which they collectively had to pay monetary compensation to Athens. That this post-480 event did not concern the Olympic festival *per se*, despite the publication of the stone at Olympia, is an obvious conclusion, since Boiotian victors are uniformly listed according to *poleis* in Olympian inscriptions before 296 BCE[127] and there is no evidence for activities at the games where the Boiotians might have acted together as a group and thereby have incurred liability as a group. Instead, as an aggregate body they are concerned with some infraction for which they together had to compensate Athens.

That this Boiotian offense against Attica, as Siewert argues, must have been a collective military attack is not a foregone conclusion, however, since as we have seen, the Boiotians clearly acted collectively in non-military contexts during this period, both at sanctuaries both inside and outside Boiotia, and with the active promotion of a set of shared characteristics which had become recognizable in non-Boiotian sources by this time.[128] Moreover, no source detailing activities of this period mentions such an attack, not even Herodotus, who, as we have seen, quite carefully describes the earlier Boiotian and Chalkidian attack on Attica of 507/6 and painstakingly quotes the Athenian victory dedication *verbatim*.[129] Our lack of corroborating evidence for a Boiotian attack on Attica immediately after 480 thus destabilizes Siewert's historical reconstruction of this stone.

Siewert's discussion of his requisite third factor – Thessalian damage of Thespiai – is also problematic. Not only does Herodotus again fail to describe such an attack, but on this issue Siewert relies on the late tradition for the battle of Keressos, a battle in which the Boiotians beat back the Thessalian forces from a still unidentified spot in south-central Boiotia. Siewert places Keressos near

---

[125] Siewert 1981, 240–241 (Siewert classifies Thespiai and Plataia as political communities somewhere between *poleis* and a sort of organized kinship group, *Stammesstaat*, a term which he leaves undefined).

[126] See e.g., M. Hansen 1995, 36–37; 1996a, 74–112, esp. 77–78; 2000b, 598; for the meanings of the term *polis*, see M. Hansen 2004, 39–46; 2000a, 16.

[127] See above, this chapter and M. Hansen 1996b, 188.

[128] See Siewert 1981, 237 for the inscription as record of a post-480 Boiotian military attack against Athens.

[129] Siewert 1981, 246: "Eine ausdrückliche böotische Beteiligung an der Verwüstung Attikas berichtet Herodot nicht." For Herodotus' care in recording the 507/6 attack and Athenian victory, see my discussion of *IG* I³ 501 above.

Thespiai and then suggests that the tradition of this battle motivated the Thespians to accuse the Thessalians of unwarranted military activity at the time of this inscription.[130] Siewert himself, however, acknowledges the problematic evidence for the battle of Keressos and its date.[131] Rather than bolstering his case for a Thessalian attack on Thespiai, then, Siewert's reliance on an insecure date and traditions of the battle of Keressos weakens his arguments for the placement and context of this stone in general.

I thus reject the proposed context of 476–472 for this inscription, while accepting Siewert's *terminus post quem* of 480. On the basis of letter forms Johnston has suggested that this inscription dates to the 440s or 450s.[132] Although arguments based on letter forms are not always compelling, the form of the ν is certainly suggestive of a date in or after the middle of the century, as Jeffery indicates in her discussion of an Arkadian list of *proxenoi* from that period.[133] If we accept this more conservative date, which seems reasonable given the insecurities of the previous argument, then we can identify a change in external use of the collective regional ethnic only in the mid-fifth century. We can safely suggest that at this time non-Boiotians were starting to recognize the Boiotians collective as more than just a geographical group, although the older geographical connotations of the term were still operating during this period.

I propose a different historical context for the inscription in which a penalty imposed against the Boiotians in favor of the Athenians makes more sense. The payment implies forceful damages. With a revision of the original decree placed in the 440's or 450's, the original compensation may have involved Boiotian damage to Athenian governments established in Boiotia after the battle of Oinophyta in 458. Thucydides tells us that Athens had behaved harshly toward Tanagra after the battle by pulling down its fortification walls.[134] Later Thucydides has the Athenian Hippocrates characterize the Athenians victors at Oinophyta as οἳ τούσδε μάχῃ κρατοῦντες μετὰ Μυρωνίδου ἐν Οἰνοφύτοις τὴν Βοιωτίαν ποτὲ ἔσχον.[135] It is possible that Athenian rule in Boiotian *poleis* after Oinophyta produced *ad hoc* reprisals on the part of disenfranchised Boiotians from across the region. As for the subsequent revision of the decree, perhaps the Thespians felt they had been wrongly accused of such anti-Athenian activity and had appealed against the original judgment. This alternative proposal must remain speculative, of course, but at the same time it offers a plausible mid-fifth-century historical context for *SEG* XXVI 475 which is pinned to known historical events and which provides a setting in which the Boiotians can reasonably be characterized as a political collective by non-Boiotians.

Additional non-Boiotian evidence from later in the century, particularly Hellanikos' fragment 125 on the Athenian Apatouria, likewise suggests that the

---

[130] Siewert 1981, 246. On Keressos, see Paus. 9.14.2; Plut. *Mor.* 866 E and *Cam.* 19.2.

[131] Siewert 1981, 245, n. 101. For further discussion, see Chapter Six below.

[132] Pers. comm.

[133] Jeffery 1990, 214 (no. 31 from Lousoi).

[134] Thuc. 1.108.3.

[135] Thuc. 4.95.3.

middle of the century witnessed a change in outsiders' use of the collective regional ethnic Βοιωτοί which corresponded to a changing external conception of the group as a political decision-making body.[136] Interestingly, although Hellanikos characterizes the Boiotian collective as such, he sets his story back in time by characterizing the Boiotians in epic terms, with a Xanthios as their βασιλεὺς who fights in single combat against the Athenian βασιλεύς, Melanthos. This portrayal parallels the epic associations of the traditions of Boiotian migration found in Thucydides and other earlier sources, as we saw in Chapter Two. Hellanikos' fragment 125 thus suggests that by the late fifth century at least one communal aspect of the Boiotian collective which the Boiotians themselves promoted within their own region was also recognized by outsiders: their link to the heroicized Boiotians from epic tradition.

CONCLUSIONS

The above analysis of the regional ethnics demonstrates a significant difference in internal and external perceptions of the Boiotian collective in the Archaic and Early Classical periods; this difference decreases markedly after the middle of the fifth century. At this time a new meaning for the term emerges from epigraphic sources.

Of the examples of Boiotian use of the collective regional ethnic from the earlier period, only the *Aspis*, an epic poem thematically centered around a mythical military expedition, situates the Boiotians generally in a military context; the *Aspis* is specific only about Boiotian links to epic shields (σάκος). As we saw in Chapter Three, this connection between Boiotians and shields persists in both external and internal sources from the *Iliad* through the Early Classical period.

The remaining internal instances of the archaic and early classical ethnic highlight the connection of the Boiotians to cult in general and to Athena specifically. Five inscriptions attest to collective Boiotian activity at the Boiotian sanctuary of Apollo Ptoios, the Akraiphian sanctuary of the hero Ptoios, and the Phokian sanctuary of Apollo at Delphi. In four of these five cases, the collective ethnic is associated with Athena, both by her name or epithet inscribed on the dedication as well as by their findspots at sanctuaries where Athena was worshipped prominently.[137] Pindar too associates the Boiotians with Athena by referring to the myth of Alalkomeneus, the autochthonous founder of the Boiotian cult of Athena Alalkomeneia. Such internal usage is strikingly consistent with the near certainty of early pan-Boiotian worship of Athena at the Boiotian

---

[136] Hellanikos *FGrHist* 4 F 125, where the historian details the origins of the Athenian Apatouria and uses the collective regional ethnic to denote a Boiotian political collective; from the final form of the *Atthis*, this fragment should be dated between 412–407/6 (Gomme 1945, 6–7, n. 3, after Jacoby). For a second and more general Hellanikan use of the term, see *FGrHist* 4 F 81.

[137] I necessarily omit from this statistic the dedication from the hero Ptoios' sanctuary as I have not seen a facsimile of the piece.

Itonion. From this pattern, it is reasonable to conclude that the term did not necessarily hold definite internal political or military connotations in the Late Archaic and Early Classical periods. The sources rather suggest that internally the collective ethnics designated the Boiotians as a group based at least in part on cult. Notably, the Boiotian collective did not restrict this cultic self-representation to Boiotian sanctuaries; in at least one of the two dedications from panhellenic Delphi, the Boiotians were simultaneously concerned to represent themselves as specific associates of Athena.

From this evidence I venture to speculate further. The infrequent use of collective ethnics during the Late Archaic and Early Classical periods may indicate that, although the Boiotians had cohered to some degree, the collective was still not sufficiently cohesive to mark its unity through a common name with frequency, either inside or outside the region. The fragmentary nature of Boiotian literary and material sources prevents a secure assessment of this possibility, but with more excavation in Boiotia we will presumably have more evidence, perhaps to the contrary, as I suspect. Until then, however, we must conclude from these few attestations that self-identification was not a high priority for the Boiotian collective during the sixth and early fifth centuries BCE. This conclusion is in itself significant in assessing the unity of the group at this time.

External use of the collective ethnics from the Late Archaic and Early Classical periods corroborates this picture: to non-Boiotians the terms held primarily geographical connotations until the middle of the fifth century BCE. There is no way to tell, but it is worth asking whether or not the burgeoning solidarity between Boiotian *poleis* within Boiotia was influenced by these external perceptions of the Boiotian collective as a geographic group. At any rate, Pindar suggests that to non-Boiotians, the Boiotians were sufficiently defined as a collective that they had become an object of collective slander by 472 or 468 BCE (*Ol.* 6.89–90; fr. 83). By the second quarter of the fifth century, then, the Boiotians were recognized by outsiders as a group with a definite shared culture. This evidence *in toto* points toward a *terminus ante quem* of the Persian war period for outside recognition of Boiotian cultural unity.

Although evidence for a change in outside perception of the Boiotians in the middle of the century is limited, the inscription from Olympia (*SEG* XXVI 475) and Hellanikos' fragment 125 suggest that an additional perception of the group arose at that time. Now the Boiotians were seen as a cultural and geographic collective that could also act in unison politically. The little surviving internal evidence supports this interpretation, since the dedication of Ἐπίδαλλος from Delphi, a stone which demonstrates internal and personal use of the adjectival ethnic Βοιότιος, is best dated to the second half of the fifth century (*LSAG* 93.17).

This pattern in use of the adjectival ethnic Βοιώτιος thus supports M. Hansen's remarks on the application and meaning of regional ethnics in general as mentioned at the opening of this Chapter: regional ethnics do not necessarily signify a political or military aspect of collective identity. These factors may materialize when the ethnic is used to denote federal citizenship, but they are not always apparent, even when a federation is attested, much like the ethnic *Arkas* which was not necessarily used as a "political label," but was "primarily meant as an indication of ethnicity" even during the operation of the Arkadian federation.[138] Similarly, usage of Βοιωτοί/Βοιώτιος outlined in this chapter and in the previous discussion of Boiotians in the *Iliad* (Chapter Two) suggests that before the mid-fifth century, these terms primarily identified the Boiotians as a cultural collective, recognized as such both internally and externally. The same epigraphic evidence suggests that it was only after the mid-fifth century that the Boiotians finally merged into a political and military federation of *poleis*.[139] This conclusion encourages re-evaluation of the evidence commonly adduced for the earlier existence of a political and military Boiotian federation and thus brings me to my final chapter.

[138] M. Hansen 1996b, 190; Nielsen 1999, 30.

[139] That a change in Boiotian political organization did not occur until the mid-fifth century is also suggested by an increase in the number of later occurrences of the regional ethnic. After the late fifth and early fourth centuries, the term is used at a much greater rate, e.g., Εὐκλῆς Δάμ[ωνος] Βοιώτιος Ταναγραῖος (a third century decree, *FD* III 3.79 = *SEG* XXXII 516); Νικασιχάρης Βοιώτιος ἐκ Πλαταιᾶν (a proxeny decree, *FD* III 3.116). The increased use of this term in the fourth century may indicate that its meaning had somehow changed or had become relevant to a greater part of the region's population. On the other hand, more frequent use of the ethnic may also indicate no more than the increased "saliency" of Boiotian ethnicity during this time (see Nielsen 1999, 24, for the same in Arkadia).

CHAPTER 6
RECONSIDERING THE BOIOTIAN *KOINON*

καὶ ἡ Περικλέους εἰς Σαμίους, ἐοικέναι αὐτοὺς τοῖς παιδίοις
ἃ τὸν ψωμὸν δέχεται μέν, κλαίοντα δέ, καὶ εἰς Βοιωτούς,
ὅτι ὅμοιοι τοῖς πρίνοις· τούς τε γὰρ πρίνους ὑφ᾽ αὑτῶν κατακόπτεσθαι,
καὶ τοὺς Βοιωτοὺς πρὸς ἀλλήλους μαχομένους.

And Perikles likened the Samians to children who accept the verdict but cry,
and the Boiotians to oak trees: for just as these are broken up by knocking
against each other, so are the Boiotians by fighting against each other.

Aristotle, *Rhetoric,* 1407a4–6.

Thus far I have pieced together the late archaic and early classical material which
illuminates the development of various categories of collective identity in Boiotia
at this time: traditions of descent, territory, ties to epic, shared dialect and a common name. These sources suggest that the Boiotian *ethnos* was indeed thriving by
the late sixth century, but none of these sources, even when juxtaposed, point
toward the existence of the largely military and political federation of *poleis*
advocated in much modern scholarship. I thus now re-evaluate the main historiographic evidence normally adduced in such arguments.

I again note my debt to M. Hansen's work on Boiotia and his skepticism
toward an archaic Boiotian military and political federation; he has repeatedly
maintained that although the Boiotians had formed some sort of group by the late
sixth century, they did not actually organize a political and military federation
until the middle of the fifth.[1] He suggests that in rushing to prove the existence of
an early political and military organization, modern scholars have often conflated
early Boiotian regional awareness with the later political system; Mackil's recent
work on the economic and cultic foundations of federations complements this
view.[2] Hansen also finds the sources for Boiotian history before 525 too scanty to
support even broad speculation about Boiotian federalism in the sixth century.[3] In
what follows I hope to confirm both the insubstantiality of these sources in
further detail and Hansen's suggested chronology for the establishment of a military and political federation of *poleis* in Boiotia. I will also suggest that not only
were Boiotian *poleis* notably disunified in the late sixth century but that the
ancient sources themselves also point to the battle of Koroneia in 447/6 as the
final catalyst for the organized Boiotian federalism reflected in the Oxyrhynchus
historian.

---

[1] Hansen and Nielsen 2004, 432; M. Hansen 1995, 13, 30–31 and n. 89; see also M. Hansen
1996a, 73–116.

[2] See Mackil 2003.

[3] M. Hansen 1995, 31; for a succinct chronology of the verifiable periods of Boiotian federalism, see Hansen and Nielsen 2004, 432.

EARLIER APPROACHES

I begin by briefly sketching the more problematic issues involved in the *opinio communis*, as represented by Larsen, Ducat, Roesch, and Hammond.[4]

With *Greek Federal States* (1968), Larsen reinvigorated discussion on early Boiotian federalism and accepted an organized political federation of Boiotian *poleis* by the last quarter of the sixth century at the latest. Many of his conclusions can no longer be accepted, particularly his reliance on shared Boiotian coinage as an indicator of a unified "Confederacy," a term which to Larsen signifies an aggressive and territorial "tribal state" in the sixth century and a union of just a few "political" and "self-governing communities" in the fifth.[5] Not only are these categories amorphously defined, but the assertion that shared coin types mark federal union remains problematic, as we have seen. Further, Larsen interprets the Plataian-Athenian relationship of the late sixth century as "the first clear proof of the existence of a political union in Boiotia" and one which exemplifies the military nature of this sixth-century confederacy.[6] I discuss this problematic alliance in greater detail later in this Chapter; here I raise a related problem common to this and other earlier work on archaic Boiotian history: an openness toward retrojecting evidence from the late fifth-century historians' accounts of earlier Boiotian activity back into the sixth century, despite the absence of corroborating material, not to mention an often unquestioned reliance on literary sources from even later periods. Additional weaknesses undermine Larsen's conclusions, such as an inconsistent view of Thebes's power in the sixth century and an evolutionary view of political development from "tribal state" to *polis*.[7] Larsen's definition of the term "state" further relies on only a single late fourth-century inscription from Epidauros.[8] Although the majority of these problems appear in Larsen's general introduction and many of his later conclusions about sixth-century Boiotia remain insightful,[9] these issues, particularly his unquestioning reliance on Herodotus' and Thucydides' accounts, require reassessment.

Ducat's primary concern lay in establishing a date for a political and military federation tied to sixth-century Theban expansion.[10] After analyzing the coinage, evidence from the Ptoion sanctuaries, the *Aspis*, and the relationship between Athens and Plataia, Ducat concludes that a Boiotian military federation had been established by the late sixth century, certainly by 509, the date he advocates for

[4] For the various reasons outlined in this Chapter I do not discuss the previous arguments of Moretti (1962) and Guillon (1963) for a seventh-/early sixth-century Boiotian federation.

[5] Larsen 1968, 29.

[6] Larsen 1968, 28–29. Earlier, Larsen also assumed the existence of a sixth-century federation (Larsen 1960, 9–16).

[7] For sixth-century Theban power, see Larsen 1968, 29–30; for the development from tribal state to *polis*, see Larsen 1968, 3–7.

[8] Larsen 1968, 4 and n. 1 (*IG* IV² I 68).

[9] E.g., Larsen's comments on a weak central federal government, which perhaps consisted in "little but the leadership in war exercised by the Thebans," during the Persian wars (Larsen 1968, 31–32).

[10] Ducat 1973, 59–73.

the Plataian-Athenian agreement. He over-emphasizes the minting of coins, which he defines in modern terms and for which he assumes a central minting authority.[11] Further problems arise in Ducat's use of inconsistent terminology. He equates "confédération" with "les Béotiens" and identifies both as indices of "la structure politique commune."[12] Yet he neither defines these terms nor discusses Boiotian epigraphic and literary use of the name Βοιωτοί, despite the fact that nearly all extant Boiotian examples of the term from late sixth- and early fifth-century inscriptions originated at the sanctuary of Apollo Ptoios, a site with Ducat was familiar through the excavations of the French School. As demonstrated in the previous Chapter, usage of the common name Βοιωτοί in these inscriptions speaks against identifying the Boiotians as a political and military federation. Furthermore, although Ducat is occasionally skeptical of the evidence,[13] and while he acknowledges that religious and cultural traditions may have played a role in constructing the Boiotian collective, he nevertheless problematically maintains that the Boiotians minted coins "pour répondre aux besoins propres, principalement militaires sans doute."[14]

Neither Larsen nor Ducat took into account the cautionary comments of Roesch, one of the foremost twentieth-century scholars of Boiotian studies, who had remarked in 1965 that next to nothing was actually known about the territorial organization of Boiotia in the sixth and even the early fifth centuries. Although Roesch had also characterized late archaic Boiotian coinage as "monnaies dont le charactère fédéral est évident," which is far from the case, his lone skepticism toward our understanding of this period of Boiotian history is remarkable.[15] His warnings have gone generally unheeded; most scholars treating the archaic Boiotian collective since Roesch by and large follow Larsen and Ducat's earlier lead: Kraay, Sealey, Salmon, Buck, Bakhuizen, Mafodda, and Hammond.[16]

In the end, then, much modern scholarship on sixth-century Boiotian federalism remains plagued by problems involved in juxtaposing literary evidence from different periods and in retrojecting this evidence back into the sixth century in attempting to provide a narrative history of archaic Boiotia. These studies also fail to consider the perplexities in the chronology, dating, and significance of Boiotian shared coin types, now familiar from Chapter Three. In what follows, then, I aim to challenge this traditional conception of late sixth-century Boiotia by analyzing passages from Herodotus and Thucydides which are commonly adduced in such arguments. I also introduce material which casts the existence of a late sixth-century political and military Boiotian federation further into doubt.

---

[11] Ducat 1973, 71–72.

[12] Ducat 1973, 59, n. 1.

[13] Ducat 1973, 60.

[14] Ducat 1973, 71.

[15] Roesch 1965, 34–36 (Roesch also dates the coins about a century too early).

[16] Kraay 1976, 109, n. 2; Sealey 1976, 144; Salmon 1978, 17–34; R. Buck 1972, 94–101 (although here Buck is less definitive than in his later works); R. Buck 1974, 47–48; R. Buck 1979, 107–117, esp. 107 and 112–115; R. Buck 1985, 25–31; Bakhuizen 1989, 69; Mafodda 2000, 101–102; Hammond 2000, 81–83.

THE FIFTH-CENTURY HISTORIANS

Any analysis of the historians' accounts of the Boiotians must begin with their use of the collective regional ethnic, Βοιωτοί, since Herodotus and Thucydides narrate much of what we think we know about the sixth-century Boiotians. I thus reiterate the simple but vital observation made in the previous chapter: use of collective regional ethnics does not always denote military or political federations, even in fifth-century sources. Hansen cites two cases in point for the historians. Thucydides refers to Achaia as allied with a number of other Peloponnesian communities in 446 but elsewhere makes it clear that the Ἀχαιοί were not united in a federal body at this time.[17] Herodotus uses the regional ethnic similarly as he includes the collective Ἀχαίοι among those parties who give troops to Xerxes; this event occurred far before the Achaians had unified federally.[18] As was the case for sixth- and early fifth-century use of *ethnika*, then, one cannot assume that the late fifth-century historians consistently used regional ethnics to indicate groups acting collectively on the basis of an organized military or political superstructure; it is more likely that ethnics are more generally used to refer to residents of a region acting along regional lines, as Hansen suggests for these terms in Herodotus.[19] Each historian's use of the collective ethnic term Βοιωτοί thus demands a fresh look in tandem with analysis of their representation of the Boiotians in general.

A. The Collective Regional Ethnic in Herodotus

I begin with Herodotus, who uses the ethnic Βοιωτοί three times to refer to a group acting militarily. The single most significant Herodotean passage adduced in arguing for a sixth-century Boiotian political and military federation is 6.108.4–5, where Herodotus describes Plataian assistance to Athens around the time of Marathon and Corinth's response to subsequent Theban aggression against Plataia. In the chapter as a whole (6.108), Plataia sets its aid to Athens in the context of their earlier relationship:

> ἀλλ' Ἀθηναίων ἰρὰ ποιεύντων τοῖσι δυώδεκα θεοῖσι ἱκέται ἱζόμενοι ἐπὶ τὸν βωμὸν ἐδίδοσαν σφέας αὐτούς. Θηβαῖοι δὲ πυθόμενοι ταῦτα ἐστρατεύον ἐπὶ τοὺς Πλαταιέας, Ἀθηναῖοι δέ σφι ἐβοήθεον. μελλόντων δὲ συνάπτειν μάχην Κορίνθιοι οὐ περιεῖδον, παρατυχόντες δὲ καὶ καταλλάξαντες ἐπιτρεψάντων ἀμφοτέρων οὔρισαν τὴν χώρην ἐπὶ τοισίδε, ἐὰν Θηβαίους Βοιωτῶν τοὺς μὴ βουλομένους ἐς Βοιωτοὺς τελέειν.

But when the Athenians were sacrificing to the twelve gods, the Plataians came as suppliants and they surrendered themselves at the altar. When the

---

[17] Thuc. 1.115.1; M. Hansen 1995, 31.
[18] Hdt. 7.185: πεζοῦ δὲ τὸν Θρήικες παρείχοντο καὶ Παίονες καὶ Ἐορδοὶ καὶ Βοττιαῖοι καὶ τὸ Χαλκιδικὸν γένος ... καὶ Ἀχαιοί ... .
[19] M. Hansen 1995, 31.

Thebans heard of this, they marched against the Plataians, and the Athenians helped the Plataians. As they were about to engage in battle, the Corinthians participated because they happened to be there, and they reconciled the border of the area for them, with both sides willing to accept it, on the condition that the Thebans leave alone those of the Βοιωτοί who did not want to be counted among the Βοιωτοί. (6.108.4–5).

This final remark is crucial in analyzing Herodotean use of the Boiotian ethnic. Here the Corinthians accuse the Thebans of forcing those Boiotians (i.e. the Plataians) who did not want to be counted among the Βοιωτοί to be so: ἐὰν Θηβαίους Βοιωτῶν τοὺς μὴ βουλομένους ἐς Βοιωτοὺς τελέειν. In characterizing the Plataians as such, then, Herodotus implies that the Plataians were understood as part of the Βοιωτοί in 480 even though their *polis* had been linked to Athens since the late sixth century.[20]

Earlier sections of this same chapter corroborate this conclusion. At 6.108.1 Herodotus describes Plataia's history, including its association with Athens:

καὶ γὰρ καὶ ἐδεδώκεσαν σφέας αὐτοὺς τοῖσι ᾿Αθηναίοισι οἱ Πλαταιέες, καὶ πόνους ὑπὲρ αὐτῶν [οἱ] ᾿Αθηναῖοι συχνοὺς ἤδη ἀναραιρέατο.

For the Plataians had given themselves over to the Athenians, and the Athenians already had undergone frequent labors on their behalf (6.108.1).

At 6.108.4 the historian also details how and where the Plataians actually forged this relationship with similar terminology: ἀλλ᾽ ᾿Αθηναίων ἱρὰ ποιεύντων τοῖσι δυώδεκα θεοῖσι ἱκέται ἱζόμενοι ἐπὶ τὸν βωμὸν ἐδίδοσαν σφέας αὐτούς (but while the Athenians were making sacrifices to the twelve gods, the Plataians as suppliants were sitting on the altar and seeking protection).[21] It is thus with an understanding of this earlier implicitly protective and subsidiary relationship with Athens that Herodotus refers to the Plataians as Βοιωτῶν as he begins to close this episode at 6.108.5. The collective regional ethnic Βοιωτοί cannot indicate a military and political Boiotian organization in this passage, then, for Plataia, an Athenian subsidiary and military protectorate, is included by the term. Βοιωτοί must instead denote some other type of collective, a regional and/or cultural one, based on more than military and political criteria of inclusion.

[20] Dating the Plataian-Athenian relationship relies on Thuc. 3.68.5 where he refers back to events in this Herodotean passage (Hdt. 6.108). Thucydides notes the date of the alliance as he records the date for Plataia's destruction (427): καὶ τὰ μὲν κατὰ Πλάταιαν ἔτει τρίτῳ καὶ ἐνενηκοστῷ ἐπειδὴ ᾿Αθηναίων ξύμμαχοι ἐγένοντο οὕτως ἐτελεύτησεν (3.68.5). Some prefer to emend Thucydides' text, reading in the "eighty-third" year after the Plataians entered into a relationship with Athens (ἔτει τρίτῳ καὶ ὀκτηκοστῷ), instead of the text's: ἔτει τρίτῳ καὶ ἐνενηκοστῷ. As Hornblower notes, arguments for emendation are weak; Thucydides' text should stand as is. The preferable date for Plataian interaction with Athens is thus 519. For cases for and against emendation, see Hornblower's review where he follows Gomme (Hornblower 1991, 464–466; also see Badian 1993, 218–219, n. 18 and 222–223, n. 33); for emendation, see Shrimpton 1984, 295–303; Salmon 1978, 20–21 and notes 4–5.

[21] For Plataian citizenship in Athens, see Amit 1973, 75–78, and Hornblower 1991, 449, for a useful summary.

One further aspect of this passage merits discussion in this context. Herodotus mentions that the Lakedaimonians had originally encouraged the Plataians to seek Athenian help in the hopes of stirring up trouble between the Athenians and the Boiotians: ὡς βουλόμενοισι τοὺς Ἀθηναίους ἔχειν πόνους συνεστεῶτας Βοιωτοῖσι (6.108.3). The historian again uses the regional ethnic here and one assumes that the πόνους between the Athenians and the Boiotians to which he refers involve come sort of physical conflagration. On these grounds, one might be tempted to interpret the passage as evidence for a military body of Boiotians; yet as we have seen, the regional ethnic used in reference to the Plataians later in this same passage indicates a cultural or regional group and cannot indicate a military federation. In reading the collective ethnic here at 6.108.3 then, we can understand the Βοιωτοί more simply as an *ad hoc* military group, as was suggested in Chapters Three and Five. Such a body would have comprised bands of men from various polities in the region or even from one strong *polis*, linked by broad cultural ties, some of whom might be spurred to respond collectively to a spontaneous situation perceived as a regional threat, such as repeated Athenian meddling in Plataian (and thus southeastern Boiotian) affairs. I return to the issue of an *ad hoc* military group later in this chapter. For now it suffices to acknowledge this possible interpretation of Herodotus 6.108 and its attendant conclusion: namely, that this passage does not provide conclusive evidence for a late sixth-century political or military federation in Boiotia.[22]

Useful for comparison to Plataia is Eleutherai, a Boiotian community situated near Plataia on the border between Boiotia and Attica.[23] Eleutherai is perhaps best known as the source for the wooden image of Dionysos used in celebrating the Attic City Dionysia. The festival and its procession are generally dated to the late sixth century if not earlier, and they are often, although not unanimously, connected to the accession of Boiotian Eleutherai under Attic control. On the basis of an Attic casualty list from 447 which includes a "Semichides Ἐλευθερᾶθεν," Parker offers 447 as the *terminus ante quem* for Eleutherian citizenship at Athens, although he seems to favor an earlier date.[24] Eleutherai is relevant in discussing Plataia because of what Pausanias says about Eleutherai's accession to Attica:

> πρότερον μὲν γὰρ Ἐλευθερεῦσιν ὅροι πρὸς τὴν Ἀττικὴν ἦσαν· προσχωρησάντων δὲ Ἀθηναίοις τούτων, οὕτως ἤδη Βοιωτίας ὁ Κιθαιρών ἐστιν ὅρος· προσχώρησαν δὲ Ἐλευθερεῖς οὐ πολέμῳ βιασθέντες, ἀλλὰ πολιτείας τε ἐπιθυμήσαντες παρὰ Ἀθηναίων καὶ κατ᾽ ἔχθος τὸ Θηβαίων.

The border with Attica was formerly Eleutherai, but when they came over to the Athenians, Mt. Kithairon was then the border with Boiotia. The Eleutherians came over not because they were oppressed in war, but because they wanted citizenship at Athens and they hated the Thebans (Paus. 1.38.8).

---

[22] Hdt. 6.108.5 is often over-translated as incontrovertible proof of the existence of a Boiotian federation: e.g., How and Wells translate the phrase ἐς Βοιωτοὺς τελέειν as "to belong to the Boeotian League under Theban hegemony" (How and Wells 1912, 110).

[23] For the Boiotian construction of this and other border forts between Attica and Boiotia, see Camp 2000, 46.

[24] Parker 1996.

While Pausanias' reflections on the situation are late, they indicate that it is possible to understand the movement of a southern Boiotian community toward Athens in territorial and/or civic terms and not in terms of a Boiotian military federation. Pausanias instead specifies enmity between Eleutherai and the *polis* Thebes; he mentions nothing about an immediate or pressing territorial or military threat from a unified Boiotian military federation of *poleis*. With this comparison in mind, I return to Plataia and Herodotus' use of the collective ethnic Βοιωτοί.

In a second and often-cited passage Herodotus again identifies the Plataians as Βοιωτοί, thereby corroborating his earlier presentation of the term at 6.108. At 7.132.1 the historian lists the various groups that surrendered to Xerxes in the Persian advance through central Greece. Among those he includes are the Boiotians, yet in this military action, as we know from Herodotus as well as from other sources, not all the Boiotians were involved:

> τῶν δὲ δόντων ταῦτα ἐγένοντο οἵδε, Θεσσαλοί, Δόλοπες, Ἐνιῆνες, Περραιβοὶ, Λοκροί, Μάγνητες, Μηλιέες, Ἀχαιοὶ οἱ Φθιῶται καὶ Θηβαῖοι καὶ οἱ ἄλλοι Βοιωτοὶ πλὴν Θεσπιέων τε καὶ Πλαταιέων.

Of those giving these things (earth and water) were the Thessalians, Dolopes, Enienes, Perraibians, Lokrians, Magnesians, Melians, Phthian Achaians, Thebans, and the other Boiotians, except the Thespians and the Plataians.

While acknowledging the refusal of the Thespians and Plataians to medize, here Herodotus still includes them as part of οἱ ἄλλοι Βοιωτοί. Ducat suggests that this passage marks the exception of these two *poleis* from the Βοιωτοί as unusual, yet at the same time, Herodotus' language forces Ducat to admit that the term Βοιωτοί cannot indicate a military federation in this passage, since, as we saw above at 6.108, Plataia had been involved with Athens militarily since the late sixth century.[25] For Ducat, all other uses of the collective ethnic, both in Herodotus and in other authors, indicate a military federation. Ducat's inability to explain the seeming inconsistency in Herodotean terminology in this passage leads to the natural conclusion that Herodotus is not inconsistent but that we have rather misinterpreted the meaning of the ethnic in the *Histories* on the basis of prior assumptions about the political and military landscape in Boiotia in the Late Archaic and Early Classical periods. We can only conclude that for Herodotus the term Βοιωτοί signifies a geographic or cultural group.

Herodotus' quotation of the Athenian monument which celebrated defeat over the Boiotians and Chalkidians in 507/6 further suggests that the collective ethnic Βοιωτοί should more simply be understood to refer to a non-specific group of Boiotians in the *Histories*.[26] As noted in Chapter Five, this inscription refers to both the Boiotians and the Chalkidians as *ethne* (ἔθνεα Βοιοτῶν καὶ Χαλκι-

---

[25] "L'expression semblerait impliquer que Thespies et Platées faisaient alors partie de la Confédération. Mais comment Platées alliée indéfectible d'Athènes, le pourrait-elle?" (Ducat 1971, 69).

[26] *IG* I³ 501 (= *SEG* XXXI 28; Meiggs and Lewis 1988, no. 15).

δέον), although Χαλκιδέον must be the term for inhabitants of that *polis* and Βοιοτὸν a non-civic term with a wider regional scope. Because Herodotus quotes this inscription *verbatim*, the other instances where he describes this same battle and where he uses the collective ethnic must be colored by the general understanding of the Βοιωτοί as an *ethnos* (5.74.2; 5.77.1–4). In the end, then, it is reasonable to conclude that for Herodotus, the collective regional ethnic Βοιωτοί indicates a general group, sometimes an *ad hoc* military collective, but also more often a cultural collective which can include the seemingly renegade Plataians and Thespians.

B. Herodotus' Use of the Term *Boiotarchai*

At 9.15.1 Herodotus mentions a group of βοιωτάρχαι who participated in the battle of Plataia in 479. From the Oxyrhynchus historian we know that after 447/ 6 there were, in fact, eleven official *boiotarchs* for the later Boiotian federation.[27] On the basis of these two texts many scholars have been tempted to retroject the post-447/6 office of *boiotarch* and an accompanying federal military and political superstructure back to 479 at the latest.[28] Roesch even sets *boiotarchs* at the head of infantry and cavalry, although such organized Boiotian troops are thus far not mentioned in any published archaic or early fifth-century source.[29]

However, exactly what *boiotarch* means in this Herodotean passage is far from clear. Hansen suggests that the term could simply signify "a very old institution, like the Thessalian *tagos*, only later adapted to the federal constitution."[30] Not incidentally, Helly has argued against the early existence of a Thessalian federal *tagos* from the lack of supporting evidence, although its existence has been almost universally accepted in modern accounts.[31] Even Larsen, normally a staunch advocate of an early Boiotian military federation, is willing only to state: "we learn that the magistrates known as 'Rulers of Boeotia' existed at the time, but we do not learn how many there were nor whether they were more than Theban officials whose title proclaimed the desire to rule the Boiotians."[32]

Arguments for the existence and role of federal *boiotarchs* in the early fifth century are accordingly weak. Buck infers from Herodotus' casual mention of *boiotarchs* that they must have been representatives familiar to a wider Greek audience who had been in office for a substantial period of time before the events Herodotus describes.[33] It is of course probable that Herodotus and his late fifth-

---

[27] *Hell. Oxy.* 19.3 (Chambers); see also Thuc. 4.91.

[28] E.g., Roesch 1965, 95, who argues for the antiquity of the office; also Salmon 1978, 18; Hammond 2000. A passage from Pausanias often bolsters such arguments (Paus. 10.20.3; see e.g., Salmon 1978, 18).

[29] Roesch 1965, 95.

[30] M. Hansen 1995, 31.

[31] Helly 1995; see also Morgan 2003, 22–23.

[32] Larsen 1968, 31.

[33] R. Buck 1979, 124.

century audience were familiar with the federal institution of *boiotarch*, but it does not follow that the office was a century older than this. Further, if federal *boiotarchs* had engaged in military leadership in the early fifth century, their absence from Herodotus' account of Thermopylai is notably odd; in the *Histories* Boiotian *boiotarchs* seem to be present only at Plataia. Buck states that *boiotarchs* were in fact involved in that earlier battle, but there is no evidence for this view.[34]

If, for the sake of argument, we accept that a group of men called *boiotarchs* did exist in 479, it is alternatively possible to categorize them as *ad hoc* military leaders, chosen from prominent families of various *poleis* to lead an impromptu army on a certain pressing occasion of regional significance. This scenario could help explain the absence of *boiotarchs* at Thermopylai and their presence at Plataia in Herodotus' *Histories*. After all, in 479 the Persians were fighting on and withdrawing through Boiotian territory and depending on Boiotian hoplites, a situation which demands collective regional involvement and participation. At the same time this action may have been little more than a spontaneous gathering of neighbors with the means to defend and protect their territory. Morgan has suggested that spontaneous mobilizations of men fighting as armies occurred in early *ethne*.[35] There is thus no pressing reason to associate Herodotus' *boiotarchai* with an organized military federal superstructure.

That both ancient and modern historians color their accounts of the past with reflections of their present is unavoidable;[36] Herodotus, despite his frequent accuracy in recording inscriptions, names, and other details, is no exception. Macan long ago illustrated how Herodotus retrojects late fifth-century Athenian political offices into the past, especially in discussing Athenian *polemarchs* and *strategoi*, offices about which the historian presumably had some knowledge, given his familiarity with Athenian society and history.[37] Raaflaub too notes the difficulty in trusting Herodotus on issues of terminology, motives of characters, or even narratives of events, in the absence of contemporary and corroborating evidence from the Archaic and Early Classical periods.[38] Despite his best efforts, then, since Herodotus cannot entirely be trusted to record the details of Athenian military offices with accuracy, I am hesitant to accept his mention of *boiotarchai* as a legitimate reflection of an established military office from an area with which he was most likely less familiar. It seems more plausible that Herodotus retrojected his contemporary understanding of the late fifth-century *boiotarchs* back into his account of events from the Early Classical period.[39] In the end, then, evidence normally adduced from Herodotus in support of a sixth-century Boiotian federation is uncompelling.

[34] R. Buck 1974, 47.

[35] Morgan 1991, 146 (on Achaia); see also Morgan 2003, 37–38, 196; Morgan and Hall 1996, 164–165, 193–199.

[36] The classic ancient examples being, of course, Aristotle's and Plato's accounts of early coinage; see T. Martin 1995, 260–262.

[37] Macan 1895, vol. 1, 365–366 n. 5 [re: Hdt. 6.109] and Appendices IX.13, 177–179.

[38] Raaflaub 1998, 87–88.

[39] For the perennial question of Herodotus' sources, see Jacoby 1913; Fornara 1971; Fehling

C. Thucydides' Boiotians: the Plataian Debate

Thucydides likewise provides little help, although his account of late fifth-century hostility between Thebes and Plataia has also played a significant role in arguing for an archaic Boiotian military and political organization (Thuc. 3.52–58).[40] I propose instead that, although this section of Thucydides' narrative offers evidence for late fifth-century tension between Thebes and Plataia, neither the Plataian nor the Theban speech suggests that Thebes had pressured Plataia into joining a Boiotian military federation in the late sixth century. Rather, like Herodotus, the Thucydidean speeches in the Plataian debate indicate that the Plataians were considered part of the Boiotian collective during the late sixth and early fifth centuries. Furthermore, various exaggerations in the Thebans' speech undermine the possible trustworthiness in detail of Thucydides' Theban version of early Boiotian history. Most important, if these speeches suggest anything about a Boiotian military and political federation, it is that the federation existed only in the last third of the fifth century.

The Plataian Speech

In their opening statements, Thucydides' Plataians raise the recurrent problem of interpreting the collective ethnic in a dramatic post-519 context, for here they define themselves as Boiotians in recounting their record during the Persian wars:

τὰ δ' ἐν εἰρήνῃ καὶ πρὸς τὸν Μῆδον ἀγαθοὶ γεγενήμεθα, τὴν μὲν οὐ λύσαντες νῦν πρότεροι, τῷ δὲ ξυνεπιθέμενοι τότε ἐς ἐλευθερίαν τῆς Ἑλλάδος μόνοι Βοιωτῶν.

We were good men in peaceful times and against the Persians; we did not break the current peace first, and we were the only Βοιωτοί who rallied at that time for the freedom of Hellas (3.54.3).

That the Plataians were the sole Boiotians who fought against Persia is of course historically false, as the serpent column from Delphi attests and as Herodotus corroborates.[41] But Plataia's exaggeration does not negate its dramatic inclusion among the Boiotian collective here. Thus, as in Herodotus, here too in Thucy-

---

1989 (English translation of 1971 edition); Hartog 1988 (English translation of 1980 edition); Pritchett 1993; Fowler 1996, 80–6 and bibliography there, esp. notes 125, 130, and 134; Shrimpton 1997 with Appendix of sources; Boedeker 2000, 99–102, also with bibliography.

[40] See, e.g., R. Buck, who cites Thucydides 3.61 as "evidence from Thebes" and who infers a federal structure of an early league from Thuc. 3.63.2 (R. Buck 1979, 112, 123 and n. 7); on Thuc. 3.63.2 see R. Buck 1979, 124 and n. 12, where Buck specifies the election of federal *boiotarchs* by oligarchies in Boiotian *poleis*. The passage rather concerns Plataian alliance with Athens during the Persian Wars and Theban views on the hypocrisy of this activity (ὡς δὲ ὑμεῖς μᾶλλόν τε ἠδικήκατε τοὺς Ἕλληνας καὶ ἀξιώτεροί ἐστε πάσης ζημίας, πειρασόμεθα ἀποφαίνειν ...). See also Hammond 2000, 80–83, esp. 80.

[41] Coil 6: Πλαταιές, Θεσπιές; Hdt. 7.132.

dides the collective term Βοιωτοί does not necessarily connote political or military alliance; rather, it reflects some other kind of group of which the Plataians, partners with Athens since 519, were thought to have been part.

Thucydides' Plataian speech also casts the causes of Plataian and Theban hostilities in terms of Greek or Persian loyalties rather than membership in a federal body. The Plataians are repeatedly made to stress the differences between Medism and Hellenism, their role in Hellenism, and Theban Medism; for example, in self defense the Plataians claim:

> εἴ τέ τι ἄλλο κατ᾿ ἐκεῖνον τὸν χρόνον ἐγένετο ἐπικίνδυνον τοῖς Ἕλλησι, πάντων παρὰ δύναμιν μετέσχομεν.

And if something else dangerous happened to the Greeks at that time, we shared in all of it beyond our power (3.54.4–5).

Thucydides' Plataians emphasize their support of Hellenism by contrasting their pro-Greek actions with those of the Thebans (οἵδε):

> ἐν ἐκείνῳ δὲ τῷ καιρῷ, ὅτε πᾶσι δουλείαν ἐπέφερεν ὁ βάρβαρος, οἵδε μετ᾿ αὐτοῦ ἦσαν.

At that time when the barbarian was threatening slavery to all, these men here fought on his side (3.56.4).

This dichotomy continues throughout the speech (e.g., Plataians grouped with the other Greeks, καὶ ἡμεῖς καὶ οἱ ἄλλοι Ἕλληνες, 3.56.4; Medism v. courage in the face of the Persians, 3.56.5). Thucydides amplifies the Plataians' bold tone in the last half of the speech, where they call themselves εὐέργεται τῆς Ἑλλάδος (3.57.1–2) and οἱ παρὰ δύναμιν πρόθυμοι ἐς τοὺς Ἕλληνας (3.57.4), an echo of their similar claim at 3.54.4–5. The Plataians use this latter categorization a second time at the end of their speech, referring to themselves as οἱ προθυμότατοι περὶ τοὺς Ἕλληνας (3.59.4).[42] They furthermore describe their land as one ἐν ᾗ ἠλευθερώθησαν οἱ Ἕλληνες (3.58.5) and contrastingly criticize the Thebans as murderers (αὐθένται). The Plataians are simply not made to cast the argument in federal terms; they rather stress Greek vs. barbarian sympathies throughout their argument.

Beyond this quasi-national opposition in the Persian wars, Thucydides' Plataians emphasize a simple but long-standing civic rivalry with Thebes, and again, although one might most expect reference to a Boiotian federation in portraying such repeated conflict, there is no mention of an early federal organization, Theban or otherwise. The Plataians offer the following account of relations between the two *poleis*:

> δεομένων γὰρ ξυμμαχίας ὅτε Θηβαῖοι ἡμᾶς ἐβιάσαντο, ὑμεῖς ἀπεώσασθε καὶ πρὸς Ἀθηναίους ἐκελεύετε τραπέσθαι ὡς ἐγγὺς ὄντας ...

---

[42] See also 3.58.1 for minor emphasis on this same point.

We were seeking alliance with you when the Thebans used their force to do us violence, and you (Lakedaimonians) pushed us away and you urged us to turn toward the Athenians because they were neighbors ... (3.55.1).

The Plataians go on to describe the relationship they shared with Athens and the rights of citizenship they received from them (3.55.3–4). Here they mention only that the Athenians helped them ἐναντία Θηβαίοις (3.55.3); no specific Theban aggressions are described here or elsewhere in the speech even though the Plataians refer a second time to their sufferings at Theban hands. On this second occasion, although Thebes is identified as the oppressor, the Plataians again neither suggest nor imply that the Thebans had earlier acted as the leading power of a federal state:

Θηβαῖοι δὲ πολλὰ μὲν καὶ ἄλλα ἡμᾶς ἠδίκησαν, τὸ δὲ τελευταῖον αὐτοὶ ξύνιστε, δι᾽ ὅπερ καὶ τάδε πάσχομεν. πόλιν γὰρ αὐτοὺς τὴν ἡμετέραν κα-ταλαμβάνοντας ἐν σπονδαῖς καὶ προσέτι ἱερομηνίᾳ ὀρθῶς τε ἐτιμ-ωρησάμεθα κατὰ τὸν πᾶσι νόμον καθεστῶτα, τὸν ἐπιόντα πολέμιον ὅσιον εἶναι ἀμύνεσθαι, καὶ νῦν οὐκ ἂν εἰκότως δι᾽ αὐτοὺς βλαπτοίμεθα.

And the Thebans did many other wrongful things to us, and you yourselves know their final act, on account of which we also undergo these current problems. For they seized our city under a truce, and what is more, during a religious month, and we punished them rightly according to the law set up for everybody, namely, that it is proper to repel the attacking enemy, and we should not reasonably be harmed because of them now (3.56.1–2).

The only relationship between the two *poleis* indicated in these passages is one of general enmity (e.g., ἔχθιστοι, 3.59.4). Thucydides' Plataian speech thus does not offer proof for a late sixth-century Boiotian military federation. At the most the speech rather reflects inter-*polis* rivalry between cities of south-central Boiotia. We in fact have a great deal of corroborating evidence for such rivalry to which I will return at the close of this chapter.

The Theban Speech

Before turning to this evidence, however, I address Thucydides' Theban speech from the Plataian episode, sections of which have also been adduced in support of a late sixth-century Boiotian federation. Close analysis of the speech rather suggests that Thucydides' Theban account of Boiotian activity before 450 does not accurately reflect earlier events. While certain sections of the Theban speech certainly illuminate the beginnings of a military and political federation, these sections can only be used to argue that a federal body arose after the middle of the fifth century, since it is only in the narrative of contemporary late fifth-century events that any reference to a Boiotian institution other than a *polis* appears.[43]

---

[43] For the general lack of rhetorical skill involved in the Theban speech, see Debnar 1996, esp. 100–109.

A first problem in the Theban speech is its inaccuracy about early Boiotian history. In summarizing for the Spartans the Thebans are made to present a version of earlier Boiotian activity that is incompatible with all other ancient sources. I quote the entire passage:

ἡμεῖς δὲ αὐτοῖς διάφοροι ἐγενόμεθα τὸ πρῶτον ὅτι ἡμῶν κτισάντων Πλάταιαν ὕστερον τῆς ἄλλης Βοιωτίας καὶ ἄλλα χωρία μετ᾽ αὐτῆς, ἃ ξυμμείκτους ἀνθρώπους ἐξελάσαντες ἔσχομεν, οὐκ ἠξίουν οὗτοι, ὥσπερ ἐτάχθη
τὸ πρῶτον, ἡγεμονεύεσθαι ὑφ᾽ ἡμῶν, ἔξω δὲ τῶν ἄλλων Βοιωτῶν παρα-
βαίνοντες τὰ πάτρια, ἐπειδὴ προσηναγκάζοντο, προσεχώρησαν πρὸς Ἀθηναίους καὶ μετ᾽ αὐτῶν πολλὰ ἡμᾶς ἔβλαπτον, ἀνθ᾽ ὧν καὶ ἀντέπασχον.

We first became estranged from them because even though we founded Plataia last of Boiotia and with it other areas which we held after expelling men of mixed stock, they did not think that it was right to be ruled by us, as it was first arranged, and outside all the other Βοιωτοί they transgressed tradition when they were pressured, since they went over to the Athenians and with them did us much harm, in return for which they also suffered (3.61.2).

Here the Thebans assert that they had earlier founded and controlled all of Boiotia, a claim which no other historical source corroborates, not even Thucydides' own account of the Boiotian migration where he does not even definitively mention Thebes or the Thebans (1.12). Given the multitude of other narratives of early Boiotian settlement (e.g. Hekataios, Strabo, Diodoros) and Thucydides' own earlier description of the tradition, Thebes's contrasting claim to have dominated the entire region seems starkly tendentious and would likely have appeared so to Thucydides' audience.

Thebes's objectivity is cast into further doubt by the Thebans' subsequent account of the battle of Koroneia in 447/6. Here Thucydides' Thebans boast that they "freed Boiotia" from the Athenians at Koroneia (3.62.4). However, in the Pentekontaetia Thucydides himself had already remarked that it was actually Orchomenos and the exiles from northwestern Boiotia who were the prime movers in this Boiotian victory; he does not even mention the Thebans (1.113.1). The discrepancy between Thucydides' own narrative of events and what his Thebans say about Koroneia undermines confidence in Theban assertions about Boiotian history in the rest of this speech. Larsen explains this contradiction by saying that Thucydides' "account is sufficiently detailed so that the failure to mention the Thebans must mean that they did not take part, unless there were a few Thebans among the unnamed men who turned up to join in the attack at Coronea."[44] Given Thucydides' well-known tendency to contrast what is said in the speeches and what is said in the authorial voice,[45] we can also read this contradiction as the historian's purposeful attempt to discredit the Thebans' boasts as exaggerated bluster, particularly since Thucydides presents his own view in the

[44] Larsen 1960, 10.
[45] See e.g., Hall 1997, 37–38.

Pentekontaetia, where he attempts to correct a number of popular misconceptions.

Rather than offering an accurate account of Thebes' role in early Boiotian history, then, Thucydides' Theban speech presents a distorted picture of early activity in the region.[46] Emphasizing Theban false bravado may have in fact been part of Thucydides' point in characterizing the Thebans in this manner, since in reality Thebes must have continuously attempted to rehabilitate its reputation during the middle of the fifth century, a period in which Thebes surely needed to obfuscate charges of Medism acquired during the Persian wars. That Medism was of primary concern to Thebes is evident in the next section of their Thucydidean speech (3.62, esp. 3–6), where Thebes reacts to the Plataian charges and defensively attributes its Medism in part to insufficient governmental control over a few powerful oligarchs:

καὶ ἡ ξύμπασα πόλις οὐκ αὐτοκράτωρ οὖσα ἑαυτῆς τοῦτ᾽ ἔπραξεν, οὐδ᾽ ἄξιον αὐτῇ ὀνειδίσαι ὧν μὴ μετὰ νόμων ἥμαρτεν.

And the whole city was not in full control of itself when it did this, and it isn't right to blame the city for the things it did wrong when there were no laws (3.62.4)

The Thebans revisit their innocence slightly later as they define their action as ἀκούσιον μηδισμόν (64.5). Given Thebes's concern to separate itself from the familiar charge of Medism and the real likelihood that Thebes manipulated tradition and oral report in the fifth century because of it, uncritical acceptance of the testimony of this speech concerning Theban control over early Boiotia and Theban efforts at the battle of Koroneia becomes problematic.[47] It is thus also humorously ironic and rhetorical on Thucydides' part that the Thebans open their speech by appealing to truth.[48] In the end, then, it is preferable to accept the details of early Boiotian history in Thucydides' Theban speech as exaggerations which illuminate real exigencies of Thebes and the likely Athenian hatred felt toward the Boiotian city in the second half of the fifth century.[49]

Notably however, even these embellished Theban accounts fail to mention a federal body/*koinon* explicitly. One might be tempted to read the phrase τὰ πάτρια [Βοιωτῶν] of the Theban speech at 3.61.2 as an oblique reference to an organized political or military federation, as has often been done in traditional modern accounts. Yet in the absence of conclusive external evidence to corroborate the existence of a federal body, the phrase itself implies little, if anything, about a military aspect to the earlier Boiotian collective. Not only does the term appear in the Thebans' distorted account of Boiotian history, but its meaning is

[46] Connor takes a similar approach in interpreting the tone of the Theban speech in general (Connor 1984, 94).

[47] For the charge of Medism against Thebes, see Hornblower 1991, 456–457.

[48] 3.61.1: νῦν δὲ πρὸς μὲν τὰ ἀντειπεῖν δεῖ, τῶν δὲ ἔλεγχον ποιήσασθαι, ἵνα μήτε ἡ ἡμετέρα αὐτοὺς κακία ὠφελῇ μήτε ἡ τούτων δόξα, τὸ δ᾽ ἀληθὲς περὶ ἀμφοτέρων ἀκούσαντες κρίνητε.

[49] See Debnar 1996, 96–97, 100–101.

simply unclear, as Hornblower has noted.[50] Τὰ πάτρια could signify religious or social obligations as plausibly as military traditions. In Thucydides' account, Plataia's violation of τὰ πάτρια might simply have been understood as a stepping away from a regional religious, cultural, or social commitment toward association with Athens, and not necessarily an infraction against a federal structure.

In support of reading τὰ πάτρια as an indication of some sort of cultural tradition, I note that over the course of the Theban speech the term seems to take on new meaning. This transition is marked in the final sections of the speech where the Thebans describe the most recent event in Boiotia: their attack on Plataia. There Thucydides twice modifies the term τὰ πάτρια with κοινά (3.65.2; 3.66.1–2). In the context of the late fifth-century events on which the Thebans dwell at this point in their speech, the term may thus reflect the new post-447/6 Boiotian federal body. I shall return to this point below in treating the later sections of the speech. It is sufficient here to note the vagueness of the term τὰ πάτρια in the early portion of the Theban speech and Thucydides' addition of the modifier κοινά in the later sections where the Thebans describe late fifth-century events.

In support of the possibility that the phrase τὰ πάτρια of the Theban speech may reflect events contemporaneous to the text, despite Theban exaggerations about previous Boiotian history earlier in the speech, I offer the following analysis of the speech as it unfolds. As we will see, at the beginning of the speech the Thebans emphasize topics similar to those raised by the Plataians: Plataian inclusion in the Boiotian collective, for example, or cultural (as opposed to political) differences between the groups. By the end of their speech the Thebans have moved to late fifth-century events. I suggest that it is only in this late fifth-century context that the Thebans' language can be understood to reflect any sort of federal consciousness.

First, like the Plataians, the Thebans refer to the Plataians with the collective regional ethnic Βοιωτοί. At 3.62.1 the Thebans answer the Plataian claim to have been the only ones from the region who did not medize and who then "atticized:"

ἐπειδὴ δὲ καὶ ὁ βάρβαρος ἦλθεν ἐπὶ τὴν Ἑλλάδα, φασὶ μόνοι Βοιωτῶν οὐ μηδίσαι, καὶ τούτῳ μάλιστα αὐτοί τε ἀγάλλονται καὶ ἡμᾶς λοιδοροῦσιν. ἡμεῖς δὲ μηδίσαι μὲν αὐτοὺς οὔ φαμεν διότι οὐδ' Ἀθηναίους, τῇ μέντοι αὐτῇ ἰδέᾳ ὕστερον ἰόντων Ἀθηναίων ἐπὶ τοὺς Ἕλληνας μόνους αὖ Βοιωτῶν ἀττικίσαι.

When the barbarian came into Greece, [the Plataians] claim that they alone of the Βοιωτοί did not medize, and for this they especially praise themselves and rebuke us. But we say that they didn't medize because neither did the Athenians, and along these lines when the Athenians later went against the Greeks, they were again the only Βοιωτοί who atticized (3.62.1).

This scenario involves events of the Persian wars and the following decades which witnessed the great rise in Athenian imperialism and which culminated, in

[50] Hornblower 1991, 454–455.

central Greece at least, with the Athenian victory at Oinophyta in 458. It is thus remarkable that Thucydides' Thebans refer to the Plataians as being part of the Boiotians during this period (the mid-fifth century). Since the Plataians had been Athenian partners from the sixth century, the term Βοιωτοί here thus again cannot signify a military or political organization. Its use thus matches that of Herodotus, who employs the term Βοιωτοί to refer both to Plataians and to other Boiotians.[51]

In these opening sections of their speech, instead of referring to any kind of federal body, the Thebans also focus on ethnic differences between themselves and others. In their portrait of Boiotian civilization, the Thebans claim to have expelled earlier inhabitants of the region (ξυμμείκτους ἀνθρώπους ἐξελάσαντες, 3.61.2). The term σύμμεικτος seems to indicate men of non-Boiotian stock, for the Thebans continue by implicitly contrasting the ξυμμείκτοι ἄνθρωποι with the conquering Boiotians, some of whom are reported to have agreed to Theban rule (ὥσπερ ἐτάχθη τὸ πρῶτον, ἡγεμονεύεσθαι ὑφ' ἡμῶν ... 3.61.2). The historicity of this part of the Theban account of regional hegemony is not the issue here; rather, the contrast between Boiotian and non-Boiotian is most notable: the groups are distinguished not in federal terms but rather through perceived racial or cultural differences.

Even in the following sections of their speech the Thebans do not mention any sort of federal organization. At 3.63.1 they revisit the theme of loyalty raised by the Plataians: Greek v. non-Greek allegiance. The Thebans here accuse the Plataians of having wronged the Greeks more than they: ὡς δὲ ὑμεῖς μᾶλλόν τε ἠδικήκατε τοὺς Ἕλληνας καὶ ἀξιώτεροί ἐστε πάσης ζημίας, πειρασόμεθα ἀποφαίνειν ("we will try to show that you have been unjust to the Greeks and that you are more deserving of every punishment"). They make this charge on the basis of Plataian Atticism during the period of Athenian imperialism (Ἀθηναίους μόνους, τοὺς μὲν καταδουλουμένους τὴν Ἑλλάδα, 3.63.3–4). The Plataians and Athenians are characterized as enemies to the rest of the Greeks: the Plataians have allied with those who wrong others, i.e. these others being the rest of the Hellenes, implicitly including Thebes (τοῖς δὲ ἀδικοῦσιν ἄλλους ξυνεργοὶ κατέστητε, 3.63.4). Thus, while the animosity between the two cities is cast in quasi-military terms, it is not based on infractions against a federal military system in Boiotia.

It is only when the Thebans begin describing the actual siege of Plataia of 432–427 that their language implies an umbrella organization of some kind. This period is exactly when one might expect such clues to appear, for the account of the Oxyrhynchus historian provides a *terminus ante quem* for the Boiotian federation of 395 (the King's Peace). It is thus no surprise that Thucydides' Thebans are made to imply the existence of such a political and military federation in recounting events of the last third of the fifth century.

---

[51] Hornblower suggests that Thucydides relies heavily on Herodotus for his Boiotian history, and the similarity in terminology I have noted here may be another indication of this tendency. Hornblower also believes that in composing his speeches Thucydides essentially took most of his material for events before 431 from Herodotus (Hornblower 1995, 668–669).

The Thebans begin their description of these contemporary events at 3.65.2 where they openly address the attack on Plataia. While this passage does not explicitly mention a military federation/*koinon* per se, for the first time in Thucydides an association between military alliances and Boiotian traditions is evident:

> εἰ δὲ ἄνδρες ὑμῶν οἱ πρῶτοι καὶ χρήμασι καὶ γένει, βουλόμενοι τῆς μὲν ἔξω ξυμμαχίας ὑμᾶς παῦσαι, ἐς δὲ τὰ κοινὰ τῶν πάντων Βοιωτῶν πάτρια καταστῆσαι, ἐπεκαλέσαντο ἑκόντες, τί ἀδικοῦμεν;

> But if some of your foremost men in wealth and birth willingly called for aid, because they wanted to put an end to your outside alliance and to position you into the common pursuits of all the Βοιωτοί, then how are we in the wrong? (3.65.2).

Here the late fifth-century status of Plataia as Athens' ally is raised and contrasted to the τὰ κοινὰ τῶν πάντων Βοιωτῶν πάτρια. For the first time in Thucydides then, τὰ πάτρια are described as κοινά. As noted above, in describing earlier events in Boiotia, Thucydides' Thebans did not previously emphasize the commonality of τὰ πάτρια in this way, despite Plataia's late sixth-century relationship with Athens. This subtle shift in terminology is particularly notable in this late fifth-century context, a period when we accept the existence of a political and military Boiotian federation; with regard to this body, the Thebans' new emphasis on communal Boiotian obligation seems apposite.

It is likewise notable that even in this section of their speech the Thebans continue to characterize Plataia's contemporary obligations in ethnic terms. Thebes is made to describe the Plataian traitors as men who were seeking to restore the Plataians back to their own group: ἐς τὴν ξυγγένειαν οἰκειοῦντες (3.65.3). In other words, Thebes is now using older ethnic ties to emphasize further the newer federal obligations. The absence of this connection in the previous sections of the speech may indicate that Thucydides had not been able to characterize Plataian obligations to the Boiotian collective in this way before.

Near the end of their speech the Thebans finally juxtapose a political federation with the phrase τὰ πάτρια Βοιωτῶν. Instead of modifying τὰ πάτρια simply by κοινά, the Thebans specifically mention citizenship κατὰ τὰ τῶν πάντων Βοιωτῶν πάτρια:

> τεκμήριον δὲ ὡς οὐ πολεμίως ἐπράσσομεν· οὔτε γὰρ ἠδικήσαμεν οὐδένα, προείπομέν τε τὸν βουλόμενον κατὰ τὰ τῶν πάντων Βοιωτῶν πάτρια πολιτεύειν ἰέναι πρὸς ἡμᾶς.

> Here is the proof that we did not act in a hostile manner: for we did no one wrong, and we invited whoever wanted to be a citizen according to the traditions of the Βοιωτοί to come over to us (3.66.1).

It is only here in referring to events of 427 that the Thebans draw a connection between πολῖται and τὰ πάτρια Βοιωτῶν. This sole occurrence is surely significant and likely reflects the advent of the Boiotian military and political federation after the mid-fifth century.[52] Even here, however, a specific term is not used to refer to a federal body, e.g. κοινόν, the most common term for federations later in antiquity. The lack of this specific reference here may reflect the relative novelty of the political and military federation or even the term itself as an indicator of unified bodies of *poleis*.

In sum, these Thucydidean passages do not offer evidence for the existence of a political or military Boiotian federation before the mid-fifth century. They do seem to reflect a general period of Theban-Plataian hostility before this time, but the details from Thucydides' Theban speech about earlier Boiotian history are most likely reflections of late fifth-century Theban concerns for their reputation.[53] The terminology of the Theban speech in particular reflects the existence of some sort of military or political federal organization only in the late fifth century.

In the end, then, the accounts of Herodotus and Thucydides cannot be used as evidence for a late sixth-century Boiotian political and military federation. Doing so involves retrojecting late fifth-century accounts back into the Archaic period and ignoring other evidence from these same historians which contradicts this conclusion. The historians' reports rather suggest that a Boiotian military and political federation had come into existence some time before 427 BCE and also that the collective regional ethnic Βοιωτοί, the term usually adduced in modern accounts to signify an early Boiotian military federalism, cannot be so used, since it often denotes a cultural and/or geographic collective in historiographic narratives.

EVIDENCE FOR SIXTH-CENTURY *POLIS* RIVALRY AND INDEPENDENCE

Because the historiographic and material sources traditionally adduced in support of a sixth-century Boiotian military federation of *poleis* are ultimately inconclusive, I now raise evidence for political and military rivalry among Boiotian *poleis* which includes inscriptions, coinage, and dedications commemorating military activities of and between certain communities. These sources further destabilize the traditional view of political and military unity in archaic Boiotia.

Attesting to military capacities and rivalry between Boiotian *poleis* are a number of dedications from Olympia of inscribed armor and weapons. In the sixth century, Orchomenos dedicated a helmet there in honor of a victory over Koroneia.[54] Also in the Late Archaic period the Thebans dedicated a greave

---

[52] In his treatment of this later section of the speech, R. Buck seems to implicitly recognize this change in Theban terminology; he capitalizes Κοινά and seems to equate Κοινὰ τῶν πάντων Βοιωτῶν πάτρια with "early constitutional development" (R. Buck 1979, 124).

[53] They may also have been colored by Thebes' early fourth-century rise to power, if Thucydides' was still "alive and noticing" at that time, as Hornblower remarks (Hornblower 1995, 667).

[54] Jeffery 1990, 95, no 11: Ἐρχομένιοι ἀνέθειαν τōι Δὶ τόλυ<ν>πιōι θορōνεια[θεν]. She dates the piece "as early as the third quarter of the sixth century" on the basis of early letter forms (ε1, μ1, ν1, χ1, ρ2; Jeffery 1990, 93).

commemorating their victory over the smaller but not insignificant *polis* of Hyettos, thereby indicating the community's probable independence at that time.[55] A little before 500 BCE the Koroneians dedicated a helmet to Olympian Zeus, and the Tanagrans a shield.[56] While the occasions for the last two dedications are either not preserved or were never recorded, their use of collective civic-ethnics and the nature of the objects on which they appear suggest that they are military trophies, like the other contemporary dedications involving Orchomenos, Koroneia, Thebes and Hyettos.[57] In combination these dedications suggest that in the late sixth and early fifth centuries Boiotian *poleis* were anything but united in a military and political federation. A number of different areas in fact seem to have been involved in intra-Boiotian hostilities: the northeast (Hyettos), northwest (Orchomenos), west-central (Koroneia), and central (Thebes). Similar spoils were erected by various *poleis* throughout Greece at this time, the most notable in this context by Arkadian communities, which, as Nielsen has demonstrated, were decidedly not organized in a political federation of *poleis* at this time.[58]

Additional details stack the evidence against the existence of a Boiotian political and military federation in this period. That at least six large-sized urban settlements in Boiotia erected protective fortification walls in the sixth century may support interpreting the above evidence for inter-*polis* rivalry and aggression and highlights both these and other subzones within Boiotia that felt the need to protect their inhabitants behind defenses: Chaironeia, Haliartos, Hyettos, Plataia (south), Thebes, and Thisbe (west).[59] That these defensive walls appear in

[55] Originally published by Kunze 1967, 98–100; *SEG* XXIV 300: ΘΕΒΑΙΟΙ ΤΟΝ ΗΥΕΤΙΟΝ. For Hyettos' importance in the Late Archaic period, see Hansen and Nielsen 2004, 442–443; M. Hansen 1995, 16 and n. 17; Knoepfler 1981, 146.

[56] Jeffery dates these two dedications to roughly the same time (Jeffery 1990, 93). On the Koroneian helmet, see Hockey and Johnston 1992, 288: ϙο]ρōνε[ες] ἀνέθειαν τōι Δὶ τόλ[υ]ν-πιō[ι. They argue that the archaeological context rules out a date after 475. A date before 500 is suggested for the inscription; the manufacture of the helmet is placed in the third or fourth quarter of the sixth century. On the Tanagran shield, see Jeffery 1990, 95, no. 12, ca. 525–500; Kunze and Schleif date the piece more generally to the sixth century, noting that whichever date one prefers, this piece is our oldest historical document from Tanagra (Kunze and Schleif 1937/1938, 69; see also 72 and plate 21). Schachter speculatively links this shield to the events of 507/6, but this theory, while attractive, cannot be proven (Schachter 2003, 65).

[57] In connection with these dedications, it is also worth mentioning an inscribed shield taken from some Tanagrans: Ταναγραί[ον hελόντες (Kunze 1956, 36–37 and plates 15–16). The Boiotian provenience of this piece has recently been questioned (see Schachter 2003, 65–66, 68–69 who attributes the piece to the Athenians); if the original attribution holds, however, this shield too may reflect inter-*polis* rivalry in late sixth-century Boiotia. Another possible dedication by a Boiotian city is a Corinthian helmet, inscribed in Boiotian script, dedicated perhaps to Olympian Zeus, as read by Jeffery ([-- Ζεῦ Ὀ]λύνπι' ἄγα[λμα], Jeffery 1990, 93, n. 2). Jeffery compares the helmet to no. 11 from Boiotia, the sixth-century dedication of the Orchomenians upon their defeat of Koroneia. As the name of the dedicator/s does not survive, its inclusion in this group of dedications from Boiotian *poleis* is necessarily speculative; the piece could just as easily have been an individual offering.

[58] Nielsen 2002, 186–187, 222–222.

[59] M. Hansen identifies six communities with dated sixth-century walls or walls of Lesbian masonry: Chaironeia (Hansen and Nielsen 2004, 439; M. Hansen 1996a, 82); Haliartos (Hansen

southern as well as northern and western Boiotia may indicate that threats were perceived as coming from a variety of directions including from within the region itself.

Additionally, in terms of shared coinage, from the early fifth century onward Orchomenos, a *polis* within the geographic confines of Boiotia, mints coins that depict an ear of grain on the reverse. Although these coins are of small denomination, if there were a federation that controlled minting of shared coin types at this time, then Orchomenos was evidently acting independently, even if these small coins were intended only for use within the *polis*. Also, as is well known, during the Persian wars Thespiai and Plataia acted independently by fighting for the Greeks, as recorded on the serpent column and as corroborated by Herodotus. Thespiai's activity as an independent *polis* in the first half of the fifth century is corroborated by *SEG* XXVI 475.3–4, the decree from Olympia in which Thespiai is explicitly treated as autonomous from the Βοιωτοί, as we have seen.[60] This evidence for independent action of Orchomenos, Plataia, and Thespiai in the first half of the fifth century further strengthens the case against the existence of a unified military and political federation of Boiotian *poleis* in the late sixth and early fifth centuries.[61]

KORONEIA: A FIFTH-CENTURY TURNING POINT

As we have now seen in this and previous chapters, literary and numismatic evidence normally adduced as proof for a late sixth- and early fifth-century Boiotian federation fails to document its emergence. Methodological flaws furthermore undermine previous arguments for early Boiotian federalism; additional evidence suggests that Boiotian *poleis* were rivals working in part to consolidate their territories at this time. The first clear ancient evidence for the existence of a Boiotian federation comes from the Oxyrhynchus historian, whose account is

and Nielsen 2004, 442; M. Hansen 1996a, 86–87); Hyettos (Hansen and Nielsen 2004, 443; M. Hansen 1996a, 88); Plataia (Hansen and Nielsen 2004, 451; M. Hansen 1996a, 101); Thebes (Hansen and Nielsen 2004, 456; M. Hansen 1996a, 108–109); Thisbe (Hansen and Nielsen 2004, 458–459; M. Hansen 1996a, 112). It seems likely that at least three other sites were fortified by the late sixth century: Akraiphia (M. Hansen 1996a, 79); Koroneia (M. Hansen 1996a, 91); Orchomenos (Hansen and Nielsen 2004, 448; M. Hansen 1996a, 96–97). Bintliff argues that all large-sized urban settlements in Boiotia were walled at this time (Bintliff 1999, 19, and see fig. 4, p. 20).

[60] See Chapter Five.

[61] This evidence also corroborates Hansen's work on Boiotian "polisness;" he identifies twenty-six archaic and early classical Boiotian *poleis* and speculates that additional communities were also *poleis* (Hansen and Nielsen 2004, 433–459; M. Hansen 1996a, 74–77; Hansen's figures contrast with Bintliff's number of archaic Boiotian "proto-*poleis*" of which only twenty-five to thirty became *poleis*; Bintliff 1996, 193–224; Bintliff 1994, 207–249). Hansen demonstrates that Boiotian *poleis* were arranged in a hierarchy, some being subsidiary to others, e.g., Mykalessos, a sometimes dependent of Tanagra but also a *polis* with its own mint and territory within the Tanagran *chora* (Hansen and Nielsen 2004, 436–437, 446; M. Hansen 1995, 36–37).

traditionally understood to reflect the years 447–387. It is during the middle of the fifth century then, if not slightly later, that we should situate the establishment of a political and military federation in Boiotia.

Ancient sources suggest that the ultimate catalyst for adding a formal military and political dimension to the Boiotian *ethnos* may have been the Boiotians' victory over Athens at Koroneia in 447/6, a battle which resuscitated the region as a whole from the difficulties which had repeatedly presented themselves since the Persian wars and which had left Boiotia in a sorry state. Not only had the conduct of Boiotian *poleis* in the wars blackened the reputation of the Boiotians as a collective, but the withdrawal of the Persian land troops through Boiotia had resulted in serious damage to the region itself. After defeat at Oinophyta in 458/7 select men from Boiotian *poleis* were exiled and the strength of the entire region again suffered under Athenian occupation. The subsequent success of these exiles, banded together in northwestern Boiotia, against the Athenian Tolmides at Koroneia in 447/6 thus marked an important reversal of fortune for the Boiotian collective and provided an event around which the Boiotians could cohere militarily.

Thucydides dramatizes the late fifth-century Theban *boiotarch* Pagondas emphasizing these points while encouraging the Boiotians to fight the Athenians at Delium in 424/3; Pagondas comments on the perceived Athenian tendency to attack the weak:

πεῖραν δὲ ἔχομεν ἡμεῖς αὐτοῦ ἐς τούσδε· νικήσαντες γὰρ ἐν Κορωνείᾳ αὐτούς, ὅτε τὴν γῆν ἡμῶν στασιαζόντων κατέσχον, πολλὴν ἄδειαν τῇ Βοιωτίᾳ μέχρι τοῦδε κατεστήσαμεν. ὧν χρὴ μνησθέντας ἡμᾶς τούς τε πρεσβυτέρους ὁμοιωθῆναι τοῖς πρὶν ἔργοις, τούς τε νεωτέρους πατέρων τῶν τότε ἀγαθῶν γενομένων παῖδας πειρᾶσθαι μὴ αἰσχῦναι τὰς προσηκούσας ἀρετάς ...

We ourselves have experienced this against them (the Athenians); for example, because we defeated them at Koroneia, when they were occupying our land because of our quarreling, up to this very moment we have had great freedom in Boiotia. We ought to remember these things, and our elders must live up to their previous deeds, and our youth, sons of previously heroic fathers, must try not to disgrace their innate excellence ... . (4.92.6–7).

Here Thucydides' Pagondas is made to remind the Boiotians of the significance that the battle of Koroneia held for them as a collective; the event is implicitly cast in heroic terms through the mention of Boiotian *arete* and the concept of equaling previous victory (πρεσβυτέρους ὁμοιωθῆναι τοῖς πρὶν ἔργοις). Most important, Koroneia is characterized as having changed the way of life in Boiotia after a period of fighting between *poleis* (στασιάζω). Because there are few historical specifics in this speech, it seems reasonable to accept its general sentiments toward the battle as accurate reflections of the importance that Koroneia had come to hold in the minds of the Boiotian collective by the last quarter of the fifth century. That Thucydides dramatizes this attitude toward Koroneia indicates that it had become widespread enough to be recognized and presented to his fifth-century audience as a believable rendition of what a leading Boiotian would have said to exhort his men; Pagondas' speech would also surely have been considered successful encouragement, since Thucydides' Athenian audience was certainly still painfully aware of the disastrous Athenian defeat at Boiotian Delium. This passage thus attests to a wide recognition of Koroneia as a decisive moment in collective Boiotian history and one around which Boiotians could later rally together.

Xenophon later makes this same point in commenting on fifth-century Boiotian-Athenian military relations:

ἀλλ' ὁρᾷς, ὅτι, ἀφ' οὗ ἥ τε σὺν Τολμίδῃ τῶν χιλίων ἐν Λεβαδείᾳ συμφορὰ ἐγένετο καὶ ἡ μεθ᾽ Ἱπποκράτους ἐπὶ Δηλίῳ, ἐκ τούτων τεταπείνωται μὲν ἡ τῶν Ἀθηναίων δόξα πρὸς τοὺς Βοιωτούς, ἐπῆρται δὲ τὸ τῶν Θηβαίων φρόνημα πρὸς τοὺς Ἀθηναίους· ὥστε Βοιωτοὶ μέν, οἱ πρόσθεν οὐδ᾽ ἐν τῇ ἑαυτῶν τολμῶντες Ἀθηναίοις ἄνευ Λακεδαιμονίων τε καὶ τῶν ἄλλων Πελοποννησίων ἀντιτάττεσθαι, νῦν ἀπειλοῦσιν αὐτοὶ καθ᾽ αὑτοὺς ἐσβαλεῖν εἰς τὴν Ἀττικήν, Ἀθηναῖοι δέ, οἱ πρότερον, ὅτε Βοιωτοὶ μόνοι ἐγένοντο, πορθοῦντες τὴν Βοιωτίαν, φοβοῦνται, μὴ Βοιωτοὶ δῃώσωσι τὴν Ἀττικήν....

But, you see, ever since the misfortune of the thousand with Tolmides at Lebadeia and with Hippocrates at Delium, the Athenian attitude toward the Boiotians has been humbled, and the Theban disposition toward the Athenians has been strengthened, so that the Boiotians, who formerly would not dare to stand against the Athenians without the Lakedaimonians and other Peloponnesians even in their own land, now threaten to invade Attika by themselves, and the Athenians, who formerly overran Boiotia when the Boiotians were alone, are afraid that the Boiotians may plunder Attica (*Mem.* 3.5.4).[62]

Xenophon here marks the Boiotian efforts at Koroneia and Delium as examples of the new Boiotians: a group to be feared, even by Athenians. The historian also implies that before Koroneia (πρόσθεν), the Boiotians had no collective military cohesiveness and would fight only with the support of others. Together with Thucydides' characterization of the Boiotian *poleis* fighting against each other before Koroneia, it is difficult to believe that Xenophon reminisces here about an already powerful military federation. Instead, like Thucydides' Pagondas, Xenophon suggests that Koroneia was a psychological and organizational turning point for the Boiotian collective and that their subsequent performance at Delium solidified this new strength both for outsiders as well as themselves. Although Larsen acknowledges the psychological impact that Koroneia had on the Boiotians, he has underestimated the impetus that the battle provided for the military organization of Boiotia, as adduced from these sources.[63]

---

[62] Larsen quotes this passage but only in arguing for the psychological impact of Koroneia (see below; Larsen 1960, 11).

[63] Larsen 1960, 11.

A number of other scholars have raised the importance of 447/6 but have not considered the earlier Boiotian collective in sufficient detail. Hornblower, for example, remarks on the general "momentousness" of Koroneia in Boiotian history.[64] On the basis of the Boiotian federal political system described by the Oxyrhynchus historian, Cartledge rightly suggests that the federal structure detailed there sprang up or developed soon after 447/6, and although he views an early Boiotian federation with skepticism, he does not comment much on the earlier situation in Boiotia.[65] Corsten too identifies 447/6 as a turning point in the structure of Boiotian community, although he still defines the earlier Boiotians as a loose urban league under Theban management (an understandable characterization, given Corsten's primary interests in explicating the activities and structure of the later league).[66] Together with the evidence from the ancient sources, the weight of these scholars' opinions on the significance of 447/6 for Boiotian federalism suggests that we should indeed envision Koroneia as the event which ultimately proved the value of a permanent and structured military alliance between men from many Boiotian *poleis* as opposed to a catalyst for further sustained militarism.

Additional evidence recommends viewing Koroneia as the trigger for a final and formal formation of the military and political Boiotian federation. On the basis of Thucydides' narrative at 1.113, Larsen suggests that Orchomenos, not Thebes, initiated the rebellion from Athenian hegemony in 447.[67] The traditional interpretation of a pre-447/6 federation under Theban leadership conflicts with this view of Orchomenian influence. If Larsen is right, then before 447/6 a rather different hierarchy of power existed in Boiotia from that usually understood. This speculation indirectly supports the argument for development of a Theban-dominated military federation only after Koroneia.

Notably, Plutarch mentions a *tropaion* set up at the sanctuary of Athena Itonia commemorating Koroneia.[68] The Boiotians erected only three known monuments marking military battles: this one after Koroneia, the *tropaion* for Leuktra in 371, and the lion of Chaironeia in 338. The chronology of these monuments may suggest that Koroneia was the first battle which the Boiotians could mark as a collective. According to tradition, the Boiotians had previously been victorious at Keressos, an important battle which they could have memorialized with a *tropaion*, yet sources report no physical marker of that event.[69] Koroneia's

---

[64] Hornblower 1995, 674–675.

[65] Cartledge 2000, 402, note 15, and 403. In this context it notable that underlying Cartledge's view is an acceptance of M. Hansen's skepticism toward an early Boiotian federation.

[66] Corsten 1999, 60; in general see also 26–60, esp. 50–60.

[67] Larsen 1960, 9–17, esp. 9–12.

[68] πλησίον γὰρ ὁ νεώς ἐστιν ὁ τῆς Ἰτωνίας Ἀθηνᾶς, καὶ πρὸ αὐτοῦ τρόπαιον ἔστηκεν, ὃ πάλαι Βοιωτοὶ Σπάρτωνος στρατηγοῦντος ἐνταῦθα νικήσαντες Ἀθηναίους καὶ Τολμίδην ἀποκτείναντες ἔστησαν (Plut. *Agesilaos* 19.2). For Perikles' warning to Tolmides before Koroneia and a brief description of the battle, see Plut. *Perikles* 18.2–3.

[69] For the tradition of this battle, which has been variously dated, see the concluding remarks of this chapter. That *tropaia* did not begin appearing until the sixth century does not undermine the absence of a known collective marker for Keressos (on *tropaia*, see Hölscher 1998, 157–158).

τρόπαιον at the Itonion seems more significant in light of the apparent absence of a memorial for Keressos. Furthermore, the monument for Koroneia is the first military marker known to have been set up at the Itonion. It thus could mark the transition of that sanctuary from a *ethnos*-centered religious site to a central sanctuary for the formal military and political federation.

I thus propose the following historical reconstruction. After defeat at Oinophyta by Athens, select Boiotians were exiled to Orchomenos. These men, already linked through shared traditions of decent, territory, symbol, dialect, and a common name, began working together to overthrow Athenian military occupation of the region. The exiles thus comprised the foundation for the later military *koinon*. Tolmides' advance into central Boiotia without supporting troops offered an unforeseen opportunity to push the Athenian forces out of the region. Boiotian success at Koroneia naturally led to a more pronounced military complexion of the group by proving the worth of developing and maintaining a permanent military body in the region, as opposed to relying on the *ad hoc* mobilization of men in times of local need. Boiotia's victory over Athens at Koroneia thus served as the final catalyst in developing Boiotian military unity, a process which had begun in earnest after Oinophyta.

Certainly formal military organization of Boiotia was closely tied to political organization. In order to formulate and administer a regional army, Boiotia had to be divided into subunits according to population and means. These zones also formed the basic units for political administration. From these observations it does not necessarily follow, however, that the federal organization described by the Oxyrhynchus historian was set into place immediately after Koroneia. As Cartledge notes, the transition to a federal system may have been a rather more extended process, especially if the structure was essentially new, as I am arguing.[70] The system had developed into its full form by the early years of the fourth century, as the Oxyrhynchus account indicates. How much ideologies, e.g., oligarchic v. democratic, played a role in this development is difficult to surmise, but Cartledge's comments on Boiotian displeasure with Athenian-style democratic rule from 458/7–447/6 are intriguing. Distaste for Athens and its mode of incorporating a portion of the "proletariat" into its government may have stimulated Boiotian development of federal *isonomia* among oligarchs.[71]

---

[70] Cartledge 2000, 403.
[71] See Cartledge 2000, 406–411, esp. 409–410.

CHAPTER 7
CONCLUSIONS AND COMPARANDA

In this book I have presented evidence for Boiotian collective identity from both internal Boiotian and external non-Boiotian sources from the Early Classical period and earlier. I have suggested that rather than a developed military and political organization, at this time the Boiotians cohered as a loose *ethnos*, basing their common identity on a surprisingly consonant combination of interrelated criteria and indicia, which I briefly review here in anticipation of offering contemporaneous comparanda.

By the Late Archaic period the Boiotians claim descent from an eponymous figurehead, Βοιωτός, whose genealogy associates the group with cult through his connections to deities prominent in the central region, most notably Poseidon Onchestos, as the *Ehoiai* attests. Boiotos' descent from an Aiolid, specified as Arne in one source, is the most consistent component of his family tree. This aspect of Boiotos' descent adds a second layer of meaning to his collective importance, as his link to the Aiolidai ties the Boiotians to southeastern Thessaly.

Boiotos' Thessalian pedigree involves the second major criterion of Boiotian identity: the tradition of Boiotian migration in which Βοιωτός may have played a role as organizer, if not oikist. Through the *Iliad* and the *Ehoiai*, parts of this story date ca. 700–580. One of the most significant factors of the migration tradition is the expulsion of the Boiotians from Thessalian Arne, a legend which is mirrored in Boiotos' genealogy as son of the Thessalian Aiolid Arne and possible leader in Boiotian Arne.

The tradition of Boiotian territory also involves panhellenic recognition of Boiotian habitation of the region at the time of the Trojan expedition through acceptance of the *Iliad's* Catalogue of Ships, a formulaic set piece which depicts the Boiotians as wealthy, powerful, and populous. This criterion for Boiotian group identity thus complements indications of Boiotian interest the Trojan War saga and the Boiotians of the Catalogue, as attested in the marked retention of epicizing archaisms in the Boiotian dialect as well as in the use of the cutout shield on shared Boiotian coinage. This iconographic link between the Boiotians and the Aiakid Ajax's famed shield reinforces literary accounts which link the Boiotians to the Aiakid family through the Asopids. The cutout shape on Boiotian coinage also likely directly recalls the Boiotian provenience of Ajax's epic shield; at the same time the shape also plays on the name of the material from which epic shields were constructed and on the name of the Boiotian collective.

In tandem with these defining aspects of the Boiotian collective, Boiotian and non-Boiotian use of *ethnika*, found particularly in the *Iliad's* Catalogue of Ships, the Theban *Aspis* and in inscriptions, attests to a sense of geographic regionalism and identification with this regional and non-civic collective. *Ethnika* also mark the collective's cultic facet, an already well-documented factor in sixth-century Boiotian identity and one now reinforced by the tradition of Boiotos' descent.

By the late sixth century, then, the Boiotians had constructed a collective identity centered around genealogy, geography, links to southern Thessaly, a tradition of invasion, cult, dialect, ties to epic tradition, the Βοιωτοί of epic, specific heroic shields, and the Aiakid family. This web of interrelated factors does not point toward the existence of a formal or developed political and military federation but rather marks archaic Boiotian preoccupation with the past, descent, and territory. Historiographic and epigraphic evidence suggests that the Boiotian *ethnos* augmented its unity by adding to it a federal structure around the middle of the fifth century.

These conclusions compare to a number of regional identities in other areas of archaic Greece. Phokis provides the most illuminating comparison, for by the end of the Archaic period the Phokians had constructed a strong ethnic and territorial group identity based on various traditions, one of which was the Catalogue of Ships.[1] By this time eponymous figures named Phokos had also appeared in myth, to which some (but not all) Phokian *poleis* claimed connections through cult and myth. These connections to Phokos helped delimit the emerging group of Phokians at this time.[2] Similarly, evidence for Arkadian collective identity starts appearing in the material record at the end of the sixth century.[3] The Arkadians shared a common name, traditions of descent and territory, and aspects of a shared culture, although evidence suggests that Arkadian *poleis* also sparred during the Archaic period. Like Boiotia, Arkadian claims to ethnic unity from the late sixth and early fifth centuries helped stimulate the incorporation of a political dimension to the group at times during the fifth century, particularly in opposition to other groups.[4]

Before such collective ethnogenesis in Arkadia and Phokis, the regions consisted in multiple communities and territorial zones.[5] In Phokis, settlements differentiated themselves from their neighbors through myth and cult, occasionally forming some sort of bond with various neighbors within the larger region.[6] It is possible to deduce a similar process at work in Boiotia in the Archaic period. Unity or attempted unity of small non-contiguous communities of the region, for example, may be reflected in the victory dedications from some of the more powerful Boiotian *poleis* discussed in the preceding Chapter. The development of such subzones also helps explain Herodotus 5.79.2, without resorting to the interpretation of a Theban-dominated Boiotian federation in the sixth century. In

[1] McInerney 1999, 120–127, 162, and 154-155.

[2] McInerney 1999, 127–149; Morgan 2003, 113. This is not to de-emphasize the other layers of identity analyzed by McInerney, especially on the civic level.

[3] Morgan 1999, 382.

[4] Nielsen 2002, 54–88, 111–157, 226–228; Nielsen 1999, 16–60; Morgan 1999, 382; Morgan 2003, 39. Nielsen argues that the Arkadians did not unite "in a truly political organisation" until the fourth century (Nielsen 2002, 154).

[5] Morgan 1999, 429–430.

[6] McInerney 1999, 127–149.

this passage, after the defeat of the Boiotians and Chalkidians in 507/6, the Thebans receive an oracle from Delphi urging them to beg their "nearest" (ἄγχιστα) for help. The Thebans express surprise, saying:

οὐκ ὦν ἄγχιστα ἡμέων οἰκέουσι Ταναγραῖοί τε καὶ Κορωναῖοι καὶ Θεσπιέες; καὶ οὗτοί γε ἅμα ἡμῖν αἰεὶ μαχόμενοι προθύμως συνδιαφέρουσι τὸν πόλεμον· τί δεῖ τούτων γε δέεσθαι;

Are the Tanagrans and Koroneians and Thespians not those who live nearest us? These men eagerly wage battle, always fighting with us: why must we beg them?

Although we must be cautious about the historical accuracy of the passage, Herodotus' representation of military cooperation among a group of neighboring Boiotian communities is significant, particularly in light of the Phokian and Arkadian comparanda for regional subzones mentioned above. It may likewise be important that Herodotus does not call these communities σύμμαχοι, "allies." They are portrayed as fighting together when necessary, implicitly on the grounds of their proximity to each other and of some sort of shared identity, not on the basis of a formal military alliance. It thus seems reasonable to understand late sixth-century Boiotian communities like Thebes, Orchomenos, Tanagra, Hyettos, and even Thespiai and Plataia as *poleis* controlling nearby territory and smaller settlements, competing with their stronger neighbors within Boiotia for territory and power.

Thus, as McInerney has suggested for Phokian development, in Boiotia various sparring subzones fused as a united group through construction and use of the common traditions identified in the previous chapters. The economic component of this *ethnos*, as marked by the early shared coinage, came to prominence by the last decade of the sixth century. It was this cultural and economic collective that created the atmosphere in which the later military and political federation arose.[7]

Unlike Phokis, however, evidence suggests that various subzones in Boiotia did not finally unite in a proper political and military federation until the mid-fifth century. As we have seen, it is only around this time that the use of the term

[7] See McInerney 148–149, 154. This conclusion is not entirely opposed to some previous views of pre-federal Boiotia, for various scholars had posited some sort of religious or cultural group before the advent of a Boiotian federation. However, the date for this group was pushed back to the Early Archaic period or even to an unspecified earlier time. R. Buck, for example, speculates that an early Boiotian amphiktyony supervised the Pamboiotia and also chose delegates for participation in the Delphic amphiktyony (R. Buck 1979, 89, and note 13, where he relies only on evidence from the Hellenistic and Roman federation); Mafodda pushes the common cultural and religious traditions of the Boiotians back to a historical "Homeric age" (Mafodda 2000, 101–102). Guillon alludes to cultic activities at Thebes which he sets at the head of a sixth-century federation; he also theorizes about religious origins for the federation (Guillon 1963, 66, note 81, for Thebes as head; Guillon 1948, 27, on cult); Ducat too remarks on the Pamboiotia, the similarity of cults within Boiotia, and the close placement of Onchestos and the Itonion along a very ancient road; he rejects the emergence of a military federation from a cultural group, however (Ducat 1973, 60–61).

Βοιωτοί changes slightly in epigraphic sources. The bronze plaque from Olympia (*SEG* XXVI 475), for example, attests that in the middle of the century outsiders begin to characterize the Boiotians as some sort of political group. Moreover, the dedication of Ἐπίδαλλος from Delphi, best dated to the second half of the fifth century, may offer an insider's view of the political significance of the term (*LSAG* 93.17). Change in use of the term Βοιωτοί and in other terminology in Thucydides' Theban speeches from the Plataian episode corroborates this epigraphic shift.

Outside Phokis and Arkadia, we find a close parallel for archaic collective definition centered upon the past, descent, and cult in the Ionian cities of western Asia Minor. I need not rehearse well-known Ionian claims to common descent. I turn to the less obvious Panionion, a site near Mt. Mykale which contained an altar to Poseidon dating to the Late Archaic period. An archaic inscription found at the nearby archaic settlement Melie, located on the hillock just west of the Panionion altar, corroborates archaic activity in the area.[8] Cult activity at the site, however, may have occurred at least in the seventh century; Geometric and early archaic pottery is attested at Melie.[9] Representatives from the twelve Ionian cities of the coast are thought to have gathered here at this time, particularly to celebrate their common festival, the *Panionia*. It is not until the fourth century that we have evidence for a political function of the site.

Herodotus provides a most intriguing discussion of the military activities of the cities involved in Ionian cult activity at the Panionion. The historian describes Lydian aggression toward Miletos which began in the reign of Ardys, son of Gyges (Hdt. 1.15) but which reached its peak under Alyattes in the first half of the sixth century. The war continued for years, as Herodotus repeatedly remarks (Hdt. 1.17.1, 1.18.1, 1.19.1). Despite Miletos' inclusion among the Ionian cities, Herodotus tellingly remarks on Miletos' position during this extended period of Lydian hostility:

> τοῖσι δὲ Μιλησίοισι οὐδαμοὶ Ἰώνων τὸν πόλεμον τοῦτον συνεπελάφρυνον ὅτι μὴ Χῖοι μοῦνοι. οὗτοι δὲ τὸ ὅμοιον ἀνταποδιδόντες ἐτιμώρεον· καὶ γὰρ δὴ πρότερον οἱ Μιλήσιοι τοῖσι Χίοισι τὸν πρὸς Ἐρυθραίους πόλεμον συνδιήνεικαν.

None of the Ionians came to the aid of the Milesians in this war except the Chians. The Chians were honoring the repayment of a similar action, for formerly the Milesians had pursued war for the Chians against the Erythraians (Hdt. 1.18.3).

This passage suggests that despite common bonds of kinship and cult, the archaic Ionians were under no obligation to assist each other in times of war. Like the

---

[8] Izmir Museum no. 3757. Melie was destroyed in the Archaic period (ca. 700 BCE), perhaps because of rivalry over control of the Panionion, according to John McK. Camp (pers. comm.; on the partition of Melian territory, see Caspari 1915, 174–176; on the history and archaeology of the Panionion and Melie in general, see Kleiner, et al., 1967, 78–167; Simon 1986, 151–152).

[9] See Simon 1986, 151.

archaic Boiotian *poleis*, then, the Ionian cities do not seem to have been organized in a steady political or military federation at this time, despite common
bonds of kinship and cultural practice.

Achaia offers an additional and likewise illuminating parallel which confirms
the archaic presence of many of the trends adduced for the Boiotian *ethnos* as
well as many previously well-documented patterns in Boiotian cult. Like Boiotia,
the early Achaian *ethnos* was oriented around control of descent, and, although
Achaia does not seem to have been as concerned with territory as Boiotia, during
times of regional stress Achaian communities acted as an *ad hoc* military group.
This tendency toward Achaian "mass tactics" is even evident as late as the
Peloponnesian war, when, as Morgan remarks, local Achaian communities joined
up only when "unavoidable" and then often "passively."[10] Even so, local Achaian
communities do not seem to have formed a political federation until the end of the
fifth century.[11]

Aside from military activities, the Archaic Achaian *ethnos*, like the Boiotian
collective, shows its community through centrally located pan-Achaian cults
situated at important cultural and geographic intersections.[12] In Boiotia, this
pattern appears with the central placement of the Itonion, the Alalkomenion, and
the sanctuary of Poseidon at Onchestos. The Itonion and especially Onchestos
were located at important trade and passage junctions between the Athamantine
plain and the Kopaic basin, in part perhaps out of an interest in displaying the
cultic aspect of Boiotian identity to those traveling along the route between Attica
and Delphi.[13] These patent similarities between Boiotian and Achaian cultic
geography highlight the less obvious parallels between potential *ad hoc* group
mobilization in each area and each group's focus on descent as a criterion in
collective definition.

In terms of the ability to gather and the motives for group mobilization,
archaic Thessaly too provides an example which may help explicate late archaic
and early classical Boiotian military activity. Rather than organized from a
federal center, archaic Thessaly can be viewed as quasi-dynastic in terms of leadership and dominance of a few powerful aristocrats who mobilized certain areas
and communities within the region, as Archibald argues.[14] These areas were not
necessarily consistently cooperative, however.[15] Such a model might be useful in
considering the kind of power that Boiotian Thebes seems to have exerted in

[10] Morgan 1991, 146 (Pellene in fact remained rebellious for the entire war).

[11] Morgan 2003, 37–38, 196; Morgan and Hall 1996, 164–165, 193–199.

[12] Morgan 1991, 144–146; Morgan 2003, 113. For analysis of community-building through
cult in Phokis, Thessaly, and Arkadia, see Morgan 2003, 107–163, where she also rightly notes
that this kind of cohesion through cult is not a static phenomenon in any region.

[13] For the economic interactions behind this cult placement in Boiotia, see Mackil 2003; for
a similar study of Thessaly, see Morgan 2003, 135–142, and also 149–155 (more general remarks on economy of cult and specific examples of other sites), 162–163, 206–223. For later
cultic activity of the Boiotian *koinon*, see Beck 1997, 191–192 (who focuses on the Basileia at
Lebadeia) and Schachter 1981–1994.

[14] Archibald 2001; see also Morgan 2003, 23–24, 86–87.

[15] Morgan 2003, 87.

south and southeastern Boiotia; instead of viewing Thebes as the head of an early Boiotian federation, we might speculate that Thebes was the center of a powerful aristocratic group which repeatedly attempted to control part of the region in the Late Archaic and Early Classical periods and which later tendentiously claimed to have controlled the whole area at this time, as I have argued for the Thebans of Thucydides. Two Boiotian inscriptions that Morgan raises in the context of cultic community may bear on this issue of Boiotian aristocratic groups: one, a sixth-century dedication from the Ptoion which mentions a group of *hetairoi*, and the other, a Theban inscription from Tanagra which describes the Theban dedicands as *lektois*: chosen.[16]

EXTERNAL CATALYSTS FOR BOIOTIAN COLLECTIVE COHESION

The above selection of comparative cases for aspects of Boiotian collective identity well illustrates the plausibility of the approach I have taken in this book toward the Boiotian *ethnos*. It remains to suggest possible reasons for the evolving cohesion of the Boiotians in the Late Archaic period. I will not offer a complete answer to this complex issue in this concluding section, since the various catalysts behind Boiotian collective cohesion require full-length monographs;[17] I venture rather to raise a probable factor here which mirrors sixth-century Phokian ethnogenesis in particular. The Phokian *ethnos* defined itself partially through opposition to Lokris and particularly Thessaly. Evidence for Boiotia suggests that opposition to and interaction with outside groups during the sixth century also served to push the Boiotians toward unity;[18] not surprisingly, these groups included the Phokians and the Thessalians. Consistent hostility is not always visible between these groups and the Boiotians, and certain ambivalence if not downright imitation is sometimes apparent (e.g., the adoption of Thessalian place names and Thessalian cult figures in Boiotia). However, a marked Boiotian rivalry with these two regions is evident in archaic and early classical sources. Because Thessaly also looms large in Phokian ethnogenesis, then, I offer here a necessarily condensed account of Thessaly as a catalyst in Boiotian collective

---

[16] For the Ptoion piece, see Effenterre and Ruzé 1994, no. 69 (with bibliography). For the Tanagran dedication, see Jeffery 1990, 94, no. 7, ca. 610–550; Effenterre and Ruzé 1994, no. 70 (with bibliography). Schachter questions the Tanagran provenance of this piece, placing it in Thebes instead (Schachter 1981–1994, vol. 1, 86; 1989, 79). Morgan attributes this second piece to Hermes, although it may have been a dedication to Apollo, since Apollo gave Hermes the staff (*Hymn. Hom. Ap.* 528ff.; Morgan 2003, 163; see also Schachter 1981–1994, vol. 1, 86).

[17] For approaches to early community interactions in regions which resulted in a sense of collective unity, see Mackil 2003 and Morgan 2003, especially 168–187, 213–225.

[18] In advocating such an oppositional model for Boiotian development, I follow Barth, Hall, and McInerney (Barth 1969, 9–38; Hall 1997, 32–33; McInerney 1999, esp. 141–143, 145–146). That other sixth-century groups besides the Phokians defined themselves similarly through opposition is generally accepted; on the interesting case of the Polichnitai of western Crete see Sekunda 2000, 331–334.

articulation; a glimpse of Boiotian ambivalence toward Phokis also appears in this account.[19]

A number of aspects of Boiotian identity presented in earlier chapters raise implicit opposition to Thessaly. The tradition of Boiotian migration, which describes Boiotian settlement and migration from Thessaly, may in part reflect interregional antagonism. Boiotian use of the cutout shield, a common heroic symbol often associated with Achilles in sixth-century iconography, might also be seen as a competitive Boiotian claim to a traditionally Thessalian hero.

The Theban *Aspis* in particular expresses anti-Thessalian sentiment; here the Theban Herakles fights and defeats the Thessalian Kyknos in a mythical battle which reflects both interregional rivalries and alliances in mid-sixth-century Greece.[20] Notably, Boiotia and Phokis are presented as necessary, if not uncomfortable, allies against the Thessalian warrior, their now common enemy.[21] This fictionalized cooperation should be read against the earlier *Hymn to Pythian Apollo* which presents a markedly more hostile Boiotian-Phokis relationship. The *Aspis*, particularly given its Theban origins, may thus indicate a developing relation between the two regions during the second half of the sixth century, based in part on mutual hostility to Thessalian invasions into central Greece at this time.[22] That Theban Pindar later performed a different version of the story in which Thessalian Kyknos defeated Herakles may indicate that any amity reached between Phokis and Boiotia in the mid-sixth century was short-lived.[23]

Regardless of Phokian-Boiotian cooperation, it is clear that throughout the sixth century, but particularly in the second half, Thessaly encroached upon territories to its south that belonged to Phokis and Boiotia.[24] Phokis accordingly developed a fierce anti-Thessalian attitude, manifest in various oral traditions and in the construction of defensive walls.[25] Phokian traditions include tales of Phokian revolt against the Thessalians on Parnassos at night, and a Phokian trap for Thessalian cavalry near Hyampolis in the years before the Persian Wars. Plutarch recounts the most famous tradition of Phokian resistance in which the underdog

[19] I prepare a fuller treatment of this topic in article format.

[20] Stesichoros' earliest version of the story, being neither directly quoted nor Boiotian, provides only a probable *terminus ante quem* of the late seventh or early sixth century for the story (Schol. Pind. *Ol.* 10.19 [fr. 207 Page *PMG*]). Also see Schol. Pind. *Ol.* 10.21 (fr. 207 Page *PMG*).

[21] The *Aspis* clearly indicates Kyknos' Thessalian pedigree by mentioning the warrior's Thessalian burial place twice (lines 380–382, 472–475).

[22] Shapiro has argued that the traditions of Herakles and Kyknos and of Herakles and the Delphic tripod must be linked (and therefore analyzed) together on the basis of their connections to Delphi (Shapiro 1984b, 273). While both stories may have originally been tied to Delphi, they did not necessarily arise in the same contexts. I thus consider them separate traditions.

[23] Pind. *Ol.* 10.19.

[24] For a brief and general treatment of archaic Thessaly, see Doulgeri-Indzessiliglou 1991, 26–27. For a still useful longer discussion of early Thessaly, see Larsen 1968, 104–121; for the territorality of Thessaly in central Greece during the sixth century, see Lehmann 1983, 35–43.

[25] See McInerney 1999, 174–175, for the wall which he dates to the years before the outbreak of the Persian Wars.

Phokians defeat the Thessalians at Kleonai, thereby saving the entire region. Herodotus humorously describes how the Phokians chose sides in the Persian Wars: they simply picked the side opposite the Thessalians.[26] McInerney dates the genesis of these stories to a generation before the Persian Wars (the late sixth and very early fifth centuries) but suggests that traditions of Thessalian incursions against Phokis reflect the entire course of the sixth century, beginning with early Thessalian successes in the First Sacred War.[27] The historicity of these stories aside, it seems reasonable to accept that these traditions reflect some sort of real sixth-century (or earlier) hostility between Thessalians and Phokians over territory.

Thessalian aggression also left its mark on Boiotian tradition, most notably in the tradition of the battle of Keressos. Similar to the Phokian tradition of victory over the Thessalians at Kleonai, the tradition of Keressos records a Boiotian victory over Thessaly. As argued below, the story of Keressos reflects sixth and early fifth-century Boiotian sentiment toward Thessaly, a historical context which overlaps with McInerney's date for Phokian resistance to Thessaly. Both Boiotia and Phokis thus seem to have expressed antipathy toward Thessalian expansion in the mid- to late sixth century.

The tradition of Keressos is problematic. Pausanias briefly describes the place and event:

ἔστι δὲ ἐχυρὸν χωρίον ὁ Κερησσὸς ἐν τῇ Θεσπιέων, ἐς ὃ καὶ πάλαι ποτὲ ἀνεσκευάσαντο κατὰ τὴν ἐπιστρατείαν τὴν Θεσσαλῶν· οἱ Θεσσαλοὶ δὲ τότε, ὡς ἑλεῖν τὸν Κερησσόν σφισι πειρωμένοις ἐφαίνετο ἐλπίδος κρεῖσσον, ἀφίκοντο ἐς Δελφοὺς παρὰ τὸν θεόν ...

Keressos is a secure place in the territory of Thespiai, in which once a long time ago they prepared against the invasion of the Thessalians; since their [the Thessalians'] attempts at taking Keressos seemed hopeless at that time, they consulted the god at Delphi ... (Paus. 9.14.2).

There is little real evidence for the location of the battle. Pausanias sets the site in the vicinity of Thespiai, as does Plutarch (see below, *Mor.* 866 E–F). These sources permit no further specificity, as Fossey notes,[28] and are likewise unclear on Keressos' date. Pausanias' term πάλαι indicates only that the battle was understood to have taken place in the distant past.

Plutarch also indicates that Keressos occurred far before his time. However, in attempting specificity, he complicates the matter by offering two contradictory

---

[26] For the traditions of the night revolt and the cavalry trap, see Hdt. 8.27–28, and McInerney 1999, 175; For Plutarch's tradition, see Plut. *Mor.* 868B–D, and McInerney 1999, 176–178; for Phokian refusal to medize, Hdt. 8.30, and McInerney 1999, 176; for a summary of Phokian antipathy toward Thessaly as visible in both the literary and material records, see Morgan 2003, 131–134.

[27] McInerney 1999, 177.

[28] Fossey 1988, 163. Also see Wallace 1974, 12–14; R. Buck 1972b, 31–40 (who bases his argument for locating the site on the "purpose" of the Thessalian commander); R. Buck 1979, 10, 108.

dates. In a first description, Plutarch places Keressos in the sixth century, more than two-hundred years before Leuktra (thus ca. 571):

τοῦτο μὲν τοίνυν Βοιωτοῖς Ἱπποδρομίου μηνός, ὡς δ᾽ Ἀθηναῖοι καλοῦσιν Ἑκατομβαιῶνος, ἱσταμένου πέμπτῃ δύο λαβεῖν συνέβη νίκας ἐπιφανεστά-τας, αἷς τοὺς Ἕλληνας ἠλευθέρωσαν, τήν τε περὶ Λεῦκτρα καὶ τὴν ἐπὶ Κερησσῷ ταύτης πρότερον ἔτεσι πλείοσιν ἢ διακοσίοις, ὅτε Λατταμύαν καὶ Θεσσαλοὺς ἐνίκησαν.

Well then, on the fifth of the month Hippodromios, which the Athenians call Hekatombaion, the Boiotians happened to win two renowned victories through which they freed the Greeks: the one at Leuktra and that at Keressos, more than two hundred years before Leuktra, when they defeated Lattamyas and the Thessalians (Plut. *Cam.* 19.2).

Some reject this date as ridiculously early; others question it on the basis of Plutarch's second reference to the battle. There, after quoting Herodotus, Plutarch characterizes relations between Boiotia and Thessaly. Within the dramatic context of Thermopylai, the Thebans approach the Persians, claiming to have already medized in an attempt to save their own lives. Overhearing this, the Thessalians address the Persians too and describe their relations with the Thebans:

... καὶ Θεσσαλοὺς μεταξὺ τῶν φονευομένων καὶ πατουμένων ὑπ᾽ ἀλλήλων παρὰ τὰ στενὰ Θηβαίοις συνδικοῦντας, ὅτι τῆς Ἑλλάδος αὐτοὺς κρατουν-τὰς ἄχρι Θεσπιέων ἔναγχος ἐξήλασαν μάχῃ περιγενόμενοι καὶ τὸν ἄρχοντα Λατταμύαν ἀποκτείναντες. ταῦτα γὰρ ὑπῆρχε Βοιωτοῖς τότε καὶ Θεσσαλ-οῖς πρὸς ἀλλήλους, ἐπιεικὲς δὲ καὶ φιλάνθρωπον οὐδέν.

... and while men were being killed and trampled on by others in the narrow pass, the Thessalians testified for the Thebans, saying that the Thebans defeated them in battle, driving them out, killing their leader Lattamyas, although the Thessalians had power in Greece all the way up to Thespiai. This was what existed at that time between the Boiotians and Thessalians – there was nothing good or friendly there (Plut. *Mor.* 866 E–F; *de Hdt. mal.* 33).

Scholars suspect that Plutarch has garbled his numbers in these two passages, writing "more than two-hundred years before Leuktra" in the first passage when he actually meant "more than one-hundred years." Such an emendation would resolve both of Plutarch's passages, setting Keressos roughly at the time of the Persian wars.[29]

---

[29] Larsen 1968, 113–114 accepts this view, although his interpretation of the battle seems to be an amalgamation of both Plutarch's and Pausanias' descriptions; also see Larsen 1960, 236–237, and R. Buck 1979, 108, 118 note 13. In reaction to a Herodotean passage which implies Thessalian-Boiotian friendliness near the Persian wars, Buck has proposed an alternate date for Keressos: ca. 520 (Hdt. 7.233). In support he identifies the figure Lattamyas, called *archon* at Plut. *Mor.* 866 E, as a Thessalian *tagos* and inserts Lattamyas into his own list of *tagoi*, thereby arriving at a date of ca. 520 (R. Buck 1979, 109). However, as Buck himself notes, none of the ancient passages explicitly refers to Lattamyas' status as *tagos*; Buck's date for Keressos of ca.

Attempts at pinpointing a specific date for the battle thus seem futile, as Schachter remarks.[30] Instead of treating Keressos as an identifiable historical event, then, we should perhaps more reasonably consider it a tradition which marks an extent of time during which Boiotian hostilities toward Thessaly had reached a peak, similar to the Phokian anti-Thessalian tradition in the Late Archaic and Early Classical periods.[31] Plutarch's dates for Keressos, ca. 571 and around the time of Leuktra, may thus roughly mark the chronological period in which Boiotian anti-Thessalian attitudes had solidified and had become most relevant to the collective. In other words, "Keressos" may have become, in part, a synonym for anti-Thessalian sentiment in Boiotia during the sixth century and later, ending slightly after the King's Peace and the dissolution of the Boiotian *koinon* in 386. Plutarch's conflicting dates for the battle become irrelevant when considering Keressos as a tradition which began to define the Boiotians during the same period when other evidence for their ethnogenesis begins to appear in the record.

Further exploration of an oppositional model for archaic Boiotian cohesion requires further work, as do the other catalysts behind collective Boiotian cohesion. Other projects implied in the preceding chapters also require attention, e.g., delineating subunits of power within the Boiotian *ethnos* during the Late Archaic and Early Classical periods, as Nielsen has done for Arkadia and Morgan has summarized for Thessaly.[32] Although M. Hansen's recent work has greatly improved our knowledge about individual Boiotian *poleis*, more can still be done with these communities, especially in terms of myth as well as real excavation. Thebes, as a major *polis* center, demands particular work on all levels of evidence.[33]

I can only hope that this reassessment and redefinition of the Boiotian *ethnos* during the Late Archaic and Classical periods brings Boiotian studies more to the fore of present scholarship and helps resuscitate the Boiotians further from the (still) common Athenian charge of rustic provincialism and piggishness. In relying on genealogy, tradition of territory, symbolism, dialect, and a common name to construct their collective self-image, the Boiotians plainly parallel other less-maligned groups in late sixth- and early fifth-century Greece.

---

520 thus remains unsubstantiated. A variety of terms were used to refer to Thessalian *tagoi*, however (i.e. *archon, archos,* and *tetrarchos*; Helly *OCD,* s.v. *tagos*), see Helly 1995.

[30] Schachter 1989, 82. See Buck for a review of more scholarly arguments about the date (R. Buck 1979, 108–109 and 188, n. 13). Janko seems inclined to take evidence for Keressos from Plutarch's *Cam.* 19.2 as opposed to *Mor.* 866, on the basis of the unreliability of the latter and the brevity of the former (Janko 1986, 47 and note 52).

[31] Suggestive of this period are McInerney's phrases "in the course of the sixth century" and "within a generation of the Persian invasion" (McInerney 1999, 177).

[32] See Nielsen 1999, 51–59, and 2002, 160–307. On Thessaly, see Morgan 2001, 30–34 and the other works cited there.

[33] Despite Symeonoglou's excellent overview of the city. On big sites and the important issues involved in their analysis, see Morgan 2003, 45–85.

ICONOGRAPHIC APPENDIX

Included in the following sections (A–J) are all currently accepted images of Achilles, Ajax and Menelaos with the specified weapon from *LIMC* I, 1981 (s.v. Achilles; Aias), Boardman 1974, Carpenter 1991 and the Beazley archive database.

I omit vases which may depict individual heroes with the specified weapons but which cannot be linked to the figures with certainty and are thus questionable (e.g., where the Beazley archive prints a "?" after the hero's name, *vel sim.*). Also omitted are vases for which both a photograph was unavailable and the prose description did not clearly indicate to which figure the shield should be attributed (e.g. from Sotheby's catalogues, private collections, market sales, *vel sim.*). In the Beazley archive, a distinction is made between "shield/shield device" and "Boeotian shield;" thus, the Beazley archive inclusions here are based on the broad searches: ACHILLES and SHIELD; AJAX and SHIELD; MENELAOS and SHIELD. Dates come from *LIMC* or Beazley unless otherwise noted.

A. ACHILLES IN BLACK FIGURE WITH CUTOUT SHIELD
(in chronological order; additional media at end of section)
Total: 115

1. Beazley archive (Achilles pursues Troilos): black-figure skyphos fragments from the Athenian Akropolis, ca. 600–550 (Athens NM 1.2146; B. Graef and E. Langlotz. 1925. *Die antiken Vasen von der Akropolis zu Athen,* Vol.1. Berlin, pl. 93.2146 A-B).

2. Beazley archive (Ransom of Hektor, Achilles' armor hanging on wall): black-figure hydria, attributed to painter of London B 76, ca. 600–550 (Zurich University 4001; Carpenter, Mannack, and Mendonça 1989, 23; Beazley 1971, 32.1bis).

3. Beazley archive (Achilles and Memnon): black-figure neck-amphora, attributed to Prometheus painter, ca. 600–550 (NY Metropolitan Museum 59.11.25; Carpenter, Mannack, and Mendonça 1989, 28; Beazley 1971, 40).

4. Boardman, no. 20 (Beazley 1956, 24.1). From Ialysos, Rhodes; Achilles arming; 585–570.

5. Beazley archive (Achilles receives arms from Thetis): neck-amphora, ca. 575–525 (Louvre CP 10521; Beazley 1956, 84.4; *LIMC* VIII, pl. 11 Thetis 39 (A); Beazley 1971, 31).

6. Beazley archive (Achilles' arms, Thetis): column krater from Boiotia, attributed to painter of London B 76, ca. 575–525 (Beazley 1956, 87.17; Carpenter, Mannack, and Mendonça 1989, 24; Beazley 1971, 32). This piece may be equivalent to *LIMC* 188 (listed there as an arming scene with Thetis; Attic column krater; from Boiotia; ca. 560/550).

7. Beazley archive (Achilles' arms, Thetis): neck-amphora, ca. 575–525 (London BM 1922.6–15.1; Beazley 1956, 86.9; Beazley 1971, 32).

8. Beazley archive (Achilles and Ajax gaming): plate, attributed to Burgeon group, ca. 575–525 (Beazley 1956, 90.6; Carpenter, Mannack, and Mendonça 1989, 24; Beazley 1971, 33).

9. Beazley archive (Ajax carries Achilles' corpse): skyphos, attributed to Camel painter, ca. 575–525 (Beazley 1956, 120.5).

10. Beazley archive (Ajax carries Achilles' corpse): neck-amphora from Chiusi, attributed to Exekias, ca. 575–525 (Beazley 1956, 144.5; Carpenter, Mannack, and Mendonça 1989, 39; J. Oakley et al. 1997. *Athenian Potters and Painters: The Conference Proceedings*. Oxford, 162, figs. 7–8 A, B).

11. Beazley archive (Achilles and Penthesileia): neck-amphora, attributed to Exekias, ca. 575–525 (Beazley 1956, 144.8, 686; Carpenter, Mannack, and Mendonça 1989, 39; Beazley 1971, 60).

12. Beazley archive (Ajax carries Achilles' corpse): amphora, attributed to near Exekias, ca. 575–525 (Beazley 1956, 149.2; Carpenter, Mannack, and Mendonça 1989, 42).

13. Beazley archive (ransom of Hektor): amphora B from Vulci, attributed to near group E, ca. 575–525 (Kassel, Staatliche Museen Kassel, *Antikensammlung*, T674; Beazley 1971, 56.31bis; Carpenter, Mannack, and Mendonça 1989, 36).

14. *LIMC* 317 (scene with Troilos and/or Polyxena): Attic Tyrrhenian amphora; ca. 570.

15. *LIMC* 360 (Achilles, named, holds head of Troilos, Trojans with round shields): Attic Tyrrhenian amphora from Pescia Romana, ca. 570 (Beazley 1956, 95.6; Carpenter 1991, no. 33).

16. *LIMC* 364 (death of Troilos, Trojans with round shields): Attic Tyrrhenian amphora, ca. 570 (Beazley 1956, 95.5; Schefold 1966, no. 73a).

17. *LIMC* 191 (Thetis arming scene): Attic neck-amphora, Camtar painter, ca. 570/560 (Beazley 1956, 84.3; Boardman 1974, no. 53, Carpenter 1991, no. 298).

18. *LIMC* 225 (Achilles ambushes Troilos and Polyxena): ovoid Attic Tyrrhenian amphora, ca. 560 (Beazley 1956, 86.8; Boardman 1974, no. 55, Carpenter 1991, no. 22).

19. Schefold 1992, no. 282 (= Beazley 1956, 51.4): Achilles chasing Troilos; C painter, ca. 560.

20. *LIMC* 260 (scene with Troilos and/or Polyxena): Chalkidian amphora, ca. 560/50.

21. *LIMC* 234 (scene with Troilos and/or Polyxena): Attic hydria from Vulci, ca. 560/550 (Beazley 1956, 85.2).

22. *LIMC* 200 (Thetis arming scene; other warrior on left with round shield): Attic hydria, Archippe group, ca. 550 (Beazley 1956, 106.2).

23. *LIMC* 290 (scene with Troilos and/or Polyxena): Attic amphora from Vulci, ca. 550 (Beazley 1956, 109.24).

24. Beazley archive (Achilles and Memnon): neck-amphora from Vulci, ca. 550–500, attributed to group of Bologna 16 (*CVA* Munich 8, pls. 413.3, 416, 418.3).

25. Beazley archive (Ajax and Achilles gaming): neck-amphora, inscribed "philonides," ca. 550–500 (Munich Antikensammlungen 8952 A; Carpenter, Mannack, and Mendonça 1989, 391).

26. Beazley archive (Ajax and Achilles gaming): lekythos, ca. 550–500 (private German collection; *Muse* 1989/90 *(Annual of the Museum of Art and Archaeology, University of Missouri-Columbia)* 23/24, 53, fig. 5).

27. Beazley archive (Ajax and Achilles gaming): amphora B, ca. 550–500 (Sevres, Musée national de céramique 6405; *CVA* Sevres pl. 15.4, 7).

28. Beazley archive (Ajax and Achilles gaming): neck-amphora from Chiusi, ca. 550–500 (London BM B211, 1851.8–6.15; Beazley 1956, 256.14, 670; Carpenter, Mannack, and Mendonça 1989, 66; Beazley 1971, 113).

29. Beazley archive (Ajax and Achilles gaming): neck-amphora, ca. 550–500 (Beazley 1956, 290.2).

30. Beazley archive (Ajax carries Achilles' corpse): amphora from Fratte, ca. 550–500 (Salerno, Museo Nazionale, 148A; G. Greco and A. Pontrandolfo, eds. 1990. *Fratte, un insediamento etrusco-campano*. Modena, 198, fig. 318).

31. Beazley archive (Ajax carries Achilles' corpse): amphora, ca. 550–500 (Vatican City, Museo Gregoriano Etrusco Vaticano, G42; F. Lissarrague. 1990. *L'autre guerrier: archers, peltastes, cavaliers dans l'imagerie attique*. Paris and Rome, 89, fig. 52 A).

32. Beazley archive (Ajax carries Achilles' corpse): olpe fragment, ca. 550–500 (Louvre 9830645; F. Lissarrague. 1990. *L'autre guerrier: archers, peltastes, cavaliers dans l'imagerie attique*. Paris and Rome, 87, fig. 50).

33. Beazley archive (Ajax carries Achilles' corpse): neck-amphora, ca. 550–500 (Bologna, Museo Civico Archeologico 545; F. Lissarrague. 1990. *L'autre guerrier: archers, peltastes, cavaliers dans l'imagerie attique*. Paris and Rome, 83, fig. 43 A).

34. Beazley archive (Ajax carries Achilles' corpse): neck-amphora attributed to Antimenes painter, ca. 550–500 (Beazley 1971, 123.12ter; Carpenter, Mannack, and Mendonça 1989, 73).

35. Beazley archive (Ajax carries Achilles' corpse): neck-amphora attributed to Antimenes painter, ca. 550–500 (Beazley 1956, 269.46).

36. Beazley archive (Ajax carries Achilles' corpse): neck-amphora, ca. 550–500 (B. Cohen and H. A. Shapiro. 1995. *Mother City and Colony: Classical Athenian and South Italian Vases in New Zealand and Australia*. Christchurch, 6, no. 3 A, B).

37. Beazley archive (Ajax carries Achilles' corpse): neck-amphora, ca. 550–500 (Beazley 1956, 312.5; Beazley 1971, 136).

38. Beazley archive (Ajax carries Achilles' corpse): neck-amphora, attributed to Antimenes painter, ca. 550–500 (Beazley 1956, 270.53; Carpenter, Mannack, Mendonça 1989, 70; Beazley 1971, 118).

39. Beazley archive (Ajax carries Achilles' corpse): neck-amphora from Tarquinia, attributed to Antimenes painter, ca. 550–500 (Tarquinia, Museo Nazionale Tarquiniese RC1052; Beazley 1956, 270.54).

40. Beazley archive (Ajax carries Achilles' corpse): neck-amphora, ca. 550–500 (J. Eisenberg. 1997. *Art of the Ancient World, Royal Athena, sale catalogue* 9, 22, no. 92).

41. Beazley archive (Ajax carries Achilles' corpse): amphora A from Cervetri, attributed to Leagros group, ca. 550–500 (Vatican City, Museo Gregoriano Etrusco Vaticano 370; Beazley 1956, 367.95).

42. Beazley archive (Ajax carries Achilles' corpse): neck-amphora, attributed to painter of Munich 1512, ca. 550–500 (Munich Antikensammlungen 1512; E. Kunze-Goette. 1992. *Der Kleophrades-Maler unter Malern schwarzfiguriger Amphoren: Eine Werkstattstudie*. Mainz, pl. 48.1–2, 53.2, 68.1 A, B).

43. Beazley archive (Ajax carries Achilles' corpse): neck-amphora from Vulci, attributed to painter of Munich 1519, ca. 550–500 (Beazley 1956, 394.4; Carpenter, Mannack, Mendonça 1989, 103).

44. Beazley archive (Ajax carries Achilles' corpse): hydria from Vulci, attributed to Antiope or Leagros group, ca. 550–500 (Munich Antikensammlungen J409, 1712; Beazley 1956, 362.34, 357, 695; Carpenter, Mannack, Mendonça 1989, 96; *LIMC* VIII, pl. 358).

45. Beazley archive (Ajax carries Achilles' corpse): neck-amphora, ca. 550–500 (private collection, Japan; I. Yoshikawa. 1988. S*pecial Exhibition of Ancient Greek Vases from Japanese Collections*. Nara, 48–49, no. 14 A, B).

46. Beazley archive (Ajax carries Achilles' corpse): neck-amphora, attributed to Antimenes painter, ca. 550–500 (Baltimore, Walters Art Gallery 48.17; Beazley 1956, 271.70; Carpenter, Mannack, Mendonça 1989, 71).

47. Beazley archive (Ajax carries Achilles' corpse): neck-amphora, attributed to Antimenes painter, ca. 550–500 (Louvre F201; Beazley 1956 274.120; Carpenter, Mannack, Mendonça 1989, 71).

48. Beazley archive (Ajax carries Achilles' corpse): lekythos, ca. 550–500 (Beazley 1956, 378.261).

49. Beazley archive (Ajax carries Achilles' corpse): lekythos from Thespiai, ca. 550–500 (Athens NM CC939, 429; Beazley 1956, 379.281).

50. Beazley archive (Ajax and Achilles gaming): hydria, ca. 550–500 (NY Metropolitan Museum 56.171.29; Beazley 1956, 362.30; Carpenter, Mannack, Mendonça 1989, 96; Beazley 1971, 161).

51. Beazley archive (Ajax and Achilles gaming): amphora A, ca. 550–500 (Madrid, Museo Arqueológico Nacional, L64, 10918; Beazley 1956, 367.96, 389; Carpenter, Mannack, Mendonça 1989, 98).

52. Beazley archive (Ajax and Achilles gaming): hydria signed Leagros, ca. 550–500 (Würzburg, University, Martin von Wagner Museum 311; Beazley 1956, 362.35, 669, 695; Carpenter, Mannack, Mendonça 1989, 96; Beazley 1971, 161).

53. Beazley archive (Ajax and Achilles gaming): neck-amphora, attributed to Antimenes painter, ca. 550–500 (Beazley 1956, 270.67; Carpenter, Mannack, Mendonça 1989, 71; *CVA* Cambridge 1, pl. 12.1).

54. Beazley archive (Ajax and Achilles gaming): neck-amphora, ca. 550–500 (Liverpool, public museum; *Burlington Magazine,* September 1966, 473, fig. 36 A).

55. Beazley archive (Ajax and Achilles gaming): neck-amphora, ca. 550–500 (Paris, Cabinet des Médailles 232; Beazley 1956, 359.9).

56. Beazley archive (Ajax and Achilles gaming): oinochoe from Vulci, attributed to class of Vatican G 47, ca. 550–500 (Beazley 1956, 430.16; Carpenter, Mannack, Mendonça 1989, 110).

57. Beazley archive (Ajax and Achilles gaming): neck-amphora attributed to Eucharides, ca. 550–500 (Beazley 1956, 397.28; Carpenter, Mannack, Mendonça 1989, 104; Beazley 1971, 174).

58. Beazley archive (Ajax and Achilles gaming): neck-amphora from Vulci, ca. 550–500 (Beazley 1956, 486.1; Carpenter, Mannack, Mendonça 1989, 122).

59. Beazley archive (Ajax and Achilles gaming): lekythos from Agrigento, attributed to class of Athens 581, ca. 550–500 (Beazley 1956, 492.73; Beazley 1971, 223).

60. Beazley archive (Ajax and Achilles gaming): neck-amphora, attributed to group of Würzburg 199, ca. 550–500 (Beazley 1956, 288.14).

61. Beazley archive (Achilles with body of Patroklos): amphora, ca. 550–500 (Agrigento Museo Archeologico Regionale AG23079; L. Braccesi, et al. 1988. *Veder greco, le necropoli di Agrigento, mostra internazionale, Agrigento*, May 2 - July 31, 1988. Rome, 254, 1.2, 255–257 A, B).

62. Beazley archive (Achilles in ambush for Troilos): neck-amphora from Vulci, attributed to Affecter, ca. 550–500 (Beazley 1956, 243.45; Carpenter, Mannack, and Mendonça 1989, 62; M. Golden and P. Toohey. 1997. *Inventing Ancient Culture, Historicism, Periodization, and the Ancient World*. London, 46, pl. 9 AH).

63. Beazley archive (Achilles in ambush for Troilos): hydria from Vulci, ca. 550–500 (Beazley 1956, 363.39, 359; Carpenter, Mannack, Mendonça 1989, 96).

64. Beazley archive (Achilles and Memnon): neck-amphora, attributed to group of Würzburg 199, ca. 550–500 (Beazley 1956, 288.8; Beazley 1971, 126).

65. *LIMC* 297 (scene with Troilos and/or Polyxena): Attic hydria, ca. 550–540 (Beazley 1956, 324.29).

66. *LIMC* 876 (a); (Ajax carries dead Achilles): Attic amphora from Vulci, Exekias, ca. 545–530 (Beazley 1956, 144.6; date from Boardman 1974).

67. *LIMC* 876 (b); (Ajax carries dead Achilles): Attic amphora from Vulci, Exekias, ca. 545–530 (Beazley 1956, 144.6; date from Boardman 1974).

68. *LIMC* 871 (Ajax carries dead Achilles): amphora, ca. 540 (Schefold 1992, no. 334).

69. *LIMC* 291 (scene with Troilos and/or Polyxena): Attic hydria, ca. 540.

70. *LIMC* 295 (scene with Troilos and/or Polyxena): Attic hydria, ca. 540.

71. *LIMC* 901 (Achilles flies over the sea): Attic amphora, Leagros group, ca. 540 (BM B 240).

72. *LIMC* 645 (if hanging shield is Achilles'; scene of Hektor's ransom): Attic amphora from Vulci; group E, ca. 540–530 (*CVA* Kassel 1 pl. 21 (1701) 2; Schefold 1992, no. 316).

73. *LIMC* 888; (Ajax carries dead Achilles): Attic amphora from Orvieto; ca. 530.

74. *LIMC* 392 (Achilles and Ajax gaming): Attic bilingual amphora from Orvieto, ca. 530/520 (Beazley 1956, 254.2/*ARV²* 4.7).

75. *LIMC* 391 (Achilles and Ajax gaming): Attic amphora, group E, ca. 530/520 (*CVA* Basel 1 pl. 40.1–3).

76. *LIMC* 559 (battle of Achilles and Hektor): Attic neck-amphora from Orvieto, Amasis painter, ca. 530–520 (Beazley 1956, 152.26; Schefold 1992, no. 310).

77. Beazley archive (Ajax and Achilles gaming): hydria, ca. 525–475 (Louvre F291; *CVA* Louvre 6, pl. 70 [409].1).

78. Beazley archive (Ajax and Achilles gaming): neck-amphora, attributed to the three-line group, ca. 525–475 (NY private collection; Carpenter, Mannack, Mendonça 1989, 86; Beazley 1971, 140.6ter).

79. Beazley archive (Ajax and Achilles gaming): neck-amphora, attributed to Medea group, ca. 525–475 (Beazley 1971, 141.2bis).

80. Beazley archive (Ajax and Achilles gaming): neck-amphora from Vulci, attributed to Toulouse painter, ca. 525–475 (Carpenter, Mannack, Mendonça 1989, 87; Beazley 1971, 141.2).

81. Beazley archive (Achilles in ambush for Troilos): lekythos, ca. 525–475 (B. Knittlmayer. 1997. *Die attische Aristokratie und ihre Helden, Darstellungen des trojanischen Sagenkreises im 6. und frühen 5. Jh.v.Chr.* Heidelberg, pl. 18.4–6, BD).

82. Beazley archive (Achilles in ambush for Troilos): lekythos, ca. 525–475 (C. Haspels. 1936. *Attic Black-figured Lekythoi.* Paris, 242.25, 131, 134, pl. 41.5 A-C).

83. Beazley archive (Achilles and Penthesileia), ca. 525–475 (K. Schefold and F. Jung. 1989. *Die Sagen von den Argonauten, von Theben und Troia in der klassischen und hellenistischen Kunst.* Munich, 242, fig. 218 A).

84. Beazley archive (Ajax and Achilles gaming): lekythos, ca. 525–475 (M. Steinhart. 1996. *Topferkunst und Meisterzeichnung, Attische Wein- und Olgefasse aus der Sammlung Zimmermann.* Mainz, 77–79, no. 15).

85. Beazley archive (Ajax and Achilles gaming): neck-amphora from Vulci, attributed to redline painter, ca. 525–475 (Beazley 1956, 601.5; Carpenter, Mannack, Mendonça 1989, 141).

86. Beazley archive (Ajax and Achilles gaming): neck-amphora, attributed to red-line painter, ca. 525–475 (Brussels, Musées Royaux R314; Beazley 1956, 601.6).

87. Beazley archive (Ajax and Achilles gaming): amphora B, attributed to Leagros group, ca. 525–475 (Carpenter, Mannack, Mendonça 1989, 98; Beazley 1971, 166.108bis).

88. Beazley archive (Ajax and Achilles gaming): ca. 525–475 (Sotheby, sale catalogue, 7.–8.7. 1994, 73, no. 324).

89. Beazley archive (Ajax and Achilles gaming), lekythos, ca. 525–475 (Columbia, University of Missouri, Museum of Art and Archaeology 82.299; *Muse, Annual of the Museum of Art and Archaeology, University of Missouri-Columbia* 17, 1983, 31; *Muse, Annual of the Museum of Art and Archaeology, University of Missouri-Columbia* 23/24, 1989/90, 49, fig. 2).

90. Beazley archive (Ajax carrying Achilles' corpse): olpe, ca. 525–475 (San Antonio Museum 86.134.48; H. A. Shapiro et al. 1995. *Greek Vases in the San Antonio Museum of Art.* San Antonio, 117, no. 58).

91. Beazley archive (Ajax carrying Achilles' corpse): neck-amphora attributed to perhaps longnose painter, ca. 525–475 (Carpenter, Mannack, Mendonça 1989, 93; Beazley 1971, 152.2).

92. Beazley archive (Ajax carrying Achilles' corpse): oinochoe, ca. 525–475 (Carpenter, Mannack, Mendonça 1989, 141; Beazley 1971, 187, 301.73ter).

93. Beazley archive (Ajax carrying Achilles' corpse): neck-amphora attributed to painter of London B235, ca. 525–475 (Carpenter, Mannack, Mendonça 1989, 89; Beazley 1971, 145).

94. *LIMC* 395 (Achilles and Ajax gaming) , Attic amphora, ca. 520 (Beazley 1956, 307.56).

95. *LIMC* 592 (Achilles with Hektor tied to chariot, *eidolon* of Patroklos): Attic amphora from Vulci, ca. 520 (Beazley 1956, 330.2).

96. *LIMC* 214 (scene with Troilos and/or Polyxena): Attic amphora, ca. 520–510 (Beazley 1956, 479.3).

97. *LIMC* 304 (scene with Troilos and/or Polyxena): Attic amphora, ca. 520–10 (Beazley 1956, 273.112).

98. *LIMC* 394 (Achilles and Ajax gaming): Attic amphora, ca. 520–510 (Munich 1567).

99. *LIMC* 410 (Achilles and Ajax gaming): Attic amphora from Vulci, ca. 520–510 (Beazley 1956, 330).

100. Boardman, no. 217 (Achilles fights Memnon, Memnon with round shield, Achilles with cutout): neck-amphora of the Three-line group; no later than 510's (Beazley 1956, 320.3).

101. *LIMC* 404 (Achilles and Ajax gaming): Attic bilingual amphora from Vulci, ca. 510 (*ARV²* 11.1).

102. *LIMC* 402 (Achilles and Ajax gaming): Attic amphora, ca. 510 (Berlin 1962.28).

103. *LIMC* 224 (scene with Troilos and/or Polyxena): Attic lekythos, near Leagros group; ca. 510 (Beazley 1956, 379.272).

104. *LIMC* 586 (Achilles with Hektor tied to chariot, Patroklos' *eidolon*): Attic hydria, ca. 510 (*CVA* Boston 2 pl. 82 [916]).

105. *LIMC* 588 (Achilles with Hektor tied to chariot, *eidolon* of Patroklos): Attic lekythos from the Heraion at Delos, Leagros group, ca. 510 (Beazley 1956, 378.257; Schefold 1992, no. 313).

106. *LIMC* 591 (Achilles with Hektor tied to chariot): Attic hydria, Leagros group, ca. 510 (Beazley 1956, 362.31).

107. *LIMC* 655 (Priam visits Achilles whose shield rests against wall): hydria, Pioneer group, ca. 510 (Schefold 1992, no. 318).

108. Schefold 1992, no. 285 (Achilles murders Troilos): hydria, Leagros group, ca. 510 (Beazley 1956, 362.27).

109. *LIMC* 411 (Achilles and Ajax gaming): Attic amphora from Vulci, Leagros group, ca. 510–500 (Beazley 1956, 367, 86).

110. *LIMC* 405 (Achilles and Ajax gaming): Attic amphora from Vulci, ca. 510–500 (Beazley 1956, 385).

111. *LIMC* 725 (Achilles and Penthesileia): Attic hydria from Vulci, Leagros group, ca. 510–500 (Beazley 1956, 362.33; Boardman 1974, no. 204; Schefold 1992, no. 321).

112. *LIMC* 403 (Achilles and Ajax gaming): Attic lekythos, ca. 500 (Beazley 1956, 480).

113. *LIMC* 22 (Achilles and Chiron?): Attic hydria from Vulci, Leagros group, end of sixth century (Beazley 361, 22).

114. Schefold 1992, no. 336 = *LIMC* 1 Aias 1 80 = Beazley 1956, 338.3 (Ajax listens to Odysseus' speech on the armor of Achilles; armor set between the two men): pelike near the Rycroft painter; soon after 500 (J. Oakley et. al. 1997. *Athenian Potters and Painters*. Oxford, 68, fig. 12A).

115. Boardman 1974, no. 262 (Achilles ambushes Polyxena): lekythos by Sappho painter, early fifth century.

B. OTHER ARCHAIC MEDIA DEPICTING ACHILLES AND THE CUTOUT SHIELD

1. *LIMC* 902: Thessalian bronze figurine from Kharditsa; Athens NM 12831.

2. Schefold 1966, no. 24c: Melian neck-amphora from Delos, ca. 670 (the identification of this scene as the receipt of Achilles' armor from Thetis seems probable, as the robed figure on the right is female; the man on the left is nude; in between the two figures lie the shield and greaves). The piece is now in the Mykonos museum (see *LIMC* 506; D. Kemp-Lindemann. 1975. *Darstellungen des Achilleus in griechischer und römischer Kunst.* Frankfurt, 157).

3. *LIMC* 389: relief pithos from Thebes; Achilles steals the cattle of Aeneas, ca. 625 (ca. 650, according to Ahlberg-Cornell 1992, 53; Boston, MFA 99.505 [528]).

4. *LIMC* 721: bronze relief strip for shield from Perachora; Achilles kills Penthesileia, ca. end of seventh to mid-sixth century (Schefold 1992, no. 77; Delphi museum inv. no. 4479).

5. C. Bol. 1989. *Argivische Schilde.* Berlin, 69–70, fig. 18, pl. 60: bronze relief on Argive shield from Olympia; Achilles kills Penthesileia, second half of sixth century.

6. C. Bol. 1989. *Argivische Schilde.* Berlin, 67, pl. 64: bronze relief on Argive shield from Olympia: Thetis gives Achilles armor, second quarter of sixth century.

7. G. Richter. 1920. *Greek, Etruscan and Roman Bronzes.* New York, 20; on an Etruscan wagon (the Monteleone wagon), ca. 540, probably from a grave (R. Hampe and E. Simon. 1964. *Griechische Sagen in der frühen etruskischen Kunst.* Mainz, 53). The scene depicts a shield with a woman and a man on either side (perhaps the receipt of the armor of Achilles, as Hampe and Simon suggest (1964, 55–56; see also Karusu 1976, 29). Richter suggests that the Etruscan artist copied famous heroic scenes from Greek art (Richter 1915, 20); the scenes on this piece might not be specifically associated with Achilles.

C. ACHILLES IN BLACK FIGURE WITH ROUND SHIELD
(in chronological order)
Total: 35

1. *LIMC* 332 (a) (Ambush of Troilos and Polyxena): early Proto-Corinthian aryballos, ca. 700 (N. Coldstream, 1977. *Geometric Greece.* London, 172–3, pl. 56).

2. *LIMC* 558 (Battle between Achilles and Hektor): Korinthian cup, ca. 580.

3. *LIMC* 808 (Achilles and Memnon): middle Corinthian column-krater from Caere, ca. 580.

4. Carpenter 1991, no. 21 (Achilles ambushes Troilos), ca. 580.

5. *LIMC* 897 (Nereids and dead Achilles): Corinthian hydria from Caere, ca. 570.

6. *LIMC* 230 (Ambush of Troilos and Polyxena): Attic Tyrrhenian amphora, ca. 570–560 (Beazley 1956, 95.4).

7. *LIMC* 238 (ambush of Troilos and Polyxena): Attic Tyrrhenian amphora, ca. 570–560 (Beazley 1956, 95.1).

8. *LIMC* 307 (Ambush of Troilos and Polyxena): Attic siana cup, ca. 570–560 (Beazley 1956, 51.4).

9. *LIMC* 310 (Ambush of Troilos and Polyxena): Attic siana cup, ca. 570–560 (Louvre CA 6113).

10. *LIMC* 261 (Ambush of Troilos and Polyxena): Lakonian cup from Cerveteri, ca. 560.

11 *LIMC* 256 (Ambush of Troilos and Polyxena): Lakonian dinos from Kyrene, ca. 560–550 (Louvre E 662).

12. *LIMC* 264 (Ambush of Troilos and Polyxena): Lakonian cup fragment from Samos, ca. 560–550.

13. *LIMC* 252 (Ambush of Troilos and Polyxena): Boiotian kantharos, ca. 550 (*CVA* Berlin 4 pl. 199 [1625] 1–3).

14. *LIMC* 584 (Achilles drags Hektor): Klazomenian hydria, ca. 550.

15. *LIMC* 649 (Hektor's ransom): Attic amphora A, attributed to Rycroft painter, ca. 550–500 (Toledo 72.54; *CVA* Toledo 1, pls. 4–5, 9 a, b).

16. *LIMC* 722 (Achilles and Penthesileia): Chalkidian amphora from Etruria, ca. 550–540 (Leningrad 1479; Schefold 1992, no. 319).

17. *LIMC* 316 (Ambush of Troilos and Polyxena): Attic cup, ca. 540 (Louvre CA 3339).

18. *LIMC* 398 (a) (Achilles and Ajax gaming): Attic cup, ca. 540 (Vatican 343).

19. *LIMC* 398 (b) (Achilles and Ajax gaming): Attic cup, ca. 540 (Vatican 343).

20. *LIMC* 508 (Thetis arms Achilles with new shield): Attic amphora from Orvieto, Amasis, ca. 540 (Beazley 1956, 152.27; Boardman 1974, no. 86).

21. *LIMC* 812 (Achilles and Memnon): Chalkidian skyphos, ca. 540.

22. *LIMC* 187 (arming scene with Thetis): Attic plate from Attica, Lydos, ca. 540–530 (Athens NM 507; Beazley 1956, 112.56; Carpenter 1991, no. 296; Schefold 1992, no. 267).

23. *LIMC* 723 (Achilles and Penthesileia): Attic neck-amphora from Vulci, Exekias, ca. 530 (Boardman 1974, no. 98, Carpenter 1991, no. 321).

24. Carpenter 1991, no. 326 (Achilles attacks Memnon): Corinthian hydria, ca. 530.

25. *LIMC* 219 (Ambush of Troilos and Polyxena): Attic (?) amphora, ca. 530–520, Göttingen.

26. Beazley archive (Achilles ambushes Troilos): column-krater, attributed to painter of Villa Guilia M 482, ca. 525–475 (Louvre CP11282; Carpenter, Mannack, Mendonça 1989, 140; Beazley 1971, 296.10).

27. Carpenter 1991, no. 316 (Achilles gets into chariot with Hektor tied to back): Attic hydria, ca. 520 (Boston MFA 63.473).

28. *LIMC* 301 (Ambush of Troilos and Polyxena): Attic hydria from Corinth, ca. 520–510 (Beazley 1956, 361.17).

29. *LIMC* 303 (Ambush of Troilos and Polyxena): Attic hydria from Vulci, ca. 520–510 (Beazley 1956, 269.33).

30. *LIMC* 408 (Achilles with round, Ajax with cutout on right; Achilles and Ajax gaming): Attic krater, ca. 520–510 (Toledo 63.26).

31. *LIMC* 877 (Ajax carries Achilles): Attic amphora, ca. 510.

32. Carpenter 1991, no. 24 (*eidolon* of Achilles flies above his tomb): Attic hydria, ca. 500 (Beazley 1956, 363.37).

33. *LIMC* 244 (Ambush of Troilos and Polyxena): Attic hydria from Samos, ca. 490.

34. *LIMC* 235 (Ambush of Troilos and Polyxena): Attic cup, ca. 490–480 (NY Metropolitan Museum 57.12.14).

35. *LIMC* 246 (b); (Ambush of Polyxena): Attic lekythos, ca. 480 (Toledo 47.62).

D. AJAX IN BLACK FIGURE WITH CUTOUT SHIELD
(in chronological order)
Total: 31

1. Beazley archive (Ajax carries Achilles' corpse): skyphos from Thespiai, attributed to the Camel painter by Beazley, ca. 575–525 (Athens NM CC809, 433; Beazley 1956, 120.5).

2. Beazley archive (death of Achilles; Ajax with shield): amphora A, attributed to Exekias, ca. 575–525 (University of Pennsylvania 3442; Beazley 1956, 145.14; Carpenter, Mannack, Mendonça 1989, 40; J. H. Oakley et al. 1997. *Athenian Potters and Painters: The Conference Proceedings*. Oxford, 159–160, figs. 3–4; Beazley 1971, 60).

3. Beazley archive (preparations for suicide of Ajax): amphora, attributed to Exekias, ca. 575–525 (Bologna, Museo Communale 558; Beazley 1956, 145.18; Carpenter, Mannack, Mendonça 1989, 40; H. A. Shapiro. 1994. *Myth into Art: Poet and Painter in Classical Athens*. London 152, fig. 107 (A); Beazley 1971, 60; *LIMC* 104; Boardman 1974, 101; Carpenter 1991, 332).

4. Boardman 1974, 56 (Herakles fights Amazons, Telamonian Ajax at right with shield): Tyrrhenian amphora from Vulci, ca. 565–550 (Beazley 1956, 98.46).

5. Beazley archive (Ajax and Achilles gaming): neck-amphora, inscribed "philonides," ca. 550–500 (Munich Antikensammlungen, 8952A; Carpenter, Mannack, Mendonça 1989, 391).

6. Beazley archive (Ajax and Achilles gaming): neck-amphora, ca. 550–500 (*Burlington Magazine*, September 1966, 473, fig. 36 a).

7. Beazley archive (Ajax and Achilles gaming): amphora A, attributed to Leagros group, ca. 550–500 (Beazley 1956, 387.86; Carpenter, Mannack, Mendonça 1989, 97).

8. Beazley archive (Ajax carries Achilles' corpse): neck-amphora from Gela, ca. 550–500 (Syracuse Museo Arch. Regionale Paolo Orsi 21926; *CVA* Syracuse 1, pl. 5 (810) 3, 5).

9. Beazley archive (Ajax carries Achilles' corpse): neck-amphora fragments, ca. 550–500 (Louvre CP 10585; Beazley 1956, 271.69; F. Lissarrague. 1990. *L'autre guerrier: archers, peltastes, cavaliers dans l'imagerie attique*. Paris and Rome, 86, fig. 47a).

10. Beazley archive (Ajax carries Achilles' corpse): neck-amphora from Gela, ca. 550–500 (Syracuse Museo Arch. Regionale Paolo Orsi 24509bis; *CVA* Syracuse 1, pl. 6 (811) 1).

11. Beazley archive (Ajax carries Achilles' corpse): neck-amphora, ca. 550–500 (Munich Antikensammlungen 1512; E. Kunze-Goette. 1992. *Der Kleophrades-Maler unter Malern schwarzfiguriger Amphoren: Eine Werkstattstudie*. Mainz, pl. 48.1–2, 53.2, 68.1, a, b, u, h).

12. Beazley archive (Ajax carries Achilles' corpse): cup, ca. 550–500 (Paris, Cabinet des Médailles 333; Beazley 1956, 646.203, 650).

13. Beazley archive (Ajax carries Achilles' corpse): neck-amphora, attributed to painter of Villa Giulia M 482, ca. 550–500 (Brussels, Musées Royeaux R313; Beazley 1956, 590.8; F. Lissarrague. 1990. *L'autre guerrier: archers, peltastes, cavaliers dans l'imagerie attique.* Paris and Rome, 86, fig.46a).

14. Beazley archive (Ajax carries Achilles' corpse): neck-amphora, attributed to related to Antimenes painter, ca. 550–500 (Carpenter, Mannack, Mendonça 1989, 73; Beazley 1971, 123.12ter).

15. Beazley archive (Ajax carries Achilles' corpse): amphora from Fratte, ca. 550–500 (Salerno 148A; G. Greco and A. Pontrandolfo, eds. 1990. *Fratte: un insediamento etrusco-campano.* Modena, 198, fig. 318).

16. Beazley archive (Ajax with shield and Kassandra): neck-amphora, attributed to three-line group, ca. 550–500 (Beazley 1956, 320.4).

17. Boardman 1974, no. 100 (Achilles and Ajax play; Ajax named on right): belly amphora by Exekias, from Vulci, ca. 545–530 (Beazley 1956, 145.13).

18. *LIMC* Achilleus 876a (Ajax carries Achilles' corpse; two sides of vase show same scene): Attic amphora from Vulci, Exekias, ca. 540 (Beazley 1956, 144.6).

19. *LIMC* Achilleus 876b (Ajax carries Achilles' corpse; two sides of vase show same scene): Attic amphora from Vulci, Exekias, ca. 540 (Beazley 1956, 144.6).

20. Carpenter 1991, no 328 (Achilles dead, Ajax guards body): Chalcidian amphora, ca. 540.

21. *LIMC* Achilleus 888 (Ajax carries Achilles' corpse): Attic amphora from Orvieto, ca. 530.

22. *LIMC* 48 (*LIMC* maintains that the unnamed figure facing Hektor has a cutout shield and is probably Ajax; fighting over Patroklos): Attic krater, Exekias, ca. 530–520 (Beazley 1956, 145.19).

23. *LIMC* 41 (Ajax and Hektor fight, both figures with cutout shields): Attic amphora attributed to the Antimenes painter, ca. 525 (Beazley 1956, 272.100).

24. Beazley archive (Ajax carries Achilles' corpse): neck-amphora from Etruria, ca. 525–475 (Louvre F 270; *CVA* Louvre 5, pl. 56 (354), 8, 11).

25. Beazley archive (Ajax carries Achilles' corpse): Panathenaic amphora from Gela, attributed to Michigan painter, ca. 525–475 (Syracuse, Museo Arch. Regionale Paolo Orsi 20067A; Beazley 1971, 157.7quater).

26. Beazley archive (Ajax carries Achilles' corpse): olpe, ca. 525–475 (San Antonio Art Museum, 86.134.48; H. A. Shapiro et al. 1995. *Greek Vases in the San Antonio Museum of Art.* San Antonio 117, no. 58).

27. Beazley archive (Ajax carries Achilles' corpse): neck-amphora, attributed to Leagros group, ca. 525–475 (F. Lissarrague. 1990. *L'autre guerrier: archers, peltastes, cavaliers dans l'imagerie attique.* Paris and Rome, 86, no. 45a; H. Shapiro. 1989. *Art and Culture under the Tyrants in Athens.* Mainz, pl. 38a).

28. Beazley archive (Ajax carries Achilles' corpse): neck-amphora, attributed to Edinburgh painter, ca. 525–475 (Kanellopoulos collection, Athens; Beazley 1971, 218).

29. Beazley archive (Ajax carries Achilles' corpse): neck-amphora from Vulci, attributed to painter of London B235, ca. 525–475 (NY Metropolitan Museum 26.60.20; Carpenter, Mannack, Mendonça 1989, 93; Beazley 1971, 152.2).

30. Beazley archive (Ajax and Achilles gaming): neck-amphora from Vulci, attributed to Toulouse painter, ca. 525–475 (Carpenter, Mannack, Mendonça 1989, 87; Beazley 1971, 141.2).

31. Beazley archive (Ajax carries Achilles' corpse): lekythos, attributed to Sappho painter, ca. 500–450 (*CVA* Agrigento 1, pl. 71, 1–2).

E. AJAX IN BLACK FIGURE WITH ROUND SHIELD
(in chronological order)
Total: 7

1. *LIMC* 22 (Ajax and Aineas); middle Corinthian cup, ca. 600–500.

2. Beazley archive (Ajax and Achilles gaming side a): cup A from Vulci, ca. 575–525 (Vatican City, Museo Gregoriano Etrusco Vaticano, A343; *LIMC* Achilleus 398a; Schefold 1992, figs. 330–31a).

3. Beazley archive (Ajax and Achilles gaming, side b): cup A from Vulci, ca. 575–525 (Vatican City, Museo Gregoriano Etrusco Vaticano, A343; Schefold 1992, figs. 330–31b).

4. *LIMC* 46 (Ajax and Hektor fight over Patroklos); Attic amphora of the Leagros group, from Vulci, ca. 550–500 (Beazley 1956, 368.106; Munich *CVA*, pls. 36 and 39).

5. Beazley archive (Ajax and Kassandra): olpe from Vulci, ca. 550–500 (Leiden, Rijksmuseum van Oudheden PC54; *CVA* Leiden 2, pl. 82.1–3; *LIMC* Aias II 37).

6. *LIMC* 61 (Ajax and Poseidon, probably): Attic cup, attributed to Amasis painter, ca. 540.

7. *LIMC* Achilleus 877 (Ajax carries Achilles' corpse): Attic amphora, ca. 510.

Not included:

LIMC 74 (because figures are unnamed; as *LIMC* notes); Melian amphora, ca. 660.

LIMC 76 (Ajax and Odysseus [?]: *LIMC* does not accept reading), Attic amphora, Munich painter, ca. 520 (Beazley 1956, 311.2).

F. ACHILLES IN RED FIGURE WITH CUTOUT SHIELD
(in chronological order)
Total: 10

As mentioned above, vases are omitted when the shield cannot be attributed to Achilles with certainty.

1. Beazley archive (Achilles and Ajax gaming): amphora A from Vulci, ca. 550–500 (Beazley 1963, 11.1, 1618; Carpenter, Mannack, Mendonça 1989, 151; Beazley 1971, 321).

2. Beazley archive (Achilles and Ajax gaming): amphora A from Etruria, ca. 550–500 (London BM B193; Beazley 1963, 4.8, 1617; Carpenter, Mannack, Mendonça 1989, 66, 320; Beazley 1971, 113, 320).

3. *LIMC* 890 (Ajax carries Achilles' corpse; probably, although shield is difficult to see): Attic amphora from Cerveteri, ca. 520 (Beazley 1963, 11.3).

4. Beazley archive; *LIMC* 342 (Achilles, Troilos, Polyxena): Attic cup from Vulci, attributed to Kachrylion potter, ca. 525–475 (London BM E13; Beazley 1963, 109 and 1626; Carpenter, Mannack, Mendonça 1989, 173; H. A. Shapiro. 1989. *Art and Culture under the Tyrants in Athens*. Mainz, pl. 55c I).

5. *LIMC* 804 (weighing of the fates of Achilles and Memnon by Hermes, if figure on left is Achilles): Attic cup from Caere, ca. 520–510 (Beazley 1963, 72.24).

6. *LIMC* 655 (ransom of Hektor): Attic hydria, ca. 510 (Fogg Art Museum 1972.40).

7. Beazley archive (exterior depicts voting for armor of Achilles; interior shows Odysseus getting the armor): cup from Cervetri, attributed to Douris, ca. 500–450 (Boardman 1975, no. 285.2; Beazley 1963, 1569 and 429.26; Carpenter, Mannack, Mendonça 1989, 116; for the large bibliography on this vase, see the Beazley archive).

8. Beazley archive (Thetis and Hephaistos with arms of Achilles): cup from Vulci, attributed to Foundry painter, ca. 500–450 (Boardman 1975, no. 262.1; Beazley 1963, 400.1, 1651, 1706; Carpenter, Mannack, Mendonça 1989, 230; Carpenter 1991, fig. 88 (1); Beazley 1971, 370).

9. Carpenter 1991, no. 28; Beazley 1963, 369.3 (Achilles ambushes Troilos): Attic cup by Brygos, ca. 480.

10. *LIMC* 833 (Achilles and Memnon): Attic krater from Vulci, ca. 470 (Beazley 1963, 290.1)

G. ACHILLES IN RED FIGURE WITH ROUND SHIELD
(in chronological order)
Total: 44 (#20 counted twice, see below)

1. Beazley archive; *LIMC* 567 (Achilles and Hektor fight): Attic oinochoe from Cervetri, ca. 550–500, Beazley archive; ca. 520, *LIMC*; (Paris, Cabinet des Médailles, 458; Beazley 1963, 12.10; Carpenter, Mannack, Mendonça 1989, 152; Beazley 1971, 321).

2. Schefold 1992, no. 275; Beazley 1963, 54.4: (Briseis and Achilles): belly amphora by Oltos, ca. 525–500.

4. Beazley archive (Achilles pursues Troilos): lekythos, ca. 525–475 (Palermo, Mormino Collection 674; F. Giudice, S. Tusa and V. Tusa. 1992. *La collezione archeologica del Banco di Sicilia*. Vol. 1. Palermo, 260–261, figs. 184–187; II, 157, E13).

5. Beazley archive (Achilles, Antilochos, Nestor, Iris): cup from Vulci, ca. 525–475 (Berlin, Antikensammlung F2264; *CVA* East Berlin I, pls. 1–3; Beazley 1963, 60.64; Carpenter, Mannack, Mendonça 1989, 164; Beazley 1971, 326).

6. Beazley archive; *LIMC* 565 (Achilles and Hektor fight); Attic volute krater from Cerveteri, attributed to the Berlin painter) ca. 525–475 (archive), ca. 490 (*LIMC*), (Beazley 1963, 206.132; Carpenter, Mannack, Mendonça 1989, 194).

7. Beazley archive; *LIMC* 369 (Death of Troilos); Attic cup, attributed to Oltos painter, ca. 525–475, (Louvre G 18; Beazley 1963, 1599.11 and 61.68; Carpenter, Mannack, Mendonça 1989, 81).

8. *LIMC* 419 (Achilles and Ajax gaming): Attic cup, ca. 510 (Beazley 1963, 1626.115).

9. *LIMC* 424 (a); (pursuit of Troilos): Attic cup from Vulci, ca. 510 (Beazley 1963, 90.33).

10. *LIMC* 424 (c); (pursuit scene): Attic cup from Vulci, ca. 510 (Beazley 1963, 90.33).

11. Beazley archive; *LIMC* 266 (Achilles and Polyxena): Attic hydria from Vulci, attributed to Berlin painter, ca. 525–475 (Beazley archive); ca. 500 (*LIMC*), (Beazley 1963, 210.174; Carpenter, Mannack, Mendonça 1989, 195; Beazley 1971, 510).

12. *LIMC* 425 (Achilles and Ajax gaming): Attic hydria, ca. 500 (Beazley 1963, 1634.75).

13. *LIMC* 423 (Achilles and Ajax and statue of Athena): Attic amphora, late sixth century (Bryn Mawr *CVA* 1 pl. 30 (610) 2).

14. Beazley archive; *LIMC* 426 (Ajax and Achilles gaming): Attic lekythos from Athens, ca. 500–450 (Louvre MNB 911, E10; C. Haspels. 1936. *Attic Black-figured Lekythoi*. Paris, pl. 40.1a-b; Carpenter, Mannack, Mendonça 1989, 211; Beazley 1963, 301.1).

15. *LIMC* 830; Boardman 1975, no. 2.2; (Achilles and Memnon): Attic cup from the Athenian agora, signed by Gorgos, ca. 500 (Beazley 1963, 213.242.1634).

16. Beazley archive; (Athena, Thetis, Hephaistos with armor): Attic pelike from Cerveteri, ca. 500–450 (Rome, Mus. Naz. Etrusco di Villa Giulia 50441; Beazley 1963, 293.41; Carpenter, Mannack, Mendonça 1989, 211).

17. Beazley archive; (Thetis with armor): neck-amphora, ca. 500–450 (Beazley 1963, 1656.2bis; Carpenter, Mannack, Mendonça 1989, 250; J. M. Barringer. 1995. *Divine Escorts: Nereids in Archaic and Classical Greek Art*. Ann Arbor, pls. 150–155).

18. Beazley archive; (Achilles kills Troilos at altar, pictured with round shield twice): cup from Vulci, ca. 500–450 (Perugia, Museo Civico 89; Beazley 1963, 1595, 320.8, 313; Carpenter, Mannack, Mendonça 1989, 214).

19. Beazley archive; (Achilles and Odysseus, hanging shield probably fully round): cup from Vulci, ca. 500–450 (London BM E56, 1843.11–3.61; Beazley 1963, 44.180; Carpenter, Mannack, Mendonça 1989, 240; *CVA* London BM 9, pls. 41–42; Beazley 1971, 375).

20. Counted twice since scenes are different on either side:

Beazley archive (Hektor and Achilles fight; on other side embassy to Achilles; round shield pictured twice): stamnos, attributed to Triptolemos painter, ca. 500–450 (Beazley 1963, 361.7; Carpenter, Mannack, Mendonça 1989, 222; *CVA*, Basel 3, pls. 22.1–6, 23.1–6; K. Schefold and F. Jung. 1989. *Die Sagen von den Argonauten, von Theben und Troia in der klassischen und hellenistischen Kunst*. Munich, 198–199, figs. 180A-B).

21. *LIMC* 566 (Achilles and Hektor fight): Attic stamnos from Vulci, ca. 490 (Beazley 1963, 207.137).

22. Beazley archive; *LIMC* 658 (ransom of Hektor): Attic cup fragments, ca. 500–450 (Beazley archive), ca. 490 (*LIMC*), (Louvre G 153; Beazley 1963, 460.14; Carpenter, Mannack, Mendonça 1989, 244).

23. Beazley archive; *LIMC* 659 (Ransom of Hektor, Achilles' arms on wall behind him): Attic skyphos from Cervetri, attributed to Brygos painter, ca. 500–450 (Beazley archive), ca. 490 (*LIMC*), (K. Schefold and F. Jung. 1989. *Die Sagen von den Argonauten, von Theben und Troia in der klassischen und hellenistischen Kunst*. Munich 1989, 232–233, figs. 208 A-B; Beazley 1963, 380.171; Boardman 1975, 248).

24. *LIMC* 734 (Achilles and Penthesileia): Attic hydria from Falerii, ca. 490 (Beazley 1963, 209.169).

25. Beazley archive; *LIMC* 344 (Achilles, Troilos and Polyxena): Attic cup, attributed to Brygos painter, ca. 500–450 (Beazley archive), ca. 480 (*LIMC*), (Louvre G 154; Carpenter, Mannack, Mendonça 1989, 224; Beazley 1963, 369.3).

26. *LIMC* 473 (Patroklos leaves Achilles): Attic stamnos from Vignanello, ca. 480 (Beazley 1963, 188.63).

27. *LIMC* 564 (Achilles and Hektor fight): Attic cup, ca. 480 (Beazley 1963, 402.23).

28. *LIMC* 570 (Achilles and Hektor fight): Attic cup from Vulci, ca. 480 (Beazley 1963, 449.2).

29. *LIMC* 345 (Achilles Troilos and Polyxena): Attic pelike, ca. 470 (Beazley 1963, 581.4).

30. Beazley archive; *LIMC* 729 (Achilles and Penthesileia): Attic kalyx-krater, ca. 500–450 (Beazley archive), ca. 470 (*LIMC*) (Fitzwilliam museum GR 3.1971; Beazley 1963, 550.3; Carpenter, Mannack, Mendonça 1989, 257; Beazley 1971, 386).

31. *LIMC* Aias I 71 (Achilles' armor on ground; Ajax and Odysseus): Attic cup from Caere, first quarter of the fifth century (Beazley 1963, 429.26).

32. Beazley archive; *LIMC* 515 (Thetis gives Achilles new armor): Attic pelike from Kamiros, ca. 500–450 (Beazley archive), ca. 470–460 (*LIMC*), (Beazley 1963, 586.36; Boardman 1975, 332; Carpenter, Mannack, Mendonça 1989, 263).

33. *LIMC* 521 (Thetis gives Achilles new armor): Attic volute krater from Tarquinia, ca. 460 (Beazley 1963, 615).

34. *LIMC* 733 (Achilles and Penthesileia): Attic cup from Vulci, ca. 460 (Beazley 1963, 879.1).

35. *LIMC* 831 (a) (Achilles and Memnon): Attic kalyx-krater, ca. 460 (Beazley 1963, 591.13).

36. *LIMC* 831 (b) (Achilles and Memnon): Attic kalyx-krater, ca. 460 (Beazley 1963, 591.13).

37. *LIMC* 367 (Death of Troilos); Attic amphora, ca. 460–450 (Beazley 1963, 530.23).

38. *LIMC* 512 (Thetis gives Achilles new armor): Attic rhyton, ca. 450 (Beazley 1963, 766.6).

39. *LIMC* 832 (Achilles and Memnon): Attic kalyx-krater, ca. 450.

40. *LIMC* 840 (Achilles and Memnon): Attic cup, ca. 450.

41. *LIMC* 519 (Thetis gives Achilles new armor): Attic hydria, ca. 440.

42. *LIMC* 420 (Achilles and Ajax gaming): Attic column-krater from Gela, ca. 430–420 (Beazley 1963, 1114.9).

43. *LIMC* 518 (Thetis gives Achilles new armor): Attic lekane from Kertsch, ca. 420 (Pushkin museum II 1 b 715).

H. AJAX IN RED FIGURE WITH CUTOUT SHIELD
Total: 1

LIMC 14 (scene of Aias' departure for war): Attic cup; Oltos painter, ca. 520–500 (Beazley 1963, 61.75).

I. AJAX IN RED FIGURE WITH ROUND SHIELD
(in chronological order)
Total: 6

1. Beazley archive; *LIMC* 36 (Ajax and Hektor battle): Attic stamnos from Todi, attributed to Smikros, ca. 550–500 (Beazley archive), ca. 500 (*LIMC*), (Beazley 1963, 20.3, 1620; Carpenter, Mannack, Mendonça 1989, 154; Beazley 1971, 322).

2. Beazley archive (Ajax and Achilles gaming): lekythos from Athens, ca. 500–450 (Louvre MNB 911, E10; C. Haspels. 1936. *Attic Black-Figured Lekythoi*. Paris, pl. 40.1 A-B; Beazley 1963, 301.1, 303; Carpenter, Mannack, Mendonça 1989, 211).

3. *LIMC* 37 (battle between Ajax and Hektor): Attic cup, ca. 480 (Beazley 1963, 437.74).

4. Beazley archive; *LIMC* 43; Carpenter 1991, no. 306 (Ajax and Hektor's duel interrupted): Attic amphora from Vulci, attributed to the Kleophrades painter, ca. 500–450 (Beazley archive), ca. 480 (*LIMC*); (Beazley 1963, 182.5, 1631; Carpenter, Mannack, Mendonça 1989, 186; J. H. Oakley et al. 1997. *Athenian Potters and Painters: The Conference Proceedings*. Oxford, 349, figs. 11–13; Beazley 1971, 340).

5. Boardman 1975, 304.2; Beazley 1963, 361.7 (Ajax and Hektor): stamnos by Triptolemos painter; ca. 480–470.

6. *LIMC* 105 (suicide): Attic lekythos, ca. 460.

J. MENELAOS IN BLACK AND RED FIGURE

Included are all currently accepted images of Menelaos with a shield in black-figure and red-figure vase painting from the Beazley archive database.

I. Menelaos with cutout shield (2 total)

1. Beazley archive (Menelaos and Helen): black-figure cup, compare to Lysippides Painter, ca. 550–500 (M. Steinhart. 1996. *Topferkunst und Meisterzeichnung, Attische Wein- und Olgefasse aus der Sammlung Zimmermann*. Mainz, pl. 2, no. 5).

2. Beazley archive (Menelaos and Helen): black-figure neck-amphora, attributed to Antimenes painter, ca. 550–500 (Los Angeles County Museum A 5933.50.7; Beazley 1956, 273.108; Carpenter, Mannack, and Mendonça 1989, 71).

II. Menelaos not certainly with a cutout shield himself; other warrior on vase possibly with the cutout shield (8 total)

1. Beazley archive (Menelaos and Helen): black-figure pyxis from Chiusi, ca. 575–525 (lost publication record); *LIMC* IV 546, Helen 296 (drawing).

2. Beazley archive (recovery of Helen, Menelaos perhaps with cutout shield): black-figure amphora b from Vulci, ca. 575–525 (Vatican City, Museo Gregoriano Etrusco Vaticano, 350; Beazley 1956, 140.1, 686; Carpenter, Mannack, and Mendonça 1989, 38; Beazley 1971, 58).

3. Beazley archive (recovery of Helen, Menelaos with sword, other warrior with cutout shield): black-figure neck-amphora from Etruria, attributed to Antimenes painter, ca. 550–500 (Berlin, Antikensammlung, F1842; Beazley 1956, 273.110; Carpenter, Mannack, and Mendonça 1989, 71; Beazley 1971, 119; *LIMC* Helen 297 [b]).

4. Beazley archive (recovery of Helen, Menelaos with sword, other warrior with cutout shield): black-figure neck-amphora fragment attributed to Antimenes painter, ca. 550–500 (University of California, Berkeley, Robert H. Lowie Museum F1842A; Beazley 1956, 273.107).

5. Beazley archive (recovery of Helen, Menelaos, other warrior with cutout shield): black-figure neck-amphora from Vulci, attributed to Antimenes painter, ca. 550–500 (NY Metropolitan Museum 69.233.1; Beazley 1956, 271.75; Carpenter, Mannack, and Mendonça 1989, 71; *LIMC* IV pl. 349, Helen 315 [b]).

6. Beazley archive (recovery of Helen, Menelaos, other warrior with cutout shield): black-figure neck-amphora from Vulci, attributed to Antimenes painter, ca. 550–500 (BM B244; Beazley 1956, 271.74; Carpenter, Mannack, and Mendonça 1989, 71).

7. Beazley archive (recovery of Helen, Menelaos, other warrior with cutout shield): black-figure neck-amphora, attributed to Antimenes painter, ca. 550–500 (Beazley 1956, 273.109, 691; Beazley 1971, 118).

8. Beazley archive (Menelaos and Paris; bodies of warriors, cutout shields): black-figure amphora A, attributed to manner of Leagros Group, ca. 525–475 (Munich, Antikensammlungen J380; *CVA* Munich 1, pls. 45.2, 46.2, 47.3, 52.6; *LIMC* VIII pl. 563, Menelaos 12a).

BIBLIOGRAPHY

Ahlberg-Cornell, G. 1992. *Myth and Epos in Early Greek Art: Representation and Interpretation (SIMA* 100). Jonsered.

Allen, A., and J. Frel. 1972. "A Date for Corinna," *CJ* 68: 26–30.

Allison, J. W. 1997. "Homeric Allusions at the Close of Thucydides' Sicilian Narrative," *AJP* 118: 499–516.

– 1989. *Power and Preparedness in Thucydides.* Baltimore.

Amit, A. 1973. *Great and Small Poleis: A Study in the Relations between the Great Powers and Small Cities in Ancient Greece.* Brussels.

Anderson, B. R. O'G. 1983. *Imagined Communities: Reflections on the Origin and Spread of Nationalism.* London.

Anderson, J. K. 1995. "The Geometric Catalogue of Ships," in J.B Carter and S. P. Morris, eds. *The Ages of Homer: A Tribute to Emily Townsend Vermeule.* Austin: 181–191.

Archibald, Z. H. 2001. "Space, Hierarchy, and Community in Archaic and Classical Macedonia, Thessaly, and Thrace," in R. Brock and S. Hodkinson, eds. *Alternatives to Athens: Varieties of Political Organization and Community in Ancient Greece.* Oxford: 212–233.

Arnold-Buicchi, C. 1992. "The Beginnings of Coinage in the West: Archaic Selinus," in H. Nilsson, ed. *Florilegium Numismaticum: Studia in Honorem U. Westermark edita.* Stockholm: 13–19.

Arnold-Biucchi, C., L. Beer-Tobey, and N. M. Waggoner. 1988. "A Greek Archaic Silver Hoard from Selinus," *ANSMN* 33: 1–35.

Ashton, R. 2000. "More Pseudo-Rhodian Drachms from Central Greece: Haliartos (again), Chalkis, and Euboia uncertain (?)," *NC* 7th series 160: 93–116.

– 1997. "More Pseudo-Rhodian Drachms from Mainland Greece," *NC* 7th series 157: 188–191.

– 1995. "Pseudo-Rhodian Drachms from Central Greece," *NC* 7th series 155: 1–20.

Babelon, E. 1907. *Traité des monnaies grecques et romaines,* vol. 2.1. Paris.

Badian, E. 1993. *From Plataea to Potidaea: Studies in the History and Historiography of the Pentecontaetia.* Baltimore: 109–123.

– 1989. "Plataea between Athens and Sparta," in H. Beister and J. Buckler, eds. *Boiotika. Vorträge vom 5. Internationalen Böotien-Kolloquium zu Ehren von Professor Dr. Siegfried Lauffer.* Munich: 95–111.

Bakhuizen, S. C. 1989. "The Ethnos of the Boeotians," in H. Beister and J. Buckler, eds. *Boiotika. Vorträge vom 5. Internationalen Böotien-Kolloquium zu Ehren von Professor Dr. Siegfried Lauffer.* Munich: 65–72.

– 1979. "On Boiotian Iron," in J. Fossey and A. Schachter, eds. *Proceedings of the Second International Conference on Boiotian Antiquities (Teiresias* Suppl. 2). Montréal: 19–20.

– 1976. *Chalcis-in-Euboea: Iron and Chalcidians Abroad.* Leiden.

Ballabriga, A. 1990. "La question homérique. Pour une réouverture du débat," *RÉG* 103: 16–29.

Barth, F., ed. 1969. *Ethnic Groups and Boundaries: The Social Organization of Cultural Difference.* London.

Beazley, J. D. 1971. *Paralipomena: Additions to Attic Black-Figure Vase-Painters and to Attic Red-Figure Vase-Painters.* Oxford.

– (1942²) 1963. *Attic Red-Figure Vase-Painters.* (first English ed. 1942; first ed. 1925, Tübingen). Oxford.

– 1956. *Attic Black-Figure Vase-Painters.* Oxford.

Beck, H. 1997. *Polis und Koinon. Untersuchungen zur Geschichte und Struktur der griechischen Bundesstaaten im 4. Jahrhundert v. Chr (Historia* Einzelschriften 114). Stuttgart.

Beloch, K. J. (1893–1904²) 1912–1927. *Griechische Geschichte,* 4 Vols. Strasbourg.

Bintliff, J. 2005. "Explorations in Boiotian Population History," *AW* 36.1 (Studies in Honor of John M. Fossey I): 5–17.

– 1999. "Pattern and Process in the City Landscapes of Boeotia from Geometric to Late Roman Times," in M. Brunet, ed. *Territoires des cités grecques. Actes de la table ronde internationale organisée par l'École Française d'Athènes (BCH* Suppl. 34). Athens and Paris: 15–33.

– 1996. "The Archaeological Survey of the Valley of the Muses and its Significance for Boeotian History," in A. Hurst and A. Schachter, eds. *La montagne des Muses.* Geneva: 193–224.

– 1994. "Territorial Behavior and the Natural History of the Greek *Polis,*" in E. Olshausen and H. Sonnabend, eds. *Stuttgarter Kolloquium zur historischen Geographie des Altertums.* Amsterdam: 207–249.

Blinkenberg, C. 1931. *Lindos: Fouilles et recherches, 1902–1914.* Vols. 1–2, *Les petits objets.* Berlin.

Boardman, J. 1983. "Symbol and Story in Geometric Art," in W. Moon, ed. *Ancient Greek Art and Iconography.* Madison: 15–36.

– 1975. *Athenian Red Figure Vases, the Archaic Period: A Handbook.* London.

– 1974. *Athenian Black Figure Vases: A Handbook.* London.

Boedeker, D. 2000. "Herodotus's Genre(s)," in M. Depew and D. Obbink, eds. *Matrices of Genre: Authors, Canons, Society.* Cambridge, Mass.: 97–114.

Bol, P. C. 1989. *Argivische Schilde* (Olympische Forschungen 17). Berlin.

Bonnechere, P. 2003. *Trophonios de Lébadée: Cultes et mythes d'une cité béotienne au miroir de la mentalité antique.* Leiden and Boston.

Borchhardt, H. 1977. "Frühe griechische Schildformen," in H.-G. Buchholz and J. Wiesner, eds. *Kriegswesen I: Schutzwaffen und Wehrbauten (Archaeologia Homerica* 1, ch. E). Göttingen: 1–56.

Bourguet, É., ed. 1929. *Fouilles de Delphes.* Vol. III.1, *Inscriptions de l'entrée du sanctuaire au trésor des Athéniens.* Paris.

Bousquet, J. 1991. "Inscriptions de Delphes," *BCH* 115: 167–181.

Bowie, A. M. 1993. "Homer, Herodotus, and the Beginnings of Thucydides' *History,*" in H.D. Jocelyn, ed. *Tria Lustra: Essays and Notes Presented to John Pinsent* (Liverpool Classical Papers 3). Liverpool: 141–147.

Bowra, C. M. 1957. "Asius and the Old-Fashioned Samians," *Hermes* 85: 391–401.

Breglia, L. 2005. "The Amphictyony of Calaureia," *AW* 36.1 (Studies in Honor of John M. Fossey I): 18–33.

Breglia-Pulci Doria, L. 1986. "Demeter Erinys Tilphussaia tra Poseidon e Ares," in *Les grandes figures réligieuses. Fonctionnement pratique et symbolique dans l'antiquité* (Annales littéraires de l'Université de Besançon 329, Centre de Recherches d'Histoire Ancienne 68, Lire les Polythéismes 1). Paris: 107–126.

Brock, R., and S. Hodkinson, eds. *Alternatives to Athens: Varieties of Political Organization and Community in Ancient Greece.* Oxford.

Bron, C. 1992. "La gent ailée d'Athéna Poliade," in C. Bron and E. Kassapoglou, eds. *L'image en jeu: de l'antiquité à Paul Klee.* Lausanne: 47–84.

Bruce, I. A. F. 1967. *An Historical Commentary on the "Hellenica Oxyrhynchia."* London.

Buck, C. D. (1955²) 1973. *The Greek Dialects: Grammar, Selected Inscriptions, Glossary.* London.

– 1909. "An Archaic Boeotian Inscription," *CP* 4: 76–80.

Buck, R. J. 1985. "Boeotian Oligarchies and Greek Oligarchic Theory," in J. M. Fossey and H. Giroux, eds. *Proceedings of the Third International Conference on Boiotian Antiquities.* Amsterdam: 25–31.

–   1979. *A History of Boiotia*. Edmonton.
–   1974. "Boeotarchs at Thermopylae," *CP* 69: 47–48.
–   1972. "The Formation of the Boeotian League," *CP* 67: 94–101.
–   1972b. "The Site of Ceressus," in J. M. Fossey and A. Schachter, eds. *Proceedings of the First International Conference on Boiotian Antiquities*. Montréal: 31–40.
–   1968. "The Aeolic Dialect in Boiotia," *CP* 63: 268–280.
Buckler, J. 1996. "The Battle of Koroneia and its Historiographical Legacy," *Boeotia Antiqua* 6: 59–72.
Burkert, W. 1976. "Das hunderttorige Theben und die Datierung der Ilias," *WienStud* 89: 5–21.
Burnett, A. P. 2005. *Pindar's Songs for Young Athletes of Aigina*. Oxford.
Burzacchini, G. 1992. "Corinna in Roma," *Eikasmos* 3: 47–65.
–   1991. "Corinniana," *Eikasmos* 2: 39–90.

Campbell, D. A. 1992. *Greek Lyric IV: Bacchylides, Corinna, and Others*. Cambridge, Mass.
——. 1982. *Greek Lyric I: Sappho and Alcaeus*. Cambridge, Mass.
Camp, J. McK. 2000. "Walls and the *Polis*," in P. Flensted-Jensen, T. H. Nielsen, and L. Rubinstein, eds. *Polis and Politics: Studies in Ancient Greek History, Presented to Mogens Herman Hansen*. Copenhagen: 41–57.
–   1994. "Before Democracy: Alkmaionidai and Peisistratidai," in W. Coulson, O. Palagia, T. L. Shear, Jr., H. A. Shapiro, and F. Frost, eds. *The Archaeology of Athens and Attica under the Democracy* (Oxbow Monographs 37). Oxford: 7–12.
Carpenter, T. H. 1991. *Art and Myth in Ancient Greece: A Handbook*. London.
Carpenter, T. H., T. Mannack, and M. Mendonça. (1982²) 1989. *Beazley Addenda: Additional References to ABV, ARV² and Paralipomena*. Oxford.
Carter, J. 1972. "The Beginnings of Narrative Art in the Geometric Period," *BSA* 67: 25–58, pls. 5–12.
Cartledge, P. 2000. "Boiotian Swine F(or)ever? The Boiotian Superstate 395 BC," in P. Flensted-Jensen, T. H. Nielson, and L. Rubinstein, eds. *Polis and Politics: Studies in Ancient Greek History, Presented to Mogens Herman Hansen*. Copenhagen: 397–415.
Casevitz, M. 1985. *Le vocabulaire de la colonisation en grec ancien*. Paris.
Caspari, M. O. B. 1915. "The Ionian Confederacy," *JHS* 35: 173–188.
Chadwick, J. 1958. "Mycenaean Elements in the Homeric Dialect," in E. Grumach, ed. *Minoica: Festschrift zum 80. Geburtstag von Johannes Sundwall* (Schriften der Sektion für Altertumswissenschaft 12). Berlin: 116–122.
Chambers, M., ed. 1993. *Hellenica Oxyrhynchia (post Victorium Bartoletti)*. Stuttgart and Leipzig.
Chantraine, P. (1968²) 1999. *Dictionnaire étymologique de la langue grecque: histoire des mots*. Paris.
–   1948. *Grammaire homérique*. Vol. 1, *Phonétique et morphologie*. Paris.
Clayman, D. L. 1993. "Corinna and Pindar," in R. M. Rosen and J. Farrell, eds. *Nomodeiktes: Greek Studies in Honor of Martin Ostwald*. Ann Arbor: 633–642.
–   1978. "The Meaning of Corinna's Ϝέροια," *CQ* n.s. 28: 396–397.
Cohen, E. E. 2000. *The Athenian Nation*. Princeton.
Coldstream, J. N. 1994. "Prospectors and Pioneers: Pithekoussai, Kyme and Central Italy," in G. R. Tsetskhladze and F. De Angelis, eds. *The Archaeology of Greek Colonisation: Essays Dedicated to Sir John Boardman*. Oxford: 47–59.
Collins, D. 2004. "Corinna and Mythological Innovation," *APA* Abstracts.
Colvin, S. 2004. "Social Dialect in Attica," in J. H. W. Penney, ed. *Indo-European Perspectives: Studies in Honour of Anna Morpurgo Davies*. Oxford: 95–108.
–   2000. "The Language of Non-Athenians in Old Comedy," in D. Harvey and J. Wilkins, eds. *The Rivals of Aristophanes: Studies in Athenian Old Comedy*. London: 285–298.
–   1999. *Dialect in Aristophanes: The Politics of Language in Ancient Greek Literature*. Oxford.

Connor, W. R. 1993. "The Ionian Era of Athenian Civic Identity," *PAPhS* 137: 194–206.

–   1984. *Thucydides*. Princeton.

Cook, E. F. 2004. "Near Eastern Prototypes of the Palace of Alkinoos," *AJA* 108: 43–77.

–   1995. *The Odyssey in Athens: Myths of Cultural Origins*. Ithaca.

Cook, R. 1937. "The Date of the Hesiodic Shield," *CQ* 31: 204–214.

Corsten, T. 1999. *Vom Stamm zum Bund: Gründung und territoriale Organisation griechischer Bundesstaaten*. Munich.

Cosmopoulos, M. B. 2001. *The Rural History of Ancient Greek City-States: The Oropos Survey Project* (BAR International Series 1001). Oxford.

Crielaard, J. P. 1995. "Homer, History and Archaeology: Some Remarks on the Date of the Homeric World," in J. P. Crielaard, ed. *Homeric Questions: Essays in Philology, Ancient History and Archaeology*. Amsterdam: 201–288.

Crouwel, J. H. and M. A. Littauer. 1979. *Wheeled Vehicles and Ridden Animals in the Ancient Near East*. Leiden.

Csapo, E. 1993. "A Postscript to 'An International Community of Traders in Late 8th–7th c. B.C. Kommos,'" *ZPE* 96: 235–236.

–   1991. "An International Community of Traders in Late 8th-7th c. B.C. Kommos in Southern Crete," *ZPE* 88: 211–216.

Daumas, M. 1998. *Cabiriaca: recherches sur l'iconographie du culte des Cabires*. Paris.

Day, J. W. 2000. "Epigram and Reader: Generic Force as a (Re-)Activation of Ritual," in M. Depew and D. Obbink, eds. *Matrices of Genre: Authors, Canons, and Society*. Cambridge, Mass.: 37–57.

Debnar, P. A. 1996. "The Unpersuasive Thebans (Thucydides 3.61–67)," *Phoenix* 50: 95–110.

Denniston, J. D. 1954. *The Greek Particles*. Oxford.

Dickey, E. 1996. *Greek Forms of Address from Herodotus to Lucian*. Oxford.

Dittenberger, W. 1906. "Ethnika und Verwandtes," *Hermes* 41: 78–102, 161–219.

–   1892. *Inscriptiones Graecae VII: Megaridis, Oropiae, Boeotiae*. Berlin.

Drachmann, A. B. 1903. *Scholia Vetera in Pindari Carmina*. Vol. 1. Amsterdam (reprint 1969, Amsterdam).

Ducat, J. 1973. "La confédération béotienne et l'expansion thébaine à l'époque archaïque," *BCH* 97: 59–73.

–   1971. *Les kouroi du Ptoion: Le sanctuaire d'Apollon Ptoieus à l'époque archaïque*. Paris.

Doulgeri-Indzessiliglou, A. 1991. "La Thessalie à l'époque archaïque," *Dossiers d'archéologie* 159: 26–27.

Ebbinghaus, S. 2005. "Protector of the City, or the Art of Storage in Early Greece," *JHS* 125: 51–72.

Edwards, G. P. 1971. *The Language of Hesiod in its Traditional Context*. Oxford.

Effenterre, H. van. 1997. "Aspects of Archaic Boeotia," from J. Bintliff, ed. *Recent Developments in the History and Archaeology of Central Greece, Proceedings of the Sixth International Boiotian Conference* (BAR International Series 666). Oxford: 135–137.

Effenterre, H. van, and F. Ruzé. 1994. *Nomima: Recueil d'inscriptions politiques et juridiques de l'archaïsme grec I*. Rome.

Ellis, J. R. 1991. "The Structure and Argument of Thucydides' Archaeology," *CA* 10: 344–375.

Étienne, R. and D. Knoepfler. 1976. *Hyettos de Béotie et la chronologie des archontes fédéraux entre 250 et 171 avant J.-C.* (*BCH* Suppl. 3). Athens and Paris.

Evans, A. 1892–1893. "A Mykenaean Treasure from Aegine," *JHS* 13: 195–226.

Farnell, L. R. 1921. *Greek Hero Cults and Ideas of Immortality*. Oxford.

Fehling, D. 1989. *Herodotus and His "Sources:" Citation, Invention, and Narrative Art*, trans. J. G. Howie (ARCA Classical and Medieval Texts, Papers, and Monographs 21). Leeds.

Feyel, M. 1942. *Contribution à l'épigraphie béotienne*. Le Puy.

Finnegan, R. H. 1977. *Oral Poetry: Its Nature, Significance and Social Context.* Cambridge.

Fontenrose, J. E. 1959. *Python: A Study of Delphic Myth and its Origins.* Berkeley and Los Angeles.

Forbes, R. J. 1964. *Studies in Ancient Technology.* Vol. 9. Leiden.

Fornara, C. 1977. *Translated Documents of Greece and Rome: Archaic Times to the End of the Peloponnesian War.* Baltimore and London.

–   1971. *Herodotus: An Interpretive Essay.* Oxford.

Forrest, G. 1956. "The First Sacred War," *BCH* 80: 33–52.

Fortenberry, C. D. 1990. "Elements of Mycenaean Warfare." Ph.D. diss., University of Cincinnati.

Fossey, J. M. 1992. *Concordances and Indices to Inscriptiones Graecae VII.* Chicago.

–   1988. *Topography and Population of Ancient Boiotia.* Chicago.

–   1973–1974. "The End of the Bronze Age in the South West Kopais," *Euphrosyne* 6: 7–21.

Foucart, P. 1885. "Inscriptions de Béotie," *BCH* 9: 403–433.

Fowler, B. H. 1957. "Thucydides 1.107–108 and the Tanagran Federal Issues," *Phoenix* 11: 164–170.

Fowler, R. L. 1998. "Genealogical Thinking, Hesiod's *Catalogue*, and the Creation of the Hellenes," *PCPS* 44: 1–19.

–   1996. "Herodotus and His Contemporaries," *JHS* 116: 62–87.

Frazer, J. G. 1898. *Pausanias' Description of Greece,* 6 Vols. New York.

Gantz, T. 1993. *Early Greek Myth: A Guide to Literary and Artistic Sources.* Baltimore.

Gardner, P. 1918. *A History of Ancient Coinage, 700–300 B.C.* Oxford.

Garland, R. 1992. *Introducing New Gods: The Politics of Athenian Religion.* London.

Gentili, B. and L. Lomiento. 2001. "Corinna, Le Asopidi (*PMG* 654 col.III.12–51)," *QUCC* 68: 7–20.

Gerber, D. E. 1970. *Euterpe: An Anthology of Early Greek Lyric, Elegiac, and Iambic Poetry.* Amsterdam.

Gilula, D. 1995. "Comic Food and Food for Comedy," in J. Wilkins, D. Harvey, and M. Dobson, eds. *Food in Antiquity.* Exeter: 386–399.

Giovannini, A. 1969. *Étude historique sur les origines du catalogue des vaisseaux* (Travaux publiés sous les auspices de la Société suisse des sciences humaines 9). Bern.

Gjongecaj, S., and H. Nicolet-Pierre. 1995. "Le monnayage d'argent d'Egine et le trésor de Hollm (Albanie), 1991," *BCH* 119 (études): 283–338.

Gomme, A. W. 1945. *A Historical Commentary on Thucydides.* Vol. 1. Oxford.

Grote, G. 1865–1870. *A History of Greece* (reprint from the 2nd London ed.). New York.

Guillon, P. 1963. *Le bouclier d'Héraclès et l'histoire de la Grèce centrale dans la période de la première guerre sacrée.* Aix-en-Provence.

–   1958. "Corinne et les oracles béotiens: la consultation d'Asopos," *BCH* 82: 47–60.

–   1943. *Les trépieds du Ptoion.* Paris.

Hainsworth, J. B. 1988. "The Epic Dialect," in J. B. Hainsworth, A. Heubeck, and S. West, eds. *A Commentary on Homer's* Odyssey. Vol. I. Oxford: 24–32.

–   1967. "Greek Views of Greek Dialectology," *Transactions of the Philological Society* 65: 62–76.

Hall, J. M. 1997. *Ethnic Identity in Greek Antiquity.* Cambridge.

–   1995. "The Role of Language in Greek Ethnicities," *PCPS* 41: 83–100.

Halliday, W. R. 1928. *The Greek Questions of Plutarch.* Oxford.

Hammond, N. G. L. 2000. "Political Developments in Boeotia," *CQ* n.s. 50: 80–93.

Hampe, R. and E. Simon. 1964. *Griechische Sagen in der frühen etruskischen Kunst.* Mainz.

Hansen, M. H. 2000a. "The Concepts of City-State and City-State Culture," in M. H. Hansen, ed. *A Comparative Study of Thirty City-State Cultures.* Copenhagen: 11–34.

–   2000b. "Conclusion: The Impact of City-State Cultures on World History," in M. H.

Hansen, ed. *A Comparative Study of Thirty City-State Cultures*. Copenhagen: 597–623.
- 1996a. "An Inventory of Boiotian Poleis in the Archaic and Classical Periods," in M. H. Hansen, ed. *Introduction to an Inventory of Poleis. Acts of the Copenhagen Polis Centre 3.* Copenhagen: 73–116.
- 1996b. "City-Ethnics as Evidence for Polis Identity," in M. H. Hansen and K. Raaflaub, eds. *More Studies in the Ancient Greek Polis. Papers from the Copenhagen Polis Centre 3.* Stuttgart: 169–196.
- 1995. "Boiotian Poleis: A Test Case," in M. H. Hansen, ed. *Sources for the Ancient Greek City State. Acts of the Copenhagen Polis Centre 2.* Copenhagen: 13–63.
Hansen, M., and T. H. Nielsen, eds. 2004. *An Inventory of Archaic and Classical Poleis*. Oxford.
Hansen, O. 1989. "The meaning of Corinna's Ϝέροια Reconsidered," *HSF* 102: 70–71.
Hansen, P. A. 1983. *Carmina Epigraphica Graeca: Saeculorum VIII–V a. Chr. n.* Vol. 1. Berlin.
Hartog, F. 1988. *The Mirror of Herodotus: The Representation of the Other in the Writing of History*, trans. J. Lloyd. Berkeley and Los Angeles.
Head, B. V. (1887[2]) 1911. *Historia Numorum: A Manual of Greek Numismatics*. Oxford.
- 1888. *Catalogue of Greek Coins: Attica, Megara, Aegina*, R. S. Poole, ed. Bologna.
- 1887. *Historia Numorum: A Manual of Greek Numismatics*. Oxford.
- 1881. *Chronological Sequence of the Coinage of Boiotia*. London (originally published in *NC* 3rd Series 1, 1881: 177–275).
- 1884. *Catalogue of Greek Coins of the British Museum: Central Greece*. (BMC Central Greece), R. S. Poole, ed. London.
Healy, J. F. 1978. *Mining and Metallurgy in the Greek and Roman World*. London.
Helly, B. 1995. *L' état thessalien: Aleuas le Roux, les tétrades et les tagoi*. Lyon.
- 1991. "Les cités antiques de la Thessalie," *Les dossiers d'archéologie* 159: 30–43.
Henderson, W. J. 1995. "Corinna of Tanagra on Poetry," *AClass* 38: 29–41.
Hepworth, R. 1998. "The 4th Century BC Magistrate Coinage of the Boiotian Confederacy," *Nomismatika Chronika* 17: 61–96.
Higgins, R. 1957. "The Aegina Treasure Reconsidered," *BSA* 52: 42–57.
Higgins, M. D. and R. Higgins. 1996. *A Geological Companion to Greece and the Aegean*. Ithaca.
Hind, J. G. F. 2001. "Centaurs, Satyrs and Nymphs on the Early Silver Coins of Thasos and the tribes of Mount Pangaion," *NC* 7th series 161: 279–287.
Hirschberger, M. 2004. *Gynaikon Katalogos und Megalai Ehoiai*. Munich.
Hockey, M., A. Johnston, et. al. 1992. "An Illyrian Helmet in the British Museum," *BSA* 87: 281–291, pls. 19–27.
Hoekstra, A. 1999. Reprint. "Initial Digamma," in I. J. F. de Jong, ed. *Homer: Critical Assessments.* Vol. 1. London: 237–255 (originally printed in 1964 in *Homeric Modifications of Formulaic Prototypes: Studies in the Development of Greek Epic Diction* (Verhandelingen der Koninklijke Nederlandse Akademie van Wetenschappen, afdeling Letterkunde, vol. 71, no. 1). Amsterdam: 42–58.
Holleaux, M. 1887. "Tête de femme trouvée dans les ruines du sanctuaire d'Apollon Ptoos," *BCH* 11: 1–5, pl. 7.
- 1885. "Fouilles au temple d'Apollon Ptoos," *BCH* 9: 520–524.
Holloway, R. R. 2000. "Remarks on the Taranto Hoard of 1911," *Revue belge de numismatique et de sigillographie* 146: 1–8.
Hölscher, T. 1998. "Images and Political Identity: The Case of Athens," in D. Boedeker and K. A. Raaflaub, eds. *Democracy, Empire, and the Arts in Fifth-Century Athens*. Cambridge, Mass.: 153–183.
Horden, P. and N. Purcell. 2000. *The Corrupting Sea: A Study of Mediterranean History*. Oxford and Malden, Mass.
Hornblower, S. 1995. "Thucydides and Boiotia," in A. C. Christopoulou, ed. *Επετηρίς της Εταιρείας Βοιωτικών Μελετών, Τόμος Β, Τεύχος α΄, Β΄ Διεθνές Συνέδριο Βοιωτικών Μελετών, Λιβαδειά, 6–10 Σεπτεμβρίου 1992*. Athens: 667–678.

– 1991–. *A Commentary on Thucydides.* Vols. 1–2. Oxford.

Horrocks, G. 1997. "Homeric Dialect," in B. Powell and I. Morris, eds. *A New Companion to Homer.* Leiden.

Householder, F. W. and G. Nagy. 1972. *Greek: A Survey of Recent Work.* The Hague.

How, W. W. and J. Wells. 1912. *A Commentary on Herodotus.* Oxford.

Howgego, C. J. 1995. *Ancient History from Coins.* London.

– 1990. "Why Did Ancient States Strike Coins?" *NC* 7th series 150: 1–25.

Howie, J. G. 1998. "Thucydides and Pindar: The *Archaeology* and *Nemean 7*," in F. Cairns and M. Heath, eds. *Papers of the Leeds International Latin Seminar 10: Greek Poetry, Drama, Prose, Roman Poetry.* Leeds: 75–130.

Hunter, V. 1982. *Past and Process in Herodotus and Thucydides.* Princeton.

– 1980. "Thucydides and the Uses of the Past," *Klio* 62: 191–218.

Hurwit, J. M. 1985. "The Dipylon Shield Once More," *CA* 4: 121–126.

Huxley, G. L. 1969. *Greek Epic Poetry.* London.

Iakovidis, E. 2001. *Gla and the Kopais in the 13th Century B.C.* (Library of the Archaeological Society of Athens, Vol. 221). Athens.

– 1992. "The Mycenaean Fortress of Gla," in J. P. Olivier, ed. *Mykenaïka: Actes du IXᵉ Colloque international sur les textes mycéniens et égéens organisé par le Centre de l'antiquité grecque et romaine de la Fondation hellénique des recherches scientifiques et l'Ecole Française d'Athènes, Athens, 2–6 October 1990* (*BCH* Suppl. 25). Athens and Paris: 607–616.

Jacoby, F. 1923–1958. *Die Fragmente der griechischen Historiker.* Berlin.

– 1913. "Herodot," *RE* Suppl. 2: 205–520.

Jameson, M. H., D. R. Jordan, and R. D. Kotansky. 1993. *A Lex Sacra from Selinous.* Durham.

Janko, R. 1992. *The Iliad: A Commentary.* Vol. 4, books 13–16. Cambridge.

– 1986. "The *Shield of Herakles* and the Legend of Cycnus," *CQ* n.s. 36: 38–59.

– 1982. *Homer, Hesiod, and the Hymns.* Cambridge.

Jarva, E. 1995. *Archaiologia on Archaic Greek Body Armour.* Rovaniemi.

Jeffery, L. H. 1990. *The Local Scripts of Archaic Greece: A Study of the Origin of the Greek Alphabet and its Development from the Eighth to the Fifth Century.* Rev. ed. with a Suppl. by A.W. Johnston (originally published 1961). Oxford.

Johnston, A. W. 1979. *Trademarks on Greek Vases.* Warminster.

Jones, S. 1997. *The Archaeology of Ethnicity: Constructing Identities in the Past and Present.* London.

Kallet, L. 2001. *Money and the Corrosion of Power in Thucydides: The Sicilian Expedition and Its Aftermath.* Berkeley, Los Angeles, and London.

Kallet-Marx, L. 1993. *Money, Expense, and Naval Power in Thucydides' History 1–5.24.* Berkeley, Los Angeles, and Oxford.

Karakasidou, A. N. 1997. *Fields of Wheat, Hills of Blood: Passages to Nationhood in Greek Macedonia, 1870–1990.* Chicago.

Karusu, S. 1976. "Ein frühes Bild des Achilleus?" in *Mitteilungen des Deutschen Archäologischen Instituts, athenische Abteilung* 91: 23–30.

Kearns, E. 1989. *The Heroes of Attica* (*BICS* Suppl. 57). London.

Keesling, C. M. 2003. *The Votive Statues of the Athenian Acropolis.* Cambridge.

Kemp-Lindemann, D. 1975. *Darstellungen des Achilleus in griechischer und römischer Kunst.* Bern and Frankfurt.

Kilian, K. 1983. "Weihungen aus Eisen und Eisenverarbeitung im Heiligtum zu Philia (Thessalien)," in R. Hägg, ed. *The Greek Renaissance of the Eighth Century B.C.: Tradition and Innovation. Proceedings of the Second International Symposium at the Swedish Insititute at Athens.* Stockholm: 131–147.

Kilinski, K, II. 2005. "In Pursuit of the Boeotian Cantharus," *AW* 36.2: 176–212.
– 1992. "Teisias and Theodoros: East Boiotian Potters," *Hesperia* 61: 253–263.
– 1990. *Boeotian Black Figure Vase Painting of the Archaic Period*. Mainz.
Kim, H. 2001. "Archaic Coinage as Evidence for the Use of Money," in A. Meadows and K. Shipton, eds. *Money and Its Uses in the Ancient Greek World*. Oxford: 7–21.
Kirk, G. S. 1990. *The Iliad: A Commentary*. Vol. 2, books 5–8. Cambridge.
– 1985. *The Iliad: A Commentary*. Vol. 1, books 1–4. Cambridge.
Kirkwood, G. M. 1974. *Early Greek Monody: The History of a Poetic Type*. Ithaca.
Kleiner, G., P. Hommel, and W. Müller-Wiener. 1967. *Panionion und Melie*. Berlin.
Knoepfler, D. 2000. "Oropodoros: Anthroponymy, Geography, History," in S. Hornblower and E. Matthews, eds. *Greek Personal Names: Their Value as Evidence* (Proceedings of the British Academy 104). Oxford: 81–98.
– 1992. "Sept années de recherches sur l'épigraphie de la Béotie (1985–1991)," *Chiron* 22: 411–503.
– 1981. Review of R.J. Buck's *A History of Boeotia*. *Gnomon* 53: 140–150.
Kock, T., ed. 1880. *Comicorum Atticorum Fragmenta*. Vol. 1. Leipzig (reprint 1976, Utrecht).
Kossatz-Deissman, A. 1981–. "Achilleus," *Lexicon Iconographicum Mythologicae Classicae*. Vol. 1. Zurich and Munich: 37–200.
Kraay, C. 1976. *Archaic and Classical Greek Coins*. London.
– 1966. *Greek Coins*. New York.
Krentz, P. 1989. "Athena Itonia and the Battle of Koroneia," in H. Beister and J. Buckler, eds. *Boiotika. Vorträge vom 5. Internationalen Böotien-Kolloquium zu Ehren von Professor Dr. Siegfried Lauffer*. Munich: 313–317.
Kroll, J. H. 2001. "Observations on Monetary Instruments in Pre-Coinage Greece," in M. S. Balmuth, ed. *Hacksilber to Coinage: New Insights into the Monetary History of the Near East and Greece*. New York: 77–91.
Kroll, J. H. and N. M. Waggoner. 1984. "Dating the Earliest Coins of Athens, Corinth and Aegina," *AJA* 88: 325–340.
Kunze, E. 1967. "Helme," in *Bericht über die Ausgrabungen in Olympia* VIII. Berlin: 111–134, pls. 50–72.
– 1967a. "Waffenweihungen," in *Bericht über die Ausgrabungen in Olympia* VIII. Berlin: 83–110, pls. 30–49.
– 1967b. "Kleinplastik aus Bronze," in *Bericht über die Ausgrabungen in Olympia* VIII. Berlin: 213–250, pls. 106–119.
– 1956. "Schildbeschläge," in *Bericht über die Ausgrabungen in Olympia* V. Berlin: 36–68, pls. 15–16.
Kunze, E. and H. Schleif. 1937/1938. "Waffenfunde," in *Bericht über die Ausgrabungen in Olympia* II. Berlin: 67–103, pls. 20–43.
Kurke, L. 1991. *The Traffic in Praise: Pindar and the Poetics of Social Economy*. Ithaca.

Lacroix, L. 1958. "Le bouclier, emblème des Béotiens," *RBPhil* 26: 7–30.
Lang, M. 1995. "War Story into Wrath Story," in J. B. Carter and S. P. Morris, eds. *The Ages of Homer: A Tribute to Emily Townsend Vermeule*. Austin: 149–158.
Larsen, J. A. O. 1968. *Greek Federal States*. Oxford.
– 1960. "Orchomenos and the Formation of the Boeotian Confederacy in 447 B.C." *CP* 55: 9–16.
Larson, J. 2002. "Corinna and the Daughters of Asopus," *SyllClass* 13: 47–62.
Larson, S. L. 2002. "Boiotia, Athens, the Peisistratids, and the *Odyssey's* Catalogue of Heroines," *GRBS* 41 (2000): 193–222.
Lauffer, S. 1980. "Inschriften aus Boiotien (II)," *Chiron* 10: 161–182, pls. 3–8.
– 1976. "Inschriften aus Boiotien," *Chiron* 6: 11–51, pls. 1–6.
Lazarides, P. 1965. "᾿Αρξαιοτητές καὶ μνημεῖα Θεσσαλίας· ῾Ιερὸν ᾿Αθηνᾶς ᾿Ιτωνίας (Φίλια-Καρδίτσης)" *ArchDelt* 20 B: 311–313.

Lazzarini, M. L. 1976. *Le formule delle dediche votive nella Grecia arcaica*. Rome.
Le Rider, G. 1989. "À propos d'un passage des *Poroi* de Xénophon: la question du change et les monnaies incuses d'Italie du Sud," in G. Le Rider, K. Jenkins, N. M. Waggoner, and U. Westermark, eds. *Kraay-Mørkholm Essays: Numismatic Studies in Memory of C. M. Kraay and O. Mørkholm*. Louvain: 159–172.
Leaf, W. 1886. *The Iliad*. Vol. 1, books 1–12. London.
Leekly, D. and N. Efstratiou. 1980. *Archaeological Excavations in Central and Northern Greece*. Park Ridge, New Jersey.
Lehmann, G. A. 1983. "Thessaliens Hegemonie über Mittelgriechenland im 6. Jh. v. Chr.," *Boreas* 6: 35–43.
Lefkowitz, M. R. 1991. *First Person Fiction: Pindar's Poetic "I."* Oxford.
Lenfent, D. 1993. "Le vocabulaire du pouvoir personnel chez Euripide," *Ktèma* 18: 29–40.
Lexicon Iconographicum Mythologicae Classicae. 1981–. Vol. 1. Zurich and Munich.
Lippold, G. 1909. "Griechische Schilde," in *Münchener archäologische Studien (dem Andenken Adolf Furtwänglers)*. Munich.
Lobel, E. and D. Page. 1955. *Poetarum Lesbiorum Fragmenta*. Oxford.
Lorber, C. 2000. "The Goats of 'Aigai'," in S. M. Hurter and C. Arnold-Biucchi, eds. *Pour Denyse: Divertissements numismatiques*. Bern: 113–133.
Lorimer, H. L. 1950. *Homer and the Monuments*. London.
Lowenstan, S. 1992. "The Uses of Vase-Depictions in Homeric Studies," *TAPA* 122: 165–198.

Macan, R. W. 1895. *Herodotus: The Fourth, Fifth and Sixth Books*. Vols. 1–2. London.
Mackie, C. J. 1996. "Homer and Thucydides: Corcyra and Sicily," *CQ* n.s. 46: 103–113.
Mackil, E. M. 2003. "*Koinon* and Koinonia: *Mechanisms and Structures of Political Collectivity in Classical and Hellenistic Greece*." Ph.D. diss., Princeton University.
Maehler, H. 1989. *Pindari carmina cum fragmentis*, part 2 (after B. Snell). Leipzig.
Maffoda, G. 2000. *Il koinon beotico in età arcaica e classica: storia e istituzioni*. Rome.
Maffre, J.-J. 1975. "Collection Paul Canellopoulos: vases béotiens," *BCH* 99: 409–520.
Malkin, I. 2001. *Ancient Perceptions of Greek Ethnicity*. Cambridge, Mass.
–   1998. *The Returns of Odysseus: Colonization and Ethnicity*. Berkeley, Los Angeles and London.
–   1994. *Myth and Territory in the Spartan Mediterranean*. Cambridge.
–   1987. *Religion and Colonization in Ancient Greece*. Leiden.
Marcadé, J. 1953. *Recueil des signatures de sculpteurs grecs*. Vol. 1. Paris.
Marchant, E. C. 1905. *Thucydides, Book 1*. London.
Martin, R. 2005. "Pulp Epic: The *Catalogue* and the *Shield*," in R. Hunter, ed. *The Hesiodic Catalogue of Women: Constructions and Reconstructions*. Cambridge: 153–175.
Martin, T. R. 1995. "Coins, Mints, and the *Polis*," in M. H. Hansen, ed. *Sources for the Ancient Greek City State. Acts of the Copenhagen Polis Centre* 2. Copenhagen: 257–291.
–   1985. *Sovereignty and Coinage in Classical Greece*. Princeton.
Mazarakis Ainian, A. 2002. "Recent Excavations at Oropos (northern Attica)," in M. Stamatopoulou and M. Yeroulanou, eds. *Excavating Classical Culture: Recent Archaeological Discoveries in Greece* (BAR International Series 1031, Studies in Classical Archaeology 1). Oxford: 149–178.
–   1997. *From Rulers' Dwellings to Temples: Architecture, Religion and Society in Early Iron Age Greece*. Jonsered.
McConnell, B. E. 1978–1979. "Fortifications of the Lake Kopais Drainage Works," *Dartmouth Classical Journal* 11: 73–103.
McInerney, J. 2001. "*Ethnos* and Ethnicity in Early Greece," in I. Malkin, ed. *Ancient Perceptions of Greek Ethnicity*. Cambridge, Mass: 51–73.
–   1999. *The Folds of Parnassos: Land and Ethnicity in Ancient Phokis*. Austin.
Meiggs, R. and D. M. Lewis. 1969² (1988). *A Selection of Greek Historical Inscriptions to the End of the Fifth Century B.C.* Oxford.

Mellink, M. J. 1989. "Archaeology in Anatolia," *AJA* 93: 105–133.
Merkelbach, R. and M. L. West, eds. 1990. *Hesiodi Fragmenta Selecta*. Oxford.
–   1967. *Fragmenta Hesiodea*. Oxford.
Momigliano, A. 1978. "The Historians of the Classical World and Their Audiences," *ASNP* 8: 59–75.
Moretti, L. 1962. *Ricerche sulle leghe greche (Peloponnesiaca, Boetica, Licia)*. Rome.
–   1957. *Olympionikai, i vincitori negli antichi agoni olimpici* (Atti della Accademia nazionale dei Lincei 8.2). Rome.
Morgan, C. 2003. *Early Greek States Beyond the Polis*. London and New York.
–   2001. "Symbol and Pragmatic Aspects of Warfare in the Greek World of the 8th to 6th Centuries BC," in T. Bekker-Nielsen and L. Hannestad, eds. *War as a Cultural and Social Force: Essays on Warfare in Antiquity* (Historisk-filosofiske Skrifter 22, The Royal Danish Academy of Sciences and Letters). Copenhagen: 20–44.
–   1999. "Cultural Subzones in Early Iron Age and Archaic Arkadia?" in T. H. Nielson and J. Roy, eds. *Defining Ancient Arkadia*. Acts of the Copenhagen Polis Center 6. Copenhagen: 382–456.
–   1997. "The Archaeology of Sanctuaries in the Early Iron Age and Archaic *Ethne*: A Preliminary View," in L. G. Mitchell and P. J. Rhodes, eds. *The Development of the Polis in Archaic Greece*. London and New York: 168–198.
–   1991. "Ethnicity and Early Greek States: Historical and Material Perspectives," *PCPS* 37: 131–163.
Morgan, C. and J. M. Hall. 1996. "Achaian *Poleis* and Achaian Colonisation," in M. H. Hansen, ed. *An Introduction to an Inventory of Poleis*. Acts of the Copenhagen Polis Center 3. Copenhagen: 164–231.
Morpurgo-Davies, A. 1993. "Geography, History and Dialect: The Case of Oropos," in E. Crespo, J. L. García Ramón, and A. Striano, eds. *Dialectologia Graeca: Actas del II Coloquio Internacional de Dialectologia Griega*. Madrid: 261–279.
Morris, C. D. 1888. *Thucydides, Book 1*. Boston.
Moustaka, A. 1983. *Kulte und Mythen auf Thessalischen Münzen*. Würzburg.
Myres, J. L. 1941. "Hesiod's 'Shield of Herakles': Its Structure and Workmanship," *JHS* 61: 17–38.

Nagy, G. 2004. *Homer's Text and Language*. Champaign-Urbana.
–   1992. "Homeric Questions," *TAPA* 122: 17–60.
Nielsen, T. H. 2002. *Arkadia and Its Poleis in the Archaic and Classical Periods*. Göttingen.
–   2000. "Epiknemidian, Hypoknemidian, and Opountian Lokrians. Reflections on the Political Organisation of East Lokris in the Classical Period," in Flensted-Jensen, P., ed. *Further Studies in the Ancient Greek Polis*. Papers from the Copenhagen Polis Centre 5. Stuttgart: 91–120.
–   1999. "The Concept of Arkadia – the People, Their Land, and Their Organisation," in T. H. Nielsen and J. Roy, eds. *Defining Ancient Arkadia*. Acts of the Copenhagen Polis Centre 6. Copenhagen: 16–79.
–   1997. "*Triphylia*. An Experiment in Ethnic Construction and Political Organisation," in T. H. Nielson, ed. *Yet More Studies in the Ancient Greek Polis*. Papers from the Copenhagen Polis Centre 4 (*Historia* Einzelschriften 117). Stuttgart: 128–162.
–   1996. "Was There an Arkadian Confederacy in the Fifth Century B.C.?" in M. H. Hansen and K. A. Raaflaub, eds. *More Studies in the Ancient Greek Polis*. Papers from the Copenhagen Polis Centre 3 (*Historia* Einzelschriften 108). Stuttgart: 39–61.
Nielsen, T. H. and J. Roy, eds. 1999. *Defining Ancient Arkadia*. Acts of the Copenhagen Polis Centre 6. Copenhagen.
Nielsen, T. H. and J. Roy. 1998. "The Azanians of Northern Arkadia," *ClMed* 49: 5–44.
Nilsson, M. P. 1951. *Cults, Myths, Oracles, and Politics in Ancient Greece*. Lund.

Osborne, M. J. and S. G. Byrne, eds. 1994. *Lexicon of Greek Personal Names*. Vol. 2. Oxford.
Osborne, R. 1996. *Greece in the Making, 1200–479 B.C*. London.

Paasi, A. 1986. "The Insitutionalization of Regions: A Theoretical Framework for Understanding the Emergence of Regions and the Constitution of Regional Identity," *Fennia* 164: 105–146.
Page, D. L. 1959. *History and the Homeric Iliad* (Sather Classical Lectures 31). Berkeley and Los Angeles.
– 1953. *Corinna* (Society for the Promotion of Hellenic Studies Suppl. 6). London.
Paley, F. A. (1861²) 1883. *The Epics of Hesiod*. London.
Palmer, L. R. 1980. *The Greek Language*. London and Boston.
Papalexandrou, N. 1999. "Listening to the Early Greek Images: The "Mantiklos Apollo" Reconsidered," in *AIA Abstracts from the 98th Annual Meeting, AJA* 101: 345–346.
Parker, R. 1996. *Athenian Religion: A History*. Oxford.
Perlman, P. 2000. *City and Sanctuary in Ancient Greece: The Theorodokia in the Peloponnese* (Hypomnemata 121). Göttingen.
Plassart, A. 1958. "Inscriptions de Thespies," *BCH* 82: 107–167.
Pleiner, R. 1969. *Iron Working in Ancient Greece* (Sborník Národního technického muzea v Praze 7). Prague.
Price, M. and N. Waggoner. 1975. *Archaic Greek Coinage: The Asyut Hoard*. London.
Pritchett, W. K. 1993. *The Liar School of Herodotus*. Amsterdam.
– 1985. *Studies in Ancient Greek Topography, part V* (University of California Publications: Classical Studies 31). Berkeley, Los Angeles and London.
– 1982. *Studies in Ancient Greek Topography, part IV: Passes* (University of California Publications: Classical Studies 28). Berkeley, Los Angeles and London.
– 1980. *Studies in Ancient Greek Topography, part III: Roads* (University of California Publications: Classical Studies 22). Berkeley, Los Angeles and London.
– 1969. *Studies in Ancient Greek Topography, part II: Battlefields* (University of California Publications: Classical Studies 4). Berkeley and Los Angeles.
Psoma, S. 1999. " Ἀρκαδικόν," *Horos* 13: 81–96.

Raaflaub, K. A. 1998. "The Thetes and Democracy (a Response to Josiah Ober)," in D. Castriota, I. Morris, and K. A. Raaflaub, eds. *Democracy 2500? Questions and Challenges*. Dubuque: 87–103.
Raubitschek, A. E. 1949. *Dedications from the Athenian Acropolis: A Catalogue of the Inscriptions of the Sixth and Fifth Centuries B.C*. Cambridge, MA (reprint 1999, Chicago).
Raubitschek, A. E. and I. K. Raubitschek. 1966. "Early Boeotian Potters," *Hesperia* 35: 154–165.
Rawlinson, G. 1875. *History of Herodotus*. Vol. 4. London.
Rayor, D. J. 1993. "Corinna: Gender and the Narrative Tradition," *Arethusa* 26: 219–231.
Richardson, R. 1896. "Inscriptions from the Argive Heraeum," *The American Journal of Archaeology and of the History of the Fine Arts* 11: 42–61.
Richter, G. M. A. 1949. *Archaic Greek Art against its Historical Background: A Survey*. New York.
Ridder, A. de. 1896. *Catalogue des bronzes trouvés sur l'Acropole d'Athènes*. Paris.
Ridgway, D. 1992. *The First Western Greeks*. Cambridge.
Ridley, R. T. 1981. "Exegesis and Audience in Thucydides," *Hermes* 109: 25–46.
Roesch, P. 1982. *Études béotiennes*. Paris.
– 1965. *Thespies et la confédération béotienne*. Paris.
Roller, D. W. 1990. "The Boiotian Pig," in A. Schachter, ed. *Essays in the Topography, History and Culture of Boiotia* (Teiresias Suppl. 3). Montréal: 139–144.
– 1989. *Tanagran Studies*. Vol. 1, *Sources and Documents on Tanagra in Boiotia* (McGill University Monographs in Classical Archaeology and History 9). Amsterdam.

Rolley, C. 1986. *Greek Bronzes*, trans. R. Howell. London.
Rose, V. 1886. *Aristotelis Fragmenta*. Leipzig.
Rumpel, I. 1883. *Lexicon Pindaricum*. Leipzig.
Russo, C. F. (1950²) 1965. *Hesiodi Scutum* (Biblioteca di studi superiori 9). Florence.

Sakellariou, M. V. 1990. *Between Memory and Oblivion: The Transmission of Early Greek Historical Traditions*. Athens.
Salmon, P. 1978. *Étude sur la confédération béotienne (447/6–386): Son organisation et son administration* (Académie royale de Belgique, Mémoires de la classe des lettres, Vol. 63, fasc. 3). Brussels.
Schachter, A. 2005. "The Singing Contest of Kithairon and Helikon: Korinna, fr. 654, col. i and ii.1–11: Content and Context," in K. Antje, A. Lukinovich, and A.-L. Rey, eds. *Koruphaioi Andri. Mélanges offerts à André Hurst*. (Recherches et Rencontres 22). Geneva: 275–283.
–   2003. "Tanagra: The Geographical and Historical Context: Part One," *Pharos* 11: 45–74.
–   1994. "The Politics of Dedication: Two Athenian Dedications at the Sanctuary of Apollo Ptoieus in Boeotia," in R. Osborne and S. Hornblower, eds. *Ritual, Finance, Politics: Athenian Democratic Accounts Presented to David Lewis*. Oxford: 291–306.
–   1990. "Tilphossa: The Site and its Cults," *Cahiers des études anciennes* 24: 333–340.
–   1989. "Boiotia in the Sixth Century B.C.," in H. Beister and J. Buckler, eds. *Boiotika. Vorträge vom 5. Internationalen Böotien-Kolloquium zu Ehren von Professor Dr. Siegfried Lauffer*. Munich: 73–86.
–   1981–1994. *Cults of Boiotia* (*BICS* Suppl. 38), 4 Vols. London.
–   1978. "La fête des *Pamboiotia*: le dossier épigraphique," *Cahiers des études anciennes* 8: 81–107.
–   1967. "A Boeotian Cult Type," *BICS* 14: 1–16.
Scheffer, C. 1992. "Boeotian Festival Scenes: Competition, Consumption, and Cult in Archaic Black Figure," in R. Hägg, ed. *The Iconography of Greek Cult in the Archaic and Classical Periods. Proceedings of the First International Seminar on Ancient Greek Cult* (*Kernos* Suppl. 1). Athens and Liège: 117–141.
Schefold, K. 1992. *Gods and Heroes in Late Archaic Greek Art*, trans, A. Griffiths. Cambridge and New York.
–   1966. *Myth and Legend in Early Greek Art*, trans. A Hicks. London.
Schmidt, G. 2002. *Rabe und Krähe in der Antike: Studien zur archäologischen und literarischen Überlieferung*. Wiesbaden.
Seaford, R. 1994. *Reciprocity and Ritual: Homer and Tragedy in the Developing City-State*. Cambridge.
Sealey, R. 1976. *A History of the Greek City-States ca. 700–338 BC*. Berkeley, Los Angeles and London.
Segal, C. 1998. *Aglaia: The Poetry of Alcman, Sappho, Pindar, Bacchylides, and Corinna*. Lanham, Maryland.
Sekunda, N. V. 2000. "Land-use, Ethnicity, and Federalism in West Crete," in R. Brock and S. Hodkinson, eds. *Alternatives to Athens: Varieties of Political Organization and Community in Ancient Greece*. Oxford: 327–347.
Seltman, C. T. (1933²) 1955. *Greek Coins: A History of Metallic Currency and Coinage down to the Fall of the Hellenistic Kingdoms*. London.
Shapiro, H. A. 1984. "Herakles and Kyknos," *AJA* 88: 523–529, pls. 68–69.
–   1984b. "Herakles, Kyknos and Delphi," in H. A. G. Brijder, ed. *Ancient Greek and Related Pottery: Proceedings of the International Vase Symposium in Amsterdam, 12–15 April 1984* (Allard Pierson Series 5). Amsterdam: 271–274.
Shrimpton, G. S. 1997. *History and Memory in Ancient Greece* (McGill-Queen's Studies in the History of Ideas 23). Montréal and Buffalo.
–   1984. "When Did Plataea Join Athens?," *CP* 79: 295–304.
Siapkas, J. 2003. *Heterological Ethnicity: Conceptualizing Identities in Ancient Greece*. Uppsala.

Siewert, P. 1981. "Eine Bronze-Urkunde mit elischen Urteilen über Böoter, Thessaler, Athen und Thespiai," in A. Mallwitz, ed. *Bericht über die Ausgrabungen in Olympia X*. Berlin: 228–248 and pl. 24.

Simon, C. G. 1986. "The Archaic Votive Offerings and Cults of Ionia." Ph.D. diss., The University of California, Berkeley.

Simpson, R. H. and J. F. Lazenby. 1970. *The Catalogue of Ships in Homer's* Iliad. Oxford.

Slater, W. J. 1969. "Futures in Pindar," *CQ* n.s. 19: 86–94.

–   1969b. *Lexicon to Pindar*. Berlin.

Smith, A. D. 1986. *The Ethnic Origins of Nations*. Oxford and New York.

Smith, C. F. 1900. "Traces of Epic Usage in Thucydides," *TAPA* 31: 69–81.

Smith, T. J. 2004. "Festival, What Festival? Reading Dance Imagery as Evidence," in G. Davies and S. Bell, eds. *Games and Festivals in Classical Antiquity* (BAR International Series 1220). Oxford: 9–23.

Snell, B., ed. 1986. *Tragicorum Graecorum Fragmenta*. Vol. 1. Göttingen.

Snodgrass, A. M. 1967. *Arms and Armor of the Greeks*. London and Baltimore (reprint in 1999 with new material located in Afterword: 131–141).

–   1998. *Homer and the Artists: Text and Picture in Early Greek Art*. Cambridge.

–   1980. *Archaic Greece: The Age of Experiment*. London.

–   1964. *Early Greek Armour and Weapons from the End of the Bronze Age to 600 B.C.* Edinburgh.

Snyder, J. M. 1984. "Korinna's 'Glorious Songs of Heroes,'" *Eranos* 82: 125–134.

Solmsen, F. and E. Fraenkel. 1930. *Inscriptiones Graecae Ad Inlustrandas Dialectos Selectae*. Leipzig.

Sordi, M. 1968. "Aspetti del federalismo greco arcaico. Autonomia e egemonia nel koinón beotico," *Atene e Roma* 12: 66–75.

Sparkes, B. A. 1967. "The Taste of a Boeotian Pig," *JHS* 87: 116–130.

Spier, J. 1990. "Emblems in Archaic Greece," *BICS* 37: 107–129, pls. 4–6.

Spyropoulos, T. 1973a. "Εἰδήσεις ἐκ Βοιωτίας," *AAA* 6: 375–395.

———. 1973b. "Archaeological Reports: Some Boiotian Discoveries," *Teiresias* 3: 2–6.

———. 1972. " ᾿Αρξαιοτητές καὶ μνημεῖα Βοιωτίας-Φθιώτιδος· Κορώνεια-Ιτώνιον," *Delt* 27B: 317–318.

Stanley, K. 1993. *The Shield of Homer: Narrative Structure in the* Iliad. Princeton.

Stefanakis, M. 1999. "The Introduction of Coinage in Crete and the Beginning of Local Minting," in A. Chaniotis, ed. *From Minoan Farmers to Roman Traders: Sidelights on the Economy of Ancient Crete* (Heidelberger althistorische Beiträge und epigraphische Studien 29). Stuttgart.

Steup, J., ed. 1897. *Thukydides*. Vol.1 (after J. Classen). Berlin.

Stewart, A. 1998. "Nuggets: Mining the Texts Again," *AJA* 102: 271–282.

Strøm, I. 1992. "Obeloi of Pre- or Proto-Monetary Value in the Greek Sanctuaries," in T. Linders and B. Alroth, eds. *Economics of Cult in the Ancient Greek World: Proceedings of the Uppsala Symposium 1990* (Acta Universitatis Upsaliensis, *Boreas* 21). Uppsala: 41–51.

Stroud, R. S. 1998. *The Athenian Grain-Tax Law of 374/3 B.C.* (*Hesperia* Suppl. 29). Princeton.

–   1984. "An Argive Decree from Nemea Concerning Aspendos," *Hesperia* 53: 193–216.

Stubbings, F. H. and A. J. B. Wace. 1962. *A Companion to Homer*. London.

Symeonoglou, S. 1973. *Kadmeia I: Mycenaean Finds from Thebes, Greece, Excavation at 14 Oedipous Street* (Studies in Mediterranean Archaeology 35). Gothenburg.

Talbert, R. J. A., ed. 2000. *Barrington Atlas of the Greek and Roman World*. Princeton.

Tatman, J. L. 2000. "Silphium, Silver and Strife: The History of Kyrenaika and its Coinage," *The Celator* 14.10: 6–24, 36.

Taübler, E. 1927. *Tyche. Beigebunden ist 'Die Archäologie des Thukydides.'* Leipzig.

Taylor, M. C. 1997. *Salamis and the Salaminioi: The History of an Unofficial Athenian Demos*. Amsterdam.

Teffeteller, A. 1995. "Helikon's Song, Korinna fr. 654 PMG," in A. C. Christopoulou, ed. *Επετηρίς της Εταιρείας Βοιωτικών Μελετών, Τόμος Β, Τεύχος α', Β' Διεθνές Συνέδριο Βοιωτικών Μελετών, Λιβαδειά, 6–10 Σεπτεμβρίου 1992*. Athens: 1073–1080.

Theokharis, D. 1967. " Ἀρχαιοτητὲς καὶ μνημεῖα Θεσσαλίας: Ἀνασκαφὴ ἱεροῦ Ἀθηνᾶς παρὰ τὴν Φίλιαν," *AD* 22 B2: 295–29.

–   1965. " Ἀρχαιοτητὲς καὶ μνημεῖα Θεσσαλίας: Ἱεροῦ Ἀθηνᾶς Ἰτωνίας (Φίλια-Καρδίτσης)," *AD* 20 B2: 311–313.

–   1964. " Ἀρχαιοτητὲς καὶ μνημεῖα Θεσσαλίας: Ἱερὸν Ἀθηνᾶς ἐν Φίλιᾳ Καρδίτσης," *AD* 19 B2: 244–249.

–––––. 1963. " Ἀρχαιοτητὲς καὶ μνημεῖα Θεσσαλίας: Φίλια (Καρδίτσης)," *AD* 18 B1: 135–139.

Thomas, R. 1992. *Griechische Bronzestatuetten*. Darmstadt.

Thompson, M., O. Mørkholm, and C. M. Kraay. 1973. *An Inventory of Greek Coin Hoards*. New York.

Treister, M. Yu. 1996. *The Role of Metals in Ancient Greek History (Mnemosyne Suppl. 156)*. Leiden.

Ure, A. D. 1935. "More Boeotian Geometricising Vases," *JHS* 55: 225–228.

–   1929. "Boeotian Geometricising Vases," *JHS* 49: 160–171, pls. 9–13.

Ure, P. N. 1927. *Sixth and Fifth-Century Pottery From Rhitsona*. London.

Vanderpool, E. 1971. "An Athenian Decree in Phocian Stiris," *AAA* 4: 439–443.

Venencie, J. 1960. "Inscriptions de Tanagra en alphabet épichorique," *BCH* 84: 589–616.

Vian, F. 1945. "Le combat d'Héraklès et de Kyknos d'après les documents figurés du VIe et du Ve siècle," *REA* 47: 5–32.

Vickers, M. 1985. "Early Greek Coinage. A Reassessment," *NC* 7th series 145: 1–44.

Vidal-Naquet, P. 1981. "Slavery and the Rule of Women in Tradition, Myth and Utopia," in R. L. Gordon, ed. *Myth, Religion and Society. Structuralist Essays by M. Detienne, L. Gernet, J.-P. Vernant and P. Vidal-Naquet*. Cambridge: 187–200.

Visser, E. 1997. *Homers Katalog der Schiffe*. Stuttgart.

Vottéro, G. 1998. *Le dialecte béotien (7e s.–2e s. av. J.-C)*, 2 Vols. (Collection d'études anciennes 18, 23). Nancy.

–   1996. "Koinès et Koinas en Béotie à l' époque dialectale (7e–2e s. av. J.-C.)," in C. Brixhe, ed. *La Koiné grecque antique*. Vol. 2 (Collection d'études anciennes 14). Nancy: 43–92.

Wachter, R. 2001. *Non-Attic Greek Vase Inscriptions*. Oxford.

Wallace, P. W. 1979. *Strabo's Description of Boiotia: A Commentary*. Heidelberg.

–   1974. "Hesiod and the Valley of the Muses," *GRBS* 15: 5–24.

Wallace, W. 1962. "The Early Coinages of Athens and Euboia," *NC* 7th series 2: 23–42.

Wartenberg, U. 1995. *After Marathon: War, Society, and Money in Fifth-Century Greece*. London.

Webster, T. B. L. 1967. *The Tragedies of Euripides*. London.

–   1958. *From Mycenae to Homer*. London.

Wees, H. van. 2000. "The Development of the Hoplite Phalanx: Iconography and Reality in the Seventh Century," in H. van Wees, ed. *War and Violence in Ancient Greece*. London.

–   1998. "Greeks Bearing Arms: the State, the Leisure Class, and the Display of Weapons in Archaic Greece," in J. Fisher and H. van Wees, eds. *Archaic Greece: New Approaches and New Evidence*. London: 333–378.

West, M. L. 1996. "The Berlin Corinna," *ZPE* 113: 22–23.

–   1995. "The Date of the *Iliad*," *MusHelv* 52: 203–219.

–   1990. "Dating Corinna," *CQ* n.s. 40: 553–557.

–   1988. "The Rise of the Greek Epic," *JHS* 108: 151–172.

–   1985. *The Hesiodic Catalogue of Women: Its Nature, Structure, and Origins*. Oxford.

– 1972. *Iambi et Elegi Graeci Ante Alexandrum Cantati.* Vol. 2. Oxford.

– 1970. "Corinna," *CQ* n.s. 20: 277–287.

West, S. 1985. "Herodotus' Epigraphical Interests," *CQ* n.s. 35: 278–305.

Wever, J. de, and R. van Compernolle. 1967. "La valeur des termes de 'colonisation' chez Thucydide," *AntCl* 36: 461–523.

Whallon, W. 1966. "The Shield of Ajax," *YCS* 19: 7–36.

Whitehead, D. 1986. *The Demes of Attica, 508/7–ca. 250 B.C.: A Political and Social Study.* Princeton.

Whitley, J. 2005. "Archaeology in Greece," *AR* 51: 1–118.

Wilamowitz-Möllendorff, U. von. 1905. "Lesefrüchte," *Hermes* 40: 116–176.

– 1895. *Euripides: Hercules furens.* Vol. 1. Berlin.

– 1886. "Oropos und die Graer," *Hermes* 21: 91–115.

Wilkins, J. 2000. *The Boastful Chef: The Discourse of Food in Ancient Greek Comedy.* Oxford.

Willcock, M. M. 1995. *Pindar: Victory Odes.* Cambridge.

Willcock, M. 1978. *A Commentary on Homer's Iliad, Books I-IV.* London.

Wright, W. 2001. "Silphium Rediscovered," *The Celator* 15.2: 23–25.

INDEX OF SOURCES

I. LITERARY SOURCES AND TEXTS

Aeschylus
  Prometheus Bound 725: 47

Alkaios (LP)
  fr. 129.1– 9: 73
  fr. 325: 133–134

Asios
  fr. 2 PEG: 21

Athenaeus
  10.417: 9

Bacchylides: 81–82, 127, 134, 155–157
  5. 187–194: 155–157
  9: 82

Cratinus (Kock)
  fr. 310: 9, 155

Eupolis (Kock)
  fr. 300: 47

Hekataios *FGrHist* 1
  fr. 119: 47

Hellanikos *FGrHist* 4
  fr. 51: 22, 58, 65
  fr. 125: 160–162

Herakleides Kreticos (Pfister)
  1.22–27, 29: 104

Herodotus
  1.18.3: 192–193
  5.77: 151
  5.79.1–5.81.3: 31, 83, 190–191
  6.108: 168–171
  7.132.1: 171
  9.15.1: 172–173

Hesiod
  Aspis: 10, 31, 50–52, 62, 67, 80, 97–100,
    106–107, 109, 114–115, 117, 119,

131, 140, 161, 166, 189, 195
  dialect: 114–115, 117, 119
  interpolation: 51
  relationship to *Ehoiai*: 97–98
  13: 99
  23–35: 98
  139–321: 99
  197: 140
  380–382: 51
  471–475: 51
  Theogony: 119, 156
  Works and Days: 119

Hesiodic *Ehoiai* (MW): 17–18, 22, 25–26, 28–
    29, 40–48, 52, 61–65, 81, 97–98,
    127, 147, 189
  fr. 10a.96: 21
  fr. 34: 21
  fr. 218: 41–44, 46–47, 52, 61–65
  fr. 219: 18, 23, 47
  fr. 344: 156

Hymn. Hom. Ap.: 18, 114–115, 119, 195

Hymn. Hom. Dem.: 119

Iliad: 10, 31, 41–50, 52, 57–62, 64–65, 67, 79,
    85, 87, 90–101, 104, 106–107, 109, 114,
    117, 119, 122, 127, 130–131, 143, 148–
    152, 161–162, 189–190
  Athenian influence: 45–46
  Catalogue of Ships: 18, 23, 28, 32–41, 45,
    48, 50, 52, 58–62, 64–65, 93, 107,
    109, 119, 122, 148, 150, 189–190
  textualization of: 33, 41, 43, 149
  epithets: 34, 44–45, 98, 124
  5.706–710: 48, 93
  7.8–10: 42–47
  7.132–142: 42–45
  7.219–225: 93–97, 99, 106, 131
  10.260–271: 104
  13.495: 151
  13.685–686: 49–50
  13.699–700: 49–50

II. INSCRIPTIONS

GENERAL INDEX